Ruling Nature, Controlling People

Luregn Lenggenhager

Ruling Nature, Controlling People
Nature Conservation, Development and War
in North-Eastern Namibia since the 1920s

Basel Namibia Studies Series 19

Basler Afrika Bibliographien 2018

This work was accepted as a PhD thesis by the Faculty of Arts and Social Sciences, University of Zurich in the spring semester 2017 on the recommendation of the Doctoral Committee: Prof Dr Gesine Krüger, University of Zurich (main supervisor) and Prof Dr Michael Bollig, University of Cologne.

©2018 The authors
©2018 The photographers
©2018 Basler Afrika Bibliographien

Basler Afrika Bibliographien
Namibia Resource Centre & Southern Africa Library
Klosterberg 23
PO Box
4051 Basel
Switzerland
www.baslerafrika.ch

The Basler Afrika Bibliographien is part of the Carl Schlettwein Foundation

All rights reserved.

Efforts were made to trace the copyright holders of illustrations and maps used in this publication. We apologise for any incomplete or incorrect acknowledgements.

Cover image: Former Buffallo Base in the Bwabwata National Park
Photographer: Sabine Hiller

ISBN 978-3-906927-00-8
ISSN 2234-9561

Contents

Foreword by Maano Ramutsindela	VII
Acknowledgements	X

1 Introduction — 1
- Historiographical Landscapes — 4
- Constituting an Archive of the Caprivi — 22
- Structure of the Book — 31

2 Nature and Development before 1965 — 32
- Creating an Image of Abundant Nature and Peace — 36
- What to Do with the Caprivi? 1915–1939 — 43
- Leslie Trollope and the Caprivi's 'Distinctiveness', 1939–1952 — 56
- Putting Caprivi on South Africa's Map, 1945–1966 — 63
- Odendaal Commission, 1962–1964 — 73
- The Caprivi in the Aftermath of the Odendaal Commission — 81
- Summarising Early South African Rule — 86

3 Nature and War (1965–1980s) — 88
- Geographies of Science, Nature and War — 89
- Living and Working in the Caprivi — 98
- Protecting Rivers and Forests — 111
- Summarising Environmental Interventions in the Context of War — 126

4 Wildlife and War (1975–1990) — 128
- The Diminishing Wildlife Populations in the Caprivi — 129
- Saving Wildlife? — 137
- The Proclamation of National Parks in the 1980s — 158
- Towards Post-colonial Wildlife Conservation — 170

5 Nature and Peace? — 173
- The Caprivi after Independence — 175
- Narratives of Development — 188

Mapping and Bordering in Conservancies and Peace Parks	203
Nature and Violence	217
Summarizing Narratives of Violence and Development	223

6 Conclusion 225

Abbreviations 233

Sources 234

Bibliography 237

List of Figures and Maps 256

Maps 256

Index 259

Foreword

The 21st century is witnessing the revival of war talk in nature conservation. This talk comes from different sources, including the nature conservation lobby group and the security establishment. The conservation lobby group made up of ecologists, conservationists, government agencies, donors, philanthropists and so on are concerned with the high rate of biodiversity loss. Accordingly, they have declared war for conservation, which means waging war on anything and anybody who threatens biodiversity or contributes to its decline. In this war talk, war has amongst others been declared on alien species that threaten, say, indigenous forests and sources of freshwater. Nowhere is this war talk more pronounced than in the decline in wildlife, especially elephants and rhinos. While concerns with the decline in biodiversity arose from the need to ensure the integrity of ecosystems and the health of the planet, there has been a shift towards seeing the loss of biodiversity as a threat to national and global security.

At the end of the Cold War, the security establishment in powerful countries such as the United States began to draw the links between the deterioration of the environment and national security.[1] The reasoning is as follows: environmental degradation leads to scarcity of resources that in turn become a recipe for conflict over scarce resources. Such conflict results in mass migration that destabilizes nation-states, and therefore posing a risk to national security. In this context national security has been redefined to include environmentally-induced risks to nation states. According to a similar logic, the decline in wildlife impacts on national as well as global security. The security establishment argues that wildlife becomes a security issue because illicit wildlife trade threatens national economies but also would finance global terrorist organizations. Thus, the war on poaching is not limited to curbing the loss of wildlife but is also integral to the war on terror. This war by conservation as Duffy[2] calls it is 'a proactive, interventionist militarized response that is spatially amorphous and extends well beyond protected areas and into the land and communities surrounding them'. Indeed, conservation areas around the world are becoming highly militarized. In South Africa's Kruger National Park, which is a core of the Great Limpopo Transfrontier Park (GLTP), both the concentration of rhinos and the rampant rhino poaching have resulted in the GLTP becoming highly militarized. The GLTP is a premier peace park project, which has become a war zone due to the violence that has ensued as a result of militarization[3]. The militarization

---
[1] Dably, S. (2009), *Security and environmental change*. Cambridge: Polity.
[2] Duffy, R. (2016), War, by conservation. *Geoforum,* 69(2): 238–248.
[3] Büscher, B. and M. Ramutsindela (2016), Green Violence, Rhino Poaching and the War to Save Southern Africa's Peace Parks. *African Affairs,* 115(458): 1–22

of protected areas involves the recruitment and training of locals as the paramilitary but also as informants for intelligence networks involved in anti-poaching campaigns.

Luregn Lenggenhager's book, *Ruling Nature, Controlling People: Nature Conservation, Development and War in North-Eastern Namibia since the 1920s* reminds us that the conservation-security nexus, which is currently receiving growing scholarly attention, and that is also crucial to the conservation lobby group and the security apparatus, has a much longer history in Southern Africa. The book shows that this nexus should be understood as a significant part of the unfolding political drama. It confirms that nature conservation does not take place in a political vacuum: ideas and practices of conservation derive their potency from prevailing ideologies and socio-political struggles. As the case study of the Caprivi shows, the quest for the control of nature and local people has spatial imprints that connect various places towards an ideologically and militarily determined future. The Caprivi is an isolated and remote region but its environmental, political and military history can only be fully understood within the broader South African sphere of influence. Expressed differently, the Caprivi should be conceptualized within the wider historiographies of Southern Africa. It was an important geopolitical site for South Africa's occupation of Namibia and for its battle against liberation movements in the region.

The Caprivi region provided a platform on which apartheid South Africa exerted its power through the military, environmental science and the narratives of local economic development. These earlier narratives have been carried forward into present-day communal conservancies and transfrontier conservation projects. Current scholarship on Namibia's communal conservancies celebrates them as innovative and as local development strategies. Though these conservancies have been subjected to scrutiny[4], their political history is often forgotten while not much attention is given to how apartheid-era nature conservation projects in the Caprivi form an important thread in the tapestry of peace parks in post-independence Southern Africa. Lenggenhager's book takes issue with developmental narratives of community-based natural resources management projects such as conservancies as well as those of peace parks. These narratives have long been used to incorporate local people into the ideology of the state and to weaken possible local resistance to conservation projects. Local people have generally played a number of roles in nature conservation, including acting as informants, as wildlife guards, and as co-managers. The nature of their roles varied according to the type and dimensions of conflict in a particular nature conservation area.

---

[4] Mosimane A.W. and J.A. Silva (2014), Boundary Making in Conservancies: The Namibian Experience. In M. Ramutsindela (ed.), *Cartographies of Nature: How Nature Conservation Animates Borders.* New Castle upon Tyne: Cambridge Scholars Publishing: 83–111.

The challenge for the growing body of scholarship on the militarization of protected areas is twofold. First, there is a need to understand how this process unfolds under quite different political conditions, and to identify what is common among military operations in conservation spaces across time. Second, the militarization of protected areas is underpinned by a particular perspective of environmental science, which provides much of the data critical to the process of militarization. Data on the decline of the number of species and on the loss of habitats are important for effective conservation. The strategies adopted to deal with environmental problems however connect such data to political goals at local, national, regional and international levels. These goals complicate our understanding and also our analysis of the militarization of protected areas. Through its analysis of historical materials from the Caprivi, this book widens avenues through which we can overcome this.

Maano Ramutsindela, University of Cape Town

Acknowledgements

This book is the result of several years of research, intellectual exchange and co-operation across two continents. I would like to take this opportunity to thank all the people who contributed to it and made these years such a wonderful and enriching experience. First and foremost, I would like to express my deepest gratitude to all the people who took the time to share their memories, experiences and thoughts with me – whether in formal interviews or in informal discussions – in Namibia, South Africa, Switzerland, Germany, Zambia, Botswana and elsewhere. Without your help and support, this book would not have been possible.

Gesine Krüger, Frank Schubert and Hanni Geiser offered me a supportive and stimulating academic home at the History Department of the University of Zurich. Throughout these years, Gesine and Frank were always on hand to give me immeasurably valuable inputs, critiques, feedback and encouragement at every stage of my work, while Hanni was always available to answer any organisational or administrative questions. Thank you for making my doctoral studies such a successful and enriching time for me and giving me all the freedom and guidance I needed. My thanks also go to all the staff at the History Department as well as to my colleagues in the Doktoratsprogramm Geschichte. A very special thank goes to Michael Bollig, who was not only prepared to be my second examiner, but who also invited me on several occasions to come to Cologne to discuss my work with him and the highly inspirational group of students and researchers at the University of Cologne. I am also particularly grateful for the detailed and thought-provoking reviews of my dissertation, which Gesine Krüger and Michael Bollig wrote. These were extremely helpful when preparing my study for publication.

Further I want to thank the people in Basel who have supported me since my time as an undergraduate student at the University of Basel. For over ten years now, Giorgio Miescher has been an encouraging, supportive and thought-provoking colleague and friend. His constant support and engagement was crucial to my academic career and my fascination for Southern Africa. This thanks also goes to Dag Henrichsen and Lorena Rizzo, who have supported me over many years in numerous ways and shared their deep knowledge of Namibian history with me on countless occasions. A special thank also goes to the entire staff at the Centre for African Studies Basel and the Basler Afrika Bibliogrpahien.

I would further like to thank the people at the History Department and in the Humanities Research Centre at the University of the Western Cape in Bellville, South Africa for inviting me as an Associate Researcher for the duration my PhD studies. Patricia Hayes, Ciraj Rassool, Leslie Witz and Premesh Lalu encouraged me to think deeper and further and helped me to build an understanding of South Africa's many pasts. At the University of Cape Town I met Maano Ramutsindela, who constantly encouraged me to forge ahead with my project and reminded me of the relevance of my topic, including for contemporary Southern African politics.

A very special thank you goes to Riedwaan Moosage, who made me feel at home in Cape Town and who proved to be a constantly caring and intellectually stimulating support at all stages of this project. I also want to thank my other friends and collegues in South Africa, especially Phindezwa Mnyaka, for welcoming me to her town and critically engaging with my project.

I want to thank Werner Hillebrecht and all the staff of the National Archives in Namibia for guiding me through their holdings and helping me to find what I needed. I am grateful for all my friends and colleagues in Windhoek, including Martha Akawa, Helvi Elago, Napandulwe Shiweda, Romie Nghitevelekwa, Memory Biwa and many more. A special thank you goes to my old friend Timo Mashuna, who was always around whenever I needed him.

Many more collegues and good friend commented on and added to the drafts of this study at various stages and in various ways – thank you so much for your motivating support Melanie Böhi, Lukas Zürcher, Emelie Danielsson, Anna Vögeli, Kirsten Rüther and many more.

My research trips in the Caprivi would not have been possible without the generous help of Bennett Kangumu (UNAM Campus Katima Mulilo), Beaven Munali (IRDNC) and Lieneke Eloff de Visser. They not only helped me to find my way around the area, but were also crucial in securing me access to people and information for which I was looking. I further want to thank all of the staff at the various community camps and the Cheshire Homes in Katima Mulilo, who made sure I felt secure and well looked-after during my stays in the Caprivi. My research over many years and in different countries was made possible by the financial support of the Doktoratsprogramm Geschichte at the University of Zurich, the University of Zurich's Nord-Süd-Kooperation, and the Swiss-South African Joint Research Programme.

Nthabiseng Moriri was a great help with the transcriptions and Michael Wenk assisted me with the maps. Patrick Grogan's language editing was crucial for this book; his patience, endurance and precision with my English and his critical comments on content and structure led this book come to a good end. Throughout the publication phase of this book, the BAB Publishing House gave me all the support I could wish for. A special thanks to Petra Kerckhoff and the entire team at the BAB as well as to Chris Saunders for his detailed comments on content and language. The publication was financially supported by the 'Doktoratsprogramm Geschichte' of the University of Zurich.

Last but not least, I am very thankful to have had so many good colleagues, friends and family members who have supported me through all of this work. It would not be possible to name you all – but all of you contributed and made it possible. James Merron, who accompanied me on my very first trip to the Caprivi and remained involved in my thesis right up to its publication, Samuel Bachmann for his constant support, Sarah Reid, Jacob Geuder, Manuel Raemy, Thomas Böhm, Peter Oderinde, Matthias Knecht, Oladimeji David Adisa, Valentin Kone, Fulvio Santimaria, Sebastian Schanzer and all the other friends, who lived with me, shared their thoughts, and kept me running. Finally, my very special thank goes to Silva Lieberherr and to my parents, Luzia and Christian, as well as to my siblings. I owe you all my greatest thanks.

1 Introduction

On an extraordinarily hot day in 1974 in a small village close to Katima Mulilo, the administrative centre of what was then called the Eastern Caprivi, a South African-controlled 'homeland' in the extreme north-east of Namibia, a South African ichthyologist and nature conservationist gathered the local schoolchildren around a crocodile carcass which he had found during the previous night.[1] His intention was to show the learners how to dissect a crocodile, but when he cut open the animal's stomach he was left terrified. What he had found was a sharp artillery grenade, which he only managed to deactivate at the last second. After this initial shock he recalled how the grenade must have entered the stomach of the crocodile. He himself was responsible; as crocodiles commonly destroyed the nets which he used to collect fish specimens for his research, he had asked friends from the South African Defence Force (SADF) who were stationed in the region to stuff some fish with grenades. Later, when the crocodiles ate the fish, they would be blown up. Only once, however, did this tactic appear not to have worked.[2]

Stuffing fish with grenades in order to blow up crocodiles was probably not exactly what Eschel Rhoodie, a journalist and press officer for the South African government, meant by "men of vision" who would bring "civilization" to the South African-occupied territory when he wrote in 1967 about Namibia's "almost limitless potential recognized by men of vision who have taken a sincere and abiding interest in it. [Namibia] is in the truest sense a last frontier for if man can survive and prosper in this hostile environment, then there are no areas left on this earth that cannot be civilized as well."[3] Rhoodie's description succinctly relates South Africa's attitude towards its occupied territory of Namibia during the apartheid period – a final "frontier" characterised by a "hostile environment" which needed to be tamed and civilised in order to release its "limitless potential".[4] The ichthyologist and the

---

[1] By using the term 'Namibia' to refer to the area of the modern nation-state of that name – even when referring to a time when the territory was not yet officially known as such – I follow a common practice among historians in describing former colonies by their current names (see e.g.: Wallace, M. (2011), *A History of Namibia*. London: Hurst, p. 8 or Silvester, J., M. Wallace and P. Hayes (1998), Trees Never Meet: Mobility and Containment, an Overview 1915–1946. In P. Hayes, J. Silvester, M. Wallace and W. Hartmann (eds.), *Namibia under South African Rule: Mobility and Containment, 1915–46*. Oxford, Windhoek and Athens OH: James Currey, Out of Africa and Ohio University Press, p. 3–50).

[2] This story was told to me repeatedly by many of my interviewees. See e.g.: Interview with HS, 10.03.2014, George, all interviews were conducted by the author. For more on the interviews, see p. 31 and the list on p. 234.

[3] Rhoodie, E. (1967), *South West: The Last Frontier in Africa*. Pretoria: Vortrekkerspres, Preface.

[4] Rhoodie (1967): Preface.

military officers in the above episode both played their roles within South Africa's multi-faceted approach towards finding and utilising the resources of Namibia and maintaining its power over the region. As such, the story serves anecdotally to introduce questions which are at the heart of this study.

This book is about how the utilisation and conservation of the natural environment, as well as research on nature, became, along with the military occupation, a central component of apartheid South Africa's policies to expand its power over areas of northern Namibia which it considered to be its frontier with 'communist', 'dark' Africa;[5] or, in the words of Eschel Rhoodie again, to protect "Western Civilization" from "abortive invasions of South West Africa by terrorists [...] armed to the teeth with Russian and Chinese weapons".[6] The book focuses on the Caprivi Strip, a region which was only attached to South African-occupied territory by a small stretch of land which linked it to the rest of Namibia. Unless otherwise noted, I use the term 'the Caprivi' to refer to the entire geographical region of the 'Caprivi Strip', consisting of the present-day Namibian 'Zambezi Region' (formerly the 'Caprivi Region', under South African rule known as the 'Eastern Caprivi' or 'East Caprivi') and the area that is commonly known as 'West Caprivi', today split between the two Namibian regions of 'Zambezi' and 'Kavango East'. The area's unique geography saw it considered by the South African government as even more remote than the rest of Namibia, or even "beyond the last frontier".[7] At the same time, the Caprivi's geographical position rendered it an area of central geopolitical and military importance for South Africa during Namibia's war of liberation which lasted from the 1960s until shortly before the country's independence in 1990.[8]

This study engages with and traces what can be thought of as three trajectories relating to the Caprivi Strip's pasts.[9] The first trajectory, with its focus on a seemingly peripheral region of the apartheid state, contributes to a better understanding of the diverse practises which the South African state employed to control its border regions. This is crucial for a

---

[5] E.g.: Rhoodie (1967) and Green, L. (1952), *Lords of the Last Frontier: The Story of South West Africa and its People of all Races*. Cape Town: H.B. Timmins. See also: Gewald, J.-B. (2013), Beyond the Last Frontier: Major Trollope and the Eastern Caprivi Zipfel. In M. de Bruijn and R. van Dijk (eds.), *The Social Life of Connectivity in Africa*. Basingstoke: Palgrave.

[6] Rhoodie (1967): Preface.

[7] This term was also employed by Jan-Bart Gewald to describe how the Caprivi was viewed by the South African administration in the 1930s. See: Gewald (2013).

[8] While the exact beginning of the war is disputed the official end was in 1989.

[9] These different trajectories are, however, not clearly separable from each other. Instead, they are interwoven and mutually constitutive. Such an understanding of different non-hierarchical and multiple interpretations of information draws loosely on Gilles Deleuzes' theory of "lines of flights" (Deleuze, G. and F. Guattari (1987), *A Thousand Plateaus*. Minneapolis: University of Minnesota Press, p. 9–10).

critical understanding of South Africa's policies and methods of governance, which were also defined and contested in, and through, its so-called peripheries. I thus agree with Alan Lester's argument that the "[s]tudies of material, symbolic, personal and discursive flows connecting South to Southern Africa are one way into more complete historical geographies of Southern, rather than just South Africa".[10]

One such set of practises was the South African authorities' surveying and mapping of the Caprivi's nature, whether in search of potential economic profit, for military or geopolitical reasons, or for the protection of wildlife. By highlighting these practices, my second trajectory shows that the seemingly competing fields of economic 'development' or 'modernisation', natural science and nature conservation, and the heightened militarisation of the area required and generated close and multi-layered forms of interaction.[11]

Following on from this historical claim, my third trajectory posits that similar discourses of economic development, wildlife conservation, and the securitisation of wildlife areas continue to shape the two major nature conservation initiatives in post-apartheid Southern Africa, namely community conservation and trans-frontier conservation areas. I add a historical understanding to a highly-contested political and economic debate which continues throughout Southern Africa and especially in the Caprivi. This debate examines the role which market-based nature conservation should and can play for the improvement in living conditions of the rural poor and questions whether this approach only serves the interests of the powerful.[12]

---

[10] Lester, A. (2003), Historical Geographies of Southern Africa, *Journal of Southern African Studies*, 29(3): 595–613 (here 609).

[11] Most of my interviewees used the term 'nature conservation' for everything related to the protection of flora and fauna, particularly wildlife. The same wording is found in most official texts and titles; these use the terms "nature conservation officers" or "nature conservation units" for persons or bodies primarily concerned with the (spatial) protection of wildlife. The fields of forestry and fishery as well as other related aspects of nature conservation each had their own terms and titles. If not stated otherwise, I will henceforth use the term 'nature conservation' in line with its common meaning to signify the protection of flora and fauna, in the context of this book this means especially the protection of wildlife.

[12] Market-based or neo-liberal interventions in nature conservation have been widely discussed by scholars in recent years, see for example in a Southern African context: Büscher, B. (2013), Transforming the Frontier. Peace Parks and the Politics of Neoliberal Conservation in Southern Africa. Durham and London: Duke University Press; Ramutsindela, M. (2007), *Transfrontier Conservation in Africa: At the Confluence of Capital, Politics and Nature*. Wallingford and Boston MA: CABI; Ramutsindela, M. and M. Shabangu (2013), Conditioned by neoliberalism: a reassessment of land claim resolutions in the Kruger National Park. *Journal of Contemporary African Studies*, 31(3): 441–456. For a global approach, see e.g.: Castree, N. (2008), Neo-liberalisation of Nature I and II. *Environment and Planning*, A40(1): 131–173 and 153–173 or Haynen, N., J. McCarthy, W.S. Prudham, P. Robbins (2007), *Neoliberal Environments: False Promises and Unnatural Consequences*. London: Routledge.

By engaging with these trajectories, this book offers a detailed history of the Caprivi and its position within a broad South African sphere of influence. Furthermore, it also contributes to a better understanding of apartheid South Africa's policies in and from the perspective of its peripheries. In so doing, I seek to offer a historical approach to underpin the ongoing intense political and scholarly discussions on community conservation, neo-liberal nature conservation and transfrontier conservation areas.

Historiographical Landscapes

To circumscribe the Caprivi's twentieth-century pasts within a single national or thematic historiographical context would be to disregard most of the arguments which will be made in this study.[13] Instead, this thesis is based on an understanding of the Caprivi's past as inextricably tied to the wider historiographies of Southern Africa. There are three main bodies of historiography which I consider as most relevant to the region. Chief among these is the still-nascent historiography on South Africa's apartheid era and its aftermath. An engagement with the Caprivi's twentieth-century past can not only contribute to a better understanding of how South Africa exerted its power within Southern Africa, but also on how governance of remote areas impacted upon centres of power within South Africa itself. With the Eastern Caprivi being directly governed by the Department of Bantu Affairs in Pretoria – and between 1976 and 1980 even as a pseudo-independent so-called homeland – this book will also add to the growing literature on apartheid South Africa's homelands.[14] As William Beinart correctly stated, South African homelands also need to be rethought of "in a longer perspective" which incorporates their "precursors and legacies"; moreover, their histories must be discussed outside of a mere "critique of 'homeland' policy", but should still be "imbricated with other local and national dynamics".[15] A number of factors mark the case of the Eastern Caprivi as unique in this regard. Not only was Eastern Caprivi the only South African homeland (administrated directly through Pretoria) situated

---

[13] A related point, as I will discuss below, is that the division between history and historiography must be critically questioned. See also: Lalu, P. (2009), *The Deaths of Hintsa: Postapartheid South Africa and the Shape of Recurring Pasts*. Cape Town: HSRC, p. 10.

[14] For an overview of the most recent research on homelands and on how former homelands are approaching their pasts, see the edited volume: Ally, S. and A. Lissoni (eds.) (2018), *New Histories of South Africa's Apartheid-Era Bantustans*. New York: Routledge and the contributions to the *Journal for Southern African Studies* (2015): Homelands as Frontiers: Apartheid's Loose Ends, 41(5), particularly the editorial: Jensen, S. and O. Zenker (2015), Homelands as Frontiers: Apartheid's Loose Ends, *Journal for Southern African Studies*, 42(5): 937–952.

[15] Beinart, W. (2018), Beyond 'Homelands': Some Idea's about the History of African Rural Areas in South Africa. In: S. Ally and A. Lissoni (eds.) (2018), *New Histories of South Africa's Apartheid-Era Bantustans*. New York: Routledge, p.1–17 (here 1).

outside of what is generally considered as apartheid South Africa's core territory, but the region was, and still is, part of Namibia – and, most significantly, its northern territories – and, as such, is entangled with the country's colonial and national historiographies. Thirdly, the book provides a regional history of the Caprivi, an area which must always be understood as forming part of a larger transborder region. In the following sections, I will outline some of the relevant lines of research which have been followed in these various directions and show how they have become interlinked in recent years.

South Africa

History writing during South Africa's apartheid period – excluding the apartheid state's own ideological appraisals and histories – was marked by two major lines of thought, namely the liberal tradition and a leftist 'revisionist' or 'radical' approach.[16] The latter emerged as particularly influential in the 1970s and 1980s, partly as a critique of the seminal work of liberal historiography in South Africa, the two-volume *Oxford History of South Africa*, which was published in 1969 and 1971.[17] These two volumes largely broke with earlier liberal ideas, which regarded European settler history as the only relevant antecedent of modern South Africa, instead emphasising the histories of other groups.[18] Nevertheless, the volumes continued to adhere to the notion that twentieth-century racism in South Africa, and its particular manifestation in the form of apartheid, was rooted in Afrikaner frontier experience, in particular their 'treks' out of the Cape Colony.[19]

---

[16] For examples of Afrikaner nationalist history, see e.g.: Krüger, D.W. (1969), *The Making of a Nation*. Johannesburg: Macmillan or Jaarsveld, F.A. (1981), *Van Van Riebeeck tot P.W. Botha*. Johannesburg.

[17] Thomson, L. and M. Wilson (eds.) (1969), *Oxford History of South Africa*, Vol. 1. Oxford: Oxford University Press; Thomson, L. and M. Wilson (eds.) (1971), *Oxford History of South Africa*, Vol. 2. Oxford: Oxford University Press.

[18] Earlier writings by black intellectuals, such as Sol Plaatje (Plaatje, S. (1914), *Native Life in South Africa*. London: King and Son) or Davidson D.T. Jabavu (Jabavu, D.D.T. (1928), *The Segregation Fallacy and Other Papers*. Lovedale) focussed on the experiences of non-white people. See Hamilton, C., B. Mbenga and R. Ross (2010), The production of preindustrial South African History. In C. Hamilton, B. Mbenga and R. Ross, (eds.): *The Cambridge History of South Africa, Volume 1, from early times to 1885*. Cambridge: Cambridge University Press, p. 1–62. See also: Visser, W. (2004), Trends in South African Historiography and the Present State of Historical Research. (Paper presented at the Nordic Africa Institute, Uppsala).

[19] In the same year in which the *Oxford History of South Africa* was published, Martin Legassick submitted his highly influential doctoral dissertation on the Griqua state, in which he debunked this 'frontier' tradition. His thesis is widely regarded as the starting point of revisionist historiography in Southern Africa. The dissertation was eventually published in 2010: Legassick, M. C. (2010), *The Politics of a South African Frontier: The Griqua, the Sotho-Tswana, and the Missionaries, 1780–1840*. Basel: Basler Afrika Bibliographien.

This situating of the origins of apartheid doctrine exclusively within the context of nineteenth-century Afrikaner experience was a central point of critique for a group of mostly young radical historians, who linked racist white supremacy in South Africa also to British imperialism and underlined connections between class, race and capitalist expansion.[20] Furthermore, they showed convincingly how it was the decline of native reserve economies during and after the Second World War which led to difficulties for the white settler industry accessing a cheap labour force. They thus argued that the introduction of apartheid in 1948 constituted an adjustment of long-standing segregation polices to new economic realities.[21] Via such reasoning, the native reserves-come-homelands entered more into the focus of historians, although initially mostly in the form of an examination of their structural function within the capitalist system of white supremacy.[22] However, with a global move towards an approach to 'history from below' and the emergence of the New Left and their interpretation of social history in the 1970s, scholars of South Africa soon turned their attentions to the histories of 'common' people. At first research was undertaken primarily on urban areas and mines and, from the mid-1980s, also on the native reserves and homelands.[23] Significantly, however, none of these studies examined the Eastern Caprivi, South Africa's only directly-controlled homeland in Namibia.

This revisionist historiography influenced and was reinforced by a more radical, black activist interpretation of South African history.[24] In the 1970s Steve Biko called for a rewriting of "the history of the black man", this time not as a history written by "white liberals" presenting black history as one of the deterioration of their black counterparts.[25] Instead he urged for a "positive history" of black experiences and critically questioned the possibility of a multi-racial history.[26] In spite of such contradictions and contestations, radical historiogra-

---

[20] See e.g.: the review of the *Oxford History of South Africa* by Marks, S. (1972), Liberalism, Social Realities, and South African History, *Journal of Commonwealth Studies*, 10(3): 243–249.
[21] See e.g.: Legassick, M. C. (1974), Legislation, Ideology, and Economy in Post-1948 South Africa, *Journal of Southern African Studies*, 1: 5–35.
[22] Legassick, M. C. and H. Wolpe (1976), The Bantustans and Capital Accumulation in South Africa, *Review of African Political Economy*, 7: 87–107.
[23] Onselen, C. (1982), Studies in the Social and Economic History of the Witwatersrand, 1886–1914. Johannesburg: Longman; the edited volume: Beinart, W., P. Delius and S. Trapido (eds.) (1986), Putting a plough in the ground: Accumulation and Dispossession in rural South Africa, 1850–1930. Johannesburg: Ravan.
[24] See also: Tsotsi, M.W. (1981), *From Chattel to Wage Slavery. A new approach to South African History*. Maseru: Lesotho Printing and Publishing Co.
[25] Biko, S. (1987). *I Write what I Like: A Selection of His Writings* (first published 1978). Johannesburg: Heinemann, p. 28–31.
[26] Biko (1987): 29 and 19–26.

phy – and with it, history as a discipline – became an important site for political and social activism in the final years of apartheid.[27]

After the official end of apartheid in the early 1990s, many scholars observed a dramatic decline of radical historiography or, even more generally, of history as praxis, as a subject or mode of thought.[28] However, the state of post-apartheid history writing looks far less pessimistic when notions of what can be part of South African historiography are broadened or when ideas of how to think about the past are considered in more diverse terms than those proposed by the academic history of the 1980s.[29] Within such broader reconceptions of what belongs to history, new areas, methods and questions are being discussed within enlarged circles, which now include not only academic historians, but also representatives from other academic fields, museums, archives, heritage bodies, and the wider public.[30] This not only allowed for new critiques of social history to emerge, but also for a reinclusion of other research topics and an interrogation of the ways in which history has constituted itself as a discipline.[31] Furthermore, new foci have been added to the mere search for historical explanations for and interpretations of the raise, constitution and struggle against apartheid. Such new thinking questioned the implications of apartheid for post-apartheid historiography and has consequently engaged with the question of how to think to the future while at the same time being caught in the constraints of a colonial, violent, and authoritarian past.[32]

Similar considerations led Premesh Lalu to question whether "the task of re-narrating pasts could be effectively pursued through the discourse of history". Furthermore, he asked: "Was it, in other words, possible to elaborate a concept of the post-apartheid as a distinct

---

[27] For example, the Marxist Theory Seminars, which were held from 1988 at University of the Western Cape in Cape Town, brought together activists and Marxist scholars and regularly attracted up to 500 attendees. Nash, A. (1999), Dilemmas of the Left Academy: A Report on the 1998 Socialist Scholars Conference, *African Sociological Review*, 3(1): 168–198.

[28] Most prominently, the narrative of this 'crisis' was formulated in an edited volume which was based on a workshop held in Copenhagen in 2004, see: Stolten, H. E. (ed.) (2007), *History Making and Present Day Politics: The Meaning of Collective Memory in South Africa*. Uppsala: Nordiska Afrikainstitutet. See also a critical review: Du Toit, A. (2010), The Owl of Minerva and the Ironic Fate of the Progressive Praxis of Radical Historiography in Post-Apartheid South Africa, *History and Theory*, 49: 266–280.

[29] Witz, L. (2008), Review of Stolten, H.E., History Making and Present Day Politics, *African Studies Review*, 51: 186–188.

[30] For an overview, see the introduction to the edited volume of papers presented at the South African Contemporary History and Humanities Seminar, a weekly seminar that has been hold at University of Western Cape since 1993: Witz, L., J.R. Forte and P. Israel (2016), Epistemological Restlessness: Trajectories in and out of History. In J.R. Forte, P. Israel and Witz, L. (eds.) *Out of History Re-imagining South Africans Pasts*. Cape Town, HSRC, p. 1–30.

[31] Witz et al. (2016): 11–13.

[32] Lalu (2009): 7–10.

ethico-political displacement of a prior violence by way of the discourse of history?"[33] Lalu thus pointed to the dilemma facing academic historians, who, in speaking for the colonised, perpetuate colonial and apartheid power structures inevitable in and inherent to their discipline.[34] Addressing this dilemma requires critical engagement with the (colonial) archive as well as with methods of knowledge production and storage practiced under the apartheid regime, a task on which I will elaborate further in the discussion of my archival sources below. It further needs to involve a combination of detailed historical research and analyses of history's reflection and public representation in a post-apartheid society.[35]

This study aims to provide such a detailed history of the Caprivi, while also discussing how histories were used, re-modelled or silenced by the powerful actors, narratives and visions of post-apartheid nature conservation discourse. In short, by incorporating the post-apartheid and post-independence context of the region into the writing of its apartheid history, I aim to address one of the key questions which Lalu raised: "where would we mark the ends of apartheid?"[36]

With my focus on the Caprivi, a region which was often seen as far removed from the centres of apartheid power, I additionally discuss the geographical limits of apartheid South Africa, which were often seen as being the boundaries of 'white' South Africa. South Africa's diverse historiographies, particularly those concerned with apartheid, have often been criticised for being self-contained and unwilling to seek parallels with other colonial contexts in Africa and beyond.[37] In his influential book, *Citizen and Subject*, the political scientist Mahmood Mamdani urged scholars to look in more complexity at the wider history of Africa so as to better understand that of South Africa – or, in his words, "to problematize both sides of every dualism (e.g. between South Africa and Africa) by historicizing it, thereby underlining the institutional and political condition for its reproduction and for its transformation".[38]

---

[33] Both quotes: Lalu (2009): 8.
[34] As formulated, among others, by Rassool, C. (2010), Power, knowledge, and the politics of public pasts, *African Studies*, 69: 79–101 and Lalu (2009).
[35] See also: Worden, N. (2012), *The Making of Modern South Africa, Fifth Edition*. Malden: Wiley-Blackwell, p. 7.
[36] Lalu (2009): 26.
[37] Mamdani, M. (1996), *Citizen and Subject: Contemporary Africa and the Legacy of Late Colonialism*. Princeton: Princeton University Press.
[38] Mamdani (1996): 299. Mamdani was criticised by historians for his supposedly simplistic and positivist understanding of history, for example by: Cooper, F. (1997a), Review: Citizen and Subject: Contemporary Africa and the Legacy of Late Colonialism by Mahmood Mamdani, *International Labor and Working-Class History*, 52: 156–160. In "not examining the past for cracks in structures of power or for possibilities of mobilization" (Cooper 1997: 159), Mamdani presents history as being "closed".

Mamdani deconstructed enduring and influential ideas about Africa's internal differences, in so doing taking South Africa to be a part of Africa in order "to establish the historical legitimacy of Africa as a unit of analysis".[39] According to Mamdani, only this reconsideration of South Africa in its African context would make it possible to study the world "from Africa".[40] Moreover, he argued that the studying and teaching of African history as the history of the "Bantu", namely as the history of Africa north of South Africa's border at the Limpopo, had been central to apartheid South Africa's education curriculum and was still being reinforced in the post-apartheid era through a perpetuation of ideas of South African exceptionalism.[41] In order to overcome such a colonial distinction between an imagined 'white South Africa' and 'the rest of Africa', it is not only important to see how South Africa and other African countries shared common histories, as Mamdani suggested, but also to understand South Africa from a perspective emanating from beyond its own centres of power and from outside its national boundaries.[42] Hence the context which Lorena Rizzo described for Kaoko, another region in northern Namibia which was often understood as a periphery, arguably also applied to the Caprivi as a 'remote' area which was also a dynamic site "where power relations and constellations came to the fore and remained contested".[43] By researching such power relations, constellations and contestations in relation to South Africa's environmental policies towards the Caprivi, I intend not only to avoid the trap of South African exceptionalism, but also to depart from the idea that South African history ends at the Limpopo or, in the case of the country's former colony of Namibia, at the so-called Red Line.[44]

The dominant narrative of a 'white' South Africa ending at its northern borders might also be seen as a reason for the surprising lack of interest shown towards Namibia within South African historiography, despite the fact that Namibia was under South African control for most of the twentieth century and was part of South Africa during the heavily-

---

[39] Mamdani (1996): 11.
[40] Mamdani (1996): 31.
[41] Mamdani, M. (1998), Is African studies to be turned into a new home for Bantu education at UCT? (Text of remarks at the Seminar on the Africa Core of the Foundation Course for the Faculty of Social Sciences and Humanities, University of Cape Town).
[42] For Namibia, this limit of South Africa power might be considered to have lain at the veterinary border (the so-called Red Line) which divided the area where white settlers lived from the 'communal lands' of northern Namibia. Miescher, G. (2012a), *Namibia's Red Line. The history of a veterinary and settlement border.* New York: Palgrave.
[43] Rizzo, L. (2012), Gender and Colonialism: A History of Kaoko in North-Western Namibia, 1870s–1950s. Basel: Basler Afrika Bibliographien, p. 2. The name 'Kaoko' or 'Kaokoveld' is commonly used for a (eco-)region within the Namibian Kunene Region. 'Kaokoland' was the name of an apartheid homeland in the same region.
[44] Miescher 2012a.

researched apartheid period.⁴⁵ South African historiography has long failed to understand the importance of South Africa's only colony, Namibia, for its own past as a colonising power, and for the establishment and maintenance of apartheid.⁴⁶ Recently, however, a group of scholars of Namibia and Southern Africa have called for an increased focus on Namibia's role within South Africa's past. They proposed the concept of a 'South African empire' by which to analyse Southern African history, not only from the vantage points of its centres in South Africa, but also from the perspectives of its 'backwaters' in Namibia and other regions under less direct forms of South African control.⁴⁷ They underline that empire "has expressed itself through networks of people, things and ideas that have moved between and circulated within metropoles and peripheries of imperial systems, as colonial cultures were created, and in which empire was constituted in the colonies."⁴⁸ In this book, I will retrace such networks and movements between the so-called periphery – in this case, the Caprivi – and the centres in South Africa and, as such, contribute to a better understanding of the complex relations between South Africa and its only colony, Namibia.

Namibia

The German colonial period and the decades of resistance against South African occupation triggered academic debate and research on Namibian history from a comparatively early stage.⁴⁹ A dominant topic of critical history writing was, on the one hand, the German

---

45 South Africa's direct political and military rule over Namibia began with the conquest of the former German colony during the First World War and ended after decades of armed resistance with the founding of the independent Republic of Namibia in 1990. Although the nature of Namibia's legal and administrative status within South Africa as well as South Africa's internal politics shifted several times during this period, this era is commonly referred to as the 'South African period' in Namibian history. See: Silvester et al. (1998) and Wallace (2011).
46 Henrichsen, D., G. Miescher, C. Rassool, L. Rizzo (2015), Rethinking Empire in Southern Africa, *Journal for Southern African Studies*, 41(3): 431–435 (here 431).
47 See the special issue on the South African Empire: *Journal for Southern African Studies*, 41(3). In its introduction, the editors highlighted that, while Namibia in particular was considered to constitute the periphery of South Africa, the territory was itself entangled in non-South African networks of power. This was especially the case through the Namibian liberation movement, which established bases in and received support from various regional powers, see: Henrichsen et al. (2015): 433. For a critical engagement with the question of whether the term 'empire' is helpful for a better understanding of Namibia's role in South Africa's past, see: Lalu, P. (2015), Empire and Nation, *Journal of Southern African Studies*, 41(3): 437–450.
48 Henrichsen et al. (2015): 432. See also: Lenggenhager, L. (2016), Circulating Nature: From North Eastern Namibia to South Africa and Back, 1960-1990. In: M. Ramutsindela, G. Miescher and M. Boehi (eds.), *The Politics of Nature and Science in Southern Africa*. Basel: Basler Afrika Bibliographien: 87–105.
49 One of the first general histories of Namibia from a non-colonialist perspective was written by the radical South African journalist Ruth First in 1963 (First, R. (1963), *South West Africa*. Baltimore: Penguin), followed eight years later by Israel Goldblatt's *History of South West Africa* (Goldblatt,

colonial era, especially the genocide during the Southwest African War between 1904 and 1908.[50] On the other hand, the emergence of a (national) history of resistance became the focus of many historians working on Namibia.[51] Unlike in South Africa itself, Namibian historiography soon began to account for some aspects of South African rule in Namibia, particularly in relation to the migrant labour system.[52] After the country's independence in 1990, scholars of Namibian history intensified their discussion of South African rule and began to challenge the assumption that the country's history could simply be reduced to an extension of South African social history.[53] In a seminal edited volume on *Namibia under South African Rule* which was published in 1998, many aspects of the first decades of South

---

I. (1971), *History of South West Africa from the Beginnings of the Nineteenth Century*. Cape Town: Juta & Co.). Almost half a century later Marion Wallace published her critical general history of the area which is now Namibia which covered the period up to the country's independence in 1990 (Wallace 2011). Wallace thoroughly surveyed most of what has been written on Namibia's past and carefully avoided falling into the trap of writing a single national narrative of the Namibian nation.

50 See e.g.: Drechsler, H. (1966), *Südwestafrika unter deutscher Kolonialherrschaft*. Stuttgart: Steiner; Bley, H. (1968), *Kolonialherrschaft und Sozialstruktur in Deutsch-Südwestafrika 1894–1914*. Hamburg: Leibniz Verlag. Debates relating to the genocide are ongoing, see e.g.: Krüger, G. (1999), *Kriegsbewältigung und Geschichtsbewusstsein: Realität, Deutung und Verarbeitung des deutschen Kolonialkriegs in Namibia 1904 – 1907*. Göttingen: Vandenhoeck und Ruprecht; Zeller, J. and J. Zimmerer (eds.) (2003), *Völkermord in Deutsch-Südwestafrika: Der Kolonialkrieg in Namibia und seine Folgen*. Berlin: Ch. Links; Böhlke-Itzen, J. (2004), *Kolonialschuld und Entschädigung: Der deutsche Völkermord an den Herero 1904–1907*. Frankfurt am Main: Brandes und Apsel. For an updated overview of literature on the genocide, see the 2016 third edition of: Zeller et al. (2003): 263–268.

51 Such a nationalist and anti-colonialist historical historiography often incorporated all histories of resistance into a single linear narrative, starting from the earliest conflicts between white travellers and local inhabitants, before moving on to Hendrik Witbooi's fight against the German colonial administration, and culminating in SWAPO's successful struggle which ultimately led to the founding of an independent Namibia. See e.g.: Katjavivi, P.H. (1988), *A History of Resistance in Namibia*. Paris: UNESCO. Only long after independence did a more critical examination of Namibian resistance begin. See e.g.: Dobell, L. (2000), *Swapo's Struggle for Namibia, 1960–1991: War by Other Means*. Basel: P. Schlettwein Publishing or Williams, C.A. (2015), *National Liberation in Postcolonial Southern Africa. A Historical Ethnography of SWAPO's Exile Camps*. Cambridge: Cambridge University Press. An overview of the most recent historical debates on the history of Namibian resistance is provided in the volume edited by: Silvester, J. (ed.) (2016), *Reviewing Resistance in Namibian History*. Windhoek: UNAM Press.

52 See e.g.: Moorsom, R. (1972), Underdevelopment, Contract Labour and Worker Consciousness in Namibia, 1915–72. *Journal of Southern African Studies*, 4(1): 52–87; or publications in related fields such as that by the Namibian anthropologist Robert Gordon: Gordon, R.J. (1977), *Mines, Masters and Migrants: Life in a Namibian Mine Compound*. Johannesburg: Ravan. Still, as Gesine Krüger, among others, has argued, the dominant role of the genocide in Namibian historiography as well as the heavy restrictions and even bans imposed (by the South African authorities) on any critical form of research on the South African period led to a clear underrepresentation of the era in Namibian history writing (Krüger (1999): 14).

53 Silvester et al. (1998): 13.

African rule were discussed. However, in the preface to the volume, the editors emphasised that all aspects of South African rule could not be covered and acknowledged that "no Kavango, no Caprivi or Khoisan history is represented".[54] Moreover, the entire Namibian War of Liberation, the introduction of apartheid in Namibia as well as its decline in the last years of South African occupation also remained undiscussed in the book. Nevertheless, the book's diverse contributions made it clear that the patterns of a settler colony had not been broadly applicable across Namibia. This was especially the case for the Caprivi and other regions in the north of the country, which together were never seen as suitable for the settlement of white farmers.[55]

Since Namibia's independence, many studies have been conducted on aspects of the histories of regions which lay beyond white settler areas.[56] As Giorgio Miescher argued, although many of these studies were highly valuable contributions towards a deeper understanding of the histories of people who have long been neglected, they often adopted 'ethnic' groups as units of analysis or were circumscribed by the geographical boundaries of the former homelands.[57] Over recent years this critique was countered by new research which understood 'homeland' or 'ethnic' histories within the broader frameworks of north-

---

[54] Hayes, P. J. Silvester, M. Wallace, W. Hartmann (eds.) (1998), *Namibia Under South African Rule, Mobility and Containment, 1915–1946*. Oxford: James Currey. p. ix.

[55] Silvester et al. (1998): 13. See also: Krüger, G. and Henrichsen, D. (1998), "We Have Been Captives Long Enough. We Want to be Free": Land, Uniforms and Politics in the History of Herero in the Interwar Period. In P. Hayes, J. Silvester, M. Wallace and W. Hartmann (eds), *Namibia under South African Rule: Mobility and Containment, 1915–46*. Oxford, Windhoek and Athens OH: James Currey, Out of Africa and Ohio University Press, p. 149–74.

[56] With her 1992 dissertation, *A History of the Ovambo of Namibia, c. 1850–1935*, Patricia Hayes turned the focus to areas in the north of the country. Along with her study, social anthropologists, in particular, have added substantively to the writing of histories of areas outside of the white farming areas. See: Gordon, R.J. and S. Douglas (1992), *The Bushmen Myth: The Making of a Namibian Underclass*. Oxford: Westview; Bollig, M. (2005), *Risk Management in a Hazardous Environment. A Comparative Study of Two Pastoral Societies*. New York: Springer; Dieckmann, U. (2007), *Hai||om in the Etosha Region: A history of colonial settlement, ethnicity and nature conservation*. Basel: Basler Afrika Bibliographien; and, in the case of Caprivi, the two dissertations by Julie Taylor and Gertrud Boden: Taylor, J.J. (2012), *Naming the Land: San Identity and Community Conservation in Namibia`s West Caprivi*. Basel: Basler Afrika Bibliographien and Boden, G. (2004), Prozesse sozialen Wandels vor dem Hintergrund staatlicher Eingriffe: Eine Fallstudie zu den Khwe in West Caprivi/Namibia. (PhD Thesis, University Cologne).

[57] Miescher (2012a): 6 and Gewald (2013). Similar discussions have also taken place in relation to histories of homelands within South Africa, see: Beinart (2018). As reasons for this focus on 'ethnic' groups, Miescher gave the studies' focus on oral history as well as the holdings of local archives, which are still organised by homelands. Examples of such an understanding of 'ethnic history' which are also partly based on oral history include e.g.: Erichsen, C. W. (2005), *The Angels of Death Has Descended Violently Among Them*. Leiden: African Studies Centre and, in many respects, Kangumu, B. (2011), *Contesting Caprivi: A History of Colonial Isolation and Regional Nationalism in Namibia*. Basel: Basler Afrika Bibliographien. I will discuss Kangamu's book below.

ern Namibia and its interactions with the rest of the country, the cross-border region shared with Angola, and the wider Southern African region.[58] By providing detailed deeper regional histories, these newer studies transposed the often strictly contained ethnic or national histories into wider regional contexts. Such understandings also shed light on people who were often absent in earlier history writing because they did not clearly fit into – or even contradicted – the supposed boundaries of an 'ethnic' group or homeland.[59] Other studies explored particular aspects of history from beyond the Red Line during the South African occupation which were not geographically or 'ethnically' bound, including environmental aspects and infrastructure development.[60]

This study follows on from these studies by aiming to understand the Caprivi's history in the twentieth century as being integrated within the frameworks of northern Namibia and the cross-border region it shares with Botswana, Angola and Zambia as well as its role within South and Southern African history. By addressing the particular topic of nature and nature conservation, I aim to depart from a narrowly-defined history of the region determined by the geographical and ethnical demarcations of the colonial and apartheid administrations.

The Caprivi Strip

The general narrative of Namibian historiography outlined above is also reflected in the few scholarly works which explicitly explore the Caprivi's past. Prior to independence, only very limited historical research was done on the area, which was partly a result of restricted

---

[58] On Kaoko's history within a (northern) Namibian context, see e.g.: Rizzo 2012 and Bollig, M. and A. Olwage (2016), The Political Ecology of Hunting in Namibia's Kaokoveld: From Dorsland Trekkers' Elephant Hunts to Trophy Hunting in Contemporary Conservancies. *Journal of Contemporary African Studies*, 34: 61–79. For newer studies within a transborder framework, see e.g. Napandulwe Shiweda's dissertation: Shiweda, N. (2011) Omhedi: Displacement and Legitimacy in Oukwanyama Politics, Namibia, 1915–2010. (PhD thesis: University of the Western Cape) or Williams (2015). In relation to southern Namibia, see: Biwa, M. (2012), 'Weaving the past with threads of memory': narratives and commemorations of the colonial war in southern Namibia. (PhD thesis: University of the Western Cape).

[59] For example, Gregor Dobler's work on the formation of a trader elite in north-central Namibia: Dobler, G. (2014), Traders and Trade in colonial Ovamboland, 1925–1990: Elite Formation and the Politics of Consumption under Indirect Rule and Apartheid. Basel: Basler Afrika Bibliographien or Miescher, G. (2006), The Ovambo Reserve Otjeru (1911–1938), The Story of an African Community in Central Namibia, BAB Working Paper, 1.

[60] Kreike, E. (2013), *Environmental Infrastructure in African History: Examining the Myth of Natural Resource Management in Namibia*. New York: Cambridge University Press; McKittrick, M. (2015), An Empire of Rivers: The Scheme to Flood the Kalahari, 1919–1945. *Journal of Southern African Studies* 41(3): 485–504; McCullers, M. (2012), Lines in the Sand: The Global Politics of Local Development in Apartheid Era Namibia, 1950–1980. (PhD thesis, Emory University).

access to both the region itself and information on it.⁶¹ Most of the texts which were concerned with the Caprivi's history were written by representatives of the South African authorities or by missionaries.⁶² Especially the lengthy, amateurishly-written manuscript by C.E. Kruger, a former South African native commissioner in the Caprivi, proved to be a source of detailed information, although it was unsurprisingly written from the subjective perspective of the South African government.⁶³ While only published after independence, the publications by Maria Fisch, a long-serving doctor, missionary and anthropologist in north-eastern Namibia, provided a similarly biased 'colonial' perspective on the Caprivi's past.⁶⁴

Academic history writing on the Caprivi mostly began after independence, and, similar to the rest of Namibian historiography, was initially – and, in many regards, still is – primarily concerned with narrow ethnic histories, which often lacked a wider regional or Southern African focus.⁶⁵ Possibly also triggered by the political crisis in the Caprivi in the late 1990s, during which the Caprivi secessionist movement gained momentum, the area's history has since entered more into the focus of scholarly debate and has been linked more frequently to a regional framework.⁶⁶ For example, a highly useful paper which explored the Caprivi's

---

61 Especially in relation to the Namibian War of Liberation, the South African regime sought to tightly control and restrict information. For an overview of information politics in Namibia under apartheid rule, see: Heinze, R. (2014), "It Recharged Our Batteries": Writing the History of the Voice of Namibia, *Journal of Namibian Studies*, 15: 25–62.
62 Kruger, C.E. (1984) History of the Caprivi Strip 1890–1984 (unpublished manuscript, NAN, Private Accessions, A.0472, 1984). As exceptions, it is worth mentioning two 'ethnic' histories which were written in the 1970s: a history of "the BaSubiya", a group of people living in Botswana, the Caprivi Strip and Zambia, by Daniel Shamukuni, a Botswanan teacher and community worker (Shamukuni, D.M. (1972), The BaSubiya, *Botswana Notes and Records*, 4: 161–184), and a Master's thesis written at the University of Stellenbosch on the 'Mafwe' people (Pretorius, J. (1975), The Fwe of the Eastern Caprivi Zipfel (MA thesis, Stellenbosch)). With their focus on ethnic history, both authors did not directly oppose apartheid policies or South Africa's occupation of Namibia and hence might have enjoyed easier access to information.
63 Kruger (1984).
64 Fisch's history of the Caprivi during the German colonial period, in particular, adopts a perspective in which Kurt Streitwolf, the first German commissioner in the Caprivi, is celebrated as a source of development and civilisation (Fisch, M. (1996), *Der Caprivizipfel während der deutschen Zeit, 1890–1914*. Cologne: Rüdiger Köppe). Fisch also published a short history of the South African period in the Caprivi, which I will discuss on p. 188 ff. (Fisch, M. (1999), *The Secessionist Movement in the Caprivi: A Historical Perspective*. Windhoek: Namibia Scientific Society).
65 See e.g. Chris Maritz's short article on relations between the 'Subia' and 'Fwe' groups (Maritz, C. (1996), The Subia and Fwe of Caprivi, *Africa Insight*, 26(2): 177–186) or the two contributions by Caprivian scholars to the *Public History, Forgotten History* Conference in Windhoek in 2000: Sehani, M. 'The Mafwe/Mayun Crisis: Rival Histories and the Assertion of Identity in the Caprivi' and Sasa, D. 'The Mayeyi Chieftainship'.
66 That a focus on the history of one particular geographical area or group of people is not necessarily of less relevance or value is shown, for example, by the highly informative and thoroughly-researched study by the social anthropologist Gertrud Boden on the 'Kwe' group in the West

role within Southern African political history in closer detail was Ashley Jackson's 2001 article on *Bechuanaland, the Caprivi Strip and the First World War*.⁶⁷ In 2003 Lawrence Flint published an insightful article on pre- and early-colonial Caprivi within the broader context of Lozi state-building.⁶⁸ Also focused on the multi-layered relations between Zambia's Western Province and the Caprivi during the South African occupation and especially in post-independence Namibia are Wolfgang Zeller's series of articles on the Caprivi as a borderland region.⁶⁹

In recent years two major books on the Caprivi were published which were both highly relevant for this study. In 2011 the Caprivian historian Bennett Kangumu published his seminal dissertation on the history of Caprivi from pre-colonial times until the 1990s.⁷⁰ His book is clearly the most thorough historical research hitherto undertaken on the area, and the Eastern Caprivi in particular, and made use of an extensive array of archival material from archives in Namibia, Botswana, South Africa and Zambia, as well as many oral sources. Kangumu's focus is clearly on what could be framed as local Caprivian topics, especially those concerned with questions of belonging and identity among the region's different population groups. This subject has become of particular interest in relation to the Caprivi secessionist movement, especially the treason trials of the secessionists, as well as to conflicts among different 'Traditional Authorities' in the Caprivi.⁷¹ In doing so, Kangumu's

---

Caprivi (Boden 2005). With her extensive political, historical and economic background chapter, she provides one of the most detailed histories of the Western Caprivi. Prior to this publication there had been very few works on the Western Caprivi's history, see e.g. the socio-linguistic study by Matthias Brenzinger (Brenzinger, M. (2003), The Khwe History: A Struggle for Recognition: Report to the Legal Assistance Centre, Windhoek. University of Cologne: Institute for African Studies) and the Master's thesis by the social anthropologist Ina Orth (Orth, I. (1999), Landrechte und Identität bei südafrikanischen Wildbeutern: Eine Fallstudie zu den Kxoe in West Caprivi (Namibia) (MA thesis, University of Cologne) as well as some historical notes in the clearly biased memoirs of former military personnel, e.g.: Breytenbach, J. (1997): *Eden's exile: One Soldier's Fight for Paradise*. Cape Town: Queillerie Publishers.

⁶⁷ Jackson, A. (2001), Bechuanaland, the Caprivi Strip and the First World War, *War & Society*, 19(2): 109–142. The article was barely referenced in any other publications on the Caprivi's history, which again points to the isolation in which the Caprivi's past has hitherto been researched.

⁶⁸ Flint, L. (2003), State-Building in Central Southern Africa: Citizenship and Subjectivity in Barotseland and Caprivi. *International Journal of African Historical Studies*, 36(2): 393–428.

⁶⁹ See, among others: Zeller, W. (2007), Chiefs, Policing and Vigilantes: "Cleaning Up" the Caprivi Borderland of Namibia. In L. Buur and H.M. Kyed (eds.), *State Recognition and Democratization in Sub-Saharan Africa: A New Dawn for Traditional Authorities?* New York: Palgrave: 79–104; Zeller, W. (2009), Danger and Opportunity in Katima Mulilo: A Namibian Border Boomtown at Transnational Crossroads, *Journal of Southern African Studies*, 35(1): 133–154. For a synthesis, see: Zeller, W. (2015), *What Makes Border Real – In the Namibia-Zambia and Uganda-South Sudan Borderlands*. Helsinki: Unigrafia.

⁷⁰ Kangumu (2011).

⁷¹ Kangumu, (2011): 20. For more on the secessionist movement and the disputes between different traditional authorities, see Chapter 5. The term 'traditional authorities' is used throughout this

book at times falls into an overly narrow understanding of the Caprivi's past as a history of – as he refers to it in the title – "colonial isolation" based on the histories of different so-called ethnic groups and their respective interactions with the local colonial administration. Nevertheless, his history of the Caprivi touches on many other broader issues, particularly the role of the Witwatersrand Native Labour Association (WNLA). The second highly relevant book is the social anthropologist Julie J. Taylor's dissertation about the interplay of history, politics, identity and the environment in western Caprivi.[72] Based on extensive field research among the San population of the western Caprivi, Taylor critically engaged with the more recent history of 'San' and their struggle for land and resources. Her book not only provides a history of the San groups in the area, but, even more crucially for this study, offers a critical approach to recent nature conservation and mapping projects undertaken by the many conservation non-governmental organisations (NGOs) in the area.

Nature (and Space) as a Field of Historical Research

Human understandings of nature have changed not only over time, but also across space.[73] Debates about the essence of nature and its relationship to human society and culture have been central to (western) philosophy and anthropology from at least the time of their emergence as academic disciplines and, in many regards, much earlier. In 1967 Clarence J. Glacken published a monumental work on the history of the concepts of nature and culture from "ancient times to the end of the 18th century", in which he argued that questions arising from the human relationship with nature have always been fundamental to what he described as "western thought".[74] Tellingly, it took a trained geographer, to produce one of the most cited and seminal works in the emerging field of environmental history.[75] In

---

book for ethnically defined political entities which are officially recognised by the government and headed by a 'chief'. In the Caprivi, a traditional authority is often referred to as a *Khuta* or *Kuta*.

[72] Taylor (2012)

[73] For example, in relation to the Namaqualand region of South Africa, see: Cousins, B., M.T. Hoffman, N. Allsopp, R.F. Rohde (2007), A synthesis of sociological and biological perspectives on sustainable land use in Namaqualand, *Journal of Arid Environments*, 70(4): 834–846.

[74] Glacken, J.C. (1967), *Traces on the Rhodian Shore: Nature and Culture in Western Thought from Ancient Times to the End of the Eighteenth Century*. Berkeley: University of California Press, p. vii.

[75] Other key early works for the establishment of environmental history as an academic field include Roderick Nash's *Wilderness and the American Mind*, also published in 1967, and Donald Worster's *Dust Bowl* (1977) and *Nature's Economy: A Study of Ecological Ideals* (1978), which all focus on the environmental history of rural North America. A more global perspective was taken most prominently by Alfred Crosby in his book on biological exchange and invasion, *The Columbian Exchange* (1972), and in his *Ecological Imperialism* (1986) on the role of ecology and nature in European imperial and colonial expansion. For an overview of environmental historiography in other geographical regions, see e.g.: Locher, F. (2009), Environmental History: The Origins, Stakes, and Perspectives of a New Site for Research, *Revue d'histoire Moderne et Contemporaine*,

the preface to his book, Glacken outlined three general ideas about the natural environment and its relationship with human society, of which the last is concerned with "men as geographic agent[s]".[76] It was in this section that he discussed the impact of humans on the environment, arguing that nature is both spatial and geographical at its core. Thus, from the establishment of environmental history as a field of research within the discipline of history, space was seen as a crucial prism through which to understand "the history of the mutual relations between humankind and the rest of nature".[77]

Whether history was happening in nature, with nature or by nature, it also always occurred through its spatiality.[78] Thus, by taking into account the ability of geography and natural science as practices to assist in better understanding the past, environmental historians brought back into the study of history the "material and cultural significance of the natural world".[79]

In the context of general African historiography, the new focus on the materiality and spatiality of the natural environment, as proposed by environmental historians and historical geographers, was met with scepticism. This perspective appeared to be worryingly close to an environmental determinist understanding of African people as mere 'products of nature', deprived of the humanity which was ascribed to Europeans.[80] For Frantz Fanon, for example, it was clear that even colonial language had "dehumanized" Africans by invoking such ideas. In his 1971 book *The Wretched of the Earth*, Fanon highlighted that "[i]n plain talk, he [the colonized] is reduced to the state of an animal. And consequently, when the

---

56(4): 7–38 or, in greater detail, the edited volume: McNeill, J.R and E.S. Maudlin (eds.) (2014), *A Companion to Global Environmental History*. Chichester: Wiley-Blackwell.

[76] Glacken (1967): vii. The other two were the notion of "a designed world" and the concept of environmental influence on humankind.

[77] As the field of environmental history was defined by J.R. McNeill (2003: 6). On the interrelatedness of environmental history and historical geography, see also: Williams, M. (1994), The relations of environmental history and historical geography, *Journal of Historical Geography*, 20(1): 3–21 and McNeill, 2003: 9.

[78] This reflects a fundamental concern within environmental history, namely the question of to which degree human beings shape nature or, conversely, to what extent the natural environment shapes human societies. The latter point was explored by neo-environmental determinists such as Jared Diamond (*Guns, Germs and Steel*, 1997 and *Collapse*, 2004) and Jeffery Herbst (*States and Power in Africa*, 2000). Other scholars proposed combinations of both positions, arguing for *middle grounds* in which nature and culture are understood to influence each other or for more process orientated approaches of *environmental infrastructuring* or *environing* (Kreike 2013). See also: White, R. (1991), *The Middle Ground: Indians, Empires and Republics in the Great Lakes Region, 1650–1815*. Cambridge: Cambridge University Press.

[79] Beinart, W. and J. McGregor (2003), Introduction. In W. Beinart and J. McGregor (eds.), *Social History and African Environments*. Athens: Ohio University Press, p. 7.

[80] Beinart et al. (2003): 7.

colonist speaks of the colonized he uses zoological terms. [...] In his endeavours at description and finding the right word, the colonist refers constantly to the bestiary."[81]

It only became possible to allay this fear of reviving colonial representations of Africans as an integral part – or even victims – of nature through an understanding of nature and geography as agents of history in their own right. This emerged when two major developments in politics and historiography fell in tune with environmental history.[82] In the 1970s environmentalism grew as a political movement at the same time as social history as well as cultural and later postcolonial theory became influential in the writing of (environmental) history in and of Africa. Also reflecting these global historiographical trends in the 1970s, the writing of Africa's environmental history thus became more focused on people as agents in the shaping of their natural environment.[83] With this new focus on the individual actor, alternative themes emerged, including some explicitly drawn from African contexts – for example, on the ideas and practices of pre-colonial societies concerning the shaping of their landscapes and the search for survival strategies – while other topics which had previously been discussed primarily from the perspective of the colonial powers were rethought under the new premises.[84] New research focussed in particular on the role played by ecological science and conservation for both colonial rule and the African responses and resistance to it as well as more generally on relations between nature and culture in

---

[81] Fanon, F. (1963), *The Wretched of Earth* (translation of the French original of 1961). New York: Grove, p. 7.

[82] Beinart et al. (2003): 7–8. Prior to the 1980s, historical geography and environmental history were also both met with significant scepticism in Germany, where supposed connections between people and land remained too closely associated with national socialist theories of 'blood and soil' and 'lebensraum'. Theories which posited a 'natural' bond between people and the land which they cultivate were based on Friedrich Ratzel's idea of 'lebensraum' and had been adopted by Nazi ideologues such as Karl Haushofer. They provided a 'scientific' basis for Nazi Germany's geopolitical ambitions (Osterhammel, J. (1998), Die Wiederkehr des Raums, *Neue Politische Literatur*, 43 (3): 379–381).

[83] One of the first major works to emerge from this new perspective was: Kjekshus, H. (1977), *Ecology, Control and Economic Development in East African History: The Case of Tanganyika 1850–1950*. London: Heinemann. However, the left wing of the rising global environmental movement faced a contradiction: on the one hand, the protection of nature had become central to leftist politics, while, on the other hand, more Marxist-leaning scholars in Africa called for more efficient extraction of natural resources in Africa by Africans in order to make up for the long-standing Western underdevelopment of Africa, as argued, for example by Walter Rodney in his influential book: Rodney, W. (1972), *How Europe Underdeveloped Africa*. London: Bogle-L'Ouverture Publications.

[84] For a very early example, see Ford, J. (1971), *The Role of the Trypanosomiases in African Ecology: A Study of the Tsetse Fly Problem*. London: Clarendon. Later examples include Anderson, D.M. and D.H. Johnson (1988), *The Ecology of Survival: Case Studies from Northeast African History*. Boulder: Westview, or a study by the social anthropologist De Waal, A. (1989), *Famine That Kills: Darfur, Sudan, 1984–1985*. New York: Oxford University Press.

settler societies.[85] Such directions of research were fuelled by growing global awareness of so-called planetary boundaries or limits and the increasing urgency for humankind to act immediately in order to save the planet.[86]

While the fact that human beings have a negative impact on many aspects of nature is rarely questioned anymore, the discussion on what and who is actually causing the damage – and the corresponding question of how to react to the realisation that the world's natural resources are in fact limited and non-renewable – remains highly contested, not only among ecologists, but also among social scientists and historians; nevertheless, many scholars agree that it is exactly this coupling of nature and resources that lies at the heart of the question.[87] A powerful concept which has emerged from this debate has been that of the Anthropocene, an idea which has enabled a framing of the argument that humankind's influence on the environment has been so strong that this must now be recognised in a new conceptualisation of geological time.[88] For the writing of environmental history and the understanding of environmental change, the concept represented the idea which Jason W. Moore described as green arithmetic – "formulating history as the aggregation of human and natural relations" – or the even more simplistic notion that "Society plus Nature = History".[89] The concept has been rightly criticised for its understanding of humanity (and nature) as single entities, an approach which disregards inequalities among

---

[85] In 1989 the Journal for African Studies (JSAS) published a special issue under the title *Politics of Conservation in Southern Africa*, 15(2). See also: MacKenzie, J.M. (1988), *The Empire of Nature: Hunting, Conservation and British Imperialism*. Manchester: Manchester University Press; or, for a more recent work on science and colonialism: Harries, P. (2007), *Butterflies and Barbarians: Swiss Missionaries and Systems of Knowledge in South-East Africa*. Athens: Ohio University Press.

[86] Most prominently formulated by the Club of Rome (Meadows, D.H., G. Meadows, J. Randers and W.W. Behrens (1972), *The Limits to Growth*. New York: Universe Books) or, even earlier and in a more radical form from a neo-Malthusian perspective on overpopulation, by: Ehrlich, P.R. (1968), *The Population Bomb*. New York: Ballantine Books. This underlying assumption of a rapidly degrading planet has been increasingly adopted by more and more scholars and public figures, e.g. in a rather optimistic argument which strongly believes in the potential of technological solutions: Rockström, J., W. Steffen, K. Noone, Å. Persson, F. S. Chapin, E. Lambin, T. M. Lenton, M. Scheffer, C. Folke, H. Schellnhuber, B. Nykvist, C. A. De Wit, T. Hughes, S. van der Leeuw, H. Rodhe, S. Sörlin, P. K. Snyder, R. Costanza, U. Svedin, M. Falkenmark, L. Karlberg, R. W. Corell, V. J. Fabry, J. Hansen, B. Walker, D. Liverman, K. Richardson, P. Crutzen, and J. Foley. (2009), Planetary Boundaries: Exploring the Safe Operating Space for Humanity. *Ecology and Society*, 14(2); for a broader audience: Gore, A. (2006), *An Inconvenient Truth: The Planetary Emergency of Global Warming and What we can do about it*. New York: Rodale; or in the highly provocative and radically market-orientated: Wilson, E. O. (2016), *Half-Earth: our planet's fight for life*. New York: Liveright.

[87] Moore, J. W. (2016), Anthropocene or Capitalocene? Nature, History, and the Crisis of Capitalism. In J. W. Moore, *Anthropocene or Capitalocene? Nature, History, and the Crisis of Capitalism*. Oakland: PM Press.

[88] Crutzen, P.J. and E.F. Stoermer (2000), The Anthropocene, *Global Change Newsletter*, 41: 17–18.

[89] Moore (2016): 4.

humans (and different species) arising from factors such as class, gender and Western hegemony.[90] As such, many critics see the idea of the Anthropocene as ignoring the political context of environmental questions.[91] In other words, the concept carries with it the danger of presenting environmental issues as "a socio-political arrangement" in which ideological contestation and struggles are replaced by "techno-managerial planning" and "the space for political contestation, debate and reorientation" is restricted.[92] On a theoretical level, such concerns have been met by new, amended concepts such as the Captialocene (or the Age of Capitalism), which aims to overcome a clear dichotomy, informed by the notion of "human exceptionalism", between nature and human society. Instead, these scholars propose a more interwoven paradigm which understands capitalism as a way of organising nature or "as a multispecies, situated, capitalist world-ecology".[93] In simpler terms, they appeal for an integrated understanding of systems of oppression, such as capitalism or racism, that sees these as being inseparably linked to the oppression of animals and nature. In order to "take equality seriously", they argue, it needs to be extended to non-human nature.[94]

Within such discourses, engagement with the history of nature conservation also shifted, particularly in relation to the spatial protection of biodiversity as practiced in nature conservation areas.[95] Nature conservation had long been primarily researched in the con-

---

[90] Andreas Malm, for example, showed in his history of the rise of steam power in nineteenth-century Britain how the shift from water energy to fossil fuels was intentionally undertaken by factory owners to maintain a hold of the means of production. He then went on to illustrate how the system of mass extraction of natural resources was brought into being by a small group of people – namely, wealthy, white, British men. The obvious implication is that it has not been 'humanity' as such which has proven to be a danger to the environment, but rather a small group of elites. (Malm, A. (2016), *Fossil Capital: The Rise of Steam Power and the Roots of Global Warming*. London: Verso).

[91] E.g.: Moore (2016) and Lövbrand, E., S. Beck, J. Chilvers, T. Forsyth, J. Hedren, M. Hulme, R. Lidskog and Vasileiadou, E. (2015). Who speaks for the future of Earth? How critical social science can extend the conversation on the Anthropocene, *Global Environmental Change*, 32: 211–218.

[92] Lövbrand et al. (2015): 215.

[93] Moore (2016): 6. The term *Capitalocene* was coined among others by Donna Harraway, who later also critizised it as be in too strongly focused on humans, see e.g.: Haraway, D. (2015), Anthropocene, Capitalocene, Plantationocene, Chthulucene, *Environmental Humanities*, 6(1): 159–165.

[94] Torres, B. (2007), Making a Killing: The Political Economy of Animal Rights. Oakland: AK. p. 1; Nilbert, T. (2002), Animal Rights/Human Rights: Entanglements of Oppression and Liberation. Oxford: Rowman & Littlefield.

[95] For definitions of the different categories of protected areas, see the website of the International Union for the Conservation of Nature (IUCN): www.iucn.org/theme/protected-areas/about/protected-areas-categories [accessed 03.01.2018]. In this book, I will generally use the term 'nature conservation area' to cover all of these categories, while I will also use official or common local terms which were or continue to be used in the spatial and temporal contexts to which I refer and which may differ from the present definitions provided by the IUCN. Such terms include 'nature / game reserves', 'national parks', 'wildlife areas'.

text of colonialism, settler societies, and especially empire.[96] However, not only was it now acknowledged how "ecology and empire went hand in hand", but also recognised were the particular places in which ecology – and, with it, nature conservation – were produced. This in turn, had a significant impact upon the construction of an imperial nature space.[97]

As a new turn towards community-based conservation occurred in Southern Africa in the late 1980s, histories of nature conservation in the region became more focused on the role of individuals within conservation practice and policy.[98] In recent years, the trend towards militarised and top-down conservation has led political scientists and geographers to turn their focus once more to structural and economic aspects of nature conservation.[99] My study aims to elucidate the particular historical and geographical context of such conservation practices.[100]

In relation to the manner in which I engage with nature and history in this study, two points should be emphasised. Firstly, nature cannot be understood only as either a social construct or as an all-defining force of history.[101] Instead, history and nature are concepts which influence each other.[102] In other words, just because all nature has a history does not necessarily mean that nature is defined only by its history, nor by its constructiveness or the discourse of it; instead, there is also a "nature in a realistic sense [...] an independent order of nature".[103] In this study, however, rather than elaborating on the agency of nature in history, I will focus on how society, and particularly politically and militarily powerful actors, made use of nature in practical as well as discursive ways.[104] This leads to a second point,

---

[96] MacKenzie (1988); Neumann (1996), for more recent approaches to nature conservation and imperialism, see: Steinhart (2006), Beinart et al. (2007); Gissibl, B. (2016): *The Nature of German Imperialism: Conservation and the Politics of Wildlife in colonial East Africa*. New York: Berghahn.

[97] Coron, W., G. Miles and J. Gitlin, (1992), Becoming West: Toward a New Meaning for Western History. In: G. Miles, J. Gitlin (eds.), *Under an Open Sky: Rethinking America's Western Past*. New York, p. 12.

[98] Anderson, D.M. and R. Grove (eds.) (1987), *Conservation in Africa: People, Policies and Practice*. Cambridge: Cambridge University Press; Carruthers, J. (1995), *The Kruger National Park: A Social and Political History*. Pietermaritzburg: University of Natal Press.

[99] E.g. Duffy, R. (2010), *Nature Crime: How We're Getting Conservation Wrong*. New Haven and London: Yale University Press; Büscher (2013), Lunstrum (2014), Ramutsindela (2007), Ramutsindela and Shabangu (2013).

[100] See also Büscher (2013).

[101] See for example Escobar, A. (1999), After Nature: Steps to an Antiessentialist Political Ecology, *Current Anthropolgy*, 40(1): 1–30 (here 2–3).

[102] Moreover, both concepts are also intricately entwined with the notions of space and landscape, as illustrated, for example, by: Bollig, M. (2009), Visions of Landscape: An Introduction. In M. Bollig and O. Bubenzer (eds.), *African Landscapes: Interdisciplinary Approaches*. New York: Springer, p. 1–40 (here 24–29).

[103] Escobar (1999): 3.

[104] Unsurprisingly, these interactions altered the region's natural environment, which in turn influenced the ways in which nature was exploited and discussed.

one which reflects the historian John McNeill's claim that interest in environmental history often derives from anxiety about contemporary social problems.[105] In the case of the Caprivi, new means of and visions for conservation brought about new social problems. Any attempt to analyse these problems calls for a deeper understanding of the historical interactions between nature and people in the area. This study therefore aims to produce a history of how people have interacted with and made use of nature in a region which experienced a long-running war and a racist occupation, and which, with its abundance of wildlife, was also consistently perceived by its various rulers throughout most of the twentieth century, and even into the early twenty-first century, as both a final bastion of "unspoiled nature" and a potential reservoir for natural resource extraction.[106]

Constituting an Archive of the Caprivi

In recent years, the influence of the colonial archive on post-colonial historiography and knowledge production has been rigorously debated.[107] As Ann Laura Stoler accurately declared, "documents were not dead matters once the moment of their making had passed", but "they could be requisitioned to write new histories" and "could be reclassified for new initiatives".[108] Research on archival records must always question the assumptions of and aims behind the archive and its methods of classification and ordering over time, while simultaneously trying to read the gaps in its collections and study 'absence' as a source in its own right. This means that it is not sufficient to analyse only the documents which are found in the archive, but that the historian should also always engage with 'missing' documents and search for "alternative archives".[109]

Important to note here is that by finding "alternative archives", I do not refer to the process of supplementing or questioning written documents with oral interviews and observations. Instead, I interpret all the various written, oral and visual sources equally and in relation to each other, a method which allows for critical engagement with all of these documents in

---

[105] McNeill, J.R. (2003), Observations on the Nature and Culture of Environmental History, *History and Theory*, 42(4): 5–43 (here 43).

[106] On the recurring trope of Namibia as "unspoiled nature", see also: Lenggenhager, L. (2009), Empty Landscapes, Wild Animals an Unspoiled People: Motifs in Namibian Tourism Advertising. In: G. Miescher, L. Rizzo and J. Silvester, *Posters in Action: On the History of Production, Circulation and Reception of Namibian Posters*. Basel: Basler Afrika Bibliographien, p. 31–44.

[107] See e.g. the edited volume: Hamilton, C., V. Harris, J. Taylor, M. Pickover, G. Reid and R. Saleh (eds.) (2002): *Refiguring the Archive*. Dordrecht: Kluwer.

[108] Stoler, A.L. (2009), *Along the Archival Grain: Epistemic Anxieties and Colonial Common Sense*. Oxfordshire: Princeton University Press, p. 3.

[109] Hamilton, C., V. Harris, G. Reid (2002), Introduction. In: C. Hamilton, V. Harris, J. Taylor, M. Pickover, G. Reid and R. Saleh (eds.), *Refiguring the Archive*. Dordrecht: Kluwer, p. 16.

both their own right and in relation to the contexts of production and archival practice in which they were found. By doing so, I seek not to create an alternative history, but rather to take into account the production and preservation of the archive as a part of the discipline which blurs the supposedly clear line between historiography and history.[110]

This study is based on archival and field research, mostly in Namibia and South Africa and, to a lesser degree, in Botswana, Zambia and Angola between 2011 and 2015. The information which I compiled during my research in Southern Africa can be roughly grouped into three categories which I will discuss in the following sections respectively: interviews; informal discussions and observations; and written and visual archival material. Together, these different types of archival data constitute my primary sources for this study. In general, I treat the interviews, which I will discuss at some length below, in the same manner as written documents, from which they only differ in form and not in what they can potentially say about the past.[111] Most written documents originate from state-run archives and originate from colonial and apartheid collections, while many of my interviewees worked for the South African state. As such, my sources bear practical, methodological and theoretical challenges, especially in relation to my stated intention to understand South Africa's policies and methods of governance as they were defined and contested in and through its 'peripheries', a task which must, paradoxically, still rely on archival material originating from the centres of power of the South African state.

Interviews

Over the course of my research, I conducted forty-two formal interviews with thirty-eight different people.[112] Most of the interviews were taped, with only a few interviewees not agreeing to be recorded. Reasons given for not allowing me to record included a lack of trust in me keeping the information confidential; or so-called customary reasons. The latter explanation was mainly the case for chiefs, who argued that it would not be permissible for their voice to be replayed. All but a very few interviews were conducted in English or, more occasionally, in German; hence no interpreter was usually needed.[113] Although the majority of my interviewees spoke English fairly well, this was not a first language for most or for me. In some instances, I later discussed particular aspects of the interviews with other

---

[110] Lalu (2009): 10.
[111] See also: Miescher (2012a): 15 and for a more detailed discussion on the role of oral interviews in African historiography: Cohen, D.W., S.F. Miescher and L. White (2001), Introduction: Voices, Words, and Historiography. In: L. White, S. Miescher and D.W. Cohen (eds.), *African Words, African Voices. Critical Practices in Oral History*. Bloomington: Indiana University Press, p. 1–27.
[112] A detailed list of all interviews can be found at the end of the book.
[113] In the few instances when I required an interpreter, this service was provided by either a family member or an acquaintance of the interviewee.

speakers of the first languages of my respective interviewees. This was especially helpful with regards to clarifying names of people and places. In three cases, I conducted written interviews by e-mail because the interviewee either lived too far away or was unavailable when I was in the area. Most of the interviews took place in the Caprivi, in Windhoek, or in South Africa, where many of the people who used to work in the Caprivi currently live. The interviews normally lasted between half an hour and two hours and were conducted at the place of residence or work of the interviewees.

Although most of my interviewees gave me consent to publish their full names, I decided to render them as anonymously as possible. The use of pseudonyms was not suitable, however, for two reasons. Firstly, inventing pseudonyms is considered problematic as it would lend me, as the researcher, the power to name my interviewees. Furthermore, chosen pseudonyms may not always account for all aspects of an individual's gender(s), language(s), class(es) and race(s).[114] Secondly, in the case of the Caprivi, family names reveal information about an individual's village, class or language group. Hence, in order to make up full names, I would have had to decide on the degree to which the pseudonym should also be associated with the attributions expressed by the interviewee's real name. To avoid such problematic choices, I chose to use initials instead. Although even initials cannot fully anonymise an individual, they do render personal details more confidential to a broader readership. However, most of the people whom I interviewed knew each other personally – or at least worked and lived during the same period in the same geographical area – and it will thus be unavoidable that they will recognise some of my other interviewees. Nevertheless, I argue that the consequences of being openly named are potentially more harmful and unpredictable, especially at a time in which digital archives and online full-text search machines are becoming increasingly important.[115]

The people whom I interviewed were diverse in terms of their function, class and socio-economic background, level of education, age, and position within society. However, with only one exception, they were all male. This extreme gender bias is partly explainable by the method with which I chose interviewees, the particular topic of my research, and my own gender. Primarily, it shows how disproportionately male-dominated the fields of nature con-

---

[114] For a discussion of the ethical challenges of naming, see: Lahman, M.K.E., K.L. Rodriguez, L. Moses, K.M. Griffin, M.B. Menoza and W. Yacoub (2015), A Rose by any other Name is still a Rose? Problematizing Pseudonyms in Research, *Qualitative Inquiry*, 21(5): 445–453.

[115] See also: Lahman et al. (2015): 450–451. There are a few instances in this book when it would not have made sense to use a person's initials instead of his/her full name. This was the case when an interviewee discussed openly accessible archival material which he/she had produced, was referred to in relevant archival records, or spoke solely in their capacity as a representative of an institution, organisation or company.

servation and tourism were, and in many regards still are.[116] Moreover, it also points towards a gap in both my own research and academic research in general, which was not possible to address in the scope of this study, namely a failure to fully understand the gendered structures which are inherent in nature conservation and to engage with the roles, memories and interpretations of women who have been active in the field. Over recent decades, environmental history as a discipline, particularly as practiced in (former) colonies, was rightly criticised for being ignorant of women as historical subjects and for its gender-biased methodology, which failed to comprehend the gendered nature of history and historiography.[117] The scholarly reaction to these shortcomings can be summarised in two main strands. Firstly, the 'Women, Environment and Development' (WED) or 'ecofeminist' perspective upheld the notion of a 'special relationship' between women and the environment and saw women as the 'natural' custodians of the land.[118] The second strand attempts to reflect gender considerations in the tools, methods, and statistics used in nature conservation and development policies.[119] Both of these lines of argument should be criticised for depoliticising gender and depriving the concept of its emancipatory and feminist background, in particular by targeting women as a homogenous and undifferentiated social category.[120] To avoid these pitfalls, the specific histories and power structures behind the exclusion of women as well as resistance to these structures should be addressed in more detail, as should the forces which uphold the patriarchal structures which are still prevalent in nature conservation, such as its close links to military activity or, more recently, neo-liberal politics.[121]

---

[116] For a critical examination of gender in community-based nature conservation and tourism in Namibia, see: Sullivan, S. (2001), Gender, ethnographic myths & community-based conservation in a former Namibian 'Homeland'. In D.L Hodgson (ed.), *Rethinking pastoralism in Africa*. London: James Currey, p. 142–164 or Khumalo, K. and W. Freimund (2014), Expanding Women's Choices through Employment? Community-Based Natural Resource Management and Women's Empowerment in Kwandu Conservancy, Namibia, *Society & Natural Resources*, 27(10): 1024–1039. For a more general overview of the topic, see: Tucker, H. and B. Boonabaana (2012), A Critical Analysis of Tourism, Gender and Poverty Reduction, *Journal of Sustainable Tourism* 20(3): 437–455.

[117] Leach, M. and C. Green (1997), Gender and Environmental History: From Representation of Women and Nature to Gender Analysis of Ecology and Politics, *Environment and History* 3(3): 343–70.

[118] Shiva, V. (1988), *Staying Alive: Women, Ecology and Survival in India*, New Delhi: Zed Press. For a critique of these approaches, see: Leach (1997).

[119] Resurreccion, B.P. and R. Elmhirst (2008), Gender, Environment and Natural Resource Management. New Dimensions, New Debates. In B.P. Resurreccion and R. Elmhirst, (eds.), *Gender and Natural Resource Management: Livelihoods, Mobility and Interventions*. London: Earthscan, p. 3.

[120] Resurreccion et al. (2008): 4.

[121] For a thorough discussion on feminist political ecology, see the edited volume: Harcourt, W. and I.L. Nelson (eds.) (2015), *Practising Feminist Political Ecologies: Moving Beyond the 'Green Economy'*. London: Zed Books. See also Lunstrum (2015) and, on militarisation and feminism, Dowler, L. (2012), Gender, militarization and sovereignty, *Geography Compass*, 6 (8): 490–99.

I did not aim for any sort of representivity when selecting my interviewees.[122] Instead, I sought to obtain a diverse range of interpretations and memories of the past as well as insights into the historical and contemporary contexts of the lives of the people to whom I talked. All interviewees had in common the fact that they were – or remained – involved in some way in the use, research or protection of nature in the Caprivi. This also informed some of my guiding questions. These circulated around the general topics of my research and included queries into areas such as the interviewees' personal experiences and memories of working in the field of nature conservation, their interpretation of past and contemporary nature conservation interventions and policies, and their ideas and visions for the future. Such questions had to be adjusted according to the very diverse backgrounds of the people to whom I spoke.

Because many held various functions at different times, there are no clear-cut lines between different groups of interviewees. Nevertheless, they can be roughly grouped into two categories. The first included people who used to work or still are working in the Caprivi or those who advised about, took decisions on or otherwise impacted upon nature conservation or closely-related fields in the Caprivi. These included Caprivian game guards who worked for the local administration, South African conservation experts and ex-government officials who were based in the region, as well as government officials who oversaw conservation and forestry in Namibia. This group also included representatives of conservation NGOs.

The second group consisted of public persons who were not directly involved in nature conservation in the Caprivi, but could give some information on its administrative and political context, as well as those who took or still take a political position within conservation discussions. Interviewees in this group included chiefs and other personnel of Traditional Authorities, party politicians, and other opinion-makers, such as unionists or pastors. South African military personnel who were based in the region during the Namibian War of Liberation as well as former independence fighters are also included in this group. I struggled in particular to arrange interviews with former South African military officials, to whom I had little access and who were often not willing to participate in formal interviews.[123] To explore some of their memories, I therefore additionally had to refer to soldiers' memoirs and relevant secondary literature.[124]

---

[122] See also Miescher (2012a), 14.
[123] My e-mails and telephone calls often remained unanswered and meetings were cancelled at short notice.
[124] See e.g.: Eloff De Visser, L. (2011), Winning Hearts and Minds in the Namibian Border War. *Scientia Militaria*, 39(1): 85–100. See also e.g. Thompson, J.H. (2006), *An Unpopular War. From afkak to bosbefok. Voices of South African National Servicemen*. Cape Town: Zebra Press.

The decision to interview a specific person was taken if the individual concerned was referenced in archival documents, held a particular function in the government or in a NGO, or was recommended by other informants. With the oldest interviewees being in their nineties, the interviews allowed me to approach a wide range of aspects concerning nature conservation for the time period from the 1950s until the present.

Informal Discussions and Observations
Alongside these formal interviews, I talked to many other people informally and took notes from these conversations. Informal discussions of this nature were crucial to help me to better understand the diverse and sometimes contested memories expressed in the interviews as well as the information which I found in written archival material. Furthermore, informal discussions allowed me to gain access to the views of persons who did not want to be formally interviewed. It was these informal discussions which served to deepen my understanding of the contexts in which the histories I was describing took place and to obtain insights into stories which otherwise remained untold. Particularly in the case of former South African soldiers and military personnel, it was crucial to talk informally, either in the Caprivi or while looking together at physical reminders of the war zone, such as old fighter jets now held in the South African Airforce Museum or at photographs taken in the region.

Talking to persons at the very places from where their memories originated also allowed me to better understand the overlapping contexts shared by physical space and memories. With this in mind, I spent several months in the Caprivi, mostly staying at communal campsites. To stay on these camp grounds also gave me the opportunity to gain further insights into current community-based tourism and conservation initiatives and to stay in close proximity to the national parks. To visit and stay at these very diverse settings – including, among many others, former and current military camps, government buildings, luxury lodges, missionary stations, national parks, and air force bases – served to further deepen my understanding of the area. Travelling within the Caprivi by car and public transport also gave me a sense of the physical space and distances between these various settings.

Archival Material
Extensive archival research was the third, and in many ways most important, pillar of my research. The bulk of my archival material stems from the National Archives of Namibia (NAN). Most of the official documents concerning the Caprivi for the time when it was directly governed from Pretoria (1939–1980) were transferred from Pretoria to the NAN in 2001. Of particular interest for the scope of this book were documents from the Caprivi homeland

administrations (1972–1980), including those from the Caprivi Agriculture and Forestry (CAF) and the Caprivi Native Affairs and Magistrate (CNAM) departments.[125] For the time prior to the establishment of the homeland, some relevant files were stored under the records of the Katima Mulilo Magistrate (LKM). I also used further documents from the records of the South West African Administration (SWAA) and its Directorate of Nature Conservation and Tourism (NTB) as well as from various other miscellaneous holdings.

Some documents concerning the Caprivi had not (yet) been transferred to Namibia, but I could access these at the National Archives of South Africa (NASA) in Pretoria. These records remained in South Africa because they generally belonged to larger archival series such as the Commission Reports (KC), which also include records from the Commission for South West Africa (SWA).[126] In other cases it was not clear why files had not been transferred to Namibia, among them documents on the Caprivi which are still kept among the records of the Secretary of Native Affairs (NTS) or the Department of Native Administration and Development (BAO).

Besides the two main archives which I visited in Windhoek and Pretoria, I consulted smaller archives, such as the Documentation Centre of the South African National Defence Force (SANDFDOC) in Pretoria, which holds the military records of both the South African Defence Force (SADF) and the South West African Territory Forces (SWATF). As access to most of these files was still restricted and the few documents which I succeeded in getting declassified often turned out to be empty folders, I also accessed the unofficial and unstructured archives of the South African Air Force Museum in Cape Town, which holds many visual documents relating to SADF garrisons in Namibia. I further visited the archives of the Livingstone Museum in Livingstone (LM) and the National Archives of Zambia (ZAR) and Angola (ANA).

Maps are a particularly insightful type of archival documents in the context of a debate on nature conservation, development and warfare as their production has played an influential role in all three areas. The maps I discuss in this book range from simple sketch maps produced by nature conservation officials in the field to detailed military maps based on aerial photography to high-gloss promotional maps released by conservation NGOs. Although maps are among the most common forms of media, mapping has long been neglected in visual studies. Social and cultural geographers in particular, but also historians and sociolo-

---

[125] In its proclamation as a self-governing homeland in 1976, the homeland was officially named as 'Eastern Caprivi' or, in Afrikaans, 'Oos-Caprivi' (Republic of South Africa (ed.) (1976), *Government Gazette*, 129(5022), 19.03.1976. Pretoria: Government Printer). Two years later it changed its name to Lozi Republic. In most contemporary documents, the homeland is referred to as 'East Caprivi' or 'Eastern Caprivi'. See also Kangumu (2011): 123.

[126] According to personal comments by NASA staff in Pretoria.

gists, have long remained concerned with a critique of photography, painting or film, while continuing to read maps as "an unquestionably 'scientific' or 'objective form of knowledge creation"[127]. It was only from the late 1980s that a small group of researchers from various fields started to theorise maps as constructed visual representations and mapping as more of a social practice than a mere scientific technique. Echoing the work of Michel Foucault and Jacques Derrida, John Brian Harley discussed mapping as a practice of negotiating relations of power and knowledge production in a detailed and influential series of articles.[128] He described maps as social documents and underlined the importance of taking into account their historical and technical contexts.[129] This has opened up space for broader and more inclusive concepts of cartography, including 'non-scientific' practices of map-making such as imaginary mapping, narrative mapping, map art, and even active attempts at counter-mapping, some of which will be discussed in the final chapter of this book.[130] While the consideration of such 'alternative' methods is gaining importance in various academic disciplines, especially in human geography and social anthropology, retracing their historical trajectories remains difficult as these cartographic practices rarely resulted in physical maps and are thus less likely to have left paper trails in any archives.[131]

It is important to recognise that the practice of mapping, as well as the map itself, is never simply a visualisation of what exists, but always serves an interest. As Denis Wood argued, "[b]ecause these interests select what from the vast storehouse of knowledge [...] the map will represent, these interests are embodied in the map as presences and absences".[132] By drawing certain (new) borders onto the map and leaving others out, mapmakers create (new) spatial realities. The credo of critical cartography "that maps *make* reality as much as they represent it" thus underlies both my historical research on mapping and my approach to the use of maps as sources.[133]

---

[127] Harley, J. B. (1989), Deconstructing the Map, *Cartorgaphica*, 26(2): 1; Perkins, C. (2004), Cartography: Cultures of Mapping: Power in Practice, *Progress in Human Geography*, 28: 384.

[128] For the most influential article, see: Harley (1989). See also: Crampton, J.W. (2001), Maps as Social Constructions. Power, Communication and Visualization, *Progress in Human Geography*, 25(2): 236.

[129] Harley, J.B. (1990), Cartography, Ethics and Social Theory, *Cartographica*, 27(2): 14.

[130] On map art and counter-mapping, see: Wood, D. (2006), *The Power of Maps*. New York: Guilford Press. On counter-mapping in conservation, see: Peluso, N. (1995), Whose woods are these? Counter-mapping forest territories in Kalimantan, Indonesia, *Antipode*, 27(4): 383–406 and Taylor (2012).

[131] Perkins (2004): 386.

[132] Wood (1992): 1.

[133] Crampton, J.W. and J. Krygier (2006), An Introduction to Critical Geography, *ACME. An international E-Journal for Critical Geographies*, 4(1): 15.

Ethnic Terminology

As for many colonial and post-colonial contexts, the question of how to refer to so-called ethnic groups is a challenging one. That the use of ethnic labels represents a problematic reinforcement of colonial and apartheid concepts which categorised people into clearly defined and distinct ethnic groups is widely accepted in academic literature.[134] However, it is also broadly acknowledged that avoiding any references to so-called ethnic groups is not a viable solution. As the legal scholar Julian Jonker argued for a South African context, to do so would constitute a "failing attempt to articulate a marginalized subjectivity while refraining from deploying apartheid categories".[135] Colonial archives which relate to Namibia and the Caprivi are replete with such categories, containing a confusing array of names for the various 'tribes', 'races', 'ethnic groups' recognised by the colonial and apartheid administrations.[136] In this book, I refer to such 'ethnic' terminology when these labels are unavoidable for my argument, usually when individuals directly referred to themselves by these terms or understood ethnicity as a defining characteristic of identity.[137]

In the Caprivi, the ethnic terms which came up most frequently were those of the five groups which have been politically, administratively and legally recognised as traditional authorities. These include the two groups in the present-day Zambezi Region which were officially recognised by the colonial authorities, the 'Masubia' (also known as Subia, Subiya, Masubiya, Kuhane or Bekuhane) and the 'Mafwe' (also known as Fwe), whose traditional authorities are seated in Bukalo and Linyanti respectively. Two traditional authorities which split off from the Mafwe were recognised after Namibia's independence, the 'Mayeyi' (or Yei, Yeyi, Bayeyi or Mayeye) and the 'Mashi' (or BaMashi or Mayuni), whose traditional authorities are seated in Sangwali and Choi respectively. There are also further groups which are currently campaigning for the recognition of their traditional authorities, including the 'Totela' (or Matotela) and the 'Khwe' (or Barakwengo, Barakwena or Kwe, who are often also referred to by the more generic 'San' or 'Bushmen') of the Western Caprivi. A further officially recognised traditional authority, the 'Mbukushu' (or Mambukushu or Hambukushu), is based just outside of the region in Andara but its jurisdiction incorporates parts of the Western Caprivi.[138]

---

[134] For an overview on the debates around ethnicity and ethnic terminology, see e.g.: Keese, A. (2010), Introduction. In A. Keese (ed.), *Ethnicity and the long-term perspective: The African Experience*. London: Peter Lang, p. 9–25. See also: Wa Thiong'o, N. (2009), The Myth of Tribe in African Politics, *Transition*, 101: p. 16–23.

[135] Jonker, J. (2005), Excavating the Legal Subject, *Griffith Law Review*, 14(2): 187–212 (here 193).

[136] Kangumu (2011): 14.

[137] This also applies to my use of the terms 'white' and 'black', which in many instances remain unavoidable when discussing Southern African histories.

[138] Kangumu (2011): 14. See also Figure 3, p. 256.

Structure of the Book

The particularities and availability of my various sources is also reflected in the structure of this book. Chapter 2 on 'Nature and Development' relies heavily on colonial and early-apartheid written governmental records as well as on secondary literature relating to these periods. In this chapter, I elaborate on the colonial and early apartheid administrations' policies towards Caprivian nature until the 1960s. I show how these policies developed from a late-colonial approach, with its emphasis on modernisation, into a narrative which underlined the need to promote Caprivian self-reliance and self-governance within the framework of apartheid's central policy of separate development. The shifting nature of these policies and the constant restructuring of the governmental institutions which were responsible for implementing them meant that numerous reports on the Caprivi's natural environment were produced, the analysis of which primarily informs this chapter.

Oral interviews as well as maps come into focus in Chapter 3 on 'Nature and War'. This chapter is concerned with South African endeavours to exploit the Caprivi's natural resources and how these were interlinked with the increasing militarisation of the region in the period roughly from 1965 to 1980. Especially in relation to the fields of forestry and fishery, I show how the region became the object of detailed ecological research. I examine not only the memories of labourers, researchers and military personnel who were involved in this research, but also the data which they produced, including maps, surveys and aerial photographs.

In Chapter 4 on 'Wildlife and War', oral interviews play an even more central role. This is not only because written archival material on the Caprivi in the 1980s is rarely available in state archives, but also due to a comparatively large number of interviewees who were prepared to share their memories from this period. In this chapter, I explore the impact of the SADF's presence in the Caprivi on the region's wildlife and show how the close links between military and nature conservation officials in the 1980s laid a basis for post-independence conservation polices in the area, particularly through the proclamation of two nature conservation areas shortly before independence.

In Chapter 5 on 'Peace and Nature', I discuss how mapping, research on nature, discourses of economic development, and processes of securitisation and militarisation continue to shape present-day nature conservation in the Caprivi. To this end, I supplemented oral interviews with informal discussions and the analysis of NGO and media reports. Relevant state archival material, however, was barely accessible for the post-independence period due to legal restrictions.

The conclusion, Chapter 6, summarises the main arguments of the book before it opens the discussion of some relevant questions that were beyond the immediate scope of my research.

2 Nature and Development before 1965

This chapter is primarily concerned with the first decades of South African rule over the Caprivi and the change from a system of late-colonial indirect rule to the establishment of apartheid's separate development policies in the mid-1960s. After the Union of South Africa took control of Namibia during the First World War, governance arrangements in the Caprivi altered several times before the eastern part of the region was put under the direct administration of South Africa's Native Affairs Department in Pretoria in 1938. The western Caprivi, meanwhile, continued to be governed from Windhoek as part of the Union mandate territory of South West Africa.

It was during this time (1930) that South Africa established the Eastern Caprivi Zipfel (ECZ) as a so-called Bantu reserve, a status which would only change in the 1970s, when the region became a 'self-governing' homeland according to the recommendations of the Odendaal Report of 1964.[1] While Bennett Kangumu characterised this first period of South African rule until the Odendaal Report as a time of "total neglect", I would rather understand it as a period marked by the sort of ambivalent administration typical for many colonial contexts of indirect rule.[2] Although the Caprivi had long been presented by the South African government as lying "beyond the last frontier", it was still entangled within the networks of the British Empire as well as within the Southern African networks of power of its South African occupier.[3] In the rhetoric of British colonialism in particular, the advent of indirect rule saw a change from the "politics of conquest" to "politics of consent".[4] The result was the establishment and strengthening of 'native courts' or 'traditional administrations', which, in many cases, managed to carve out for themselves powerful positions in the space between the local population and the colonial administration.[5] As I will show in this chapter, this system of indirect rule allowed South Africa to control the Caprivi at minimal cost to itself, while at the same time positioning itself to take advantage of any potential future economic or geostrategic benefits which the region might offer. As such, South Africa's policies towards the Caprivi reflected a general tendency in indirectly-ruled areas all

---

[1] Kangumu (2011): 92.
[2] Kangumu (2011): 13, 127.
[3] Gewald (2013): 87; Witz, L. (2015), Hunting for Museums, *Journal of Southern Africa Studies*, 41(4): 671–685; Henrichsen et al. (2015): 433.
[4] As described, for example, in relation to Malawi by John McCracken (McCracken, J. (2012), *A history of Malawi, 1859–1966*. Woodbridge: James Currey, 216–218.
[5] John Ilife described a similar system in relation to colonial Tanganyika in as early as 1979 (Iliffe, J. (1979), *A Modern History of Tanganyika*. Cambridge: Cambridge University Press).

over colonial Africa to appropriate a territory's natural resources and strategic value while attempting to keep administrative costs as low as possible.[6]

At least for the period up to the 1950s, no economic resources of any significant value or geostrategic importance were found in the Caprivi, but the many reports and surveys which were undertaken by the South African administration suggest that the occupation authorities were on the lookout for potential opportunities for economic development.[7] Generally, these accounts broadly substantiate Adam Ashforth's analysis of South African commission of inquiry reports. Ashforth argued that the discourse which these reports helped to establish was simultaneously concerned with "the making of substantively true propositions about material and social reality while also elaborating practical means to achieve specific ends within the context of that reality".[8] Hence, the aims of state power can be revealed through a careful reading of these reports. While in the reports on the Caprivi no areas of potential were clearly defined, such reports were important for creating a context in which colonial power could be established and in which potential profits could be detected.

At the same time, in order to win the loyalty of local inhabitants and particularly the chiefs, the South African authorities needed to sustain a narrative of 'civilisation' 'modernisation' and 'development'. The three terms were all used concurrently and interchangeably by South African officials, although their connotations changed over the time. The term 'civilisation' was used in the discourse of South African officials over the entire period until at least the late 1960s and signified not only economic endeavours, but also more general attempts to 'uplift' local people, including the provision of missionary or 'western' education.[9] The other two concepts continue to occasion intense academic debate on their different connotations and the way in which they influenced each other, with the general consensus now being that both played an important role for the establishment and maintenance of (colonial) power and control.[10] Without going into further detail on this debate, it

---

[6] McCracken (2012) and Myers, J.C. (2008), *Indirect Rule in South Africa: Tradition, Modernity, and the Costuming of Political Power*. Rochester: University of Rochester Press, p. 4.

[7] On the methodological challenges of using such reports as historical sources, see also p. 43 ff.; on an early example of this sort of report, the report of the South African Native Affairs Commission of 1904–1905, see: Krüger, G. (2009), *Schrift, Macht, Alltag: Lesen und Schreiben im kolonialen Südafrika*. Köln, Weimar, Wien: Böhlau-Verlag, particularly 263–266.

[8] Ashforth, A. (1990), *Politics of Official Discourse in Twentieth-Century South Africa*. Oxford: Clarendon Press, p. 4.

[9] For an example, see: Rhoodie (1967); for an overview of the ongoing debate among political scientists on the role of 'civilisation' discourses for imperialism, see e.g.: Gallo, E. (2014), Civilisation and empire: A challenging nexus, *Human Figurations*, 3(1).

[10] For a focus on British- and French-ruled Africa in the 1930s–1960s, see e.g.: Cooper, F. (1997b), Modernizing Bureaucrats, Backward Africans and the Development Concept. In F. Cooper and R. Packard (eds.), *International Development and the Social Sciences*. Berkeley: University of California Press, p. 64–92.

is important to underline here that the concept of 'development' was never clearly defined and was enacted in many different forms in the colonised world.[11]

Especially in the context of British colonies during the time period under discussion here, development entailed aspects of 'active modernisation', or what Frederick Cooper described as "actions [...] that were most often seen as technical but which also constituted authoritarian interventions into African society in the name of the general good", as occurred in many colonial contexts in the nineteenth and early twentieth centuries.[12] Especially after the Second World War, colonial development policies became linked to a more hegemonic vision for the future, one which envisioned the establishment of a politically-legitimate and economically-productive empire through the economic development of (particularly) rural Africa.[13] Thus, as Cooper illustrated, development was no longer discussed as a "colonial initiative" or as a set of measures which could be implemented through political decisions, but rather as a "universal social process" to be facilitated and directed by human agents, while actually being "driven by history".[14]

Similar debates about the meaning of modernisation and development also marked South African rule over Namibia. Lorena Rizzo and Michael Bollig described how South Africa's policies of colonial encapsulation and marginalisation in north-western Namibia during the first half of the twentieth century also involved state-led initiatives to modernise the region, such as vaccination programmes, hunting laws, and road construction.[15] Bollig

---

[11] Although, as Cooper reminds us, for African colonial administrations and particularly for the metropolitan centres of colonial power in London and Paris, 'development' was initially not seen as the product of a complex and fluid process of social interaction, but rather as a "flat, unchanging, primitive landscape" (Cooper 1997b: 65). Development was thus presented as something which had to be brought *to* Africa, *for* Africans.

[12] Cooper (1997b): 65.

[13] Cooper (1997b), 75. Such a late colonial 'push' mainly by the British colonial administration for the development of their colonies in order not to lose them, especially after India gained its independence in 1947, manifested itself in particular in the form of huge agricultural and energy projects. See e.g.: Esselborn, S. (2004), Koloniale Landschaft und industrielle Landwirtschaft. Das Groundnut Scheme. In F. Uekötter (ed.), Ökologische Erinnerungsorte. Göttingen: V&R: 219–250 or Fontain, J. (2015), *Remaking Mutirikwi: Landscape, Water and Belonging in Southern Zimbabwe*. London: James Currey; on Mozambique, see: Isaacman, A.F. and B.S. Isaacman (2013), *Dams, Displacement, and the Delusion of Development: Cahora Bassa and Its Legacies in Mozambique, 1965–2007*. Athens, OH: Ohio University Press. This understanding of 'development' was also adopted by post-independence governments throughout Africa in the 1960s, see e.g. Tischler, J. (2013), *Light and Power for a Multiracial Nation. The Kariba Dam scheme in the Central African Federation*. Basingstoke: Palgrave Macmillan.

[14] Cooper (1997): 64.

[15] Rizzo (2011); Bollig, M. (1998b), The Colonial Encapsulation of the North-Western Namibian Pastoral Economy, *Africa: Journal of the International African Institute*, 68(4): 506–536 and Bollig, M. (2013), Conserving the Margins of Empire: Knowledge Production, Visions and Practices of Species Protection in North-Western Namibia (unpublished paper presented at the South African

also noted a shift in South Africa's understanding of the function of such development practices, from seeing them as a political tactic to intervene in local political contestations to ultimately regarding them after the Second World War as a 'de-politicised' endeavour to be practiced by 'experts' as part of a much broader development strategy.[16]

With South Africa's implementation of the apartheid system from 1948, which was based on the notion of 'separate development', the development discourse became an even more central aspect of South African policy, especially in relation to the economic development of the so-called homelands, which were – according to the logic of apartheid – envisioned to become self-reliant.[17] South African officials in Namibia therefore increasingly saw their role as being to establish spaces in which Africans were to 'develop' on their own. At the same time, with South Africa having been entrusted with holding the territory 'in trust', the South African authorities needed to show that their rule in northern Namibia provided no benefit to their own country and that their administration of the area was 'supportive' of and 'non-exploitative' towards local inhabitants. As such, the discourse and praxis of development became a central focus through which power-relations and questions of governance were discussed and disputed. For example, in relation to South African water politics in Namibia, Molly McCullers showed that "disputes over development were, at their root, contestations of sovereignty."[18] Furthermore, she demonstrated how effectively this sort of development narrative and its implementation on the ground could be used to manipulate local inhabitants and ultimately control their land.

Empire Workshop, Basel). On early South African development projects in Southern Africa, see also: McKittrick, M. (2013), An Empire of Rivers: Climate Anxiety, Imperial Ambition, and the Hydropollitical Imagination in Southern Africa 1919–1950 (unpublished paper presented at the South African Empire Workshop, Basel 2013) and McKittrick (2015).

[16] Bollig (2013). On the 'scientification' and simultaneous 'depoliticisation' of South Africa's policies towards non-whites, see also: Ashforth (1990).

[17] H.F. Verwoerd, prime minister of South Africa from 1958 until 1966 and often seen as the 'architect of apartheid', explained in 1950 that "[o]ur first aim as a Government is [...] to lay the foundation of a prosperous producing community through soil reclamation and conservation methods and through the systematic establishment in Native territories of Bantu farming on an economic basis" (quoted in Pelzer, A.N. (ed.) (1966), *Verwoerd Speaks: Speeches 1948–1966*. Johannesburg: AFP Publishers, p. 24). Such interventions into the development of agriculture were not new to South Africa and had been carried out since at least the beginning of the twentieth century, see, e.g.: Beinart, W. and C. Bundy (1987), *Hidden Struggles in Rural South Africa: Politics and Popular Movements in the Transkei and Eastern Cape, 1890–1930*. London: James Currey. These policies were often described as a cause for resistance against apartheid in South Africa, see Mbeki, G. (1964), *South Africa: The Peasants' Revolt*. Baltimore: Penguin Books, and Redding, S. (2006), *Sorcery and Sovereignty: Taxation, Power, and Rebellion in South Africa, 1880–1963*. Athens: Ohio University Press.

[18] McCullers (2012): 11.

The Caprivi's natural environment and, in particular, its wildlife were seen by South African officials as especially suited vehicles for potential development. In the Caprivi, lines of conflict and systems of power manifested themselves over and over again in contestations over hunting regulations and other laws pertaining to the use of natural resources. For example, the South African authorities could support a pliant local elite and perpetuate its power through the establishment of a favourable legal framework for hunting and the use of natural resources, and, in so doing, tighten the South African state's overall grip on the region. This chapter will show that the Caprivi's natural environment and its potential uses were of importance to its various rulers from as early as before the First World War.

However, before examining a chronological narrative of nature as a contested field of governance in the area, it is worth exploring an alternative and parallel narrative, one which idealised the abundant Caprivian nature of a chronologically unspecified time in which people were said to have lived together in peace and harmony.

Creating an Image of Abundant Nature and Peace

References to nature 'when it was still good' came up in most of my interviews as well as in many written documents as a parallel or contrast to the more recent situations being described. These images of an abundant nature, often situated in an unspecified 'time before', all share striking similarities, whether originating from the earliest European descriptions of the Caprivi, the oral histories of people living there, or contemporary descriptions from the twenty-first century.

The image which dominates among all these various descriptions is that which depicts the Caprivi as a region of robust nature and abundant wildlife, a natural environment which was in harmony with its inhabitants and was capable of providing them with all the necessary supplies for life. The following statement from the head of one of the four recognised traditional authorities in the Zambezi Region in 2014 illustrates this narrative's central assumptions:

> There was a time, before, when there was abundance of wildlife, when people knew where the animals were and when they needed time to rest, a time when chiefs were deciding on such matters [wildlife and hunting] and when we all lived in harmony.[19]

The quote suggests three aspects which are central to this idealised vision of Caprivian nature, namely a high population of game, the notion that people could live in peace and harmony with nature, and a reference to a chronologically-unspecified and romanticised

---

[19] BS, 14.05.2014, Sangwali.

"time before". 'A time before' or an era 'before colonial times' does not necessarily refer to the historical time before the region came under colonial rule. Instead, such narratives refer to romanticised images of nature, which run parallel to and in resonance with the social and political histories of the region, from which various actors draw at different times in order to support their respective demands and convictions.[20] When I enquired from my interviewees as to which time they meant, their answers were often ill-defined and they vaguely referred to a pre-colonial time, but sometimes also to a period "before the South Africans came" or "before it [the Western Caprivi] was declared a conservation area".[21]

An analogous image is the colonial construction of 'unspoiled' African nature, which follows a direct line from Herodotus' description of Africa as the place of "beasts" to modern-day safari marketing campaigns which depict the continent as the "kingdom of animals".[22] Besides inventing an Africa which is close to nature and thus defined in opposition to civilisation, such a narrative assumes that the continent as a whole has been "unchanged since time began" and thus outside of history.[23]

The Power of Game: Chiefs and Local Knowledge

A frequent point of reference for my interviewees who claimed to represent groups which had previously relied heavily on hunting and the gathering of field fruits was the elaborate knowledge of nature which they maintained that their ancestors had possessed. Speaking of "the times before there were parks", TC, an elderly village headman in the Western Caprivi, said that people had "surviv[ed] on hunting and collecting field fruit". He remembered that:

---

[20] The idea that pre-colonial African nature was abundant and harmonious was, and continues to be, reflected in many environmental histories, against which the destructive effects of European expansion in the late-nineteenth century is contrasted. As an example, see: Kjekshus (1977). For an overview of this so-called apocalyptic school of environmental history, see: MacKenzie, J.M. (1997), Empire and the Ecological Apocalypse: The Historiography of the Imperial Environment. In T. Griffiths, L. Robin (eds.), *Ecology and Empire: Environmental History of Settler Societies*. Edinburgh: Keele University Press: 215–128.

[21] Among others: TC, 11.05.2014, Mutjiku; AC, 20.05.2014, Kongola; BS, 14.05.2014, Sangwali.

[22] For a general discussion on this topic, see e.g.: Pieterse, N. (1995), *White on Black. Images of Africa and Blacks in Western Popular Culture*. New Haven: Yale University Press. In relation to northern Namibia, see Hayes, P. (2000), Camera Africa: Indirect Rule and Landscape Photographs of Kaoko. In G. Miescher und D. Henrichsen (eds), *New Notes on Kaoko*. Basel: Basler Afrika Bibliographien: 48–76; in relation to Southern Africa in general, see also: Rassool, C. and L. Witz (1996), South Africa: A World in One Country: Moments in International Tourist Encounters with Wildlife, the Primitive and the Modern. *Cahiers d'Études Africaines*, 36(143): 335–371.

[23] Rassool et al. (1996): 349. As I will show repeatedly in this study, such representations have been advantageous, not only for colonial powers, but often also for a range of other actors. For example, in many tourism advertisements for destinations in Southern Africa, notions of "timeless" or "unspoiled" nature continue to be invoked (see Chapter 5).

In our culture, the culture of the old people, our lives depended on wild animals, because we had to hunt them and eat them. We did not plough [...]. With our people the men hunted and the women collected, that was how we could survive. Our hunting was with bow and arrow that meant that you could kill an animal here and shoot another one there. But [...] they did know what exactly was happening, not like the poachers today.[24]

That TC spoke of a time before there were parks indicates that he was not referring to the pre-colonial period, but to a time before the proclamation of the Western Caprivi Game Reserve. Although this occurred in 1964, he explained later in the interview that he only became aware of the reserve with the building of South African military bases in the area in the 1970s, which suggests that he was probably referring to an even more recent time. More importantly, the quote shows the significance to which he attached the knowledge of his forefathers, with which he contrasted the acts of "poachers", who, at the time to which he referred, were mostly white South African military personnel.[25] AC, a community activist working for an NGO in the Western Caprivi, where he also grew up, remembered that before the Namibian War of Liberation started in the 1960s, his family would search for fruits in Angola and Botswana. They had also known where to find animals and hunted them for their meat.[26] According to AC, this knowledge had been lost when they were no longer allowed to cross international borders during the war.

Many interviewees in areas where agriculture tended to be more important than hunting or gathering highlighted the role which traditional authorities would have played in controlling the region's natural resources. The regulation of hunting activities within local communities was often presented as a fundamental characteristic of chiefly authority, not only by the chiefs themselves, but also in literature.[27] Chief BS referred repeatedly to the deep knowledge which the chiefs had in "those times" and how important it was for him to maintain this to sustain "harmony within the community and with nature".[28] In the same vein, another chief explained that: "Large game was royal game. The chief was in charge of quotas and he knew how to do it. There was always enough meat, but we never overhunted. Small animals were taken care of by the headmen, they were hunting them for the pot of the community."[29] A former chief of the Mafwe Traditional Authority, claimed that from the time after the Second World War, "[a]nimals were protected by the government.

---

[24] Both quotes: TC, 11.05.2014, Mutjiku.
[25] See Chapter 4.
[26] AC, 20.05.2014, Kongola.
[27] See e.g.: Hinz, M.O. (2003), *Without Chiefs there would be no Game: Customary Law and Nature Conservation*. Windhoek: Out of Africa.
[28] BS, 14.05.2014, Sangwali.
[29] JM, 28.05.2014, Choi.

It was a joint venture with the help of the chiefs and that is why we still have animals. I protected Lupala".[30] As such, a chief's knowledge of wildlife became an argument for vesting him with state-sanctioned authority. This can also be seen in the way in which RM spoke of so-called "royal game", namely large game animals such as elephants and giraffes which could not be legally hunted by anyone other than chiefs according to the game laws of 1926. RM remembered that there "were selected animals for the chiefs like the giraffes, the elephants, and the hippo. Ordinary people were not allowed to kill them. If you killed those animals the tribal authority would take you through questioning and you would be punished because those animals were selected for the chiefs."[31]

The legal scholar Manfred O. Hinz used a statement from a former chief in the Caprivi as the title for his book, "Without chiefs there would be no game".[32] In his study he conducted interviews with, among others, representatives of traditional authorities in the Zambezi Region, many of whom also describe the importance of the traditional authorities' knowledge for the management of natural resources, particularly game. They too recall a time when there were still many animals and people could hunt all but some of the large game reserved for the chief or his appointed hunters.[33] The study was commissioned by Namibia's Ministry of Environment and Tourism (MET) to develop a scientific basis for future environmental legislation. It started out from the assumption that traditional authorities should have an "accepted space to play an active role in administrating and managing natural resources" and that the recognition of these rights should be based on "memories and practices" which "survived" the "many inroads into the traditional ways of life" and which "can be employed to administer and manage natural recourses today and in the future".[34] The study's reliance on such memories and its emphasis on the role of traditional authorities also helped chiefs to assert the right to oversee the management of natural resources and, in so doing, fulfil the role ascribed to them in the stated aim of the study. This reflects a resort to an imagined pre-colonial 'tradition', a trend which is often seen in postcolonial contexts as a means of assigning power to traditional authorities.[35]

---

[30] RM, 29.05.2014, Chinchimane. Lupala is an island in the Kwando River which today forms part of the Nkasa Lupala National Park.
[31] RM, 29.05.2014, Chinchimane.
[32] Hinz (2003).
[33] Hinz (2003): 54–55.
[34] Hinz (2003): 6.
[35] Brubaker, R. and F. Cooper (2000), Beyond "Identity", *Theory and Society*, 29: 1–47. The power which has been vested in traditional authorities in Namibia since the 1990s is especially reinforced through constant references to their 'traditional' functions in the control of natural resources, particularly game (see also Chapter 5).

Traditional authorities' claims to the right to control wildlife are based on twentieth-century history, as I have shown above, but are also supported by pre-colonial narratives and memories. An emphasis on the natural features of the land is apparent in many histories of the region, particularly in so-called local historiographies.[36] These histories were important for chiefs to assert their belonging to lineages of power, but also helped to explain migrations and patterns of settlements. An abundance of wildlife, in particular, was often mentioned as a main reason for why leaders and their subjects settled in a particular area. The "Tjaube Chronicle", a text on the history of the Tjaube group, whose members used to live between the Kavango and Kwando rivers before probably moving further west in the eighteenth century, records how their king searched for land.[37] First, "he found a lot of game there: elephants, buffalos, lions, leopards and all the animals were very ferocious." As these frightened him, he sought help to "forge weapons" so that his people could "fight those very ferocious animals". He was also said to have organised the assistance of two further groups, "the Djo knowing how to kill hippos, and the Canikwe knowing how to kill fish with nets".[38] Similar accounts can be found in the "Chronicle of the Gciriku", a history referred to by a group which currently lives in the central Kavango valley. The chronicle states that their forefathers "only used to cultivate small gardens and mainly lived on meat".[39] In search of better land, they discovered the Kavango River valley and "they were very much amazed". As a result, they returned to the Okavango River to tell their people that "that country was just abounding in wildlife".

Similar histories also exist for the area which is now the Zambezi Region. In the historiography of the Masubia, it is told how it took years of searching before they found their "promised land" close to the Chobe River, where they henceforth settled.[40] As D.M. Shamukumi described: "The BaSubyia found the Chobe River a natural food store flowing with milk and honey. Hippo, fish of various species, different kinds of bucks, birds and other creatures were abounded."[41]

---

[36] E.g. for Kavango, see: Fleisch, A. and W.J.G. Möhlig (2002), *The Kavango Peoples in the Past. Local Historiographies from Northern Namibia*. Cologne: Rüdiger Köppe. Such historiographies were often handed down orally within 'royal' families. In the twentieth century, some of these were written down by the respective families in the vernacular and then sometimes translated by anthropologists or missionaries.
[37] Rudolf Haushiku, a descendant of the Tjaube, recorded the chronicle in writing and gave it to a mission station in 1954. It was translated and published in Fleisch et al. (2002).
[38] Both quotes: Fleisch et al. (2002): 40–41.
[39] Both quotes: Fleisch et al. (2002): 67–68.
[40] Shamukuni (1972): 162.
[41] Shamukuni (1972): 163.

Early Descriptions of the Caprivi's Nature and German Colonial Visions

An imaginary of a poetic, beautiful and particularly abundant nature in the Caprivi was reinforced by early European descriptions of the area. In his travelogue of his trip to the region in the late-nineteenth century, Emil Holub, a Czech hunter and collector, described how the vegetation of the Chobe valley was "luxuriant and quite tropical"[42] and that the "animal life" was "everywhere abundant". [43] He went on to report on the many animal tracks which he found, the birds which he recognised, and the beautiful landscapes which he encountered. In 1895 the Swiss geographer Alfred Bertrand travelled up the Zambezi, "penetrating the kingdom of the Barotsi [...] and surveying a part of this country."[44] He declared that he expected to find himself "in a virgin country" the moment he crossed the Zambezi at Kazungula on his way to Shesheke and the rapids of Katima Mulilo, but, unlike Holub, did not describe the landscape, concentrating instead on chronicling his hunting endeavours and the game which he encountered. In the vicinity of Shesheke, just north of present-day Katima Mulilo, his party sighted wildlife; "[f]or several days now we cross a zone wherein we encounter gnus and zebras by hundreds – a splendid sight".[45] It was also in this region that "a troop of gnus [...] had to suffer the disastrous consequences of their curiosity; we have stocked our larder extensively".[46] Similar descriptions of beautiful country with an abundance of wildlife can be found in David Livingstone's account of his two trips into the area in 1851 and 1853, as well as in that of one of the early European traders in the area, James Chapman.[47]

Descriptions of Caprivian nature did not change appreciably after the region was allocated to the colonial territories of the German Reich by the Anglo-German Treaty of 1890.[48] One of the earliest German colonial travellers to the area was Kurt Streitwolf, who was commissioned to officially claim the territory for the German Reich by establishing a police station and colonial office. In his published report on the 'expedition' which he thus undertook at the behest of Bruno von Schuckmann, the colonial governor of the German Reich in Namibia, Streitwolf presented his description of what would later become named as the Caprivi. He described the area in a much less positive light than earlier travellers had done,

---

[42] Holub, E. (1975), *Seven Years in South Africa: Facsimile Reproduction of the 1881 Edition*. Johannesburg: Africana Book Society, p. 111. The book was originally published in Czech in Prague in 1880 under the title "Sedm let v jižní Africe".
[43] Holub (1975): 111.
[44] Bertrand, A. (1899), *The Kingdom of the Barotsi, Upper Zambezia, A Voyage of Exploration in Africa*. London: T Fisher Unwin, p. 2. The book was originally published in French in 1898.
[45] Bertrand (1899): 80.
[46] Bertrand (1899): 88.
[47] Livingstone, D. (1857), *Missionary Travels and Researches in South Africa*. London: J. Murray and Chapman, J. (1868), *Travels in the interior of South Africa*. London: Bell and Daldy.
[48] In line with the General Act of the Berlin Conference in 1885, the area that later became the Caprivi Strip had initially fallen under the British colonial sphere of influence.

but still underlined its copious wildlife and, occasionally, its beauty. In his report Streitwolf described his first impression of the area as "very discouraging [...] only swamp and reed", but on the same page still noted that it was "very pretty".[49] Significantly, Streitwolf repeatedly wrote of the value of the geographical and ecological knowledge of the local population, an asset of which he thought the German colonial regime should take full advantage. In his description of a settlement which had been abandoned shortly before his arrival in the colony, Streitwolf declared that "the natives fully appreciate such strategic places, as they generally have an excellent sense for the terrain". In Streitwolf's narrative, the local residents had only left this valuable place because they feared the "expansion of white culture".[50]

Streitwolf often described the area in poetic terms: "Innermost peace everywhere. The lean lechwes, of which there are hundreds strolling through the bush, wait inquisitively for the lonely wanderer. From deep in the bush comes the deep sound of the hippopotamus".[51] Simultaneously, however, he never neglected to remain alert to the potential benefits of the land for himself, including those provided by game: "The many lechwes offered us an excellent opportunity to hunt".[52] On his way back to Windhoek, in the area which today forms the western Caprivi, Streitwolf again highlighted the large numbers of game: "On the way back I could see how plentiful the game was here".[53] The wildlife here was so abundant that for once he even refrained from shooting at it, as his party had enough meat. He commented on this apparently unusual situation by observing that it was occasionally fine to simply enjoy the sight of game without firing a shot.

In his conclusion, Streitwolf offered a lengthy description of the Caprivi, starting with an extensive account of its natural environment and local population and finishing with an assessment of the potential economic value of the entire area for its German colonisers.[54] Although he observed a potential for agriculture, cattle farming, cotton production and forestry, he was convinced that these sectors would not prove to be of significant value to the colony because the area was too isolated and difficult to reach. Furthermore, he observed that due to its climate and the presence of the malaria disease, the region would hardly be suitable for "white farming".[55] The only potential profit he saw in what would become the Caprivi lay in the approximately ten thousand "natives" living there. However, he regretted that they numbered so few as he predicted that the region's fertile soil could easily have fed

---

[49] Streitwolf, K. (1911), *Der Caprivizipfel*. Berlin: Süsserott, p. 53. Own translations of the German original.
[50] Streitwolf (1911): 60.
[51] Streitwolf (1911): 172. A lechwe is a type of antelope.
[52] Streitwolf (1911): 172.
[53] Streitwolf (1911): 177.
[54] Streitwolf (1911): 221–229.
[55] Streitwolf (1911): 232.

one hundred thousand inhabitants, who together, he argued, could have been of high value to the German colony as a "native labour recruitment district".[56] With this conclusion, Streitwolf anticipated some of the central concerns of successive rulers in the Caprivi: the constant but – especially in relation to the search for a labour force – mostly unsuccessful hunt for potential ways to take advantage of the area's resources, an often fruitless endeavour which contrasted sharply with regular and hopeful attestations to the Caprivi's abundance of wildlife and natural riches.

Elements of this idea of an environment with copious wildlife and natural resources, which was, however, too remote to utilise, run like a thread through the region's past and will be discussed repeatedly in various contexts in the following chapters. As we will see, the reasons for invoking this image as well as the people who have done so have changed over time, but it continues to manifest itself over and over again. For example, in 2018 Wikipedia described the Caprivi Strip in the following manner:

> The area is rich in wildlife and has mineral resources. Of particular interest to the government of Namibia is that it gives access to the Zambezi River and thereby a potential trading route to Africa's East Coast. However, the vagaries of the river level, various rapids, the presence of Victoria Falls downstream and continued political uncertainty in the region make this use of the Caprivi Strip unlikely, although it may be used for ecotourism in the future.[57]

What to Do with the Caprivi? 1915–1939

South African rule over Namibia began with the fall of the German colonial authority and the declaration of martial law in July 1915. The implication of the South African invasion during the First World War for the Caprivi was that the region lost its primary geo-strategic function as a German wedge between British colonial territories and would henceforth remain surrounded by allied territories until the independence of Zambia and Botswana in the mid-1960s.[58]

---

[56] Streitwolf (1911): 234.
[57] https://en.wikipedia.org/w/index.php?title=Caprivi_Strip&oldid=802112531 [permanent link to the version accessed on 08.01.2018]
[58] Caprivi was also the location of the first Allied occupation of enemy territory in the First World War, a development which occurred after some members of the Northern Rhodesian Police, the BSAC's security force, gathered at Sheshcke on 21 September 1914 and requested that the German Resident hand over Schuckmannsburg without them having to resort to the use of force. The Northern Rhodesia Police was supported by the Bechuanaland Protectorate Police (BPP) under the command of the High Commissioner of the Bechuanaland Protectorate. For a detailed study of the Caprivi's role in the First World War, see: Jackson (2001).

From 1915 until 1921 the Caprivi, like the rest of Namibia, was officially placed under South African martial law. On the ground, however, the exact administrative situation was less clear and remained contested throughout the war, particularly between the Bechuanaland Protectorate and the British South Africa Company (BSAC).[59] After the war, control of the Caprivi was transferred to the British-ruled Bechuanaland Protectorate from 1921 to 1929 and the territory was divided administratively into Eastern Caprivi and Western Caprivi, but after only eight years of Bechuanaland rule, both parts were returned to the control of the Windhoek-based South West African Administration.[60] In 1939, the East Caprivi was put under the direct administration of the South African Department for Native Affairs in Pretoria, while the West Caprivi remained indirectly governed through South African-controlled South West Africa and its native commissioner in Rundu.[61]

A study of the Caprivi during this early period of South African rule over Namibia serves to illustrate succinctly the range of policies applied by South Africa towards northern Namibia. Collectively, these can be described as ambivalent: in the Caprivi, for example, the South Africa authorities in official reports downplayed the region's economic potential and bemoaned the high costs of governance, but also initiated a series of surveys, reports and reconnaissance trips in search of potential ways to make use of the area and keep its population 'calm' and 'loyal' at minimum cost.[62]

Becoming Part of the "Dark Areas" – Early South African Rule over Northern Namibia

With South Africa's invasion in Namibia in 1915, and even more so after Pretoria was granted a League of Nations mandate to govern the colony in 1920 Namibia was ruled in an increasingly divided manner. The central and southern sections of the territory were regarded as part of 'South Africa proper', an area in which white farming was promoted and Africans, at least in theory, were only to exist as labourers. Beyond this region to the

---

[59] On the one hand, it seemed that the Bechuanaland Protectorate was not willing to hand over the Caprivi Strip to the BSAC, whose claim was supported by Chief Lewanika of the Barotse in Zambia, who had ruled over the area during the pre-colonial era. On the other hand, many Caprivi headmen and chiefs appeared to prefer to remain under the rule of the Protectorate for fear of harsher treatment under the BSAC and Lewanika. See: Jackson (2001): 125–132.
[60] The exact date of the transfer of control of the Caprivi to the Bechuanaland Protectorate is not entirely clear, as it was mentioned in only two proclamations from 1922. These referred retroactively to 1 January 1921 as the date of the transfer (Kangumu 2011, 76). The respective terms 'Eastern Caprivi' and 'East Caprivi' as well as 'Western Caprivi' and 'West Caprivi' were used interchangeably in literature and archival documents. In this book, I refer to these areas as the 'Eastern Caprivi' and 'Western Caprivi'.
[61] There are different views on why this happened: Kangumu (2011): 92–96.
[62] See also: Myers (2008): 16–37.

north marked, from a South African perspective and in the words of a magistrate in Outjo in 1924, the start of the "dark areas".[63] Officially, these were known as the 'Northern Native Territories' and were closed off to white settlers.[64] In order to better understand the specific situation in the Caprivi, it is first important to situate the region within this broader context of early South African occupation in Namibia.

The so-called Red Line which divided Namibia into two sections – the police zone in the south and the northern territories – was a central feature of Namibia's colonial history. Miescher described how new laws introduced in 1916 began to turn the Red Line from a porous boundary which existed only on the map into a clearly-defined and closed border.[65] From 1916, all Europeans and Africans who lived south of the Red Line were no longer allowed to enter the northern territories without a permit, while Africans from the north were not allowed to enter the police zone without permission.[66] The South African administration later defined all territory beyond the old police zone borders, which had been established during the German colonial period, as well as all wildlife reserves as generally closed to white settlers, with only seventy-two Europeans still allowed to remain living outside the police zone.[67] These were mostly farmers who could prove that they had already settled there under German rule as well as some missionaries.[68]

Because of the spread of lung sickness into the northern areas of European settlement, the export of cattle from Namibia to South Africa was banned completely from 1915. In 1917 this ban was lifted for certain areas, but remained in force for the northernmost parts of the police zone. To return to a situation in which all white farmers south of the Red Line would be allowed to export cattle and meat, it was adjudged that the Red Line would henceforth have to be more strictly controlled. To do so, South Africa not only established new police stations along the Red Line in the 1920s, but also introduced livestock-free buffer zones north of the Red Line. As I will show below, this measure also impacted upon the Western Caprivi.[69]

---

[63] Quoted in: Miescher (2013): 147.
[64] See also: Miescher (2013): 142–146.
[65] Miescher (2013): 92–93.
[66] Miescher, G. (2012b), Facing Barbarians: A Narrative of Spatial Segregation in Colonial Namibia. *Journal of Southern African Studies*, 38(4): 769–786 (here 774).
[67] The term *police zone* was adopted by South Africa as a direct translation of the original German-language *Polizei-Zone* (the area which was under colonial police control) and remained in use until Namibia's independence. Its exact boundaries shifted several times. See Miescher (2012a) and (2013).
[68] Miescher (2013): 94.
[69] Miescher (2013): 134–138.

The South African occupation from 1915 had a diverse range of impacts on the different regions of Namibia and the various population groups living in them. The division between the police zone in southern and central Namibia and the territories to the north was particularly crucial in this regard. In the police zone, South Africa sought to present itself as a "mature, responsible and civilized power" in order to underpin its claim over Namibia in the eyes of the international community.[70] This had to manifest itself not only in relation to the treatment of the defeated German settlers, but also with regards to the African population. Scholars generally see this initial period of South African rule as having provided a narrow window of opportunity for Africans within the police zone to perform acts of resistance and, in some cases, regain some of their flocks or herds of livestock which they had lost through the German occupation.[71] For the Herero-speaking population in particular, processes of social and cultural reconstruction in the post-genocide context also accelerated during this period.[72] Indeed, during this time, the South African military occupiers seemed to be more restrained than their German predecessors, but these few years of more "paternalistic rule"[73] or "mild liberalism"[74] in the police zone ended with the granting of a new legal basis for South Africa's League of Nations mandate in Namibia on 1 January 1921.[75] This also heralded the introduction of a series of South African rules throughout the colony to regulate migrant work, segregate and control the local population, and extract as much wealth as possible from the territory.[76]

However, to the north of the Red Line, especially in the area which was named by the colonisers as 'Ovamboland', South African dominance was entrenched immediately from 1915, when a Resident Commissioner was first stationed in Ondangwa.[77] While South African forces managed to occupy Ondonga and install a commissioner in Ondangwa and at

---

[70] Silvester et al. (1998): 22–23.
[71] Silvester et al. (1998): 22–23; Krüger et al. (1998): 149–174; Miescher (2013): 91; Emmett, A. (1988), Popular Resistance in Namibia. In B. Wood (ed), *Namibia 1884–1984: Readings on Namibia's History and Society*, London: Namibia Support Committee: 224–258; Wallace (2011): 211–215, Dieckmann (2007), Krüger (1999): 194–202, Gordon (1992).
[72] For a detailed study of these processes, see: Krüger (1999): 183–264.
[73] Silvester et al. (1998): 22–23.
[74] Wallace (2011): 205.
[75] Miescher (2013): 91.
[76] Wallace (2011): 205, Silvester et al. (1998): 22.
[77] Miescher (2013): 91. The term 'Ovamboland' was created by the German colonial administration to name the area of north-central Namibia in which the so-called Ovambo people were assumed to live. Parts of this area became a homeland with the name of 'Ovambo' in 1968. Today the area is commonly referred to as 'the North', while the term 'Ovamboland' is also still used. This area correlates more or less with the territory of the four present-day Namibian regions of Oshikoto, Oshana, Ohangwena and Omusatio, which are often jointly referred to as the 'Four-O regions'. Parts of northern Ovamboland are now located within Angola. See also: Hayes (1992).

Namakunde without using military force – probably also due to a severe drought which hit the north of the colony in 1915 and which may have incapacitated any potential resistance – this was not the case for Oukwanyama. Here the new colonial power had to send a large force to defeat the resistance led by the Oukwanyama king, Mandume, who died in battle on 5 February 1917.[78]

With the historiography of this period focusing mainly on the impact of South African colonial policies on the division between the police zone and Ovamboland, the effects of those policies in other areas of northern Namibia remain largely vague or have been assumed to be similar to those in the central-north.[79] For example, Marion Wallace wrote of Oukwanyama as an exception to South African policy in Ovamboland, which she described as generally "cautious, usually non-interventionist, and even tinged with a certain amount of paternalism".[80] She described South African policies towards Kaoko and Kavango in similar words, while failing to mention the Caprivi.[81] In focusing more on the different contexts of the various northern territories, Lorena Rizzo argued that, unlike the regions of the central-north, Kaoko as well as Kavango "remained uncontained in terms of the role they were to play within the colony's economy and society."[82]

What was common to all areas north of the Red Line was that the colonial authorities saw them as unsuitable for white farming. This meant that instead of establishing a 'settler colony' in northern Namibia, different forms of administration and alternative ways to render these areas to be of benefit to the colonial regime had to be found.[83] While the densely-populated Ovamboland became an important source for cheap migrant labour, the role of the other northern regions during colonial times – Kaoko, Kavango and the Caprivi – within South Africa's political and economic perspectives remained unclear.[84] As such, the political

---

[78] See also: Vigne, R. (1998), "The Movable Frontier": The Namibia-Angola Boundary Demarcation 1926–1928. In P. Hayes, J. Silvester, M. Wallace and W. Hartmann (eds), *Namibia under South African Rule: Mobility and Containment, 1915–46*. Oxford, Windhoek and Athens OH: James Currey, Out of Africa and Ohio University Press: 289–304. See also: Hayes (1992): 205, Shiweda (2011): 1–10.
[79] Silvester et al. (1998): 18.
[80] Wallace (2011): 210.
[81] Wallace (2011): 211. The name 'Kaoko' has often been used to describe the geographical area of the Kaokoveld in north-western Namibia. Under the South African occupation, the region was known as Kaokoland and became a homeland of the same name in the 1970s. Today, this area forms part of the Kunene Region.
[82] Rizzo (2012): 124.
[83] Silvester et al. (1998): 18.
[84] More recent research has shown that after 1925, at least the western parts of Kavango also became an important source for labour, see: Likuwa, K.L. (2015), Colonialism and the Development of the Contract Labour System in Kavango. In J. Silvester (ed.), *Reviewing Resistance in Namibian History*. Windhoek: UNAM Press: 105–126.

situation in northern Namibia, particularly in regions which offered less immediate returns of economic profit for the colonisers, resembled that of other non-settler colonies in Africa. In such areas, often called protectorates rather than colonies, control of the local population was not achievable through the appropriation of land, the exclusion of 'natives' from the rights of citizenship, or their forced integration into the structures of agrarian settler capitalism. Unlike such measures of direct or "immediate despotism", control of the population in non-settler areas was thus enforced in an indirect or mediated manner.[85] This meant that land became or remained communally managed, peasants were supposedly 'free', and local authorities were installed or shored up so that they would apply a version of customary law as defined or approved by the colonial state.[86] In this context, labour generally constituted the most important commodity.[87]

The first decades of South African rule in northern Namibia must be understood within this context of indirect despotism, in which the means for the immediate control of local populations were vested in traditional leaders. South Africa's main interests in such areas were the potential sources of labour which they offered and, to a lesser degree, any local natural resources through which economic benefits could be obtained for South Africa.[88] As both labour and raw materials were to be procured at a minimal administrative cost, indirect rule was seen as a promising solution.[89] However, as the developments in the Caprivi itself showed, the administration of the region remained cost-intensive and the potential benefits for its colonisers had not yet been discovered.

A Time of 'Freedom'? Life under the Bechuanaland Protectorate, 1921–1929

Unlike the rest of northern Namibia, the Caprivi was governed by the Bechuanaland Protectorate from 1921 to 1929. This period is of particular relevance as it resurfaced in many memories and reports as a comparison or more positive counter-example to what happened subsequently under direct South African rule. In 1929, shortly before the control of the

---

[85] Mamdani (1996): 17.
[86] Mamdani (1996): 18.
[87] Mamdani (1996): 17. Lorena Rizzo has referred to the laboured articulation of clear policy towards the north-western region of Kaoko as an 'ambivalent' or 'hesitant' process: Rizzo (2012): 125. In relation to Kaoko, see also: Bollig, M. (1998a), Power and Trade in Precolonial and Early Colonial Kaokoland 1860s–1940s. In P. Hayes, J. Silvester, M. Wallace and W. Hartmann (eds), *Namibia under South African Rule: Mobility and Containment, 1915–46*. Oxford, Windhoek and Athens OH: James Currey, Out of Africa and Ohio University Press: 175–194; On Kavango: Eckl, A. (2000), What Happened to Kavango's Early Colonial History? The Colonial Production of Kavango Land and Peoples, 1891–1951. (unpublished paper, Windhoek).
[88] See also the following studies on migrant workers and mining: Moorsom (1972) and Gordon, R.J. (1977), *Mines, Masters and Migrants: Life in a Namibian Mine Compound*. Johannesburg: Ravan.
[89] Miescher (2013): 143.

Caprivi was given back to the South West African Administration, the Resident Magistrate of the Bechuanaland Protectorate in the Caprivi, J. W. Potts, conducted an extensive reconnaissance trip in the company of the Administrator of South West Africa, Albertus Werth, and other officials to prepare for the territory's hand-over to the South African authorities in Windhoek.[90] While travelling through the entire Caprivi to Luhonono (Schuckmannsburg), which was at the time the Caprivi's administrative centre, they met the Caprivi's recognised chiefs to "give them the opportunity of asking questions with regards to the laws they would be expected to observe" under the new administration.[91] This way of incorporating chiefs, via consultations, into practices which enforced state power was evident on many other occasions in the Caprivi.[92] Arguably, this gave traditional authorities the impression that they were being listened to and the corresponding opportunity to raise issues of concern, while also offering the colonial authorities the chance to present themselves as supportive of the chiefs and gain insights on which topics were relevant to local rulers. The colonial administration thus sought to impose laws on Africans, not only through the direct application of so-called native laws, but also, as J.C. Myers argued, through the chiefs, "as one of them".[93] In this regard, the colonial authorities needed to identify areas in which they could reinforce the power of loyal chiefs, with reports from such meetings or hearings playing a crucial role in revealing suitable opportunities to do so.[94]

Significantly, the only question which was raised by any of the three chiefs whom Potts and his entourage met – or, at least, was regarded as important enough by Potts to be mentioned in his report – concerned game laws.[95] When M. Chadwick, the then de facto representative of the South West African Administration in the Eastern Caprivi, summoned Chief Lifasi Simata Mamili for a meeting on 7 October 1929 in Luhonono, Mamili "enquired as to what game laws his people would be expected to observe and he was told that he would be given full particulars in due course".[96] As an explanation for this question and his reac-

---

[90] NAN, SWAA, A503/4, Caprivi Zipfel: Handing over to the South West African Administration. 26 October 1929.
[91] NAN, SWAA, A503/4, Caprivi Zipfel: Handing over to the South West African Administration. 26 October 1929.
[92] See also Ashfroth (1990): 8–11.
[93] Myers (2008): 18.
[94] On South African commission reports, see also: Ashforth (1990); Krüger (2009): 263–266.
[95] The party met Chief Andara II (sometimes referred to as Dimbu II) of the Mbukushu in Andara (the chief in charge of the Western Caprivi, whose headquarters were located outside of the Caprivi), Chief Mamili of the Mafwe in Schukmannsburg (today, Luhonono), and Chief Liswaninyana of the Subyia in Kasane (since he was not allowed to travel to Luhonono because of a smallpox outbreak). These were the only three chiefs in the region who were officially recognised by the colonial administration.
[96] NAN, SWAA, A503/4, Caprivi Zipfel: Handing over to the South West African Administration. 26 October 1929, p. 10.

tion to it, Potts added in brackets that the entire Caprivi "will be made a game reserve".[97] It remains unclear as to why Potts, and possibly also Mamili, thought that the SWAA would proclaim Caprivi as a game reserve as no other documents made any mention of such plans. Nevertheless, it demonstrates that game laws were seen as an important issue by both the colonial authorities and the chiefs. Indeed, as I will discuss below, Mamili's premonition was partly justified when, after the change of governing power, the SWA game laws of 1927 were also introduced in the Caprivi.[98] Although this legislation was primarily aimed at white hunters within the police zone, it also affected the northern territories, where the hunting of all animals was forbidden unless written permission was granted by the local magistrate.[99] The stricter control of firearms and application of hunting laws would later play a significant role in informing opposition to and resistance against South African rule in northern Namibia.

The time prior to the introduction of these laws, particularly the nine-year period during which the Caprivi was under the control of the Bechuanaland Protectorate, have been and continue to be remembered by many Caprivians as a time of progress and minimal direct colonial repression which offered some 'freedom' to residents in the Caprivi.[100] This was mainly a result of government investment in schools and health infrastructure and, crucially for the focus of this study, also marked a period in which people were allegedly permitted to possess weapons and ammunition.[101] To better understand this rather weak control exercised by Bechuanaland in the Caprivi, it is important to note that in the Bechuanaland Protectorate itself, the impact of the colonial administration also remained very limited until the 1940s. At the time the primary aim of the British High Commission for Bechuanaland was to keep the protectorate 'under control' while minimising the costs of administration. This was achieved by vesting so-called 'native chiefs' with significant power and granting them far-reaching responsibilities, including over key legislation such as weapon laws.[102] Furthermore, according to Ashley Jackson, the under-staffed colonial administration

---

[97] NAN, SWAA, A503/4, Caprivi Zipfel: Handing over to the South West African Administration. 26 October 1929, p. 10.
[98] South West Africa Administrator's Office (ed.) (1927), Ordinance No 5, *Official Gazette*, 233, 20 May 1927. Windhoek: Government Printer.
[99] It is not clear how strictly this law was enforced in the Caprivi. In many later reports, it was reported that inhabitants of the Caprivi were still allowed to hunt small animals and only required permission by the chief and the South African authorities for shooting so-called 'royal game'. Consent to do so was normally granted to hunt some rhinoceroses, hippopotamuses or elephants.
[100] Kangumu (2011): 72–78.
[101] Kangumu (2011): 78.
[102] See e.g.: Jackson (2001): 125–132 and Vengroff, R. (1977), *Botswana: Rural Development in the Shadow of Apartheid*. London: Associated University Press, p. 26–32.

sought the loyalty of chiefs in order to help withstand claims by both South Africa and the BSAC for control over the territory.[103]

From SWAA Rule to Direct South African Control of the Eastern Caprivi, 1929–1939

A comparatively positive interpretation of the Caprivi's Bechuanaland period already appears to have taken hold among the Caprivian population during the subsequent period of rule by the South African-controlled South West African Administration (1929–1939). In 1938 Leslie French Trollope, the then native commissioner in the South West African Administration (SWAA) and later the first South African native commissioner and magistrate in the Eastern Caprivi, wrote an extensive report on the general living conditions and political circumstances in the region in which he expressed his regret that Caprivians had ever enjoyed such a degree of 'freedom'. He wrote how during this time "the natives enjoyed all the privileges of natives in Bechuanaland, privileges that we did not and could not continue."[104] As "privileges" he counted the loose weapons laws and the opportunities to export cattle from which Caprivians had benefited. Trollope was concerned that inhabitants of the Caprivi would demand the same rights as those enjoyed by Africans in Botswana, rather than consider themselves to be at the level of Namibians, who enjoyed fewer privileges.[105] He went on to argue that "actually our administration [SWAA] cannot appear in too favourable a light to the natives", since, unlike under the Bechuanaland Administration in the 1920s, the South West African Administration conducted no veterinary controls in the Caprivi and thus no longer allowed the export of cattle from the region.[106]

Furthermore, Trollope pointed out that the recently-introduced game laws were stricter than before and no longer allowed Africans, including even chiefs, the right to shoot any game without permission. Although he then noted somewhat contradictorily that Caprivians were still allowed to hunt small animals, he underlined in the same sentence that the buying of firearms was now forbidden and that access to ammunition had been restricted.[107] The way in which Trollope discussed hunting regulations and weapon laws alongside each other here suggests that, although colonial power manifested itself most visibly

---

[103] Jackson (2001): 125–132.
[104] NAN, SWAA, A503/4, L.F.C. Trollope, Inspection Report, 1937, p. 20.
[105] NAN, SWAA, A503/4, L.F.C. Trollope, Inspection Report, 1937, p. 21. See also e.g.: Vengroff (1977).
[106] NAN, SWAA, A503/4, L.F.C. Trollope, Inspection Report, 1937, p. 22. During the Bechuanaland period, it was possible to export cattle through Botswana. According to Trollope, it would have been too expensive for the South West African Administration to permanently station a veterinary surgeon in the Caprivi.
[107] NAN, SWAA, A503/4, L.F.C. Trollope, Inspection Report, 1937, p. 22.

through game legislation, the colonial authorities as well as Caprivians considered the right to possess firearms to be at least as significant as the right to hunt.[108] The stricter control of guns can be seen as a general tendency among Southern African colonial rulers from the late-nineteenth century, in particular during the inter-war period, and was unsurprisingly applied inconsistently according to race.[109] While colonial regimes often regarded the arming of white settlers as important for maintaining their power, armed Africans increasingly came to be seen to represent a danger to colonial authority, with even loyal chiefs being banned from owning weapons. This fear was likely further fuelled by progress in weapons technology.[110]

The strict regulation of weapons and ammunition was seen as particularly important in the Caprivi due to the threat which rising local dissatisfaction with rule from Windhoek was seen to pose to the colonial status quo. Trollope repeatedly noted that the "natives of the strip are discontent[ed]".[111] Alongside their unfavourable comparisons of South West African Administration rule with life under the governance of Bechuanaland, Trollope saw a further reason for growing discontent among Caprivians. He was convinced that, due to their unique history and geographical situation, locals were in close contact with people from neighbouring colonies, especially Zimbabwe. These links, he argued, would have exposed them to the influences of communism, especially through the 'Watch Tower' movement.[112] This movement, more commonly referred to as 'Kitawala', was a central African offshoot of the Jehovah's Witness religious sect which had become radically anti-colonial in the interwar years and had been met with strong repression from the colonial governments in the Congos, Angola, Zambia and Zimbabwe.[113] "I do not wish to suggest any 'communist peril' in the Caprivi", Trollope stated, "but a few educated natives had been to Rhodesia and one of the most discontented speakers that I had in my meetings was such a native".[114]

In addition to the implementation of the above regulations to control hunting and the possession of firearms, the about ten-year period which the Caprivi spent under the con-

---

[108] See e.g. for colonial Kenya: Steinhart, E.I. (2006), *Black Poachers, White Hunters. A social history of hunting in Colonial Kenya*. Oxford: James Currey; on hunting in Kaoko, see also: Bollig et al. (2016).
[109] Storey, W.K. (2008), *Guns, Race, Power in Colonial South Africa*. Cambridge: Cambridge University Press, p. 185–186.
[110] Storey (2008): 185–188.
[111] NAN, SWAA, A503/4, L.F.C. Trollope, Inspection Report, 1937, p. 21.
[112] NAN, SWAA, A503/4, L.F.C. Trollope, Inspection Report, 1937, p. 21.
[113] See e.g.: Higginson, J. (1992), Liberating the Captives: Independent Watchtower as an Avatar of Colonial Revolt in Southern Africa and Katanga, 1908–1941. *Journal of Social History*, 4: 55–80.
[114] NAN, SWAA, A503/4, L.F.C. Trollope, Inspection Report, 1937, p. 21.

trol of the South West African Administration had three other significant effects in the region. These were the tightening and later abolition of the so-called 'Barotse privileges', the definitive demarcation of the northern boundary with Zambia and Angola, and the forced removals of people and cattle from the Western Caprivi. All of these can be understood as measures aimed to gradually increase the colonial grip on the Caprivi by restricting the access of its inhabitants to natural resources and, as I will show below, as a means of acquiring more information on the region in the process.

'Barotse privileges' was the name for a series of special laws which allowed the so-called Barotse people from Zambia to cultivate vegetable gardens, catch fish, and collect reeds along a small strip of the Namibian side of the Zambezi River. Although these rights were referred to as an 'ancient' privilege, there was no evidence that they had ever existed before the First World War. Instead, Kangumu has argued convincingly that they had mainly served the Northern Rhodesian authorities in their efforts to maintain good relations with the Barotse Kingdom in the early twentieth century, before later acting as a gesture of mutual goodwill between the colonial authorities of the Eastern Caprivi and those of Northern Rhodesia. The 'privileges' were firstly restricted by the colonial administration in the Eastern Caprivi to people living in or around Shesheke, but shortly thereafter even these individuals also required a permit to cross into the Caprivi. According to the authorities in the Caprivi, this additional regulation was introduced to ensure that they did not bring weapons into the Caprivi. In 1933, the right to cultivate gardens was abolished and finally, in 1940, the privileges were withdrawn altogether.[115]

The second impact, which may have occurred in connection with the withdrawal of the 'Barotse privileges', was the surveying and demarcation of the Andara-Katima borderline in 1930 and 1931.[116] For the first time after a general agreement on colonial boundaries was signed at the 1886 Portuguese–German Convention, the border between Angola and Namibia was thereby precisely defined and demarcated on the ground.[117] In order to do so, the representatives of the relevant political authorities – Northern Rhodesia, South Africa via the South West Africa Administration, the Bechuanaland Protectorate and Portugal – had to first agree on the position of two beacons in Katima Mulilo and Andara.[118] Thereafter,

---

[115] NAN, LKM, N/15/39, Barotse Privileges in the Eastern Caprivi Zipfel, 14 October 1950; See also: Kangumu (2011): 109–110.

[116] This is a straight line which runs from the village of Andara (today located in the Kavango East Region) to Katima Mulilo, thus forming the Caprivi Strip's northern border with Angola and Zambia.

[117] NAN, SWAA A503/5, Re: Northern Boundary of the Caprivi Zipfel S.W.A. 22 October 1930. See also: Akweenda, S. (1997), *International Law and the Protection of Namibia's Territorial Integrity. Boundaries and Territorial Claims*. The Hague: Klewer Law International: 237–244.

[118] NAN, SWAA A503/5, Caprivi Strip Boundary. Andara-Katima Mulilo Line. Undated (1930?). The

surveyors demarcated a geodetic straight line from the beacon in Andara to that in Katima Mulilo. This line had to be cleared of bush over its entire 220-kilometre course, with the cutline needing "to be wide enough for the passage of cars."[119] Workers and two surveyors from Portugal and Namibia respectively undertook this labour-intensive task at a pace of ten kilometres per week, such that it took them several months to set all twenty-two beacons along the border.[120] Although this newly demarcated line may not yet have had an immediate impact on the local population, it nevertheless marked the basis for subsequent control of the border.

The surveying and demarcation of the northern border led to increasing colonial knowledge on the Caprivi's geography and nature. For example, the South West African Administration's surveyor general, A. G. Landsberg, stated in detail in his report on the survey where game had been found, where dense bush occurred, and which islands had been flooded during rainy season.[121] Furthermore, aerial photographs were taken, and geodetic data was collected, probably for the first time. This information, combined with the better physical accessibility afforded by the cutline, was arguably crucial for tighter colonial control of the region.[122]

The South West African Administration's third intervention targeted mainly the Western Caprivi. This region had come under more vigorous observation in the 1920s, when veterinary measurements were taken to protect white farmers just south of the Red Line from the spread of cattle diseases so that the ban on the export of their cattle could be definitely lifted.[123] The Red Line was finally codified in the Prohibited Areas Act of 1928, with the South West African Administration subsequently attempting to establish an adjoining 'stock-free' or quarantine zone.[124] However, this zone had little effect on the movement of cattle in and out of the police zone. According to Miescher, the consequent frustration on the part of the colonial authorities led to an increased willingness in the 1930s to "deploy violence against both, people and animals" inside the stock-free zone.[125]

---

reasons for the involvement of the Betchuanaland Protectorate's administration in this process remained unclear, since its territory did not border directly on the Andara-Katima Mulilo Line.

[119] NAN, SWAA A503/5, Re Northern Boundary of the Caprivi Zipfel S.W.A. 22 October 1930, p. 8.
[120] NAN, SWAA A503/5, Re Northern Boundary of the Caprivi Zipfel S.W.A. 22 October 1930, p. 9 and NAN, SWAA A503/5, Boundaries of the Caprivi Strip Survey. 12 May 1930.
[121] NAN, SWAA A503/5, Re Northern Boundary of the Caprivi Zipfel S.W.A. 22 October 1930.
[122] In 1940 the cutline was turned into a road, see: Boden (2004): 68.
[123] Miescher (2013): 134–137.
[124] Miescher (2012b): 776.
[125] Miescher (2012): 780. Michael Bollig described the implementation of such measures in the Kaoko. This involved the shooting of cattle as a punishment for not reporting cases of lungsickness. See: Bollig (1998b): 526–527.

Archival material reveals that the shooting of livestock and the forced removals, arrests and harassment of people which Miescher and Bollig described for north-west Namibia also affected the north-east, especially in the Western Caprivi, after 1935.[126] While under the governance of the Bechuanaland Protectorate, veterinary services and controls in the Western Caprivi had been conducted through Botswana's own veterinary services, this was no longer the case under the South West African Administration.[127] In the early 1930s, several cases of lung sickness occurred in Namibia which resulted in a vaccination campaign in Kavango in 1937. For this purpose, all inhabitants of the Western Caprivi had to take their cattle to the Okavango River for vaccination. However, only one year later, the colonial authorities decided to clear the entire Western Caprivi of both "stock and people".[128] Nevertheless, it seems that only pastoralists were forced to leave the area. Khwe-speakers, who mostly did not own cattle, were left unaffected by these measures.[129] It is important to note here that the control of the mobility, and settling of these pastoralists was not only aimed at protecting white farming in central and southern Namibia. Nomadic or partly-sedentary groups also appear to have posed a particular danger to the otherwise clearly-defined colonial spatial and ethnic order. A reduction of their mobility was thus seen as a priority for the colonial authorities.[130] Surprisingly, people who owned very few or no cattle but were less sedentary then the pastoralists who had to move out of the strip were not targeted by this eviction order. By the end of the 1930s, two guards had been stationed at Bwabwata in the Western Caprivi. These received the title of 'Native Guards' or 'Border Guards' and were given the role of enforcing the ban on cattle in the area as well as patrolling its borders with Angola and Botswana.[131]

In short, while the colonial authorities' knowledge of the Caprivi increased gradually during the 1930s, and some interventions on the part of the colonial authorities were carried out – including the implementation of stricter hunting and weapons laws or the forced removal of people and the shooting of cattle in the Western Caprivi – the entire region continued to be portrayed by its rulers as remote, of no value and difficult to govern.[132]

---

[126] Miescher (2012): 780.
[127] NAN, SWAA, A503/4, L.F.C. Trollope, Inspection Report, 1937, p. 22.
[128] NAN, SWAA A503/1, J.W. Potts, Caprivi Zipfel. Handing over to the South African Administration, 1929, p. 10.
[129] Taylor (2012): 66.
[130] Bollig (1998b): 509.
[131] Boden (2004): 68.
[132] See also: Lenggenhager, L. (2015), Nature, War and Development: South Africa's Caprivi Strip, 1960–1980. *Journal for Southern African Studies*, 41(3): 467–483 (here: 469).

Leslie Trollope and the Caprivi's 'Distinctiveness', 1939–1952

In 1939 the Caprivi's administrative structure changed again. While the Western Caprivi remained under the governance of the native commissioner in Rundu, control of the Eastern Caprivi was transferred to South Africa's Department of Native Affairs in Pretoria by Union Proclamation No. 147 on 1 August 1939. Shortly thereafter, the territory was officially given the name of the Eastern Caprivi Zipfel (often abbreviated as ECZ) and declared a magisterial district, before becoming a so-called Bantu Reserve in 1940.[133] In October 1939 Leslie Trollope, who had authored the reports discussed above in his earlier capacity as native commissioner for the South West African Administration, took office as the local magistrate in Katima Mulilo, the Eastern Caprivi's new administrative centre.[134] He remained in this position for more than fifteen years, with only a short break in 1946, during which his then assistant, and the later permanent magistrate, C.E. Kruger occupied the position for a year.

Promoting 'Wellbeing', Befriending the Neighbours and Protecting the Fauna

Trollope's duties were defined by the Department of Native Affairs in Pretoria as to

> (a) foster the operation of native institutions and to endeavour to improve them and make them an effective instrument of administration; (b) to combat witchcraft; (c) to control stock diseases; (d) to control the sale of ammunition; (e) to preserve the indigenous fauna; (f) to maintain friendly relations with neighbouring administrations; (g) to make proposals for the utilisation of the tribal levies; and (h) to pay attention to the Mandate from the League of Nations and the provision therein regarding the promotion of the material and moral wellbeing [sic] and the social progress of the inhabitants.[135]

It is important to contextualise these responsibilities within South Africa's broader vision for the governance of so-called native reserves. While the control of weapons and cattle diseases or the establishment of 'native' administrations were central aspects of South Africa's 'native' policies domestically and in Namibia, other aims were more particular to the specific contexts of Namibia and the Caprivi, especially the need to be perceived as being supportive of the local population so as to comply with the requirements of the League of Nation man-

---

[133] Kangumu (2011): 95–96.
[134] The old administrative headquarters established by Kurt Streitwolf at Luhonono (formerly Schuckmannsburg) were demolished in 1935 and transferred to Katima Mulilo, which was considered to be a healthier setting and less likely to be affected by annual floods.
[135] NASA, NTS 463/400/1, Eastern Caprivi Zipfel, undated, 1940 (?). Similarly quoted in: Kangumu (2011): 96. Kangumu did not indicate from where the passage originated. Gewald referred to a similar quote in an article in the Peruvian newspaper *Lima Times*. Gewald (2013): 85.

date.¹³⁶ Further considerations which were seen as particularly important in governing the Eastern Caprivi were the need to be on good terms with neighbouring territories and the protection of local fauna and flora.

Despite the fact that it was included in this list of policy goals formulated by the Department of Native Affairs in Pretoria, the "promotion of the well-being" of the Caprivi population seems not to have been a very pressing concern in the first decade of direct South African rule in the Caprivi, but, as we will see later, became of high relevance at the latest in the 1950s. However, Trollope did recognise before taking office, in as early as 1938, that "owing to their geographical position, [Caprivians] live in very difficult circumstances and are in urgent need of assistance".¹³⁷ This statement would contradict a 1939 report by another South African official, in which he described the inhabitants of the Caprivi as "fairly healthy" and the region as possessing an "abundance of wild fruits and game", while offering good harvests and presenting its residents with no danger of starvation.¹³⁸ Such inconsistencies in the portrayal of living conditions in the Caprivi might suggest that Trollope chose to depict a suffering local population which had to be 'rescued' and sustained by South Africa, as it was demanded by the mandate. Or it could suggest that the other official was portraying the South African colonial authorities in an overly positive light for the same reasons.

More pressing in the initial stages of Trollope's term (in the Caprivi) were two other tasks assigned to the magistrate in Katima Mulilo, which seem to have often been regarded as closely linked in the day-to-day work of the office, namely the protection of the local fauna and flora and the maintenance of good relations with neighbouring territories. Trollope's correspondence from the time reveals that these responsibilities were closer to his heart than any others. As magistrate, Trollope was in detailed correspondence and contact with the Bechuanaland Protectorate's district commissioners in Maun and Kasane and established close ties to the Northern Rhodesian authorities in Livingstone and Sheshebe, from where he collected his post.¹³⁹ He was also in constant exchange with many museums and scientific institutions in Southern Africa and Europe. The fact that he was such an

---

[136] There were also central aspects of so-called 'Native' or 'Bantu' Reserves in South Africa which were not – or not yet – of relevance in the Caprivi in the 1940s, namely 'betterment' and 'rehabilitation' schemes. These included the culling of cattle, which, for example, was met with strong resistance in the Transkei during the 1930s and 1940s. See: Bundy, C. (1987), Land and Liberation, Popular Rural Protest and the National Liberation Movements in South Africa 1920–1960. In S. Marks and S. Trapido (eds), *The Politics of Race, Class and Nationalism in Twentieth Century South Africa*. London and New York: Longman: 254–286 (here 268–270).

[137] NAN, A503/25, L. Trollope, Eastern Caprivi Zipfel: Control, 1938, p. 4.

[138] NASA, NTS 463/400/1, Report on Native Affairs: Eastern Portion of the Caprivi Zipfel, 1939, p. 1–2.

[139] See also: Gewald (2013): 85.

active participant in these academic networks suggests that Trollope did not only seek to act as a representative of South Africa, but also attempted to position himself within the broader (scientific) networks of the British Empire. He thus may have sought to build on the role which the Caprivi and northern Namibia played already in the work of academic institutions in Southern Africa, especially through hosting collecting and hunting expeditions which passed through the area. Leslie Witz described several such expeditions which made their way through northern Namibia for the purpose of 'collecting' game for natural history museums in London, New York and the South African town of King William's Town during the first half of the twentieth century. Using the example of the Kaffrarian Museum (today known as the Amathole Museum) in King's William Town, Witz argued that such expeditions took place within an "imperial museum network that linked London, South Africa and India."[140] The resulting collections were considered to be "representatives of the natural environment[s]" from which they originated.[141] Trollope's correspondence with Southern African academic institutions may also be seen as reflecting what Witz held to be a second imperial network – beyond that of the British Empire – which was established through South Africa's colonisation of Namibia. According to this argument, South African colonial officials "opened up Namibia as a field for collectors from South African museums".[142]

Trollope's other main focus in the Caprivi was the protection of local flora and fauna. Indeed, one of the most important cases which he investigated during his time as magistrate was related to this aim, namely a case against Simataa Mamili, who had been recognised by the South West African Administration as chief of the Mafwe in 1931 and now stood accused of poaching.[143] The outcome of this case may have informed subsequent opposition to South African nature conservation laws and was retrospectively invoked by Caprivians as proof of the colonial administration's greater interest in protecting animals than people.[144] In his first inspection trip to the Caprivi in 1937, still in the capacity of a native commissioner, Trollope had investigated the case of Chief Mamili. Government officials had repeatedly described the chief as a heavy drinker and troublemaker, but most importantly accused him of hunting so-called royal game, namely hippopotamuses and elephants, without a permit, which was prohibited under the game law of 1927.[145] The Simataa Mamili

---

[140] Witz (2015): 678.
[141] Witz (2015): 674.
[142] Witz (2015): 679.
[143] Gewald (2013): 85. As discussed above, Trollope had initially investigated Mamili in 1937 at a time before he had taken office as magistrate in the Caprivi.
[144] I will return to this point on p. 73 ff. See also: Kangumu (2011): 102.
[145] E.g.: NAN, SWAA, A503/4, L.F.C. Trollope, Inspection Report, 1937, p. 9.

case occupied Trollope's attentions during the early years of his rule in the Eastern Caprivi. One year after Trollope's first visit, Mamili had been discharged from his chiefy duties, only to be reinstalled in his position again in 1939 by South Africa's chief native commissioner as an "act of grace" when Pretoria took control of the Eastern Caprivi.[146] In 1944, after allegedly having hunted illegally again, Mamili was permanently removed from office by Piet van der Byl, the South African minister of Native Affairs, who also ordered him to leave the "Mafwe tribal area".[147] In his removal order, van der Byl said that Mamili had been drinking too much again and was generally "incompetent", but the only crime which he was accused of committing concerned illegal hunting.[148]

Not only was Trollope concerned with enforcing game laws – at least when these were allegedly transgressed by 'disloyal' chiefs – but he also collected a host of information on the region's fauna and flora, geography, and history.[149] In a report written in 1940, he expressed his concern about the diminishing numbers of wildlife:

> There is no doubt that in years gone by the Strip must have been the huntsman's paradise both for variety and numbers of game. The variety is still there, but the numbers have (with the exception of buffalo and lechwe) greatly diminished.[150]

As the main cause thereof, he referred to the considerable hunting activities of whites prior to South African rule in the region; in contrast, he deemed the "destruction" caused by the hunting which was still partially lawful for local inhabitants to be "not excessive".[151] However, in many subsequent reports, South African officials still wrote of plentiful wildlife. In these reports, descriptions of Caprivian nature and its economic potential were closely juxtaposed. Trollope and others primarily discussed agriculture and cattle farming as possible vectors of future economic development, but saw little potential for both, mainly as a result of the area's low population density and the difficulties in exporting its agricultural products due to veterinary restrictions and its remoteness.

In 1942, for the first time in the annual report to the secretary of Native Affairs in Pretoria, a paragraph was devoted to trees.[152] According to this report, the

> greater portion of the Eastern Caprivi Zipfel [...] is heavily tree covered. In parts these trees are well grown and numerous although it is doubtful whether they would be of

---

[146] Kangumu (2011): 101.
[147] NAN, Accessions, A.871, Removal Order, 17 July 1944.
[148] NAN, Accessions, A.871, Removal Order, 17 July 1944.
[149] Gewald (2013).
[150] NASA, NTS 463/400/1, Report on the Administration of the Eastern Caprivi Zipfel, 1940, p. 25.
[151] NASA, NTS 463/400/1, Report on the Administration of the Eastern Caprivi Zipfel, 1940, p. 25.
[152] NASA, NTS 463/400/1, Report on the Administration of the Eastern Caprivi Zipfel, 1942, p. 7.

interest to the timber trade, especially in view of the remoteness of the territory. Be that as it may, without trees the strip would be poor country.[153]

This quote again reveals some of the most important characteristics of early South African rule in the Caprivi and, to some degree, elsewhere in northern Namibia too. While the South African authorities were constantly on the lookout for any potential profits to be found in these areas, they also regularly disparaged them as poor and distant. The Caprivi itself was declared to be among the furthest of these isolated territories – even beyond the last frontier – and was thus regarded as even more in need of any sort of development which would ultimately render it worth the cost of its governance.

The Caprivi as an Oddity?

Many of the features of Trollope's governance in the Caprivi resembled the methods of administration applied in other parts of northern Namibia or, more generally, in other territories under indirect colonial rule. Above all, he downplayed the potential benefits which occupation of the area could provide, but continued a constant search for potential economic opportunities and resources. However, for the Caprivi, a third more unique feature is evident from many of the descriptions of the area from this time. This is the notion that the Caprivi was especially remote, useless, and distinct from the rest of South Africa and Namibia. As I will show, such ideas about the Caprivi's peculiarity often started from the assumption that the region was not only affected by similar, but deeper, problems of governance to those in other areas of Namibia, but constituted a distinct oddity in its own right.

Leslie Trollope's 1937 report provides such a description. Trollope authored this report based on the findings of an inspection trip to the Eastern Caprivi, which he had undertaken to prepare for the region's impending transfer from the control of the South West African Administration to that of South Africa's Department of Native Affairs.[154] In the report, he acknowledged that:

> The blunt fact is that our control of this small territory, remote from S.W.A. to which it is connected by a 20-mile wide elongated strip of desert, and almost completely surrounded as it is by other administrations, is wholly artificial. It is politically anomalous, economically unsound and administratively wellnigh [sic] impracticable.[155]

---

[153] NASA, NTS 463/400/1, Report on the Administration of the Eastern Caprivi Zipfel, 1942, p. 7. On South Africa's forestry policies in Namibia, see also p. 111 ff.
[154] After the hand-over of power to South Africa in 1939, Trollope became the Eastern Caprivi's first native commissioner under the direct South African administration.
[155] NAN, SWAA, A503/4, L.F.C. Trollope, Inspection Report, 1937, p. 21.

As many other officials did at the time, Trollope described the Caprivi as not merely difficult and expensive to govern, but also as unlikely to provide any economic returns for these efforts: "Insofar as the Eastern Caprivi is concerned [... its control] would necessitate a permanent minimum staff of an administrative official [...], a veterinary officer [...] and a doctor – and complementary native staff. All this for about 9,000 people".[156] With the knowledge that the administration in the Caprivi had hitherto only been staffed by himself and a few policemen and that any such further investments in personnel were highly unlikely to ever be sanctioned for the region, he concluded that:

> The Strip is no labour source for us nor an outlet for our products. [...] It is quite unsuited for European settlement and there are, as far as I know, no minerals. The most sensible thing would be to resume the negotiations, which were interrupted by the Great War, with England for an exchange of territory.[157]

The South West African Administration's outlook for the Western Caprivi – the region which, unlike the Eastern Caprivi, remained under its direct control after 1939 – was equally pessimistic. In a confidential 1944 letter to the chief native commissioner in Windhoek, Harold Edees, the then native commissioner in Rundu, described the Western Caprivi as "a useless strip of country" which "is unsuitable for agriculture away from the rivers [...] has only a meagre supply of water for the greater part of the year, and is, in consequence, unsuitable for stock".[158]

The regular changes to its administrative structures and the loss of the Caprivi's primary function as a geostrategic wedge between German- and British-ruled colonies after the First World War fed into subsequent explanations as to why the region should be regarded, in Trollope's words, as "politically anomalous".[159] The political uniqueness of the Caprivi, he repeatedly argued, derived from the fact that the area had few obvious links with the rest of South Africa or Namibia and "lies between and in the closest contact with the protectorates of Bechuanaland and Barotseland." He had reached this conclusion on the basis of his understanding of the social structures of the Caprivi's inhabitants, who had, Trollope argued, "little tribal organisation or authority, certainly nothing approaching that of the highly organised Ovambo tribes". He continued, positing that the two Caprivi "tribes" were "not very distinct" and should actually both be considered as "vassals and hangers-on of other tribes" across the borders. For Trollope, this distinctive 'ethnic' context and the fact

---

[156] NAN, SWAA, A503/4, L.F.C. Trollope, Inspection Report, 1937, p. 21.
[157] NAN, SWAA, A503/4, L.F.C. Trollope, Inspection Report, 1937, p. 21.
[158] NAN, SWAA, A503/1, H.L.P. Edees, Western Caprivi Zipfel: Control of, 1944, p. 1.
[159] This and the following quotes: NAN, SWAA, A503/4, L.F.C. Trollope, Inspection Report, 1937, p. 19–20.

that "the Administration in the Strip is so very different from that in the Union" also indicated that it would not be possible for a senior clerk from the South African Department of Native Affairs to simply become a native commissioner for the Eastern Caprivi.[160] Instead, he suggested that the Eastern Caprivi should be governed by the South West African police sergeant, E.P. Brittz, who had been stationed in the region for the previous nine years, possessed good knowledge of the area, and had proven to already have "natural resistance" against the "tropical diseases" in the Caprivi.[161]

The narrative of the Caprivi's supposed variance with the rest of Namibia and South Africa was further reinforced by its climatic and ecological distinctiveness. Trollope, for example, described Caprivian fauna as "not resembling very much" that of South Africa.[162] Indeed, the image of Caprivian flora and fauna as completely different from that found in South Africa – or even as 'tropical' – runs like a thread through descriptions of the area up until the twenty-first century.[163]

In his article on Leslie Trollope, Jan-Bart Gewald suggested an additional aspect of this 'Caprivi as oddity' narrative. Gewald argued that it was Trollope's particular style of governance and his "remarkable character" which further reinforced the idea that the Caprivi was "beyond the last frontier".[164] This, he proposed, was due to Trollope's enthusiasm for getting to know the area, his close engagement with colonial authorities from across the borders, and consequently his rather loose ties to the Department of Native Affairs in Pretoria.[165]

Such a reading of Trollope's approach to governance could imply that the narrative of Caprivi distinctiveness was a symptom of South Africa's "neglect of administrative responsibility" and the singularity of Trollope's character, as described by Gewald.[166] I propose

---

[160] NAN, A503/25, L. Trollope, Eastern Caprivi Zipfel: Control, 1938, p. 4.
[161] NAN, A503/25, L. Trollope, Eastern Caprivi Zipfel: Control, 1938, p. 4.
[162] Quoted in: Gewald (2013): 87.
[163] For example, see the German journalist and writer Rainer Bruchmann's book on Caprivi history: Buchmann, R. (2000), *Caprivi, An African Flashpoint: An Illustrated History of Namibia's Tropical Region Where Four Countries Meet*. Northcliff: self-published. The SADF also used the Caprivi as a base for 'tropical training': Kangumu (2011): 148. The notion of a 'tropical' Caprivi is not supported by ecological classification systems. According to the Köppen-Geiger ecological classifications, the Caprivi has the same warm semi-arid desert climate (BSh) which is also found in large parts of northern South Africa. The only area of South Africa or Namibia which is classified as tropical (Aw) is a very narrow strip along the South Africa–Mozambique border, to the south of Maputo. Similar patterns can be found in the classification of vegetation areas, according to which the Caprivi does not differ categorically from large parts of Namibia and South Africa.
[164] Gewald (2013): 81–93.
[165] Gewald (2013): 83–85. These aspects of Trollope's rule in the Caprivi exhibit elements of what has sometimes been described in colonial discourse as "becoming native", see e.g.: Leon, C.E. (2009), *Movement and Belonging: Lines, Places and Spaces of Travel*. New York: Peter Lang, p. 110–111.
[166] Gewald (2013), see also: Kangumu (2011): 56.

instead to situate the assumed administrative indifference within the context of the sort of 'ambivalent' administration which occurred in many supposedly peripheral areas at the edges of colonial power. In the particular case of the Caprivi under Trollope's rule, this manifested itself in a reluctance on the part of South Africa to channel administrative resources until the region's precise economic potential was ascertained. The search for anything which might prove the region's potential value thus constituted the main task for Trollope and his successors in the Caprivi until the mid-1950s.

Establishing 'good relations' with the chiefs was important in order to acquire more information about the region and thereby exert more control over it, all while expending only limited resources. In this sense, Trollope's loose ties with Pretoria, his keen interest in gaining detailed knowledge about the local area, and his close co-operation with the inhabitants and governers of neighbouring territories were conducive for the establishment of state power in the context of indirect rule.[167] That Trollope at the same time repeatedly portrayed the Caprivi as 'useless' territory and downplayed its potentials should be understood as serving to support South Africa's claim that the occupation of Namibia was a development project which was not to be pursued for the sake of profit.[168]

As I will argue in the following section, the urge to present the occupation as a development project became more pressing as opposition and resistance to South Africa's mandate grew, both within Namibia and internationally. In the following years, as I will show, the research, protection and control of the Caprivi's nature, which had hitherto been only one of many possible potentials, thus became a dominant aspect of South African policy in the Caprivi.

Putting Caprivi on South Africa's Map, 1945–1966

An interplay of global, regional and local developments shaped the trajectory of the Caprivi in the 1950s and early 1960s. Changes in world politics reconfigured South African policy towards Namibia from just after the end of the Second World War until the passing of United Nations General Assembly Resolution 2145, which terminated the South African mandate in 1966. At the same time, internal resistance against the occupation of Namibia grew through the efforts of nationalist, anti-colonial organisations in the late 1950s and the launching of an armed struggle for independence from the mid-1960s. Below I will outline the most important developments which affected the Caprivi at the international and

---
[167] Gewald (2013).
[168] McCullers (2012): 27, 128. See also: Steward, A. (1963), *South West Africa: The Sacred Trust*. Johannesburg: da Gama Publications.

regional levels until the mid-1960s. I will also explain how South Africa reacted to these by applying new strategies of governance in the Caprivi and how the area's importance for Pretoria grew in the process.

International and Regional Politics

The consolidation of anti-colonial resistance after the Second World War led to the independence of an increasing number of African nation-states, a process which marked the end of formal European colonialism in most parts of Africa. Many of the newly-established independent states, including Zambia and later Angola in particular, were to play a pivotal strategic role for the independence movement in Namibia and the liberation movement in South Africa, where the decolonisation process followed a different path. The South African Union had already become a self-governing autonomous dominion of the British Empire in 1910 and later became a colonising power in its own right.[169] In 1945, when the League of Nations reconstituted itself as the United Nations (UN), the South African prime minister, Jan Smuts, issued a request for the UN to accede to Namibia's incorporation into South Africa as its fifth province. Smuts' efforts even included the staging of a referendum, which was meant to prove the consent of the Namibian population.[170] This was not held by a democratic ballot, but through meetings with chiefs and headmen, in which they were supposedly asked whether they would prefer to be under any other government. The UN did not recognise this referendum and turned down South Africa's request by the end of 1946.[171]

The victory of Daniel F. Malan's Herenigde Nasionale Party (HNP, later 'Nasionale Party' (NP); in English, 'National Party') in the South African general election in 1948 and the subsequent implementation of the strict racial segregationist policies of apartheid impacted significantly upon Namibia, where apartheid was also gradually introduced. This affected the Namibian population in a variety of ways, most severely in the increasingly strict race laws, the far-reaching effects of an expanding migrant labour system, and the later establishment of so-called homelands for 'non-white' Namibians.

However, from immediately after the so-called referendum, internal resistance against South African rule had increased, not only in Namibia itself, but also among Namibian migrant workers in South Africa. Namibian labourers, clergy and other church figures, and a nascent black Namibian intelligentsia founded various resistance and liberation organisations.[172] The most prominent of these was the Ovambo People's Congress (OPC), which

---

[169] The Union's status as a sovereign state was granted by the Statute of Westminster in 1931.
[170] Wallace (2011): 246.
[171] Wallace (2011): 243–250.
[172] Wallace (2011): 243–250.

was established in 1957 in Cape Town and renamed the Ovamboland People's Organization (OPO) in 1959.[173] Shortly thereafter, the organisation reconstituted itself as the South West Africa People's Organisation (SWAPO), a name which emphasised its nationalist rather than ethnic approach towards realising the goal of an independent Namibia.[174] One of the organisation's founding members was Sam Nujoma, who would be elected as the first president of post-independence Namibia while Herman Andimba Toivo ya Toivo, the co-founder of the OPC, became SWAPO's general secretary.[175]

South Africa's withdrawal from the Commonwealth in 1961 and the official termination of its UN mandate in Namibia in 1966 saw it renew its interest in the northern parts of Namibia, which now came to be regarded as a strategic location which separated a 'new' South Africa, now outside the realms of the British Empire, from what it considered to be 'Black Africa'.[176]

The period from the end of the Second World War until the 1960s should thus be seen as a time of increasing South African control over Namibia, particularly of those areas to the north of the Red Line, where most Namibians lived. The corresponding growth of international and internal resistance against the South African occupation forced South Africa, in turn, to establish new strategies to maintain its control of the territory.

South African Development Strategies in Northern Namibia

As this domestic and international political context evolved in the 1950s and early 1960s, South Africa resorted to new strategies to govern northern Namibia. These can be grouped around two main goals. The first was to convince regional and international powers that South Africa was more concerned about the 'well-being' and 'development' of Namibia and its people than about any potential benefits which might accrue from the occupation for Pretoria. Secondly, South Africa sought to win the fight against emerging local resistance as well as thwart the dangers which would supposedly emanate from the newly-established independent states to the north, not only via police and military force, but also through discursive strategies. In short, South Africa thus sought to legitimise its occupation by presenting it as a good cause with the goal of developing Namibia and protecting it from the threat of communism emanating from the north.[177]

---

[173] Dobell (1998): 28–32.
[174] The exact place and date of the foundation of SWAPO are unclear. See: Dobell (1998): 28–32 and Wallace (2011): 250.
[175] Dobell (1998): 28–32.
[176] Mamdani (1996): 31.
[177] Rhoodie (1967). See also Rizzo (2012).

These two central aspects of subsequent South African policy towards Namibia are reflected in Eschel Rhoodie's 1967 book *South West: The Last Frontier in Africa*. Rhoodie, who was a journalist and press officer for the South African government, aimed to improve South Africa's international image and justify its occupation of Namibia.[178] In his preface, he described Namibia as:

> A land of grazing cattle, of different races, of fishing and mining towns, of deserts and weird mountains and practically nothing else – except of course the almost limitless potential recognized by men of vision who have taken a sincere and abiding interest in it. It is in the truest sense a last frontier for if man can survive and prosper in this hostile environment, then there are no areas left on this earth that cannot be civilized as well.[179]

He went on to describe the territory's "wide", "nameless" and "unproductive" landscapes, arguing that these promised absolutely no profit for South Africa and that the occupation represented nothing but a favour to help Namibia's "backward" people "develop" their land. By doing so, he promoted official South African government rhetoric which described the occupation as a trusteeship to contribute towards the development of the territory.[180] The second main concern of Rhoodie's book was the fight against communism and South Africa's leading role in maintaining "Western civilisation" in Namibia and protecting local people from what Rhoodie predicted would be the "abortive invasions of South West Africa by terrorists from Tanzania [...] armed to teeth with Russian and Chinese weapons".[181]

Rhoodie thus provided an example of how South Africa legitimised its occupation of Namibia and the expansion of the apartheid system into the territory with a combination of arguments for the defence against communism and the development of hitherto 'unproductive' and 'useless' landscapes. In order to understand how these two strategies translated into the control and commodification of nature in the Caprivi, it is crucial to look at some of South Africa's self-proclaimed 'development' strategies, which started to affect all regions of northern Namibia from the 1950s.[182]

The intensification of the developmental aspects of South Africa's occupation was aimed primarily at the more effective incorporation of the Namibian population into the South African migrant labour system, the strengthening of the 'ethnographical potential' ascribed to parts of the local population, and the control and capitalisation of the region's natural resources. I will outline the first two of these aims in this section, before I briefly refer to

---

[178] Rhoodie (1967).
[179] Rhoodie (1967): Preface.
[180] McCullers (2012): 128 and Lenggenhager (2015).
[181] Rhoodie (1967): Preface.
[182] Bollig (1998b) and (2013), McCullers (2012).

forestry as an example of one of South Africa's key early efforts to control and commodify northern Namibian nature.[183] I will then focus on South Africa's 'development' of the natural environment of the northern territories in greater detail in following chapters.

A primary interest for South Africa in northern Namibia was the sourcing of an additional workforce. Labour had become South Africa's most coveted resource in the region after the Second World War, with migrant workers from the area vital for the growing mining sector in South Africa and Namibia as well as for privately-owned farms in central and southern Namibia. Robert Moorsom described how the difficult agricultural situation in central-north Namibia as well as its high population density created the perfect conditions for the recruitment of cheap labour due to the fact that "wage-labour, or local petty-bourgeois activities dependent on its earnings, [had] been the only possible source of cash income for the vast majority" of its inhabitants.[184] The result was that, unlike for the Caprivi and north-west Namibia, the principal function of the South African regime in the central-north soon revealed itself as the procurement of migrant labour and the regulation of its distribution throughout Namibia and South Africa.[185]

In addition to the recruitment of migrant workers from then Ovamboland, South Africa also held a deep interest in sections of the population which were considered to be "unspoiled by western civilization".[186] This so-called ethnographic interest was mostly focussed on the north-western territory known as the Kaoko. As Lorena Rizzo argued, the socio-economic marginalisation of central and northern Kaoko intensified after the Second World War.[187] This contributed to the reduction of the region to its symbolic value for white settlers as an exotic realm, expressed primarily through the representation of its inhabitants, especially the so-called 'Himba' people.[188] This interest in people who were considered to be 'traditional' also had more practical benefits for the colonial authorities. Ethnological surveys were not only useful in finding more effective ways to strengthen South African political and economic hegemony in peripheral regions, but also for providing a scientific

---

[183] Another example is hydrology, see: McCullers (2012) and McKittrick (2013).
[184] Moorsom (1977): 65.
[185] Moorsom (1977): 56. On the former Ovamboland, see: McKittrick, M. (1998), Generational Struggles and Social Mobility. In P. Hayes, J. Silvester, M. Wallace and W. Hartmann (eds.), *Namibia under South African Rule: Mobility and Containment, 1915–46.* Oxford, Windhoek and Athens OH: James Currey, Out of Africa and Ohio University Press: 241–262.
[186] Rhoodie (1967): 22.
[187] Rizzo (2012), see also: Bollig (1998b).
[188] Rizzo (2012): 267. On white settlers' safari trips to Kaoko and to 'the Himba', see: Henrichsen, D. (2000), Pilgrimages into Kaoko: Herrensafaris, 4x4s and Settler Illusions. In G. Miescher and D. Henrichsen (eds), *New Notes on Kaoko.* Basel: Basler Afrika Bibliographien: 159–188. On Kaoko, see also the edited volume: Miescher, G and D. Henrichsen (eds.), *New Notes on Kaoko.* Basel: Basler Afrika Bibliographien.

basis for apartheid's ideologies of difference. For example, the information gathered was crucial for the later separation of Namibia's different population groups into homelands, as recommended by the Odendaal Commission in 1964. As Robert Gordon argued, ethnology "served to facilitate the transformation of power from vulgar control to management through co-optive domination of blacks".[189] Apart from the so-called Himba people, this was particularly the case for groups labelled as 'San' or 'Bushman', onto which (South African) anthropologists also projected their desires for 'exoticism' and 'otherness'.[190]

A third area of 'development' envisioned by the South African authorities can be grouped around agriculture, forestry, fisheries and wildlife.[191] After the Second World War, many colonial powers focused on such natural resources as a central field for the development of their colonies. Among such interventions, Emmanuel Kreike listed "large-scale dam, irrigation, livestock, animal, and human health, soil, wildlife, and forest conservation projects".[192] For north-central Namibia, especially the former Ovamboland, Kreike illustrated how late colonial investments in hydrological and soil conservation projects usually failed.[193] For the Caprivi, colonial forest conservation efforts are most worthy of discussion as forestry was central to South Africa's growing interest in Namibia's natural environment in the region and beyond.[194]

In 1957 South Africa sent a qualified forester, PL, to Namibia to establish a forestry office in Grootfontein, a town close to the northern border of the police zone. As a young, unmarried man, he applied for the job – according to him – out of boredom and because "it was a new country and we did not know what was going on there".[195] His main initial task was to survey indigenous trees on white-owned farms and plan an increased timber production output to supply a growing demand from the copper mines in Tsumeb.[196] At the

---

[189] Gordon, R.J. (2005), The Making of Modern Namibia: A Tale of Anthropological Ineptitude? *Kleio*, 37(1): 26–49 (here 47).

[190] 'San', otherwise known as 'Bushmen', are one of the most thoroughly researched population groups worldwide, with an extensive academic literature available on every aspect of 'San' history, society, culture, health, and life in general.

[191] See on the agriculture: Bollig (1998b). Michael Bollig and Elsemi Olwage also mentioned the control and protection of wildlife as an important aspect of South African policy towards northwestern Namibia. These served, in particular, to keep wildlife stocks sufficiently plentiful to allow for undisturbed leisure hunting by South African elites. See: Bollig et al. (2016).

[192] Kreike (2013): 5.

[193] Kreike (2013): 63–135.

[194] For a more detailed discussion of colonial forest policies in Namibia up to the 1980s, see p. 98 ff.

[195] PR, 21.04.2014, Napier.

[196] Copper and iron-ore mining in the area around Tsumeb and Otavi had been conducted since pre-colonial times and intensified under German colonial rule. Mining in the area declined during the Second World War, but recovered in the 1950s. The Tsumeb smelter complex was built in 1961 and 1962 and was commissioned in 1963, featuring integrated copper and lead sections with a refinery. By 1964, the smelter already produced more than 3,500 tons of copper and 6,000 tons of

same time, the overcutting of trees was viewed as a rising problem for the area's long-term development. This was said to occur not only on white-owned farms, but also, according to official reports, in areas beyond the police zone, such as the former 'Bushmanland' and Eastern Okavango regions.[197] Controlled timber production would henceforth be promoted as a potential vector for economic development in these areas, especially after it began to decline on white farms by the early-1960s because of increasing profits in the meat industry and a corresponding demand for grazing land.[198] Indeed, according to PL, the mapping and surveying of forests beyond the police zone became one of his major responsibilities shortly after he took office in 1957.[199] Surprisingly, this occurred before the formal cartographic surveying of the northern territories, which only began as their strategic importance increased in the late 1960s.[200]

This early start also contributed to a sense that areas to the north of the Red Line formed part of a 'new country', in which foresters would have to do everything "from scratch". As a consequence, "research was highly important".[201] For example, in the Kavango burning trials were conducted in 1959, based on statistical methods developed by the state forester in Pretoria to reduce the risk of large-scale bush fires. Plants were also imported from Australia to test their growth rates and suitability for large-scale introduction into northern Namibia. PL was convinced that if local residents continued to cut down trees at the same rate it would take only a few dozen more years until all 'indigenous' trees would be removed and there would be no more wood available. He thus sought to import fast-growing trees as replacements and identified different kinds of eucalyptus as most suitable for the local environment.[202]

In northern Namibia, PL received approval for designated forestry reserves, each with a size of several thousand hectares, in which no people would be allowed to live. Instead, the areas would be set aside for the possible future introduction of trees for timber production since, as PL claimed, "although we don't need it now, we might need it in twenty or fifty years, to introduce exotic trees for wood production".[203]

---

lead per month (Jones, R.T. and P.T. Mackey (2015), An Overview of Copper Smelting in Southern Africa. *Copper Cobalt Africa*: 499–504).

[197] PR, 21.04.2014, Napier. See also: Erkkilä, A. (2001), *Living on the Land: Change in Forest Cover in North-Central Namibia 1943–1996*. Joensuu: University of Joensuu.

[198] CG, 08.04.2014, Cape Town.

[199] PR, 21.04.2014, Napier.

[200] See also: Leser, H. (1982), Namibia, Südwestafrika: Kartographische Probleme der neuen topographischen Karten 1:50,000 und 1:250,000 und ihre Perspektiven für die Landesentwicklung. Basel: Basler Afrika Bibliographien.

[201] Both quotes: PR, 21.04.2014, Napier.

[202] PR, 21.04.2014, Napier.

[203] CG, 08.04.2014, Cape Town.

As I will demonstrate for other South African interventions in northern Namibia, these vigorous efforts to introduce more sustainable timber production assisted the colonial authorities in several ways. Firstly, it secured a steady supply of timber for the mining sector. Secondly, it was one of the earliest campaigns which sought to present South Africa's occupation as 'supportive' of local populations living in what would become homelands. Furthermore, it was also important for controlling flora in the vicinity of white farms, which were perceived to be under threat from uncontrolled weeds invading from the communal areas.

Heralding Change in the Caprivi, 1950s

As I have shown above, aspects of economic development gained importance in South Africa's policies in the northern territories of Namibia after the Second World War. While PL would be based at the forestry office in Grootfontein and conduct his trials from there for the duration of his time in office, his successors were based in the Caprivi itself, where they implemented more frequent projects in the 1960s and urged more intensive investment in economic development. Although notions of development and the 'uplifting' of the inhabitants had been presented as a solution to secure the region and render its population more dependent on South Africa from the mid-1950s onwards, it nevertheless remained unclear in which specific forms economic development should be promoted in the Caprivi.

The end of Leslie Trollope's rule in the Caprivi in 1952 heralded major changes in South African policy towards the region. Trollope had not only cooperated widely with the authorities of neighbouring territories, but had also contributed to the production of detailed knowledge on the Caprivi and its inhabitants. In 1952 Trollope was attacked at his house in Katima Mulilo by his alleged lover and never fully recovered, dying some years later while in hospital in Bulawayo.[204] The fact that he was the only colonial governor or magistrate of the Eastern Caprivi who was buried in the territory and continues to be commemorated in post-independence Namibia may indicate that he was less unpopular locally than other colonial rulers.[205] He had been sceptical of the area's economic and political value for South Africa and therefore limited himself mainly to keeping the region's social and political structures as stable as possible by not intervening too obtrusively in the lives of local people.[206]

This policy changed in 1952 when, just after the attack on Trollope, South Africa replaced him – against his will – with a new magistrate, A.B. Colenbrander. In 1954, two years after he took office, Colenbrander wrote a report on the general policy for the development

---

[204] Gewald (2013): 88.
[205] See also Kangumu (2011): 96–97. Trollope's grave in Katima Mulilo is still maintained as a tourist attraction.
[206] Gewald (2013).

of the Eastern Caprivi. Therein he stated that he wanted to draw the Department of Native Affairs' attention "to the importance of this Area in the future and the need for sound planning now in regard to its development".[207] This report was written at a time when the Caprivi's significant potential strategic value was becoming ever more noticeable for South Africa. It was also written in a year in which a South African brigadier, H.J. Zinn, anticipated that the Caprivi would become a "launch-pad and shock absorber in case of unrest/attack in surrounding areas".[208] Colenbrander also foresaw potential security threats for South Africa, particularly as neighbouring territories "might easily develop along quite different lines" than South Africa.[209] He warned in his report that, if his administration was unable to better support local people, then the Caprivi could become "a happy hunting ground for agitators" and "develop into a soft-spot" for South Africa's future maintenance of power in the mandated territory.[210]

Remarkably, these concerns did not (yet) result in Colenbrander requesting more security personnel or an increased militarisation of the Caprivi's borders, but mainly for what he called the 'uplifting' of the local population. His proposed solution for counteracting internal resistance was therefore the intensified economic and infrastructural development of the area. As early as the 1950s, some twenty years before the SADF's infamous 'Winning the Hearts and Minds' (WHAM) campaign took shape in Namibia, Colenbrander thus recognised the importance of maintaining a good relationship with the local population in order to prevent any potential future 'unrest' targeted against the South African occupation.[211]

One of the most visible of the early attempts to develop the Caprivi in line with Colenbrander's vision was the upgrading of an airfield close to Katima Mulilo and the extension of transport infrastructure to the region, developments which were closely linked to the strengthening of the Witwatersrand Native Labour Association (WNLA) post in Katima Mulilo. The WNLA's airstrip had existed since 1941. In 1954 it was renovated to further support the activities of the WNLA and the infrastructural development of the town.[212] In 1959 the South African Air Force (SAAF) extended the runway, before gaining full posses-

---

[207] NASA, NTS463/400/1, A.B. Colenbrander, General Policy and Development: Eastern Caprivi Zipfel, 20 December 1954, p. 1.
[208] Quote in: Kangumu (2011): 145.
[209] NASA, NTS 463/400/1, A.B. Colenbrander, General Policy and Development: Eastern Caprivi Zipfel, 20 December 1954, p. 3.
[210] NASA, NTS 463/400/1, A.B. Colenbrander, General Policy and Development: Eastern Caprivi Zipfel, 20 December 1954, p. 3.
[211] On the WHAM campaign, see e.g.: Eloff De Visser (2011).
[212] The renovation of the airfield also encouraged plans to export fish from the Caprivi to South Africa.

sion of the airfield in 1964 and transforming it into the M'pacha military base.[213] Further investments in infrastructure for the WNLA post included improvements in road and river transport. Significantly, most of the migrant workers recruited by the WNLA in Katima Mulilo came from outside the Caprivi Strip, especially from Angola.[214] The WNLA's activities in the Caprivi thus exercised a greater influence on the region's infrastructure than on the lives of local residents. Although migrant labour became a source of income for most families in the Caprivi, the region never became as important a source of labour as other parts of northern Namibia.[215] It was arguably this low success rate in recruiting human capital from the area which put additional pressure on the South African authorities to find alternative ways to achieve profits in the Caprivi and render the local population more dependent on South Africa.

The institutional push to implement changes in South African policy towards the Caprivi was still evident in the 1963 annual Eastern Caprivi administrative report. In the report, N.W. Boshoff, Colenbrander's successor as magistrate of the Eastern Caprivi, warned again of the potential for "disturbances" in the region, fostered by those whom he termed "political agitators from North Rhodesia".[216] He declared that:

> Although there was no incident of major importance during the year, it can be said that the winds of change are also blowing over the Caprivi. In the past the people were living in harmony and were content with what they were told by the Government and abided thereby. Today there is a feeling of discontent and restlessness evident amongst them. The people have openly declared [...] that they no longer wish to be ruled by the Government of the Republic of South Africa – and this [was said] by the chiefs and their councillors obviously instigated by agitators.[217]

This statement illustrates that Boshoff sought to sustain a narrative in which local people were portrayed as having lived in harmony with both nature and their colonial rulers, only now to be "pushed" in the wrong direction by "troublesome" outsiders.[218] To understand to

---

[213] See: Kruger (1984), chapter 11: 15, and Kangumu (2011): 142–145.
[214] Kangumu (2011): 140–144.
[215] Kruger estimated that an average of 360 migrant labourers left the Eastern Caprivi annually in the early 1960s (Kruger 1984, chapter 9: 10). Kangumu showed that in the 1970s about four per cent of the Caprivi population lived outside of the Strip (Kangumu 2011: 39). In the case of Ovamboland, in comparison, Moorsom estimated that an average of 20,000 workers were on contract outside of the homeland in the 1960s and 1970s, a figure which equated to around 30% of its male population (Moorsom 1977: 67).
[216] NASA, KC SWA 2/6, Annual Report on the Administration of the Eastern Caprivi Zipfel for 1962, 18 April 1963, p. 1.
[217] NASA, KC SWA 2/6, Annual Report on the Administration of the Eastern Caprivi Zipfel for 1962, 18 April 1963, p. 9.
[218] NASA, KC SWA 2/6, Annual Report on the Administration of the Eastern Caprivi Zipfel for 1962, 18 April 1963, p. 6–8.

what extent this assertion already indicated South Africa's plans to establish a pseudo-independent Eastern Caprivian homeland and how such observations also laid the foundations for South Africa's subsequent focus on the Caprivi's natural environment as the region's assumed primary asset, it is crucial to examine the role and function of the Commission of Enquiry into South West Africa Affairs, the so-called Odendaal Commission of 1962–1964.

Odendaal Commission, 1962–1964

The 'Commission of Enquiry into South West Africa Affairs', was named after Frans Hendrik Odendaal, who headed the commission.[219] It was established in 1962 by the South African government to plan the future spatial and administrative ordering of Namibia according to South Africa's racist policies of separate development. In practice, this meant that the commission's task was to propose potential bantustans for South West Africa.[220] The commission was composed of supposed experts in their respective fields, chosen by the South African prime minister, Hendrick Frensch Verwoerd, to display its supposedly high scientific standards.[221] Verwoerd saw the task of the commission in "promoting the material and moral welfare and the social progress of the inhabitants of SWA, and more particularly its non-white inhabitants" and, ultimately, to submit a report and a five-year plan "for the accelerated development of the various non-white groups".[222]

There are at least three important aspects concerning the Odendaal Commission which are relevant to the Caprivi in the early 1960s. Firstly, the establishment of a commission of inquiry reflected what Adam Ashforth termed a "Grand Tradition" of commissions in South Africa, namely a series of 'Native Question Commissions' which were regularly established in moments of crisis from 1902 until the early 1980s.[223]

Secondly, the statements made at the commission's public hearings in Katima Mulilo in 1963 demonstrated the extent to which Caprivian nature was seen by various speakers as relevant to the 'development' of the region. As I will show, control over the region's natural

---

[219] McCullers (2012): 135.
[220] Republic of South Africa (ed.) (1964), *Report of the Commission of Enquiry into South West Africa Affairs, 1962–1963*. Pretoria: Government Printer.
[221] The commissioners included: Johannes Petrus van Schalkwyk Bruwer, a professor of social anthropology; H.W. Snyman, a professor of medicine and public health; H.J. van Eck, the head of the Industrial Development Cooperation; P.J. Quin, an agronomist and nutritionist and a former official in the South West African Commission for Bantu Affairs. See: Horrell, M. (1963), *A Survey into Race Relations in South Africa*. Johannesburg: South African Institute of Race Relations: 231–232.
[222] NASA, Prime Minister's Office (PM) 72/EM 2/70/2, Terms of Reference of the Commission of Enquiry into the Affairs of South West Africa, 11 September 1962.
[223] Ashforth (1990).

environment was presented by the commission as a particularly promising opportunity for the South African state to provide development 'solutions'.

Thirdly, the information collected and the proposals made by the Odendaal Commission provided a basis for further decision-making in relation to South Africa's alleged development efforts in the Caprivi and, particularly in the Western Caprivi, for further socio-economic research.

The "Grand Tradition" of Commissions of Inquiry and the 'Racial Question'

Adam Ashforth's proposed "Grand Tradition" started with the South African Native Commission (1903–05) and ended with the Labour Legislation Commission in the late 1970s.[224] He defined two major criteria for a commission to have formed part of this tradition. Firstly, a commission had to be a response to a crisis or the perception of a crisis confronting the ruling orders. Secondly, the commission should have adopted a general approach towards its subject matter. Consequently, Ashforth saw "commissions of enquiry addressing the 'Native Question' as a whole, seeking strategies for state power in periods when social, economic, and political forces had forced a re-examination of the fundamental principles underlying state power."[225] Even more analytical was Adam Sitze, who described South African commissions of inquiry as "a more prosaic name for the administrative organ tasked with listening to, evaluating, and archiving the voices of the victims of abuses of illegal state activity".[226]

The Odendaal Commission fulfilled Ashforth's two main criteria in that it was a response to a supposed condition of crisis, to which it also offered a general approach towards finding a 'solution'.[227] I have already explored how South African rule in Namibia was confronted by various crises in the early-1960. Among these, in most urgent need of addressing by the apartheid state was the growing international and domestic pressure on South Africa to withdraw from Namibia.

In this context, South Africa resorted to sending experts to define 'problems', such as the assumed "underdevelopment of black people", to which they could find technical-adminis-

---

[224] The tradition's culmination in the late 1970s has been questioned by Adam Sitze, who also saw similarities with earlier commissions in the Truth and Reconciliation Commission of the late 1990. See: Sitze, A. (2013), *The Impossible Machine, A genealogy of the South African Truth and Reconciliation Commission.* Ann Arbor: Michigan University Press.
[225] Ashforth (1990): 3.
[226] In his book, Adam Sitze drew a genealogy of commissions of inquiry from those enacted by nineteenth-century British colonial authorities to the post-apartheid Truth and Reconciliation Commission (Sitze 2013: 132).
[227] McCullers (2012): 132–134.

trative solutions based on the segregationist principles of 'separate development'.[228] In this regard, Molly McCullers traced how the Odendaal Commission in Namibia picked up on the work of the Tomlinson Commission (1950–1954) in South Africa.[229] Both commissions shared the aims of giving scientific "substance to the slogans of apartheid" and proving that the creation of self-governing bantustans would offer a 'practical' solution to the 'native question'.[230] The substantive measures which they proposed included techniques of mastery, especially the production and systematisation of knowledge.[231] As I will discuss below, these measures included not only the mastery of the state over local inhabitants, but also – especially in the Caprivi – the mastery of "'Man' over 'Nature'".[232] Having learnt from the Tomlinson Commission, Verwoerd reduced the time available for the Odendaal Commission to gather socio-economic data from over five years to a single year.[233] Most importantly, the Odendaal Commission, unlike the Tomlinson Commission before it, was not tasked with looking for ways to scientifically define and divide different ethnic groups, but took these identities as given. Its focus lay instead on attempting to answer "how to make these groups commensurable with a map of geographically distinct homelands".[234]

South Africa's investments into the exploration, mapping and surveying of northern Namibia show how attempts to lend a scientific basis to 'separate development' were central to apartheid ideology and crucial for its expansion into Namibia. In turn, the Odendaal Commission not only defined the borders of future homelands, but also laid the foundations for further research into Namibia's economic potential. In the same way as the apartheid regime had sought to legitimise homeland politics in South Africa through the work of the Tomlinson Commission some ten years earlier, South Africa was searching for opportunities to promote its occupation of Namibia as a development project. However, the few contemporary academic texts on the commissions cast doubt on their findings and questioned their success in convincing an international audience of South Africa's plans for Namibia. Yet these works often criticised both commissions only for their 'scientific' calculations and not for their underlying political and social assumptions.[235] For example, in his 1966 ar-

---

[228] Ashforth (1990): 1–2.
[229] McCullers (2012): 134.
[230] Ashforth (1990): 3–4; 150–153.
[231] Ashforth (1990): 5. This argument is also based on Michel Foucault's understanding of power and knowledge, see e.g.: Foucault, M. (1975), *Surveiller et punir: Naissance de la prison*. Paris: Gallimard: 34–40.
[232] Ashforth (1990): 3–5.
[233] McCullers (2012): 134.
[234] McCullers (2012): 135.
[235] D'Amato, A. (1966), The Bantustan Proposals for South-West Africa, *Journal of Modern African Studies*, 4(2): 177–192.

ticle in the *Journal of Modern African Studies*, Anthony D'Amato attempted to "point out some of the theoretical and practical inadequacies of the Bantustan proposals over the long run".[236] However, after conducting a "careful assessment of the plan", he did not go on to criticise South Africa's subjection of Namibia to its racist homeland policies.[237] This may indicate that South African attempts to present the country's occupation of Namibia as an effort undertaken in 'good faith' with the goal of solving the so-called 'native question' and as a modernisation project supported by the principles of science had a longer-lasting and deeper impact in Namibia than the concrete plans proposed by the Odendaal Commission. By considering a set of scientific solutions to a series of assumed problems and challenges, the commission's hearings were crucial in legitimising the occupation and providing a scientific underpinning.

Public Hearings in Katima Mulilo, 1963

The representatives of the Odendaal Commission stayed in Katima Mulilo from 4 to 7 February 1963 to collect 'evidence'. This marked the beginning of the commission's fifth visit to Namibia and its only visit to the Caprivi. In Katima Mulilo, the delegation visited the catholic hospital and conducted so-called public hearings, on the first day with "local headmen" and on the next with "whites".[238] Such hearings constituted a central method of gathering evidence for the commission and also served the portrayal of apartheid South Africa as a 'civilised partner' which listened to its people. At the same time, as I have shown above, hearings also gave the apartheid state the opportunity to 'define' problems which it could later 'solve', while also offering it a chance to communicate and 'test' reactions to future policies.[239] The following examples from the public hearings demonstrate the extent to which the question of nature and wildlife conservation was presented as a site of conflict and, as such, as a potential vehicle for governance and development. Conservation offered an opportunity to provide 'solutions', especially given the economic potential which was ascribed to the protection and control of nature.[240]

The hearings began with a meeting of all the members of the *Khutas* (traditional authorities) and other people who were sanctioned by the *Khutas* to speak. Attendees included the two recognised Caprivi chiefs, Simata Simasiku Mamili and Joshua Moraliswane, their

---

[236] D'Amato (1966): 92.
[237] D'Amato (1966): 192.
[238] NASA, KC SWA, 2/6, Proposed fifth visit, February 1963, p. 1–2.
[239] Ashforth (1990): 5.
[240] In this regard, the situation in the Caprivi seems to have differed from that of north-western Namibia, where Bollig and Olwage observed a clear anti-conservationist agenda on the part of the colonial authorities during the 1960s due to the region's assumed agricultural potential. See: Bollig et al. (2016): 67–69.

respective *Ngambelas*, Mutonga David and Muniango, a so-called "secretary of the tribe", an interpreter and 315 "followers".²⁴¹ Odendaal opened the meeting by explaining that the commission had come "to find out what the needs are of the tribes here" and "what we can do to improve" them.²⁴² He then emphasised again that all the commissioners were academics and well-renowned experts in their respective fields of health, anthropology, economics, and agriculture. Thereafter, he extended an invitation to the chiefs and their entourage to speak out on their complaints and concerns. The secretary of the Masubia *Khuta*, Sepensa Lifumbela, opened the response: "The first is about the elephants and hippos, which come to eat our crops and also kill some of the members of the tribe. The second thing is about the guns or rifles."²⁴³ With this complaint about the damage caused by elephants and hippopotamuses as well as the gun laws, Lifumbela raised a topic which would be referred to repeatedly throughout the course of the hearings. The criticisms of the game laws were then taken up by the *Ngambela* of the Masubia, Kalundu Muniango, who heavily criticised South Africa for its neglect of the Caprivi in general and, in particular, for its handling of wildlife issues. Several speakers referred to incidents in which South African officials had jailed local people for shooting animals and confiscated their rifles. Furthermore, they complained, no magistrate had taken action to rectify these unfair punishments during earlier visits to the Caprivi. This failure, according to most of the speakers, had led them to lose their "trust" in the South African authorities. After Odendaal promised to send more special guns for shooting elephants, Muniango responded that the "Caprivi has been suffering for a long time even if the Commission[er] says he is going to recommend the 24 guns sent here, those guns will never come".²⁴⁴ He then went on to describe a South African official who had come "to look after the elephants, not the people" and concluded with the remark that "the people are very angry to be compared with animals, that the animals are better than people".²⁴⁵

Crucially, one underlying aim of the entire Odendaal Commission was to promote so-called 'self-governance' in the proposed homelands. The hearings were conducted as 'proof' that, in so doing, the apartheid state would fulfil the wishes of local people.²⁴⁶ Given this context, the commission's continuous portrayal of Caprivi's inhabitants as unsatisfied with their existing circumstances under South African rule should be seen as intentional. How-

---

[241] 'Ngambela' is a title signifying the chief's main counsellor and principal executive.
[242] NASA, KC SWA, 72/35, Minutes of the public hearings, February 1963, p. 1–2.
[243] NASA, KC SWA, 72/35, Minutes of the public hearings, February 1963, p. 2.
[244] NASA, KC SWA, 72/35, Minutes of the public hearings, February 1963, p. 7. To shoot an elephant or a hippopotamus required an especially large and robust rifle cartridge.
[245] NASA, KC SWA, 72/35, Minutes of the public hearings, February 1963, p. 7.
[246] McCullers (2012): 132–134; Ashforth (1990): 7–8.

ever, as the following exchange between Muniango and Odendaal illustrates, the question of game laws and firearm restrictions intermittently contradicted this carefully-constructed narrative.

> Muniango: We got a lot of troubles from elephants and hippos. They should be killed.
>
> [...]
>
> Chairman: Haven't they [the people] got rifles and ammunition?
>
> Muniango: There are very few guns here that we can use while the Caprivi is under the government of the Union [sic].
>
> [...]
>
> Chairman: What do you want to use the gun for, just to kill the elephants and the hippos? We can ask the police to shoot [them].
>
> Muniango: We can shoot them ourselves.
>
> Chairman: You want to shoot them when you find them in your lands or you want to shoot them altogether?
>
> Muniango: We want to shoot them in the forest. [...] Magistrate Mr. Vercuiel tells us that the government sent them here to look after animals, not people. [...] That is why we ask that they should give us an[other] government.
>
> Chairman: You want a government for yourselves.
>
> Muniango: No, we get another government to look after us.
>
> Chairman: So [...] you are not able to govern yourself. You want another government.
>
> Muniango: We can govern ourselves but we want another government to be our help.
>
> Chairman: But you are governing yourselves today, ain't [sic] you?
>
> Muniango: We are not governing ourselves because we are not allowed to kill the elephants, we are not allowed to kill the hippos.[247]

Given the growing opposition in the region to South African rule, it seems unlikely that South Africa ever had the intention of granting Caprivians free possession of firearms. As such, by insisting on free access to weapons, the hearing attendees were demanding a concession which they knew South Africa would never make. During the hearing, they thus managed to highlight that the traditional authorities would never be awarded the power to

---

[247] NASA, KC SWA, 72/35, Minutes of the public hearings, February 1963, p. 5.

amend gun and wildlife laws, in so doing revealing both a fundamental contradiction at the heart of South Africa's homeland policy and the fact that the region would never be granted the true independence which the commission had promised.

Although the chairman repeatedly tried to convince the hearing's attendees to approve a system of self-governance, it became clear that the representatives of the *Khutas* were not prepared to accede to this for as long as Caprivians were denied the right to possess guns and have control over wildlife. Furthermore, the speakers at the hearing were aware that South Africa would never permit the unregulated possession of arms and shooting of wildlife; or, as Muniango stated, the "government will never give us guns and rifles and ammunition and allow us to kill the hippos and elephants."[248] Both sides thus regarded the ability to determine weapon and game legislation as central to governance in the region. As the minutes of the hearings reveal, it seems that all those who were present were well aware that true sovereignty for the envisaged homeland would therefore never be genuinely considered. At the same time, the chiefs still sought to negotiate as much power for themselves as they could.

The unwillingness of the South African authorities to support chiefs in the Caprivi with weapons and ammunition is coherently explained by the fear of uprisings and the growing local support for independence movements. However, the imposition of strict game laws must also be seen in relation to South Africa's broader plans for the development of the region. Odendaal repeatedly referred to South African investments in development projects during the commission's public hearings. According to him, South Africa had invested a large sum of money into the Caprivi in the previous two years and was willing to spend even more. The commission members, however, did not agree that a portion of this amount should be used to purchase guns for the chiefs to shoot elephants.[249]

On the second day of the hearings, which was reserved for the testimony of South African officials and other whites in the Eastern Caprivi, the economic development of the area was discussed in more detail. They saw the professionalisation and scientifcation of ecological, agricultural and veterinarian issues as crucial and argued for more biological, zoological and geographical research. For example, Jack Ashwin, the manager of the WNLA post near Katima Mulilo, stated that the local "people as a whole are very much backwards" and that the only way to develop the area would be to improve their living conditions. His first suggestion was to invest in the control of the tsetse fly.[250] Later he observed that in "this

---

[248] NASA, KC SWA, 72/35, Minutes of the public hearings, February 1963, p. 6.
[249] NASA, KC SWA, 72/35, Minutes of the public hearings, February 1963, p. 7.
[250] NASA, KC SWA, 72/35, Minutes of the public hearings, February 1963, p. 18. See also: MacKenzie (1988): 225–257.

part of the country the game is diminishing rapidly".²⁵¹ As a solution, he recommended the increased surveying and control of animal movements along with the introduction of closed seasons for hunting or the proclamation of game reserves.

The native commissioner in the Eastern Caprivi, N.W. Boshoff, did not agree with this vision for wildlife protection. In his appearance at the Odendaal Commission, Boshoff immediately complained about the plans for game conservation proposed by his superiors in Pretoria. In his view, elephants and hippopotamuses were "vermin" which spread disease and destroyed crops and fields.²⁵² He proposed that Caprivians should be allowed to shoot both species, with the profits made from the resulting "harvest" of ivory to be transferred to "the tribal funds".²⁵³ In contrast, he argued, the protection of wildlife would never bring in any profit for the South African authorities and would only encourage unrest and disaffection among locals.²⁵⁴ Boshoff's views on wildlife conservation reflected policies which had already been implemented in the Kaoko, where game preservation practices were also increasingly seen as an obstacle to the development of agriculture. Elephants had even been reclassified as vermin there, with local residents given poison and guns to contribute to their destruction.²⁵⁵

During the hearings, the commission did not react to the two very different visions for the management of nature and wildlife in the Caprivi. Nevertheless, it became clear that issues around the control of wildlife had become a point of conflict, not only between the South African occupation authorities and locals in the Caprivi, but also among different individuals within the South African administration.

All in all, the Caprivi's incorporation within a general South African policy for the rule of occupied Namibia, as proposed by the Odendaal Commission, marked a concrete end to earlier 'ambivalent' policies of governance in the region. After the frequent changes to its administrative structures before 1939 and an unsuccessful search for its economic 'potential' thereafter, for the first time South Africa now treated the Caprivi as an integral part of its mandate in Namibia. Consequently, it was proposed that the entire region should become

---

[251] NASA, KC SWA, 72/35, Minutes of the public hearings, February 1963, p. 21.
[252] NASA, KC SWA, 72/35, Minutes of the public hearings, February 1963, p. 1–2
[253] NASA, KC SWA, 72/35, Minutes of the public hearings, February 1963, p. 1. The term 'tribal fund' was used for the budget of the reserves and, later, the homelands. It was funded by taxes collected in the respective reserves/homelands and administered by the traditional authorities and, later, the homeland administrations, which in turn had to report to their respective South African magistrate or commissioner. South African investments were mainly made via the Bantu Investment Trust, a state-owned investment company which allowed the South African government to stake its claim to a share of homeland revenues.
[254] NASA, KC SWA, 72/35, Minutes of the public hearings, February 1963, p. 1–2.
[255] Bollig et al. (2016): 67–69.

a 'self-governing' homeland in the foreseeable future. The Odendaal Plan and the commission's public hearings also revealed that the regulation of the region's wildlife and nature would remain a central and contested space of governance – not only in relation to the corresponding dispute over gun laws, but increasingly also as a potential vehicle for economic development.

The Caprivi in the Aftermath of the Odendaal Commission

More than a year passed between the Odendaal Commission's public hearings in Katima Mulilo and the publication of its final report in 1964. As Ashforth argued for South African commissions of inquiry in general, the publication of a final report marked the beginning of the "persuasive phase" of discourse, in which the report became "an authoritative statement relating to questions of political action, with simultaneously limiting and empowering effects."[256] In other words, the publishing of the Odendaal Report allowed the South African authorities to base subsequent policy for the Caprivi on what had already been presented as 'scientific fact'. The commission's public hearings and its final report thus had an important discursive impact on South Africa's future policies in the Caprivi. The commission defined the control of nature as a major challenge in the region, while at the same time discussing appropriate 'solutions' and linking the control of nature and wildlife to development and economic growth.

Planning the Eastern Caprivi

The Odendaal Plan had little immediate political impact on the Eastern Caprivi. As for other regions in Namibia, the plan proposed a legislative council with limited powers which would be composed of chiefs and elected representatives.[257] Within this context, Odendaal also offered what Kangumu termed a "roadmap for a Caprivi identity", namely the establishment of an Eastern Caprivi government with its own state symbols, including a constitution, flag, and national anthem.[258] However, the Legislative Assembly would only become operational nearly a decade later in 1972. In the meantime, the Department of Bantu Administration and Development in Pretoria established a Planning Committee for the Eastern Caprivi.[259] Two of the committee's main tasks highlight the focus of South African

---

[256] Ashforth (1990): 9–10.
[257] Du Pisani, A. (1986), *SWA/Namibia: The Politics of Change and Continuity*. Johannesburg: Jonathan Bell, p. 162–163 and Kangumu (2011): 112–113.
[258] Kangumu (2011): 113.
[259] This department, often simply referred to as the 'Bantu Administration', changed its name on several occasions. It was known at various times as the 'Department of Native Affairs', the 'De-

policy in the Caprivi at the time. These were the efforts to integrate the region more fully into South Africa and develop its economic potential through scientific research and infrastructural development. The composition of the Planning Committee illustrates the areas in which Pretoria saw 'developmental' potential for the Caprivi. The committee was chaired by the native commissioner for the Eastern Caprivi and included the head of the Department of Bantu Administration and Development's engineering branch, a high-ranking member from its agricultural branch, and an accountant.[260] An advisory board, which comprised of two forestry experts and a geologist, was also established.[261] The fact that the committee mainly consisted of officials with a background in the environmental and ecological sciences hints at the department's primary interests in the Caprivi by the mid-1960s. Besides the commissioner himself, all members of the Planning Committee were based in Pretoria. Unlike before 1963, when – according to the official view – local chiefs had directly 'advised' the commissioner, they were no longer given a role to play within the committee.[262] This suggests that – in contrast to the homeland narrative of 'self-reliance' and 'independence' – South Africa was increasingly interested in imposing stronger and more direct forms of control over the Eastern Caprivi in anticipation of potential political changes and growing resistance in the territory.

It is not surprising that one of the first actions which was undertaken by the newly-constituted Planning Committee was to tour the Eastern Caprivi in 1964 and compile an extensive report on the area.[263] In this report, the committee once again mapped out the most important potential sectors for development in the territory, including agriculture, forestry, roads and fishery infrastructure. As Bennett Kangumu correctly argued, the Planning Committee sought to promote the implementation of smaller infrastructure projects on the ground, in contrast to the Odendaal Commission, which had been primarily concerned with drawing up a broader policy framework.[264]

This endeavour to economically 'develop' the Eastern Caprivi and the economic potential of its natural environment was on the one hand part of South Africa's politics of 'sepa-

---

    partment of Bantu Administration (and Development)', the 'Department of Plural Relations and Development', and the 'Department of Co-operation and Development'.

[260] See Kruger (1984), chapter 12: 14. Kruger mentioned that Jan Vorster, the committee's representative from the agricultural branch, was very "experienced" as he had also been involved in the planning of the Tanzania Groundnut Scheme in the late 1940s. This project later became an infamous example of a failed large-scale colonial agricultural intervention. See: Esselborn (2004).

[261] Kruger (1984), chapter 12: 14.

[262] Kangumu (2011): 115.

[263] NASA, BAO 20/271, Verslag van die Departementele Komitee Insake die Ontwikkeling van die Oostelike Caprivi Zipfel, 21 August 1964.

[264] Kangumu (2011): 117.

rate development', through which the government wanted to create economically depended homelands, that could serve as cheap labour recruitment areas. On the other hand, particularly in the Caprivi, these endeavours arose from the South African authorities' anxiety to appease the local population in order to prevent resistance, while simultaneously rendering Caprivians ever more dependent on the apartheid state.

Planning the Western Caprivi

The recommendations and effects of the Odendaal Commission for the Western Caprivi differed from those for the Eastern Caprivi and the rest of Namibia in a number of ways. The entire Western Caprivi was declared a nature conservation area in 1963, but this decision had no noticeable consequences for conservation on the ground.[265] It remains unclear from the records who made this decision – taken at the very time when Odendaal was weighing up his proposals – and for what reasons. Based on statements by Oswald Köhler and other South African state anthropologists, Gertrud Boden argued that the proclamation of the Western Caprivi as a conservation area was primarily aimed at controlling the movement of people from across the Angolan border.[266] Although such security reasons should not be deemphasised, the decision should also be understood within the broader context of South Africa's policies towards the northern territories of Namibia.

The proclamation, I argue, formed part of the apartheid state's wider plans to keep space open for further development and potential profit-making once the northern regions of Namibia had been secured, pacified and fully incorporated into South African-controlled territory. In the 1960s, although there were signs of unrest and resistance against South African occupation in northern Namibia and international support for South Africa's racist policies was diminishing, apartheid policy-makers were still planning for a time after victory in the nascent Namibian War of Liberation. In this regard, the reports of smaller and less well-known commissions which focussed on planning for the future of the northern territories offer a different perspective on South African policies in the Western Caprivi and northern Namibia in general.

Following the publication of the Odendaal Report, the South West African Administration established a series of further commissions to explore in greater depth some of the recommendations made by the Odendaal Commission and to look for additional opportunities for economic development, especially in northern Namibia. One such commission was established in 1966 with the mandate to investigate the feasibility of tourism and nature

---

[265] Boden (2004): 79.
[266] Boden (2004): 79–80.

conservation in the so-called 'Bantu areas'.²⁶⁷ The 'Komitee van Undersoek na Toerisme en Verwante Aangeleentheit in die Bantoegebiede van Suidwes-Afrika', also referred to as the Frank Commission, ultimately sought to promote the development of tourism outside the police zone to take advantage of the growing tourism industry in Namibia, especially in the wake of the Odendaal Commission's decision to reduce the size of the Etosha nature reserve.²⁶⁸ The Frank Commission's proposals included the establishment of wildlife reserves in the homelands for reasons of both science and tourism.

The largest area which the Frank Commission recommended for a 'Bantu Nature Reserve' was the already-proclaimed Western Caprivi nature conservation area. According to the Frank Commission's report, the Odendaal Commission had not been aware that the region was in fact a game reserve when it proposed to declare the Western Caprivi a homeland for 'Khwe Bushmen'.²⁶⁹ Julie Taylor showed how the discursive association of the Western Caprivi with an idealised 'Land of the Bushmen' was reinforced after the Second World War, when South Africa's policies towards 'Bushmen' in northern Namibia shifted from violent coercion to an attempt to 'befriend' and 'protect' them for the sake of science and, later, tourism.²⁷⁰ This idea that 'Bushmen' were natural components of a broader nature which was in need of protection and preservation might have also been a reason why Dave Marée, the then Bantu Commissioner in Rundu, rejected plans for retaining the Western Caprivi as a conservation area and removing its population to the banks of the Okavango River.²⁷¹ Marée did not believe that wildlife could be protected against the will of the people living in the area. Instead, he argued that providing a homeland for the "Kgoe-Bushmen" (Khwe) would be the best way in which to protect the rare wildlife of the area, an aim which he already saw as a central ecological feature of the 'Bushman' way of life.²⁷²

Due to the Western Caprivi's unresolved administrative status, the Director of Nature Conservation in the South West African Administration requested the ecologist K. L. Tinley

---

[267] NAN, Nature Conservation and Tourism South West Africa Administration (hereafter NTB), 22/2/1, Beleidskommissie Frank, 1959–1971.

[268] E.g.: NAN, NTB, 22/2/1, Maree to Steyn, 6 August 1968. ("Commission of Inquiry into Tourism and Related Issues in the Bantu Areas of South West Africa"). On the impact of the Odendaal commission report on the Etosha park, see: Dieckmann (2007): 169–177.

[269] NAN, NTB, 22/2/1, Report Natuurbewaring en toerisme in Bantoetuislande, July 1969, p. 15.

[270] Taylor (2012): 66–7. As I will show in Chapter 4, the Khwe-speaking population of the Western Caprivi ultimately did become 'useful' for the South African authorities in another context, namely as trackers for the SADF.

[271] Similar disputes among South African officials also occurred in other areas of Namibia, particularly in Etosha, where disagreements over land use arose between the Department of Native Affairs and the Directorate of Wildlife from the 1950s onwards. See Miescher (2012a) and Dieckmann (2007).

[272] NAN, LKM, 3/3/3, Maree to Chief Commissioner of Bantu Affairs, Distrikt Okavango. Deproklaering van Natuurtuin Wes-Caprivi, 3 October 1964, p. 2.

to conduct a survey of the territory's natural and economic potential.²⁷³ Tinley stayed in the Western Caprivi for three months in 1966 and wrote an extensive report on his findings, including proposals for further use of the area.²⁷⁴ The stated purpose of his survey was "to ascertain whether anything of natural and unique value would be lost to South West Africa if the terrain was to be developed along the lines envisaged for the Okavango Native Territory".²⁷⁵ In his final report, Tinley also added a chapter on "men" – along with others on "fish", "birds", and "mammals (excluding men)" – in which he discussed the local residents "from an ecological point of view".²⁷⁶ Besides a few "Kwe Bushmen [...] that [sic] still occur today", he described all people in the Caprivi as "half civilized".²⁷⁷ Such categorisation of so-called Bushmen according to their level of 'purity' has a long history in Southern Africa, wherein this cruel logic the 'purest' were mostly considered as worth protecting, while the "half civilized" were considered as a danger and not worth to 'protect'.²⁷⁸

In particular, a group whom he labelled as "Barakwengo Hottentots" were, in Tinley's words, "no longer in harmony with the environment, and cannot live in the wild state".²⁷⁹ As too "affected by Western civilization", he saw them as no longer being of interest as objects for research or tourism, but as still constituting a threat to Caprivian nature.²⁸⁰ Contrary to Marée's opinion, Tinley warned that they would "deplete the habitat with no thought for tomorrow" unless they received "advice, guidance and encouragement in sustained self-help land use policies".²⁸¹ This disagreement between Tinley and Marée was probably more over the 'Barakwengo's' supposed degree of 'purity' than the way in which they should be treated.

---

[273] NAN, NTB, 22/2/1, Report Natuurbewaring en toerisme in Bantoetuislande, July 1969, p. 15.
[274] NAN, BB0478, K.L. Tinley, Western Caprivi Conservation Area, South West Africa: A Proposal of Natural Land Resource Land Use, August 1966.
[275] NAN, BB0478, K.L. Tinley, Western Caprivi Conservation Area, South West Africa: A Proposal of Natural Land Resource Land Use, August 1966, p. v.
[276] NAN, BB0478, K.L. Tinley, Western Caprivi Conservation Area, South West Africa: A Proposal of Natural Land Resource Land Use, August 1966, p. 30.
[277] NAN, BB0478, K.L. Tinley, Western Caprivi Conservation Area, South West Africa: A Proposal of Natural Land Resource Land Use, August 1966, p. 29–30.
[278] Gordon et al. (1992): 62.
[279] NAN, BB0478, K.L. Tinley, Western Caprivi Conservation Area, South West Africa: A Proposal of Natural Land Resource Land Use, August 1966, p. 32. See also on similar discussions by the Commission of the Preservation of Bushmen (Schoemann) 1949 – 1951: Gordon et al. (1992): 160, Miescher (2012a): 167. It is worth noting that Tinely called the group "Hottentots" a term that was used in 19th century South Africa to describe so-called "bushmen", who were supposedly "more civilized". According to this rasist categorisation the so-called Hottentots were seen as assimilated into colonial society at a very early stage, forming the basis of the so-called coloured people, and were no longer thought to exist independently by the late nineteenth century in South Africa.
[280] Gordon et al. (1992): 62.
[281] NAN, BB0478, K.L. Tinley, Western Caprivi Conservation Area, South West Africa: A Proposal of Natural Land Resource Land Use, August 1966, p. 30.

While Marée still regarded them as a constituent part of nature, and as such as no barrier to nature conservation, Tinley argued that the 'Barakwengo' had ceased to be "natural" and had thus become a threat to their environment. In the recommendations, which he made in his report, Tinley outlined his position clearly: "For the natural ecosystem to be maintained it is required that the half civilized and no longer independent Barakwengo are removed to a site outside the Western Caprivi".[282] This, he argued, was mainly for their own "welfare", but also for the better control of the area.

In his report, Tinley recommended that the Western Caprivi should be kept under state control – and not be constituted as or incorporated into a homeland – for security and veterinary reasons. Moreover, he considered the territory to be of potentially high economic value due to its very large and diverse wildlife population, which included some species which were endemic to the region and extinct in other parts of Namibia and South Africa. He remarked that these rare species – together with the 42 species of fish found in its rivers – would make the Western Caprivi a perfect place to harvest game systematically. Referring to this report, the Frank Commission recommended the removal of the "few hundred bushmen" living in the area to the shore of the Okavango River and the use of the rest of the region for further research on how to exploit timber, fish and wildlife for future hunting and tourism projects.[283]

Although the Western Caprivi remained state land, the plan to keep it open for research and tourism purposes would not be realised. Only months after the report was conducted, the area was declared a closed military zone in which army bases and airfields were to be built. At least for the Western Caprivi's immediate future, this military rezoning implied that all other land uses would be put on hold.[284]

Summarising Early South African Rule

In this chapter, I have shown how the discourse and practice of development changed over the course of the first decades of South African rule in Namibia. Until the Second World War, development discourse was linked to rather vague notions of possible economic profits

---

[282] NAN, BB0478, K.L. Tinley, Western Caprivi Conservation Area, South West Africa: A Proposal of Natural Land Resource Land Use, August 1966, p. 35.

[283] NAN, NTB, 22/2/1, Report Natuurbewaring en toerisme in Bantoetuislande, July 1969, p. 15–16.

[284] Until the mid-1980s, even high-ranking officials in the civil administration were restricted from entering this area, thus making further research and conservation efforts impossible. However, according to informal comments by former military personnel, the SADF remained engaged in nature conservation within the restricted area. See for example the monthly propaganda journal of the SADF: 'Nature Conservation in Caprivi: SADF Battles to Save our Heritage', *Paratus*, 11 (November 1982), p. 10–11; 58. See also p. 137 ff.

awaiting discovery which could render worthwhile the administrative costs of maintaining even a system of indirect rule. However, besides some surveys and negotiations with local chiefs over gun and game laws, South Africa's direct impact on the ground in the Caprivi seemed to have been low. In the 1950s, with South Africa's gradual introduction of apartheid policies in Namibia, the economic development discourse intensified, and South Africa began to invest more directly in what South African officials described as the development of the territory. These development interventions in the northern territories illustrate how South Africa's interests in Namibia and, in turn, Pretoria's colonial grip moved steadily northwards, crossing over the Red Line and proceeding as far as the Angolan border. In the course of this movement, ideas of development became increasingly linked with South Africa's urge to find 'scientific' evidence to support its apartheid policies, an effort which reached a first highpoint with the report of the Odendaal Commission.

With the apartheid state's plans to turn the Eastern Caprivi into a 'self-governing' homeland, economic development discourse also became an important aspect of what Hendrick Verwoerd termed the "guidance to self-reliance".[285] Through a series of measures white experts would provide 'support' for homelands to become economically 'independent' from South Africa. In reality, as many scholars have pointed out, the dependence of homelands on South Africa and the nature of the supposed support which they were to receive "render[ed] any semblance of economic autonomy ludicrous".[286] Instead, South Africa's homeland policies carried with them the thinly-veiled aim of "destroy[ing] African economic prospects and [stripping] blacks of citizens' rights, in order to perpetuate white rule".[287]

By the mid-1960s it had become increasingly clear that the Caprivi would be of high military strategic value for South Africa in its fight against the Namibian liberation movements and as a basis from which to contain the newly- or soon-to-become independent states to the north. From this point, the Caprivi was no longer regarded as a valueless yet expensive oddity, but as a territory with significant military and geostrategic importance which required extensive military and police control and surveillance. As I will show in the following chapter, the development and commodification of the Caprivi's nature was now also regarded as worth the expense. The growing influence of the military and its increasing entanglement with environmental research and nature conservation efforts in the Caprivi thus form the focus of the next chapter.

---

[285] Quoted in Pelzer (1966): 22.
[286] Jensen, S. and Zenker, O. (2015), Homelands as Frontiers: Apartheid's Loose Ends, *Journal for Southern African Studies*, 42(5): 941.
[287] Jensen et al. (2015): 941.

3 Nature and War (1965–1980s)

Between the late 1960s and the mid-1980s, environmental research and war served together to reinforce the Caprivi's importance for South Africa, particularly in the areas of forestry and fishery. The natural environment became a central area of concern and action for the Caprivi's various governments in the years after the release of the Odendaal Plan. Aims included the so-called modernisation of agriculture, the commodification of forestry and fishery, and the closely-related research, mapping and protection of nature.[1] Furthermore, all these areas also constituted key interests for the South African Police (SAP) and the South African Defence Force (SADF), which became highly influential actors in the Caprivi after the outbreak of the Namibian War of Liberation in 1966. In this chapter, I will thus show how the Caprivi was rendered a South African military space during this war and, increasingly, also a space in which South Africa could shape the natural environment.

The growing military strategic significance of the region and the start of the war meant that the Caprivi's natural environment became a battleground, not only for military conflict, but also due to political tensions over the management, control and representation of nature.[2] South Africa's attempts to win these battles took place on many levels. Besides the increasing militarisation of the Caprivi, South African officials invested in what they regarded as the development of the local population and sought to achieve a closer incorporation of the hitherto peripheral region into the realms of South African political, economic and epistemological power. Such strategies had their foundations in Pretoria's growing interest and investment in the Caprivi's natural resources, such as fisheries and forestry, as well as in its subsequent endeavours in the field of nature conservation (Chapter 4). To better understand these interventions, its crucial to examine how and by whom environmental data was collected. Before doing so, I elaborate on the military and administrative context in which South African environmental surveys and development initiatives took place and relate this to broader concepts of knowledge production within colonial networks. In this regard, South Africa's investments in Caprivian nature in the 1970s and 1980s should be seen in the context of the country's attempts to establish scientific networks and an ongoing exchange of objects of nature between itself and the Caprivi as the apartheid state expanded its bureaucratic control over the territory. This, in turn, allowed South Africa to claim and control 'remote' spaces through the surveying, mapping and systematic ordering of Capriv-

---

[1] See also: McCullers (2012): 10.
[2] See also: Kreike, E. (2004), War and the Environmental Effects of Displacement in Southern Africa, 1970s–1990s. In W. Moseley and B.I. Logan (eds.), *African Environment and Development: Rhetoric, Programme and Reality*. Aldershot: Ashgate: 90–110.

ian nature. Crucially, all of these trends were underpinned by the massive militarisation of the region.³

Geographies of Science, Nature and War

Environmental Science, Power and Space

In recent decades, scholars have discussed in great detail the close nature of the relationship between political and scientific claims to space.⁴ At the basis of this discussion is the argument that science and politics are powerful partners which together reinforce each other's claims to and control over 'newly' incorporated spaces. Bruno Latour aptly described this affinity in his famous assertion that native Americans viewed 'white moderns' as speaking with forked tongues: "By separating the relations of political power from the relations of scientific reasoning while continuing to shore up power with reason and reason with power, the moderns have always had two irons in the fire. They have become invincible."⁵

Expanding "geographies of science" and what belongs to it (such as people, plants, or practices) as David N. Livingstone has termed them, thus constituted new spatial and power relations.⁶ Arising from this ever-widening circulation of science and scientific practices, "a whole range of mechanisms" have been established to win credibility for the knowledge of the "faraway".⁷ The result has been that "observers have been drilled; bodies have been disciplined; pictures have been painted; photographs have been taken; maps have been charted; measurements have been standardized".⁸ Understanding South Africa's environmental research in the Caprivi as a localised example of much wider "geographies of scientific knowledge" offers a new perspective which no longer regards science in the Caprivi as

---

3   Similar interdependencies between political power, nature and the production of knowledge have been widely discussed for other colonial and imperial contexts, most prominently for the British Empire in Southern Africa, Australia and North America, see for example the edited volume: Beinart, W. and L. Hughes (eds.) (2007), *Environment and Empire*. Oxford: Oxford University Press. On mapping as a means of conquest, see: Etherington, N. (2007), Introduction. In N. Etherington (ed.), *Mapping Colonial Conquest: Australia and Southern Africa*. Crawley: University of Western Australia Press.
4   See e.g.: Bryant, R.L. (1998), Power, Knowledge and Political Ecology in the Third World: A Review, *Progress in Physical Geography*, 22(1): 79–94; Fairhead, J. and M. Leach (2003), *Science, Society and Power: Environmental Knowledge and Policy in West Africa and the Caribbean*. Cambridge: Cambridge University Press; Livingstone, D.N. (2003), *Putting Science in Its Place: Geographies of Scientific Knowledge*. Chicago: Chicago University Press.
5   Latour, B. (1993), *We have never been modern*. Cambridge, MA: Harvard University Press, p. 38.
6   Livingstone (2003): 1–13.
7   Livingstone (2003): 8.
8   Livingstone (2003): 178.

mere "provincial practice", but as an undertaking which occurred within a broader Southern African context.[9] Moreover, as surveying in the Caprivi occurred in close cooperation with the apartheid military from the 1960s to the late 1980s, Southern African geographies of war, power and environmental science became ever closer interlinked.

In the Caprivi, ecological surveys and environmental interventions became a vector through which South African power could be exercised in space. Such surveys of Caprivi's nature as well as the interventions and reactions which were based on the newly-acquired information formed a central feature of South African rule over the Caprivi and other areas of northern Namibia.[10]

Similar interventions in areas which were considered to be remote and in need of development were not new to South Africa. For example, the 'betterment' schemes or 'soil conservation' programmes which were implemented in the so-called native reserves and later homelands had attempted to regulate and control land usage.[11] Subsequent dam construction and river regulation projects can also be seen as attempts to extend the reach of South African state power through increasing the state's knowledge about and control over nature, especially in areas towards the periphery of South Africa's sphere of influence.[12]

Although South Africa's keen interest in the Caprivian nature in the second half of the twentieth century can be understood as another example from the country's long tradition of environmental interventions, the Caprivi's specific temporal, political and geographical context was also decisive.[13] South Africa's most significant interventions into the Caprivian natural environment took place at a time when neighbouring countries had already gained their independence. This also means that the scientific and economic exploitation of the region in the 1970s should not only be understood against the background of a 'western' scientific arrogance which overrode so-called African knowledge. This stereotypical colonial approach was often pinpointed by scholarly works on ecological science in imperial and colonial contexts. These presumed that colonial scientists typically disregarded local knowledge which would supposedly have been more fitting for the specific contexts in which they

---

[9] Livingstone (2003): 1–13.
[10] See also: Kreike (2004): 90–110 and Henrichsen et al. (2015).
[11] On betterment planning, see: De Wet, C.J. (1995), *Moving Together, Drifting Apart: Betterment Planning and Villagisation in a South African Homeland*. Johannesburg: Witwatersrand University Press and Beinart et al. (1987), and Beinart (2018): 11–13. In 1964 Govan Mbeki had already described such 'betterment schemes' as an important factor driving rural resistance. Mbeki, G. (1964), *South Africa: The Peasants' Revolt*. Baltimore: Penguin Books. See also: Redding, S. (2006), *Sorcery and Sovereignty: Taxation, Power, and Rebellion in South Africa, 1880–1963*. Athens: Ohio University Press.
[12] Isaacman, A.F. and B.S. Isaacman (2015), Extending South Africa's Tentacles of Empire: The Deterritorialisation of Cahora Bassa Dam. *Journal of Southern African Studies*, 41(3): 541–560.
[13] For other parts of northern Namibia, see: Kreike (2013).

worked. The result, it was argued, was that the ill-suited colonial interventions which followed ultimately led to increased resistance against overbearing colonial rule.[14]

The interviews which I conducted with former experts and environmental scientists who worked in the Caprivi in the 1970s tell a different story. Even as representatives of the apartheid state, these individuals were fully aware of the importance of local knowledge for their work and were more than willing to gather as much information on the area as possible from locals. Indeed, many Caprivians who worked for South African experts remembered that they were constantly encouraged to make use of their own 'local' or 'indigenous knowledge'. Similarly, in the British Empire, the value of so-called 'native knowledge' had been regarded highly since the interwar period and steadily gained in importance in the late colonial era.[15]

While 'local' knowledge was considered to be an important qualification for Caprivians to work for South African experts, all of the Caprivians whom I interviewed remembered their formal education, at least initially, as having being very basic and of no lasting value.[16] The clear division of knowledge into 'indigenous' and 'formal' categories on the basis of such education was reinforced by the supposed divide between 'the modern West' and 'traditional Africa' constructed in colonial, apartheid, and, later, neo-liberal thought. As Donaldo Macedo argued in 1999, this division has been drawn by those in power, but must be deconstructed via the experiences of the colonised.[17]

The attitudes of ecological experts must thus be understood within the different contexts in which they worked. Ecologists, biologist and zoologists in the Caprivi did not work exclusively for the South African state, nor solely to further the interests of Pretoria and its political aspirations to control Namibia and its inhabitants.[18] Many also worked within the

---

[14] As described, for example, by: McCracken, J. (1982), Experts and expertise in colonial Malawi. *African Affair*, 81(322): 101–116. See also: Beinart et al. (2003): 17. Patrick Harries showed in his book *Butterflies & Barbarians* that nineteenth-century missionary naturalists also did not always maintain such a clear distinction between 'western' and 'local' knowledge systems (Harries 2007).

[15] Beinart et al. (2003): 17.

[16] JL, 18.05.2014, Malengalenga and SS, 02.10.2012, Katima Mulilo. SS himself employed the term "local knowledge". There is an extensive scholarly debate on the terminology and classification of different (non-academic) knowledge systems. Different terms include 'native', 'indigenous', 'traditional', and 'local' knowledge, all of which carry with them slightly different meanings and varying applications. For an overview, see e.g. the following two edited volumes: Sillitoe, P. (ed.) (2006), *Local Science vs. Global Science: Approaches to Indigenous Knowledge in International Development*. New York: Berghahn Books and Semali, L. M. and J.L. Kinchelo (eds.) (2011), *What is Indigeneous Knowledge: Voices from the Academy*. New York: Routledge.

[17] Macedo, D. (2011), De-Colonizing Indigenous Knowledge. In Semali, L. M. and J. L. Kinchelo (eds.), *What is Indigenous Knowledge. Voices from the Academy*. New York: Routledge, p. xii–xiii.

[18] See: Beinart, W., K. Brown, and D. Gilfoyle (2009), Experts and Expertise in Colonial Africa Reconsidered: Science and the Interpenetration of Knowledge. *Africa Affairs* 108(432): 413–433 (here 424).

international networks of academia and sought to contribute important research to their respective disciplines.[19] This double role is reflected in their memoirs, in which they often position themselves as having occupied a place beyond their otherwise clearly-defined function within the apartheid bureaucracy.

According to David N. Livingstone's understanding of science and geography, it is "geography [which] makes the scientific enterprise an inescapably moral undertaking".[20] In other words, in order to account for the role which the natural sciences, especially environmental science and research played in the expansion of South Africa's apartheid policies into the Caprivi and in Pretoria's subsequent control over the region, it is important to first understand the particular geographies of the area and their accompanying histories. I will do so by first exploring the military and political contexts in which environmental research and interventions took place in the Caprivi.

The Namibian War of Liberation in the Caprivi

From the mid-1960s until Namibia's independence in 1990, the Caprivi, like other parts of northern Namibia, was a war zone. Although the entire region was not continually affected by direct combat operations, it was an area of constant insecurity in which conflict could break out at any time and in any place. While the SAP was initially in charge of security operations in northern Namibia, the SADF took command from 1974.[21] The SADF installed a very dense network of military bases in the region with the aim of keeping the local population under surveillance, securing Namibia's northern borders, and launching attacks into Zambia and Angola.[22] While raids into neighbouring countries and the securing of the border were mainly conducted by members of the SAAF, the control and surveillance of the population in the Caprivi was increasingly undertaken by paramilitary organisations and military intelligence groups.[23] In 1976, 45,000 SADF soldiers were based in the operational area of northern Namibia, not including members of the police.[24] In the second half of the 1970s, South Africa gradually began to 'namibisize' its forces and tasked the South West

---

[19] Beinart et al. (2009): 424.
[20] Livingstone (2003): 178.
[21] Dale, R. (1993), Melding War and Politics in Namibia: South Africa's Counterinsurgency Campaign, 1966–1989. *Armed Forces & Society*, 20(1): 7–24 (here 10–11).
[22] Silvester, J., M. Akawa, and N. Shiweda (2014), The Namibian Liberation Struggle. In A.J. Temu and J.N. Tembe (eds.), *Southern African Liberation Struggles: Contemporaneous Documents, 1950–1994: Volume 3*. Dar es Salaam: Mkuki Na Nyota, p. 171–178.
[23] In 1979 the *Koevoet* (Afrikaans for 'crowbar') was founded as a special SWAPOL unit. It consisted mainly of black Namibian fighters under the command of white South Africans (Wallace 2011: 291). According to Dale, it had already been established, or at least had already been in planning, in 1976 (Dale 1993: 12).
[24] Dale (1993): 12.

African Territory Forces (SWATF) and the South West African Police (SWAPOL) with supporting the military effort. Only residents of Namibia could join these organisations – within which they were grouped according to apartheid's system of racial and ethnic classification – in contrast to members of the SADF, who mostly lived in South Africa.[25]

Opposed to these forces were the South West African People's Organization (SWAPO) and its armed wing, the People's Liberation Army of Namibia (PLAN), which aimed to end the South African occupation and establish an independent state.[26] The Caprivi National Union (CANU), which was established between 1958 and 1962 and merged with SWAPO in 1964, was also involved in active resistance in the Caprivi.[27] From the beginning of the armed struggle in the mid-1960s, many Namibian civilians and PLAN fighters crossed the borders into neighbouring countries. A first SWAPO exile camp was established in Tanzania in 1964, while SWAPO founded further bases in southern Zambia, and fleetingly also in Botswana, in the 1970s.[28] Particularly after its independence in November 1975, Angola became an important host country for exiled Namibians.[29] While from at least the late 1960s these camps were also inhabited by civilian refugees from Namibia, some of them were also used by PLAN for training purposes and to launch its operations in northern Namibia.[30]

As the leading organisation in the Namibian liberation movement, SWAPO worked in close cooperation with many other (Southern) African socialist and anti-colonial movements, in particular Zambia's United National Independence Party (UNIP) and the Movimento Popular de Libertação de Angola (MPLA).[31] Similarly, South Africa's fight against the

---

[25] No Namibian passport existed until the mid-1970s, before which white Namibians were automatically awarded South African citizenship. The exact dates of the establishment of these various police and military units remain unclear. Dale (1993: 12) writes of a process which had already started in 1974, while Wallace (2011: 294–295) identifies 1980 and 1981 as the years in which SWATF and SWAPOL were respectively established, although the latter date contradicts her claim that the *Koevoet* was founded as a unit within the SWAPOL in 1979.

[26] SWAPO played an especially central role in the Namibian liberation movement after the UN General Assembly officially recognised the organisation as the sole and authentic representative of the Namibian people in 1976. For a history of SWAPO and PLAN, see: Dobell (2000). For a more general overview of the Namibian liberation struggle, see also: Silvester et al. (2014).

[27] Dobell (2000): 35 and Kangumu (2011): 201.

[28] For a general overview, see: Williams (2015): 4–5 and, in more detail, 65–148. On Zambia, see: Williams, C.A. (2011), Ordering the Nation: SWAPO in Zambia, 1974–1976. *Journal of Southern African Studies*, 37(4): 693–713. On Botswana, see: Müller, A.J. (2014), *"The Inevitable Pipeline into Exile": Botswana's Role in the Namibian Liberation Struggle*. Basel: Basler Afrika Bibliographien. On Angola, see: Shigwedha, V.A. (2017), The Aftermath of the Cassinga Massacre: Survivors, Deniers and Injustices. Basel: Basler Afrika Bibliographien.

[29] Williams (2015): 4–5.

[30] Williams (2015): 4.

[31] See e.g.: Leys, C. and J. Saul (1995), *Namibia's Liberation Struggle: The Two-Edged Sword*. London:

liberation movement did not cease at the northern borders of Namibia. The SADF fought on the side of the União Nacional para a Independência Total de Angola (UNITA) in the Angolan Civil War (1975–2002) and also sought to fight SWAPO at its camps in southern Angola and Zambia. Namibia's armed liberation struggle (1966–1990) as well as the Angolan War of Independence (1961–1974) and the subsequent Angolan Civil War, which pitted UNITA against the Cuban-backed MPLA government, are therefore often understood as a single war.[32]

From a South African military perspective, operations in northern Namibia and the Caprivi were mostly described as 'counter-insurgency' measures to secure South African-occupied territory against so-called 'terrorists'.[33] Counter-insurgency has since become a well- established strategy of warfare worldwide. In 2009, the United States Department of Defence defined it as "consisting of integrated and synchronized political, security, economic, and informational components that reinforce governmental legitimacy and effectiveness while reducing insurgent influence over the population".[34] South Africa's understanding of its military presence in northern Namibia and in the Caprivi was reflected in a similarly comprehensive counter-insurgency approach known as the 'total strategy', which called for more than the mere establishment of a local "military outpost" or "military fiefdom".[35] Besides its military components, such a strategy was also envisioned to feature 'non-combatant' elements, including political and economic measures, increased surveillance, and generally a tighter control of all activities in the area.

The SADF promoted these non-combatant aspects of its occupation as a crucial part of its 'total strategy', for which the 'Winning the Heart and Minds' (WHAM) campaign was central. This was grounded in the basic doctrine of winning "the sympathy and support of

---

James Currey, p. 2; Williams. (2015); Dobell (2000): 57–51. SWAPO probably also cooperated with the *União Nacional para a Independência Total de Angola* (UNITA) before it became an ally of the SADF after Angola's independence. Silvester et al. (2014): 183–184.

[32] In Namibia, the war is mainly referred to as the 'War of Liberation', while in South Africa the name 'Border War' or 'Bush War' is widely used in soldiers' personal accounts of the conflict. On the naming of the conflict, see: Hayes, P. (2010), Bush of Ghosts. In J. Liebenberg and P. Hayes (eds.), *Bush of Ghosts: Life and War in Namibia 1986–1990*. Cape Town: Umuzi, p. 15; Dale, R. (2014), *The Namibian War of Independence, 1966–1989: Diplomatic, Economic and Military Campaigns*. Jefferson: McFarland and Company, p. 2 and Krüger, G. (1992), Fallstudie Namibia. In: A. Harneit-Sievers (ed.), *Kriegsfolgen und Kriegsbewältigung in Afrika: Der Nigerianische Bürgerkrieg, 1967–1970*. Hannover: 221–242.

[33] Dale (1993): 10–11.

[34] Bureau of Political-Military Affairs (ed.) (2009), *United States Government Counterinsurgency Guide*. Washington.

[35] Frankel, P.H. (1984), *Pretoria's Praetorians: Civil-Military Relations in South Africa*. Cambridge: University of Cambridge Press: 104. See also: Dale (2014).

the people upon whom the insurgents depend".[36] The SADF had its own unit dedicated to this effort, the so-called Civic Action Programme which supported the SADF in non-combat activities, such as providing teaching or medical services for locals. However, as Richard Dale argued, Civic Action Programme representatives, who also wore the SADF uniform, struggled to gain the sympathy of local residents, who already knew about the brutal and abusive tactics employed by other members of the SADF or police.[37] It was here that the civil administration had an important role to play as South African government officials or civil servants were less likely to be associated with the atrocities of the SADF and the Koevoet.[38]

Towards a Caprivi Homeland

South African rule in the Caprivi in the period from 1963 to 1980 was defined by the Odendaal Commission's decision to turn the Eastern Caprivi into a self-governing homeland along the lines of a South African 'bantustan' or 'homeland'. By following the general recommendations of the earlier Tomlinson Commission, South Africa sought to establish 'homelands' – especially to the north of the Red Line, but also within the police zone – which it would recognise as formally independent 'countries'. In contrast, areas designated for whites in Namibia would be fully incorporated into South Africa.[39] The implementation of the Odendaal Plan in areas to the south of the Red Line led to the forced separation of the population into 'racially'- or 'culturally'-defined homelands, a move which was met with strong resistance.[40] For the four northern homelands of Kaokoland, Ovamboland, Kavangoland and the Eastern Caprivi, the immediate impact was less direct, although the demarcation of the homeland boundaries continues to cause conflict up to the present-day.[41] In the medium-term, the recommendations of the Odendaal Report may also have led to more radical resistance to South African occupation and further international pressure on

---

[36] Eloff de Visser (2011): 86.
[37] Dale (1993): 14 and Dale (2014).
[38] Eloff de Visser (2011): 86.
[39] See also: Silvester, J. (2015), Forging the Fifth Province. *Journal for Southern African Studies*, 41(3): 505–518, in which he showed how, after the Second World War, a number of alternative visions or options for Namibia's future were considered by South African politicians. These went beyond the dichotomous choice between national independence or full incorporation into South Africa. See also Miescher (2012a: 285–87), who showed that the Odendaal Commission's recommendations altered the character of the Red Line. While it was no longer included on maps, it now manifested itself in the form of a fence which cut through newly-demarcated homelands, including Hereroland. See also: Silvester et al. (2014): 142–152 and Wallace (2011): 262.
[40] E.g.: Kössler, R. (2000), From Reserve to Homeland: Local Identities and South African Policy in Southern Namibia. *Journal of Southern African Studies*, 26(3): 447–462. See also: Wallace (2011): 262.
[41] Wallace (2011): 262 and Katjavivi (1988): 72–76. For example, the border between the Zambezi Region and the Kawango East Region in the Western Caprivi is still disputed.

Pretoria to withdraw from Namibia.⁴² Simon Hafeni Kaukungwa, a founding member of SWAPO, made the organisation's opposition to the Odendaal Commission clear at a hearing in Ohangwena in 1964, when he openly declared that SWAPO would "reject every word and paragraph of the Odendaal Commission Report".⁴³ SWAPO, he emphasised, was not interested in a free Ovamboland, but only in the freedom of the whole of Namibia. He also warned the South African government that the establishment of bantustans would lead to the sort of "bloodshed which you have never seen before".⁴⁴

In defiance of such explicit warnings from SWAPO, but with the support of several powerful traditional leaders, the establishment of homelands in Namibia commenced after the publication of Odendaal Report.⁴⁵ The Eastern Caprivi was initially governed by the Planning Committee, which had been directly appointed by the South African Department of Bantu Administration and Development, until 1972. Thereafter, for the first time since 1939, the Caprivi was no longer ruled directly by a South African magistrate or native commissioner. This role was now filled by the Legislative Council of the East Caprivi, which included two chiefs representing the Masubya and Mafwe 'tribal' or 'ethnic' groups respectively, as well as other representatives from these two groups. An Executive Council was also constituted from further representatives of the two groups.⁴⁶ The main difference to previous administrative structures in the Caprivi was the role of the South African authorities. Their power was now executed through a Commissioner-General, who was appointed to "guide Caprivi to self-government".⁴⁷ The Commissioner-General presided over a group of white administrative directors responsible for the sectors of agriculture and works, justice and education respectively as well as one Chief Director. These directors were officially appointed as 'advisors' to their respective departments, but enjoyed almost complete power in their areas of governance through the budgetary control which they were mandated to exercise in their departments.⁴⁸ This administrative structure persisted until 1976, when the Eastern Caprivi became a supposedly 'independent', 'self-governing' yet South African-controlled homeland for the next four years, with a political structure which was very similar to

---

42 Silvester et al. (2014).
43 Quoted in: Silvester et al. (2014): 145.
44 Quoted in: Silvester et al. (2014): 145.
45 The first Namibian homeland to be established was Hereroland in 1968. By the mid-1970s, ten homelands had been created all over Namibia, with three – Okavangoland, Ovamboland and Hereroland – declared self-governing entities with their own governments, flags and anthems. The forth homeland that was decalred a self-governing homeland within Namibia was the Eastern Caprivi homeland, which was not seen as a Namibian homeland, but as a South African, as it was directly controlled by Pretoria, not through Windhoek.
46 Kangumu (2011): 123.
47 Kangumu (2011): 123.
48 Katijavivi (1988): 73.

the so-called bantustans in South Africa, such as Venda.[49] Common to all these homelands was that they were granted a pseudo-independence or self-governing status, although none were ever recognised as independent states by any state other than South Africa itself. The Eastern Caprivi (officially the Republic of East Caprivi, later renamed as the Lozi Republic) therefore received its own flag, national anthem and coat of arms, but little else changed in the territory before it was returned to the control of the South West African Administration in 1980.[50]

The establishment of the Eastern Caprivi homeland increased the direct influence which South Africa could exercise over inhabitants in the Caprivi. Under previous structures, 'traditional leaders' had been less tightly controlled by the South African authorities, at least in their daily responsibilities. Now, with the increased incorporation of 'traditional leaders' into South African structures of power, the apartheid state could shape the lives of homeland populations more profoundly.[51] Jason Myers argued that in the early years of apartheid in South Africa, such structures allowed for a more nuanced, and thus more effective, exercising of power than the unabashed "white supremacy without apologies" practiced in the 1980s by the P.W. Botha government. For Myers, "by dressing the South African state in the costuming of tribal society and the institution of chieftaincies, its actions would become those of a social form, to which those classified as Natives could be said [...] to belong." Law therefore no longer emanated from the "mouth of a colonial administrator", but was directed via a chief.[52]

A very different political structure was established in the Western Caprivi once the Odendaal Commission's proposal to turn the proclaimed game reserve into a homeland for 'Bushmen' was rejected in the mid-1960s. In 1968 the region was 'upgraded' to a game park which was officially managed from Windhoek.[53] In practice, however, the area was already an effectively closed military zone in which, at least from 1970 onwards, not even civil servants – whether from the Eastern Caprivi or from Windhoek – were allowed to enter.[54] Most residents within the park's boundaries had little choice but to find jobs and housing at one of the SADF's military bases, where they lived under direct military control.[55]

---

[49] For an overview of the historiography of the South African homelands, see: Ally et al. (2018) and Jensen et al. (2015).
[50] Kangumu (2011): 123.
[51] Kangumu (2011): 122.
[52] All quotes: Myers (2008): 18.
[53] What exactly changed through this change of name remains unclear.
[54] Taylor (2011): 73.
[55] Taylor (2011): 73. I will return to the situation in the Western Caprivi when discussing the SADF's own nature conservation policies in Chapter 4.

Living and Working in the Caprivi

South Africa's growing interest in Caprivian nature, the militarisation of the region, and the establishment of a homeland in the Eastern Caprivi led to an increasing number of South Africans coming to work in the area as well as a rise in low-wage labour for Caprivians, in the military, but also in the fields of fishery, forestry and nature conservation. The following section is based on the memories of South African and Caprivian personnel who used to work for the South African or the homeland authorities in the areas of nature conservation, forestry or agriculture. To gain an insight into their memories, I relied mostly on oral interviews. I will discuss their personal experiences in the Caprivi as well as the roles which they played within the larger context of South Africa's occupation of the Caprivi at a time in which the region was becoming of increasingly high strategic importance to the apartheid state.

Working in Forestry, Fishery and Nature Conservation

In 1967 C.E. Kruger, the South African magistrate and Native Commissioner in Katima Mulilo, anticipated that further South African personnel would be required in the Caprivi to assist in the establishment and administration of an Eastern Caprivi homeland. In preparation for this influx of civil servants, he issued a general circular on conditions in the Caprivi and the role which the newcomers would be expected to play in its governance.[56] He stated that "Europeans living here are, as things are constituted, merely doing service of the kind or the other in the general interest of the inhabitants, and, naturally, of our own country". He then went on to describe the importance of legal provisions which allowed the South African administration in the Caprivi to keep the "ruling authorities [...] under surveillance and guidance." In anticipation of the upcoming changes of administration, he also emphasised that "apart from legal provisions, however, the tribal authorities naturally look to this office as the source from which they receive instructions and general information".[57]

This idea, that the South African authorities supported the local population because Caprivians were 'naturally' dependent on South African assistance, was reflected in many accounts from white South African officials who were sent to the Caprivi in subsequent years. The dual imperative of needing to be seen to work in the interests of local people while seeking to maintain the structures of South African hegemony in the region was central to the WHAM campaign initiated in the 1970s. According to this strategy, South African officials would support local residents as part of a wider counterinsurgency campaign

---

[56] NAN, Kavango Administration (AKA), 1/5/1, For General Information, 1 September 1967.
[57] All quotes: NAN, AKA, 1/5/1/ For General Information, 1 September 1967, p. 3.

to 'pacify' them. However, a probably more significant driving force behind these efforts, as Myers argued, was the notion that "the costumed state apparatus must not only act, it must be seen to 'act as' – [thus] claiming for itself the right of representation."[58]

This study can only briefly touch upon the highly diverse, fluid and complex web of relationships which local residents established with this 'costumed state apparatus'. This is because the information which I could gain through my interviews was mostly limited to the memories of Caprivians who worked for governmental bodies in the Caprivi. Nevertheless, PL, a Caprivian who worked for many years in various positions in the homland administration and after independence became a politician, formulated a sentiment with which many of my Caprivian interviewees might have agreed. Although PL recognised that the apartheid state paid his salary and invested in what it regarded as the development of the region, he was left with the constant feeling that the very presence of South African officials in the Caprivi imparted "the stigma of oppression". Any of their actions or interventions therefore only served to remind him that Caprivians were "still colonised".[59]

Employees in the fields of forestry and nature conservation in the Caprivi in the 1970s and 1980s can be grouped into two main categories, namely those who worked for the civil administration and those employed by the military. Among the former were primarily well-educated South African experts in leadership roles as well as Caprivians, such as PL, in lower-ranking administrative positions. The civil administration also employed poorly-paid field workers and game guards. South African experts were assigned to the Caprivi by the Department of Bantu Administration and Development, while the local administrative personnel as well as the field workers were contracted by the Caprivi Government Service, the administrative arm of the homeland government.[60] The exact nature of this administrative structure, particularly in relation to the civil servants who were sent from South Africa, remains unclear and seems to have altered constantly. While some claim to have worked for the Department of Bantu Administration and Development in Pretoria, others recall having been officially employed by the Caprivi Government Service.[61] Moreover, as for all public offices within the apartheid state, all administrative bodies were further sub-divided along racial and ethnic lines.

---

[58] Taylor (2011): 45.
[59] PL, 13.05.2014, Katima Mulilo.
[60] By the term 'field worker', I refer here to uneducated or poorly-educated local workers who were employed in the field in its broadest sense. These included labourers in the areas of forestry, fishery, and nature conservation as well as so-called 'game guards'. I will discuss terminology relating to game guards as well as their working conditions in Chapter 4.
[61] BW, 10.03.2014, Sedgefield, and DP, 28.02.2014, e-mail.

Some of the first Caprivians to be employed by the Caprivi Government Service worked for its Department of Agriculture and Forestry (CAF).[62] For example, CC started his job as a field worker as a young man in 1973 and worked in nature conservation until 2005 for the entire duration of his career. He was initially employed under the South African Otto Graupner, who took office as the nature conservation officer for the Caprivi Government Service in the same year. Five further field workers began working alongside CC in the section dedicated to nature conservation from 1973. It remains unclear from the official records how many more field workers were employed by the CAF. However, the fact that they are not mentioned in the government's lists of employees may suggest that many field workers were not given permanent jobs, but were instead employed temporarily when their services were required.

In late 1972, BW and Otto Graupner were transferred from the Transvaal Provincial Administration's Division of Nature Conservation to the Caprivi. Graupner would henceforth oversee nature conservation and wildlife protection in the area, while BW took responsibility for fisheries, but they would both cooperate very closely in their work on a daily basis. BW recalled that he worked together with Graupner, who was "responsible for nature conservation development" in the Caprivi Government Service.[63] They were succeeded by DP and Danie Brits, two further South Africans. By no later than 1978, Manie Grobler and a second officer had taken over.[64] On average, there were thus around four white people working in the specific field of nature conservation in the Caprivi during the 1970s at any given time, while many more South Africans worked in closely-related roles in the local agriculture, forestry, fishery and veterinary services.

By far the largest group of 'whites' in the Eastern Caprivi in the 1970s were military and police personnel. By the mid-1970s, the SADF had built at least seven large camps and two major airbases in the territory. It was also in the Caprivi that South Africa trained some of its infamous special units, such as the Reconnaissance Commandos ('Recons'), the Battalion 32 ('Buffalo Battalion') and, at a later stage, Koevoet.[65] A former South African colonel estimated that several thousand soldiers were based in the Caprivi in the late 1970s.[66] Some of these were stationed in different camps in the countryside, but higher-ranking officers often

---

[62] Forestry, fishery and wildlife issues had previously primarily been the responsibility of the South African police or the traditional authorities. SS, 15.05.2014, Katima Mulilo, and CC, 02.11.2015, Windhoek. In the case of the Western Caprivi, so-called 'Bushmen guards' had been tasked with maintaining law and order as well as protecting game since the 1930s (Taylor 2012: 67).

[63] BW, 10.03.2014, Sedgefield.

[64] NAN, CAF, 2/10/1, Office Administration and Auxiliary Services, Staff Main File (whites), Blanke personeel, 22 September 1978.

[65] Kangumu (2011): 154.

[66] NN, 12.03.2014, Cape Town.

lived in the town of Katima Mulilo. There they could be joined by their wives and children due to legislation which allowed military personnel who were on extended tours in regions far from home to be accompanied by their families.[67] In the initial stages of the war, nature conservation tasks within the military were usually undertaken by higher-ranking officials with a personal interest in wildlife.[68] Only towards the late 1970s did more specialised professionals within the SADF begin to work explicitly on wildlife and nature conservation projects, probably supported by members of the Civic Action Programme.

Jobs in the fields of forestry, fishery, and nature conservation in the Caprivi were taken up for diverse reasons. Nevertheless, I could identify some recurring motives, especially among groups of similar employees. For most of my Caprivian interviewees, an important reason to apply for a job in these sectors was the promise of a rare secure position and wage. CC, for example, remembered that he decided to take up his job because friends who worked in nature conservation considered themselves lucky, believing that "the government would take care" of them and that they would receive paid work until their retirement.[69] The promise of a secure job is also mentioned by others who were permanently employed as field workers during the South African occupation. BN, who started in this role in 1979, said that he applied for the position because he wanted to have a "real" job instead of working as an unskilled farm labourer.[70] Both BN and CC also mentioned that they had come to like animals and enjoy being in nature, but had only realised this after they had started their jobs. BN, who had family and friends working for the Caprivi Government Service who encouraged him to apply, remembers the job application process as being very quick. He remembered:

> I took my application there [to the Caprivi Government Service] and they took my application. Just after a very short period they told me 'Okay your application has been accepted'. I think it was like Wednesday and I was told to go to Nkasa [nature conservation camp] by Friday.[71]

Officials who were sent from South Africa often mentioned their love for nature, the opportunity to work in an unfamiliar region, and the chance to "build something new" as reasons for accepting a job in the Caprivi.[72] For BW and other biologists in the area, the supposed distinctiveness of Caprivian fauna and flora provided a further motivation for taking up work in the area. This opportunity to research plants, and even animals, which did not exist

---

[67] CT, 26.03.2014, Cape Town.
[68] SM, 27.04.2014, Windhoek.
[69] CC, 02.11.2015, Windhoek.
[70] BN, 17.05.2014, near Sangwali.
[71] BN, 17.05.2014, near Sangwali.
[72] BW, 10.03.2014, Sedgefield.

in in other parts of Namibia and South Africa lent the Caprivi a high scientific regard.[73] The Caprivi also offered an unusual chance for South African scientists to conduct research in an unfamiliar region of Africa, an opportunity which had become ever rarer in the 1970s and 1980s due to a host of international boycotts against the apartheid state and its representatives, including scientists.[74] BW fused his academic interests with his willingness to support conservation "to take up this challenge and to use the opportunity to study the unknown fish life and fishery of the region and the lake and [I] would also assist with general conservation work where possible."[75]

South African experts in the Caprivi in the 1970s recalled going to great lengths to support what they framed as "educating" and "developing" locals.[76] When HS, the first trained forester in the Caprivi, commenced his work, he was convinced of the backwardness of the local inhabitants and how much they were in need of support. During an interview in 2014, he remembered: "You cannot think how backwards and poor those people were when we first came there. They didn't even use salt in 1973 and they caught the fish and dried it in the sun with all the flies and everything. Then they packed the fish on bicycles and traded it across the border". He saw his job as removed from the politics of South Africa and especially his country's military campaigns in the region, imagining his role as solely "to get the local people raised to a higher standard of living and that was my main thing in forestry".[77]

An important assumption of this sort of development narrative was that such help was not imposed, but requested by legitimate local actors, whether in the form of so-called traditional authorities, local governments, or unspecified 'local people'. BW recalled that "the request for fish research originated with local staff seeing catches of small fish and raising concern – then this request came via the Department of Bantu Affairs to the Transvaal Provincial Administration's Nature Conservation and via the director to me." The protection of rivers and other forms of nature conservation, meanwhile, were supposedly "initiated by officials stationed in Caprivi" but with "further motivation by local people".[78]

Small-town Life and the Love for Nature – Remembering 'White Katima Mulilo'

Although the Caprivi was a highly-militarised war zone in the 1970s, a recurring memory of the white officials who worked there at the time is that of living in the remote, but beauti-

---

[73] A similar 'otherness' was also attributed to flora and fauna in Kaoko. See: Bollig et al. (2016): 67.
[74] See e.g.: Haricombe, L.J. (1995), *Out in the Cold: Academic Boycotts and the Isolation of South Africa*. Ann Arbor: Information Resources Press.
[75] BW, 03.05.2013, e-mail.
[76] See also: William Beinart et al. (2009).
[77] Both quotes: HS, 10.03.2014, George.
[78] Both quotes: BW, 10.03.2014, Sedgefield.

ful small town of Katima Mulilo while supporting local people and enjoying the beautiful nature. These romanticised memories of life in a happy and well-governed community – an existence in harmony with the local population and surrounded by a wild and fascinating nature – stand in sharp contrast to many other aspects of life in the Caprivi in the 1970s, which was dominated by the brutal war which was being fought in the region and the apartheid system. As I will show in this section as well as in the following chapter, this was a war which was not only fought via military means by soldiers, but also through the policies and actions of the various administrative structures which sustained the South African occupation. Most officials in the Caprivi's civil administration were thus in some way complicit in the racist and violent structures of South African rule and contributed, as I will show, in a variety of ways to the suppression of any local calls for a democratic and independent future.

Katima Mulilo was not well connected to South Africa, with transport to the country usually only possible via SAAF-flights. To add to the town's remoteness, the Caprivi was almost entirely surrounded by militarised international borders with enemy countries. Despite this isolation, life in Katima Mulilo in the 1970s is often remembered by South Africans who lived there as having been infused with a strong sense of 'community' spirit among its ('white') residents. Katima Mulilo's small 'white community' at the time consisted of high-ranking civil servants and military officials as well as doctors, missionaries and some few businesspeople. In the memories of many of these former residents, Katima Mulilo developed into a South African outpost during the war. As DP remembered, the town

> was isolated. We were surrounded by hostile countries and to get to Caprivi by road meant going through Zimbabwe and the intense war there. We were reliant on the air force providing us lifts to Waterkloof air base in Pretoria. Veggies [vegetables] were flown in once a week, meaning that if you were not in town then – then no veggies. We slaughtered and made our own meat supplies. I developed veld sores [tropical ulcers] due to limited fresh food.[79]

But, as BW described, the 'community' supposedly experienced "hardships – such as floods preventing us to travel anywhere in the 1975/6 rainy season or blackouts – together."[80] As it is common for settler and civil servant memories of colonial contexts, this recollected sense of community allows former residents to continue to indulge in memories of a good and happy life spent in the company of people with whom they believed to have shared a common destiny. As HS recalled, "all the people there, were young people, except for the couple

---

[79] DP, 28.02.2014, e-mail.
[80] BW, 10.03.2014, Sedgefield.

of old bosses and they were all selected for some or other bloody reason to be there."[81] He then went on to describe how they organised sports events together, met to watch rugby, or went to church with each other. He concluded his reminiscences with a story of how he and his friends from the army and police all helped to build a new pub together. After its completion, "we put it full of beer and vodka and everybody came and stood there and had a few sips – that is more or less the old Caprivi."[82]

Some South African civil servants and military personnel lived in Katima Mulilo with their families, including some who married during their period of service and then brought their new wives to the Caprivi. The South African authorities supported family life in many ways, including by offering work to the wives of their employees. As BW recalled, "[s]taff of departments and army and police were motivated and lived all with their families in Katima [Mulilo], forming social structures like a church congregation, angling club, own sport events, social ladies club, readers circle, own primary school where my wife became a teacher".[83] HS, whose wife worked for the police in Katima Mulilo and both of whose children were born in Katima Mulilo, remembered the Caprivi as a perfect environment in which to raise children. The South African authorities, he recalled, were very well organised and were always ready to act in case of an emergency among the South African community in Katima Mulilo. Indeed, not only was the SAAF on constant standby for medical emergencies, but it would also fly women to Pretoria for shopping trips.[84]

One unique aspect of life in Katima Mulilo which was mentioned repeatedly by my interviewees was the town's beautiful surrounding natural environment and all the opportunities for fishing, boating, safaris and hunting which this provided. C.E. Kruger, South Africa's long-serving magistrate in the Caprivi, made it clear in his 1967 general information circular for 'white' personnel that the "charm of the natural life and features of the Caprivi Strip is one of the main attractions of service here and most of us would wish to enjoy as much of it as we reasonably can".[85] With the growing population of Katima Mulilo, its white inhabitants seem to have informally declared the town a nature conservation area in the 1960s, in which it was not permitted to cut trees, hunt, or keep dogs, except "in the case of Europeans, because their dogs are normally well cared". However, at least until 1976, when South Africa implemented a new nature conservation act, government officials were "free to fish at will" outside of Katima Mulilo.[86] According to HS, they took advantage of this

---

[81] HS, 10.03.2014, George.
[82] HS, 10.03.2014, George.
[83] BW, 10.03.2014, Sedgefield.
[84] HS, 10.03.2014, George.
[85] NAN, AKA, 1/5/1, For General Information, 1 September 1967, p. 5.
[86] Both quotes: NAN, AKA, 1/5/1/, For General Information, 1 September 1967, p. 5.

frequently and "I fished all along the rivers. I knew the area fairly well."[87] Unsurprisingly, hunting – in both its legal and illegal forms – was also a common activity. As HS recalled, "the swamps were full of game at the time and there was a big game crossing about here [near Katima Mulilo]".[88] Kruger had declared in 1967 that "the ruling attitude towards game was to conserve", but officials were allowed to "shoot a few head of game".[89]

The excitement of being in a 'wild' and 'natural' environment repeatedly came up as a decisive factor in the decisions of former residents to move to and work in the Caprivi. DP remembered that he "was very excited to be on the banks of the Zambezi River deep into the continent I loved."[90] Although Katima Mulilo took on more and more functions as an administrative centre, entertainment options in the town remained limited. As no other urban centres were within easy reach, the civil and military personnel and their families spent their free time outdoors. Many photographs and written accounts by former militaries illustrate that it was common to have a 'braai' (barbecue) on the banks of a river, to go fishing, or even to go on 'photo-safaris' in areas which were considered relatively safe, usually in the surrounds of Katima Mulilo.[91] In his semi-autobiographical memoir, the infamous South African colonel Jan Breytenbach, who commanded several special units in the Caprivi in the 1970s, noted the natural beauty of the area and how soldiers usually spent their free time in nature.[92] As he recalled: "In the early 1970s I was introduced to this remote world of wonders, of savage beauty [...]. [It was] enveloped in a cloak of primeval perfection, pristine in the purity that permeated in all its component parts – animals, bush, swamps and rivers."[93] He then described how he would spend his evenings on the deck of a boat on the Okavango River ("My dream of sundowners on the water would become a reality after all") before "turning in to the sounds of snorting hippos and splashing fishes in some isolated little creek deep inside the ancient heart of Africa".[94]

---

[87] HS, 10.03.2014, George.
[88] HS, 10.03.2014, George.
[89] NAN, AKA, 1/5/1/, For General Information, 1 September 1967, p. 5.
[90] DP, 28.02.2014, e-mail.
[91] See also: Hayes (2010): 15.
[92] Breytenbach, J. (1997): *Eden's exile: One Soldier's Fight for Paradise*. Cape Town: Queillerie Publishers. Among other roles, Breytenbach was the first commander of Battalion 32, a South African special unit consisting mainly of Angolan low-ranking riflemen and white South African and international officers deployed to support UNITA against MPLA and Cuban forces in southern Angola. Breytenbach also led the paratrooper attack on the SWAPO refugee camp in Cassinga in 1978, killing more then six hundred people, among them many children. He later became the head of the SADF's school for guerrilla warfare. See e.g.: Shigwedha (2017).
[93] Breytenbach (1997): 14.
[94] Breytenbach (1997): 122.

Educating Employees

A further common theme in the memories of white officials who served in the Caprivi during the 1970s and 1980s was their professed support and care for the well-being and prospects of Caprivians, particularly in the area of environmental education. In this regard, communication between the relevant authorities in South Africa and the Eastern Caprivi, but also among different groups within the Caprivi – such as South African officials and their Caprivian workers – are evident. Indeed, the education of Caprivians in South Africa is one of the few topics in relation to which individual Caprivians appear in official government records. As a result, rare direct written communications between Caprivians and South African officials, which otherwise seldom went beyond mere field reporting, can be found on this subject.[95]

South African officials in the Caprivi recognised the importance of 'local' or 'indigenous' knowledge, particularly in fields such as forestry, fishery or wildlife protection. At the same time, this knowledge was only acknowledged when it was in accordance with South African aims. This moulding of local knowledge, a process which was believed to be crucial to enforcing South African rule in the Caprivi, was to be enhanced by educating some Caprivians in South Africa.

The education system in the Caprivi, as well as in other parts of Namibia, mirrored that imposed on the 'black' population of South Africa, the so-called 'Bantu Education System', which was introduced by the Bantu Education Act of 1954.[96] 'Bantu Education' had at least two main goals. Firstly, the strict segregation of schooling along 'ethnic' and 'racial' lines was seen as pivotal for the maintenance of a segregated society and, as such, for the perpetuation of a system of white supremacy.[97] The second aim, as Hermann Gilomee argued, was to provide mass education in order to maintain a constant supply of semi-skilled workers.[98]

No educational qualifications were required for prospective game guards or other field workers in the Caprivi in the 1970s, but a grade nine secondary school diploma was manda-

---

[95] See e.g. reports on problem animals in: NAN, CAF, 6/19/2/2, Problem herbivores.
[96] The Eiselen Commission laid the basis for 'Bantu Education' in South Africa in the late 1940s, while the Van Zyl Commission (1958) and the Odendaal Commission (1962) applied the administrative and ideological recommendations of the Eiselen Report to the specific circumstances of Namibia. Jansen, J.D. (1995), Understanding social transition through the lens of curriculum policy: Namibia/South Africa. *Journal of Curriculum Studies*, 27(3): 245–261 (here 249).
[97] Gilomee, H. (2009), A Note on Bantu Education, 1953–1970. *South African Journal of Economics*, 77(1): 190–198.
[98] Gilomee (2009): 191. For an overview of the education system in Namibia under South African rule, particularly after 1980, see: Salia-Bao, K. (1991), *The Namibian Education System under the Colonialists*. Randburg: Hodder & Stoughton, p. 18–26 and 31–100.

tory from 1980.⁹⁹ According to the former game guards whom I interviewed, they received no initial education or training on the job.¹⁰⁰ This only commenced in 1976, when the Caprivi homeland government was given the opportunity to send some young men to South Africa to do practical training at the Manyeleti Game Reserve in today's Mpumalanga province as well as theoretical courses in nature conservation at the Cwaka Agricultural College, currently known as the Owen Sitole College of Agriculture in KwaZulu-Natal. From at least 1976, the Eastern Caprivi could send one or two students every year to these institutions, financed by the Eastern Caprivi Government Service.¹⁰¹ There the game guards received a very basic education, but this still served for some as a starting point for a career within the Eastern Caprivi homeland administration. JL, who later became a high-ranking official in the CAF, recalled that "South Africans did surveys in the homelands to find the best people to send to South Africa".¹⁰² He himself had been recommended by his headman and, when offered the opportunity, "took the call" to go to a South African agricultural school. He was impressed by the "modern" agricultural methods which he learned there and, in his own words, came back to the Caprivi as a "man of vision" who was ready to fight for the "development" of the homeland.¹⁰³ With his newly-acquired knowledge, JL's task became to convince local residents of what he had learnt as well as to identify further young men to be sent to South Africa for education and training.

The students' different personal experiences in South Africa seem to have shaped their political views on apartheid and the South African occupation of Namibia. In 1978 Conrad Puleliso Matengu was sent for practical training at Manyeleti Game Reserve. In a long letter to the secretary of the Public Service Commission in the Eastern Caprivi, Matengu soon complained about his stay at the reserve. He wrote that he had been treated badly and had not learnt anything as he had been restricted to office work. In contrast, he noted that "two whites", the manager of Manyeleti as well as the nature conservation officer in Katima Mulilo, had promised that he would receive an education which would allow him to help develop his "own country", the Eastern Caprivi. Matengu concluded the letter by emphasising that "[i]t is already a complete year now with the [East Caprivi] Government, but they [Manyeleti Game Reserve] have given me nothing. I find it very wise if I could be at home because I could be helping my people in one way or another."¹⁰⁴ His request was ignored

---

⁹⁹ NAN, CAF, 1/1 (I), Conditions for Employment, 1979. See also: SS, 15.05.2014, Katima Mulilo.
¹⁰⁰ Interview with SS, 15.05.2014, Katima Mulilo; CC, 02.11.2015, Windhoek; BN, 17.05.2014, near Sangwali.
¹⁰¹ E.g.: NAN, Administration for Caprivians (ACS), 5/3/2, Nature Conservation Students Cwaka, 7 November 1978 and NAN, ACS, 5/3/2, Albertus Mwahi, 12 June 1977.
¹⁰² JL, 18.05.2014, Malengalenga.
¹⁰³ JL, 18.05.2014, Malengalenga
¹⁰⁴ NAN, ACS, 5/3/2, Matengu to Public Service Commission, 19 October 1978.

and, a few weeks later, after his practical training had come to an end, he had to begin his theoretical lessons at Cwaka. From there he tried once more to convince his superiors in Katima Mulilo to allow him to return home, this time by addressing the conservation officer in Katima Mulilo directly. In this letter, Matengu questioned whether the officer was happy to disregard his plans for the future, to which he provided the following rhetorical answer: "Maybe yes! Just because I am a black man. If I could be a white man I could not be in this situation. I want to fight for the rights of my people, so let me come home."[105] Unsurprisingly, Matengu did not receive a response to this letter and had to remain at Cwaka for another year before he ultimately failed the course and left of his own accord.[106]

These two letters are the only references I could find to Matengu. In my 2014 interview with the conservation officer, he did not mention Matengu and, when asked, could not remember his case.[107] Nevertheless, the example of Matengu demonstrates that South Africa's plan to further appropriate Caprivian local knowledge by educating young Caprivians in South Africa was not always as straightforward as hoped for by the South African authorities. Moreover, their education in South Africa also exposed Caprivians to the currents of opposition and resistance to the apartheid state – and 'Bantu Education' in particular – which were in the process of growing into fully fledged protest movements in South African schools and other educational institutions in the 1970s, culminating most notably in the Soweto Uprisings in 1976.[108]

Being an Expert?

Further education was an issue of less relevance for the South African experts who worked in the Caprivi. Most of these South African officials had finished their higher education or professional training in South Africa before being sent to the Caprivi. The majority claimed that they were asked by their superiors or employers in South Africa to apply for a position in Namibia or the Caprivi.[109] All of the South African officials whom I interviewed saw their role as having been to 'advise' the Eastern Caprivi Government and its inhabitants on their

---

[105] NAN, ACS, 5/3/2, Matengu to Perry, 5 December 1978.
[106] NAN, ACS, 5/3/2, J.F. Parmitert to the Secretary for Agriculture and Works, Eastern Caprivi Government Service, Nature Conservation Student C. Matengu, 14 December 1979.
[107] DP, 28.02.2014, e-mail.
[108] The Soweto Uprisings were a series of demonstrations led by schoolchildren in the Soweto township in 1976. They were brutally put down by the police, who killed at least 178 protesters. On anti-apartheid resistance in South African schools and universities, see: Brown, J. (2016), *The Road to Soweto: Resistance and the Uprising of 16 June 1976*. Johannesburg: Jacana. On its consequences, see: Nieftagodien, N. (2014), *The Soweto Uprising*. Johannesburg: Jacana. See also: Gilomee (2009).
[109] E.g. DP, 28.02.2014, e-mail.

particular areas of expertise, but at the same time they often reflected openly on their own initial ignorance of the local context.[110] PL, the first state forester sent to Namibia, recalled that he was asked by his supervisor-to-be, the head forest officer in Pretoria, to apply for the job while he was still working in Gaborone in the 1950s. PL remembered that "it [Namibia] was a new country and we didn't know what was happening there."[111] Although he was considered to be an expert, he admitted that in hindsight "everything was new" to him and that he did not possess sufficient knowledge of the local environment. Similarly, BW, who was deployed to the Caprivi as a fishery expert, claimed that "I did not know the region at all but had enough practical know-how to tackle the job."[112]

BW also pointed towards a further solution, namely to rely on Caprivians to make up for the gaps in the knowledge of the South African experts. He remembered: "I found it exciting and never had problems with my staff – some had never worked before."[113] The forester HS expressed similar sentiments when he explained that "the local people you were working with, they grew up there, they knew this sort of working in the field without knowing much about it."[114] Both South African officials thus openly acknowledged the importance of the labour and know-how which their employees provided, but did not consider these contributions to be evidence of either experience or knowledge. For example, HS remembered how "I saw and I learned from the local people" how to cut mopane trees so that their branches would grow back faster, but would not accept any advice when "select[ing] a very nice site" to do the cuttings to grow a thick forest.[115]

Both BW and HS recalled that one of the most important skills which they required in the Caprivi was the ability to understand "the blacks". Both had been confident that they already knew how to "deal with the local population" from their stints working in other homelands.[116] For instance, HS prized his knowledge of "the black people" in the Caprivi because he had "worked before that long in the Transkei and assisted guys amongst this people."[117]

Although experts did rely on local workers, the latter play a very peripheral role in their memories. This was evident, for example, when BW discussed his research on fisheries and how he had "mostly worked alone for weeks in the remote floodplain". What he had actually meant by working alone in a remote area became clear in the following sentences, in which he described how he "never had problems with local population" because his "fisheries as-

---

[110] See also the discussion on colonial experts in: Beinart et al. (2009).
[111] PR, 21.04.2014, Napier.
[112] BW, 10.03.2014, Sedgefield.
[113] BW, 10.03.2014, Sedgefield.
[114] HS, 10.03.2014, George.
[115] HS, 10.03.2014, George.
[116] BW, 10.03.2014, Sedgefield.
[117] HS, 10.03.2014, George.

sistants or the four or so game guards were very loyal and did all the interpretation". Strikingly, although he claimed to have worked alone, BW thus had several assistants with him and was in constant contact with local residents in these supposedly "remote" areas. In his memories, he repeatedly highlighted the importance of "his blokes", but never recognised them as peers or colleagues.[118]

As described above, the South African experts in the Caprivi presented themselves as being in the region to support the local population at the request of the *Khutas* and the Eastern Caprivi Government. According to HS, they therefore felt accountable to locals for the effects of their projects. For example, HS recalled how he was called to a *Khuta* meeting in the late 1970s to answer the complaints of traditional leaders about restrictions which they faced in protected forest areas. He described how "[w]hen I came to the *Khuta* meeting, they looked at me and said that it is now seven, eight, nine years since all our people were taken out [of the forest reserve] and since then we were not allowed to graze the area. So, tell us now – what do we get back?"[119] HS recounted this story to illustrate the sense of accountability which he felt towards the *Khuta*. However, it can also be interpreted as another attempt to present the South African occupiers as supportive of and willing to listen to Caprivians in their capacity as mere 'advisors' to the 'traditional' authorities and the homeland government. HS may have also recalled this story to present himself in a good light despite the general failure of the South African authorities to fulfill their promise to compensate the evictees.

This narrative is contradicted, however, by many of the South African officials' other memories. For instance, HS remembered how he unsuccessfully tried to convince residents in floodplains to grow rice. He went on to describe how, "when we saw that they wouldn't really take it from us, we called in the chief. We said take your best land and we will help you – there is the tractor, there is the plough. We will plough but we'll keep a straight check on the cost at the end you going to pay for it."[120] Through such recollections, it becomes clear that chiefs in the Caprivi, as it was typical in South African homelands, functioned primarily as a vehicle through which the South African authorities could enforce measures proposed by its body of white experts. By offering the chiefs support in ploughing but compelling them to pay back the expenses, chiefs could be kept loyal yet beholden to the South African regime.[121]

---

[118] All quotes: BW, 10.03.2014, Sedgefield.
[119] HS, 10.03.2014, George.
[120] HS, 10.03.2014, George.
[121] Myers (2008).

In conclusion, the rise in employment opportunities for Caprivians in the 1970s in the Eastern Caprivi civil administration – especially in the areas of fishery, forestry, and nature conservation – as well in the military left its mark on the Caprivi in a number of ways, including in terms of its links with South Africa, the relationship between the South African authorities and Caprivians, and the interactions between different groups within the 'white community'. The many white civil servants and military personnel who were deployed to the Caprivi may have contributed to the creation of closer ties between the Caprivi and metropolitan South Africa, but their memories and the stories which they told about the area also reinforced the narrative that the Caprivi was remote and removed from the rest of South African territory.

At the same time, this relative isolation fashioned a close sense of community among the different groups of South Africans living and working in the region. Many of the former members of this community remembered leading a comfortable life in Katima Mulilo, a town which offered most of the amenities of South African small-town life as well as a fascinating natural setting. To maintain this sense of idyll, the 'white community' in the Caprivi seems to have successfully banished from its mind the ongoing war in the area as well as the racial oppression which the majority of the region's population was experiencing. Unsurprisingly, the inhabitants of the Caprivi usually appear in these idealised memories as helpful sources of 'indigenous knowledge', as members of a grateful workforce, or as thankful recipients of South African education. This, of course, masked the fact that it was during this very period that resistance against the South African occupation increased, while large sections of the population continued to live in difficult economic conditions, with few rights, and often in fear of the South African security apparatus.

Protecting Rivers and Forests

Controlling the spread of *Salvinia Molesta*, a fern which proliferates rapidly in rivers and lakes, and ensuring the sustainable use and conservation of forests were key concerns for South Africa's civil administration in the Caprivi. River and forest conservation projects allowed the authorities to present themselves as a caring government which protected the area's main economic resources – fresh water, fish and timber – while also serving the interests of the military. River and forest conservation further helped to lay the foundations for later practices and collaborations in wildlife protection and other emerging fields of nature conservation in the Caprivi.

Protecting Rivers: Controlling Salvinia Molesta

Salvinia molesta is an aquatic fern originating from South America which has been found in the river system of the Chobe, Liniyanti and Kwando rivers since the 1950s. The plant spread into the Caprivi via the Zambezi River after the construction of the Kariba Dam in 1959.[122] Having spread explosively through the region's rivers, *Salvinia* became problematic for the South African authorities for two main reasons. Firstly, its presence made it nearly impossible for boats to navigate along or across rivers, thereby rendering fishing difficult and tourism less viable. *Salvinia* thus presented a risk to many plans for economic development. Secondly, the fern posed a security threat in the eyes of the military, as it allowed enemy fighters as well as poachers to cross border rivers undetected. Research into and control of *Salvina* thus became a central area of cooperation between the civil administration and the military.

In 1967 D.S. Mitchell, a botanist from the University College of Rhodesia, undertook a major survey of the spread of *Salvinia* and outlined its "disadvantageous effects" for the Caprivi and neighbouring areas in Botswana. He concluded that

> [s]table weed mats effectively prevent the movement of boats on those parts of the river they occur. In the [Chobe] Game Reserve this makes the patrolling of one border of the Reserve difficult and the apprehension of poachers awkward, thus interfering with the full development of the area for tourism.[123]

In Botswana, tourism had started to emerge as a significant sector for economic development by the 1960s.[124] But Mitchell not only saw the serious risks which the plant posed for the the Chobe Game Reserve in Botswana, but also for affected areas in the Caprivi. He predicted that if *Salvinia* was to penetrate the swamps of the southern Caprivi, "it would be likely to endanger the habitat of the Sitatunga [a swamp-dwelling antelope]. This would seriously interfere with the development of tourism and safari hunting activities in the region."[125]

---

[122] NAN, CAF, 6/18/15/2, Botswana–South Africa Survey of Salvinia Molesta in Chobe–Linyanti–Kwando River System, 1972, p. 2.

[123] NAN, CAF, 6/18/17, D.S. Mitchell, A Survey of Salvinia Auriculata in the Chobe River System, 11 March 1967, p. 4.

[124] Mutwira, R. (1989), Southern Rhodesian Wildlife Policy (1890–1953): A Question of Condoning Game Slaughter? *Journal of Southern African Studies*, 15(2): 250–262. See also two case studies of the Moremi National Park: Bolaane, M. (2005), Chiefs, hunters and adventurers: the foundation of the Okavango/Moremi National Park, Botswana. *Journal of Historical Geography*, 31: 241–259 and Bolaane, M. (2013), *Chiefs, Hunters and San in the Creation of the Moremi Game Reserve, Okavango Delta: Multiracial Interactions and Initiatives, 1956–1979*. Osaka: National Museum of Ethnology.

[125] NAN, CAF, 6/18/17, D.S. Mitchell, A Survey of Salvinia Auriculata in the Chobe River System, 11 March 1967, p. 5.

Unlike in Botswana, the authorities in the Eastern Caprivi had yet to regard tourism as potentially lucrative, but were concerned by the harmful effects of *Salvinia* on fisheries and security. Fishery was seen as a promising area for further economic development in the Caprivi and was promoted by the South African authorities.[126] South African officials regarded the abundant surface water and rich fish fauna of the Caprivi as being of high "strategic value" for the occupied territory as a whole because other parts of it lacked these resources. Furthermore, there were also specific fish species in the Caprivi which could not be found in the rest of Namibia or in South Africa itself.[127]

From as early as the 1930s, South African academic institutions regularly organised trips to the Caprivi to collect fish specimen. However, the most systematic surveys were conducted in relation to the *Salvinia* problem in 1973 and 1977. During the course of these surveys, specimens from several hundred fish species were collected and sent to the Albany Museum in Grahamstown.[128] According to Mitchell, *Salvinia* not only prevented fishermen from using boats for fishing, but was also "competing for nutrients with plants that start the food chain ending in fish".[129] Its eradication was therefore seen as a key precondition for the development of a fishing industry as well as an opportunity for the authorities to show their support for local fishermen.[130]

The authorities' second major concern in relation to *Salvinia* was that it rendered Caprivi's border rivers difficult to patrol and control.[131] This constituted a threat for South African security in the area, which was seen to be endangered not only by poachers, but more especially by enemy combatants crossing into the Caprivi from their bases in Zambia and, later, Angola.[132] Monitoring and controlling the spread of *Salvinia* thus also became a responsibility for the military and the police.

---

[126] Van der Waal, B.C.W. (1985), Aspects of the Biology of Larger Fish Species of Lake Liambezi, Caprivi, South West Africa. *Madoqua*, 14(2): 101–144; Tvedten, I. (2002), If You Don't Fish, You Are Not a Caprivian: Freshwater Fisheries in Caprivi, Namibia. *Journal of Southern African Studies*, 28(2): 421–439.

[127] Van der Waal, B.C.W. and P.H. Skelton (1984), Check List of the Fishes of Caprivi. *Madoqua*, 13(4): 303–320 (here 303).

[128] Van der Waal et al. (1984): 313. See also: Lenggenhager (2016). Some specimens were also taken to the JLB Smith Institute for Ichthyology (now called the South African Institute for Aquatic Biodiversity) in Grahamstown for further research.

[129] NAN, CAF, 6/18/17, D.S. Mitchell, A Survey of Salvinia Auriculata in the Chobe River System, 11 March 1967, p. 5.

[130] NAN, CAF, 6/18/15/2, Botswana–South Africa Survey of Salvinia Molesta in Chobe–Linyanti–Kwando River System, 1972; NAN, CAF, 6/18/15, D. Edwards and P.L. Thomas, The Salvinia Molesta Problem in the northern Botswana and Eastern Caprivi Area, 1978.

[131] NAN, CAF, 6/18/15, Edwards, D. and P.L. Thomas, The Salvinia Molesta Problem in the Northern Botswana and Eastern Caprivi Area, 1978.

[132] A prominent case which illustrates how Namibian liberation fighters would cross the Zambezi River into the Caprivi was that of Tobias Hainyeko, the first SWAPO military commander, who

This shared interest in the fight against *Salvinia* saw an increase in levels of co-operation between civil servants, military officials and ecologists in the Caprivi. From the late 1960s until at least 1978, South African officials in the Eastern Caprivi produced an annual report, conducted surveys, established regional 'expert' networks and expanded close co-operation with the military.[133] The SAAF supported the surveys by providing aeroplanes and pilots for the production of aerial photographs documenting the distribution of *Salvinia*.[134] These photographs also served as primary data for the production of distribution maps, which subsequently informed decisions about countermeasures to be implemented against the plant. In some cases, the SAAF was also involved in spraying pesticides over *Salvinia* from helicopters.[135]

The fight against *Salvinia* also helped to strengthen ties with neighbouring territories. Colleagues from Botswana and Zimbabwe regularly joined their South African counterparts in the Caprivi to conduct surveys and implement control measure. Co-operation with Botswana's Department of Nature Conservation in Maun was particularly close. BW recalled that he maintained personal friendships with colleagues from across the border and crossed it on several occasions to meet with them.[136] On a more official level, South Africa intensified its technical and academic co-operation with Botswana.[137] Similarly, before 1975, the authorities in the Eastern Caprivi were also willing to work with the Portuguese colonial regime in Angola, to whom it offered to provide "whatever technical assistance they may require".[138]

From an ecological point of view, it seemed obvious that the effective control of *Salvinia* could only occur in partnership with surrounding territories. But transnational co-operation with 'friendly' neighbours was also in the strategic interests of the South African military. At least in relation to Botswana, the SADF regarded the *Salvinia* control project as a convenient means to be on good terms with the local population on both sides of the border. Indeed, Denzil Edwards, the assistant director of the Botanical Research Institute in Pretoria, declared in a letter to the chief of the SADF that "the project [...], I believe, is

---

was shot dead on the Zambezi in 1967 while trying to establish better lines of communication between SWAPO cells within Namibia and the exiled organisation's headquarters in Dar es Salaam. On Hainyeko's death, see Katjavivi (1988): 59–64 and Silvester et al. (2014): 165–171.

[133] BW, 10.03.2014, Sedgefield.
[134] NAN, CAF, 6/18/15/1, aerial photograph, 'Ngoma Bridge Area Showing Open Water', 1972.
[135] NAN, CAF, 6/18/15/1–2.
[136] BW, 10.03.2014, Sedgefield.
[137] NAN, CAF, 6/18/15/1, and 6/18/15/2, Correspondence between Ben van der Waal and David S. Mitchell.
[138] NAN, CAF, 6/18/15/1, and 6/18/15/2, Correspondence between Ben van der Waal and David S. Mitchell.

contributing materially to good relations between the local peoples of Botswana and South Africa".[139]

The spread of *Salvinia* was only brought under ultimate control when a biological antagonist was found and introduced into rivers in the Caprivi in the mid-1980s.[140] Attempts to control the *Salvinia* problem, which endured for some thirty years, generated a trail of detailed documentation, including correspondence, reports, memoranda and travelogues. The project has also remained prominent in the memories of many of the people involved in its implementation.[141] This can be read, perhaps, as an indication of the fundamental importance which was attached to the fern's eradication for ecological sustainability, conservation, economic development, and security. However, the project could also be interpreted as an attempt to legitimise the efforts of the civil administration in the Eastern Caprivi to procure further material and infrastructural support from the military or even as means of justifying its very existence in the first place. Both of these factors were probably crucial, as would have been many others. For example, the fight against *Salvinia* also showed the importance of documenting, structuring and mapping environmental knowledge as a means of exerting power over the 'remote' Caprivi.[142]

Mapping, as a technology of power, also reinforced the urge to draw a line between 'native' – in the sense of 'indigenous' or 'national' – vegetation and 'invasive' or 'alien' plants.[143] As Kenneth R. Olwig demonstrated, the distinction between 'native' and 'alien' flora and fauna remains central in modern scientific environmental monitoring, in which state-financed "fleets of planes [...] can patrol within and beyond the state's borders, protecting the nation from invasive pollutants of any kind, chemical or biological".[144]

---

[139] NAN, CAF, 6/18/15/1, Edwards to Chief of SADF, Request for Helicopter Support, 10 June 1977.
[140] In 1985, the biological control of Salvinia achieved its first success in the Eastern Caprivi through the introduction of a weevil which caused the Molesta mats to sink and decompose. Schlettwein, C.H.G. and Bethune, S. (1992), Aquatic weeds and their management in southern Africa: Biological control of Salvinia Moleste in the Eastern Caprivi. In: T. Matiza and H.N. Chabwela (eds.), *Wetland Conservation Conference for Southern Africa: Proceedings of the Southern African Development Coordination Conference held in Gaborone, Botsana, 3 – 5 June 1991*. Gland: IUCN: 173–188.
[141] NAN, CAF, 6/18/15/1–2, Agricultural Matters, Weed Control (Salvina Spray Project); BW, 10.03.2014, Sedgefield; DP, 28.02.2014, e-mail; CS, 15.08.2012, Windhoek.
[142] See also: Livingstone (2003).
[143] Olwig, K.R. (2003), Natives and Aliens in the National Landscape, *Landscape Research*, 28(1): 61–74. See also: Giraut, F., S. Guyot and M. Houssay-Holzschuch (2005), La Nature, les Territoires et le Politique en Afrique du Sud. *Annales. Histoire, Sciences Sociales*, 60(4): 695–717.
[144] Olwig (2003): 72. On the postcolonial nation-state and the discourse of alien people and plants, see also: Comaroff, J. and J.L. Comaroff (2001), Naturing the Nation: Aliens, Apocalypse and the Postcolonial State. *Journal of Southern African Studies*, 27(3): 627–651.

In conclusion, along with the wider interpersonal networks, new infrastructural requirements, and overlapping institutional interests which it generated, the *Salvinia* example points towards further ways in which the militarisation of the Caprivi and its environmental exploration became entangled. In particular, these imperatives converged in shared epistemological grounds which were articulated by both the civil administration and the military in the course of their efforts to control 'nature'. The acquisition of in-depth knowledge about the natural environment hence became an important means for exercising power through the intersection of counter-insurgency strategies with efforts to commodify and protect nature.[145]

Forestry and the Introduction of the Eucalyptus

Like measures to control *Salvinia*, forestry in the Caprivi witnessed elements of both co-operation and conflict between the SADF and the civil administration. It also revealed further characteristics of the relationship between the Caprivi and metropolitan South Africa. These included the importance which South Africa attached to the researching, surveying and mapping of Caprivian forests as well as to the circulation of natural specimens between the Caprivi and South African institutions.[146] Furthermore, forestry also contributed to the spatial ordering of the Caprivi according to natural features, including the exclusion and depopulation of designated 'protection' areas.

Before turning to the particular case of the eucalyptus trees which were sent to the Caprivi from South Africa, it is important to explore the contested histories of forestry and relate these to the different networks of power which have held sway in Namibia.[147] Imperial Germany was first to apply the methods of 'modern' forestry science in Namibia. At the time, in the early years of the German occupation, forestry was central to colonial projects worldwide. The British Empire also went to great lengths to promote forestry in its colonies in Southern Africa and beyond.[148] Timber was not only seen as a crucial resource for colonial economic development and maritime transport; ideologically, the planting of trees also evoked imperial visions of improvement, agriculture and civilisation.[149]

---

[145] See also more generally: Beinart et al. (2007).
[146] This circulation included the sending of Caprivian tree samples to South Africa and the introduction of trial trees from South Africa into the Caprivi, see: Lenggenhager (2016).
[147] Leslie Witz proposed the notion of dual networks of empire in his analysis of hunting in Namibia in the first half of the twentieth century by hunters and collectors working for British and South African museums: Witz (2015): 674–79.
[148] Barton, G. (2002), *Empire Forestry and the Origins of Environmentalism*. Cambridge: Cambridge University Press, p. 99–104.
[149] Bennett, B. M. (2010), The El Dorado of Forestry: The Eucalyptus in India, South Africa, and Thailand, 1850–2000. *International Review of Social History*, 55(18): 32 and Barton (2002): 99–104.

In Namibia, the German colonial regime was concerned that indigenous forests would not be sufficient to support the growing demand for timber in the colony. Although expertise was brought in from other German colonies, such as Cameroon, no clear solution presented itself for achieving increased wood production in Namibia. While some colonial officials pushed for the introduction of exotic trees, others argued that a better management of indigenous trees would maximise production.[150] Both approaches were implemented in the first decade of the twentieth century. While a forest station with its own nursery and indigenous seed store was established in every district in southern and central Namibia, trials were also conducted with 'exotic' plants, such as date palms or lilac, although such plants were only rarely used for timber production.[151]

After the First World War, the South African authorities foresaw the importance of establishing an effective forestry policy and management system to accompany an ever-rising demand for wood in Namibia. However, in the beginning South Africa was not yet willing to invest heavily in forestry and remained satisfied with leaving the German regulations unchanged until the 1950s. Only gradually did the South African authorities begin to exploit Namibian forests more systematically, including in areas to the north of the Red Line. Although there was no clear forestry policy implemented in these areas, the governing authorities in the native reserves issued a few licences to a Namibian company to cut trees in Kavango and Ovamboland in 1933 and the following years.[152]

South Africa's interest in Namibian forests increased rapidly in the 1950s, when the growing demand from the flourishing mines in Tsumeb for timber led to the overcutting of white-owned farmlands in the north of the police zone.[153] The fear that these often only recently declared farmlands would be encroached by bush led South Africa to establish a forestry station in Namibia in Grootfontein in 1957.[154] PL, who was in charge of establishing the first forestry station and nursery in Grootfontein, soon realised that he would have

---

On the use of trees by Israel in the Palestine conflict and how such practices originated in various colonial settings, see also: Braverman, I. (2008), "The Tree Is the Enemy Soldier": A Sociolegal Making of War Landscapes in the Occupied West Bank. *Law & Society Review,* 42(3): 449–482.

[150] On similar discussions in South Africa during this period, see also: Witt, H. (2014), The Role of Alien Trees in South African Forestry and Conservation: Early 20th-Century Research and Debate on Climate Change, Soil Erosion and Hydrology. *Journal of Southern African Studies,* 40(6): 1193–1214.

[151] Erkkilä, A. and H. Siikonen, (1992), *Forestry in Namibia 1850–1990.* Joensuu: University of Joensuu, p. 65–67.

[152] Erkkilä et al. (1992): 71.

[153] Overcutting was particularly severe on farmlands which had been recently demarcated by the Lardner-Burke Commission in 1947. On the commission, see: Miescher (2012a): 138–151; Erkkilä et al. (1992): 72; NAN, SWAA, A205/21, E.K. Marsh, Report on the availability of indigenous timbers for mine props in South West Africa, 1954.

[154] See also p. 63 ff.

to conduct surveys on 'indigenous' forests before he could commence with his primary task of preventing farms from being overcut. For these surveys, PL relied heavily on the support of a worker, whom he described as his "local help". Together they mapped the trees around Grootfontein and in Kavango, after which PL reached the conclusion that indigenous trees would not grow fast enough to supply the rising demand for timber.[155] Furthermore, he argued, it would be too difficult to transport heavy trunks from northern Namibia to the mines in Tsumeb. As a result, he commenced trials with imported trees from South Africa and Australia. The most prominent species which PL introduced to the region as part of this project was the eucalyptus.

The eucalyptus originates from Australia and was introduced by colonial forestry departments in most parts of the British Empire in the nineteenth century.[156] In the 1890s government foresters working for the Cape Colony's Department of Forestry initiated a programme to compare climates within the British Empire in order to find the most similar climatic regions to Southern Africa. From these they hoped to procure suitable flora for plantations in South Africa.[157] Australian plants, the colonial foresters concluded, provided the best option. As they had found eucalyptus trees to be particularly suited to the local environment, the species was soon planted all over South Africa. Because of a lack of indigenous timber amid an ever-growing demand, eucalyptus plantations also became very popular among private farmers in the early twentieth century.[158] While South African foresters and other scientists continued to travel the world in search of additional adaptable tree species, they also began to expand their planting experiments in the country's own imperial peripheries.

In 1958 the first trials to evaluate the prospects for introducing eucalyptus trees into northern Namibia were conducted.[159] Ironically, these occurred at a time when increasingly dire warnings were being expressed by scientists and the wider public in South Africa itself about the impurity which 'exotic trees' threatened to impart on supposedly pristine white settler landscapes; as a result, concerned South African citizens were beginning to take

---

[155] The most valuable indigenous tree species for timber production in North-Eastern Namibia, kiaat or bloodwood trees, have an extremely slow growth rate. Other important species in the area were leadwood and Zambezi teak. The wide-spread burkea and acacia trees were of less value for wood production. See: Le Roux, P. and M. Müller (2009), *Le Roux and Müller's Field Guide to the Trees and Shrubs of Namibia*. Windhoek: MacMillan Education.

[156] Bennett, B. M. (2011a), A Global History of Australian Trees, *Journal of the History of Biology*, 44: 125–145.

[157] Bennett, B. M. (2011b): Naturalising Australian Trees in South Africa: Climate, Exotics and Experimentation. Journal of Southern African Studies, 37(2): 265–280.

[158] Bennett (2011b): 276–77.

[159] Eucalyptus had already been introduced into south and central Namibia by the German colonial authorities. See: Erkkilä et al. (1992): 100.

matters into their own hands and eradicate 'exotic' species.[160] As Jean and John Comoroff showed, anxiety about 'alien plants' had been articulated by biologists in South Africa in as early as the 1930s. By the 1970s, the Comoroffs argued, this attitude had been widely adopted by the broader public in upper middle-class areas.[161] In contrast, concerns that 'alien plants' would destroy the local flora seem to have been less pressing in Namibia, where the planting and promotion of 'exotic' species occurred alongside efforts to prevent the local population from overcutting their own trees. Together these policies enabled the colonial regime to intensify its control over local economies and limit access to forests.[162]

By the late 1960s, PL was convinced that if logging continued in Namibia, it would take only a few dozens more years before no 'indigenous' trees would be left standing and no more wood would be available. To counter this danger, PL sought to identify adaptable, fast-growing trees for future import as replacements. After selecting different varieties of eucalyptus for this purpose, he secured approval for designated forestry reserves covering several thousand hectares. These were to be set aside for the possible future introduction of 'exotic' trees for timber production; humans, meanwhile, would not be permitted to live in the reserves. For PL, the reserves would be of long-term benefit, since "although we don't need it now, we might need it in twenty or fifty years, to introduce exotic trees for wood production."[163]

The introduction of eucalyptus was given a trial in the Eastern Caprivi in the mid-1970s. The territory's head forester, HS, had been on the lookout for rapid-growing trees which would provide timber suitable for local use, especially for the construction of houses and *kraals*. He had hoped that this would help to discourage local people from cutting down more valuable 'indigenous' trees. According to him, however, this effort was "a complete failure". Even though he claimed to have "tried just about everything and even got pamphlets from Australia on the different species", the trees did not grow well in the swamp conditions. HS was left with no choice but to content himself with at least "having tried it" and to "forget about [growing] eucalyptus up there".[164]

One of the largest and most ecologically promising designated trial areas in northern Namibia was located near Bagani, on the western shore of the Okavango River along the border of the Western Caprivi.[165] In 1974 PL conducted a trial there for eucalyptus and other fast-

---

[160] Bennett (2011a): 100 and Comaroff et al. (2001): 246.
[161] Comaroff et al. (2001): 245–246. Similar projects which aim to rid the Western Cape of invasive plants continue today.
[162] On the Transkei, see: Tropp, J. (2006), *Natures of Colonial Change: Environmental Relations in the Making of the Transkei*. Athens (OH): Ohio University Press.
[163] CG, 08.04.2014, Cape Town.
[164] All quotes: HS, 10.03.2014, George.
[165] A eucalyptus trial was also conducted in Katima Mulilo, but the trees died after only two years.

growing, dense trees. However, the introduction of eucalyptus trees to northern Namibia had remained contentious, even among the different organs of the South African regime. One year after PL had started his trial in Bagani, the SADF cut down all trees in the trial area without providing any reasons. Only later did PL apparently find out the real reason, namely that "[t]he terrorist hid behind the eucalyptus trees, because those were the densest bushes in the whole area, so the military just destroyed the trees so that the terrorists can't hide anymore".[166] Although the opportunity for enemy fighters to hide in eucalyptus plantations might not have been the only reason for the destruction of the trees, PL and HS were convinced that it was.[167] HS also recalled subsequent forestry projects which had been ended or destroyed by the SADF.[168]

Although the military and the civil administration in the Caprivi employed similar practices to rule people and control space, the SADF's destruction of eucalyptus field trials shows that they also disagreed on key issues. The example of forestry therefore exposes the apartheid state's attempts to hide its military goals behind the cloak of development and economic support; it was only desirable to sustain a narrative of economic development as long as this was not seen to pose a security threat. In the case of forestry, as soon as the economically valuable but dense eucalyptus plantations offered hostile combatants a possible place to hide, they were destroyed by the SADF without regard for their economic potential.

Making Use of 'Indigenous' Forests

In addition to conducting eucalyptus trials, another important responsibility for the foresters in the Eastern Caprivi was the research, surveying, and control of 'indigenous' forests. Prior to the 1970s, wood from these forests had mostly been used by the inhabitants for subsistence, although private companies from Botswana and Zambia had repeatedly proposed to harvest timber in the Caprivi from 1947.[169] However, only after the establishment of the Planning Committee in 1964 did officials in the Caprivi begin to see economic potential in the production of timber.[170] In 1968 Friedrich Breitenbach, Research and District Forester

---

Erkkilä et al. (1992): 134.
[166] CG, 08.04.2014, Cape Town.
[167] Other reasons could have been that the SADF needed the wood for its own use or that it had used the area as a training ground for its personnel to practice the cutting of dense woods.
[168] HS, 10.03.2014, George.
[169] Geldenhuys, C. (1977), Woodland Management Plan for the Nakabunze Reserve, Eastern Caprivi (unpublished report, George), p. 1.
[170] In his short 1947 report on timber production in the Caprivi, J.D.M. Keet of the Union Forestry Department of South Africa had been very sceptical about the area's potential for forestry due to the supposed difficulty of transporting timber from the region. See: Keet, J.D.M. (1947), *Caprivi Zipfel: Forestry and Allied Questions. Report to the Secretary of Native Affairs.* Pretoria, p. 7–8.

in the indigenous forests section of the South African Department of Forestry in George, compiled an extensive "Long-term Plan of Forestry Development in the Eastern Caprivi Zipfel".[171] The stated goal of this plan was to "provide for soil conservation and timber production through systematic protection and management of the forests, woodlands and wooded savannahs of the territory".[172] Breitenbach's plan remained the most detailed and wide-ranging forestry study in Namibia until the 1990s.[173] Three aspects are of particular interest. Firstly, the plan shows the great lengths to which the South African authorities went to compile a highly detailed survey of the region's nature. Breitenbach spent two weeks in the field, conducting surveys from the air and on the ground which covered large areas of the Eastern Caprivi. He also took over 150 colour photographs and collected more than fifty tree specimens. Secondly, these specimens were brought back to the Saasveld Herbarium in South Africa, where they were included in its South African flora collection.[174]

However, the most significant aspect of Breitenbach's plan was the spatial planning which it proposed to enforce on the basis of the forestry information gathered in the surveys. The plan recommended that protected forest reserves should cover nearly twenty per cent of the Eastern Caprivi's territory. These were to be divided by cut-lines and roads into "manageable and controllable units" and then cleared of any forms of cultivation.[175] Although Breitenbach did not state how many people would be affected, he went on to declare that "[i]nhabitants, if any, must be resettled outside the reserves. The same applies to a few small family settlements of cattle herders".[176] While he downplayed the extent of these proposed removals in his report by claiming that only a few families would be affected, he emphasised that it would be important to have uniformed staff or police officers patrolling the boundaries of the 'protected areas' to control access to them.[177]

---

[171] NAN, ARCAT, BB2598, F. Breitenbach, Long-term Plan of Forestry Development in the Eastern Caprivi Zipfel, 1968. This plan was accompanied by a reform to the Preservation of Trees and Forests Ordinance (No. 37 of 1952) in 1968 (No. 72 of 1968), in which clearly-demarcated protected forest areas were created in Namibia for the first time. See also: Erkkilä et al (1992): 76–77.

[172] NAN, ARCAT, BB2598, F. Breitenbach, Long-term Plan of Forestry Development in the Eastern Caprivi Zipfel, 1968: 1.

[173] Erkkilä et al. (1992): 123.

[174] NAN, ARCAT, BB2598, F. Breitenbach, Long-term Plan of Forestry Development in the Eastern Caprivi Zipfel, 1968: 6–7.

[175] These cut-lines were later also important for the military and wildlife conservationists in their efforts to control access to the area, see p. 63 ff. See also: NAN, ARCAT, BB2598, F. Breitenbach, Long-term Plan of Forestry Development in the Eastern Caprivi Zipfel, 1968, p. 77.

[176] NAN, ARCAT, BB2598, F. Breitenbach, Long-term Plan of Forestry Development in the Eastern Caprivi Zipfel, 1968: 77–78.

[177] NAN, ARCAT, BB2598, F. Breitenbach, Long-term Plan of Forestry Development in the Eastern Caprivi Zipfel, 1968: 87.

Though Breitenbach's plans were never fully implemented, at least four of the six proposed areas had been demarcated as forest reserves by the late 1970s.[178] According to the forester in charge, some of these areas were no longer inhabited by the 1970s: "All settlements were cleared from there [the reserves], because that was the army operational area. When I came there, there was nobody living there."[179] This indicates that some of the removals proposed by Breitenbach in 1967 were carried out, whether at the behest of the military or in order to implement the forestry proposals, or as a combination of both.

In 1972 Breitenbach returned to the Caprivi, this time in the company of another South African forestry scientist, to undertake a woodland inventory of Forests Reserve 1, an area close to Katima Mulilo which they named 'Nakabunze'. Together, they conducted a detailed census of the trees in the forest and "basically mapped the entire forest communities. For example, you would have dense wood there and open grass here then we could map it like that."[180] To do so, they drew maps directly onto aerial photographs, which had mostly been taken by the SAAF. This process served to supplement the very basic printed maps which they had at hand.[181] As the forestry scientist underlined, this was an especially useful approach in the Caprivi:

> Because I had the aerial photographs of the Caprivi I could use them as a base map, and include the data and the samples there. I could see that a line goes there and that this part is that vegetation and this part is this vegetation, so I could actually map it.[182]

This sort of mapping would not have been possible for the Kavango, for example, which formed too large a territory and for which there were not enough aerial photographs available.

After working for the apartheid state in Namibia, the co-author of the report became a professor of botany and forestry in South Africa. He remembered that most of his work in Namibia had been done "for nothing"; according to him, the maps which he had drawn and the majority of the data which he had collected were never used again and he did not know what had become of them.[183] However, in 1990 the South African Department of Water

---

[178] Geldenhuys (1977): 1.
[179] HS, 10.03.2014, George.
[180] CG, 08.04.2014, Cape Town.
[181] The aerial photographs which they used for this purpose were only available at a scale of 1:65,000. While Geldenhuys initially hoped that they could obtain most of the data directly from the interpretation of these photographs, he emphasised at the beginning of his report that this method could potentially be very misleading. Geldenhuys, C. (1990), *Woodland Management Plan for the Nakabunze Reserve, Eastern Caprivi, translation of the Africans original of 1977*. Pretoria: Department of Water Affairs and Forestry, p. 7–10 and CG, 08.04.2014, Cape Town.
[182] CG, 08.04.2014, Cape Town.
[183] CG, 08.04.2014, Cape Town.

Affairs and Forestry did publish an English-language translation of the 1977 report as the 'Woodland Management Plan for the Nakabunze Reserve'.[184] Some of its data was also subsequently used for academic publications and field guides on Namibian flora.[185]

In 1973 HS was sent to the Eastern Caprivi to conduct an even more detailed survey of the territory's forests. HS's main task was to find "usable timber" while also "collect[ing] as much ecological information" as possible.[186] He spent more than six months in the area's forests, systematically counting different types of trees and collecting leaves to send to his department's South African headquarters in Sedgefield in South Africa. While the leaf samples entered the collections of the herbarium at the botanical gardens in Sedgefield, the other information was used to produce precise maps of the local forests and their vegetation types. Researching the natural environment in this detailed manner was a rigorous and labour-intensive project, as HS explained:

> My job was to go up there, and survey on foot, with a chain. What I did was walking. I walked ten kilometres with a compass. Then five hundred meters angular [in the direction of walking] and then at night ten kilometres back to my camp again. And every 150 meters I made a fifty-metre circular survey of all the usable timber. I had a gun bearer with me all the time and everybody had to work with a gang of six people. [...] And I looked [to see] if there is any usable timber and I measured it and I dotted it down.[187]

HS was responsible for an area which his supervisor described as the most difficult region in Namibia for forestry work due to its frequent military activity, its proximity to the Angolan and Zambian borders, and the fact that the few employees in the forestry department were often ordered to perform other tasks in related areas such as agricultural development or wildlife protection.[188] The urgency with which the counting and mapping of trees was undertaken might indicate that the SADF was also involved, probably because any data which was produced also promised to be of benefit to the security forces. HS's memories reveal several aspects of this close cooperation with the SADF. Firstly, researchers had to receive 'security clearance' from the military before they could enter designated forests. Secondly, the SADF was responsible for the security of the research team while they conducted the surveys. Thirdly, collected data and plant samples were usually flown out to

---

[184] Geldenhuys (1990).
[185] Le Roux et al. (2009) and Geldenhuys, C. (1997), Sustainable Harvesting of Timber from Woodlands in Southern Africa: Challenges for the Future. *The Southern African Forestry Journal*, 178(1): 59–72.
[186] HS, 10.03.2014, George.
[187] HS, 10.03.2014, George.
[188] CG, 08.04.2014, Cape Town.

South Africa by the SAAF. Finally, the SADF and the military personnel and their families in Katima Mulilo were major potential customers for wood and other locally-produced timber products.[189]

The more detailed information on local forests which the surveys produced as well as the growing demand for timber in the Eastern Caprivi were influential in the South African authorities' decision to draw up a new set of forestry regulations, the so-called Eastern Caprivi Forest Enactment of 1975.[190] This legislation regulated the use of wood from the Eastern Caprivi and further restricted the rights of Caprivians to access and use their forests. Significantly, it also marked an official end to the small number of sawpits that had been established by the South African government in the 1930s. These had given some Caprivians the opportunity to harvest timber and manufacture planks or boats for sale.[191] HS described his efforts to end this practice:

> They [Caprivians] were not further allowed to cut their own trees, they had to come to me and I will go mark them the trees. I got a big Mercedes 4x4 and I charted the logs for them free of charge. We did everything just to get them out of the habit of doing it themselves. When they finished I go and measure up their timber for them and I got for them a market, mostly with the army blokes and the people from the Republic buying up the wood. I worked out the price and then took the cash back to them.[192]

Here HS referred to South African attempts to promote cash economies in the homelands. This, the apartheid state hoped, would make rural economies more controllable. For this reason, the infamous pre-apartheid betterment schemes for rural native reserves were retained as a central pillar of homeland policy.[193] By the 1970s, however, homeland politics had "lost almost entirely any aspect of improvement or rationalisation of land use and became instead principally instruments of coercion".[194]

---

[189] HS and CT also provided examples of the SADF's own increasing demand for wood, including the request for sizable and attractive timber with which to build bars on the military bases as well as in Katima Mulilo. Although they did not mention it, the general building of military infrastructure in the area would in all likelihood have required many large additional supplies of timber. HS, 10.03.2014, George and CT, 26.03.2014, Cape Town.

[190] NAN, CAF 6/19, Eastern Caprivi Forest Enactment, 1975.

[191] Sawpits were introduced during the early period of South African rule, probably before the Second World War. Geldenhuys (1977): 1.

[192] HS, 10.03.2014, George.

[193] Ferguson, J. (1990), The Anti-Politcs Machine: 'Development', Depoliticization and Bureaucratic Power in Lesotho. Minneapolis: University of Minnesota Press, p. 262. See also: Beinart (2018): 12–13.

[194] Furgeson (1990): 262.

However, HS's memories also reveal that South African power in the Eastern Caprivi was never absolute. For example, he remembered how

> [t]he other problem was the making of mokoro [a type of canoe] for what they [the Caprivians] cut a whole solid youthful tree. This was harder because they could sell the mokoro for a lot of money to the blokes near to the lakes and rivers for fishing. I had to get them out of this habit and I never got them out of it. They just moved their operations further out of reach and still cut the trees until eventually I saw that I'm losing the battle.[195]

By following this strategy, according to HS, Caprivians compelled him to offer them better services in order to prevent them from cutting whole trees for their boats. These included helping people to find the most suitable trees to cut and offering to transport the timber to markets.

Aware of his inability to fully enforce the new laws solely by coercive means, HS was forced to become creative in finding ways to convince Caprivians to abide by what he saw as a more sustainable way to use the forests. For example, he tried to convince people living close to forests to carve figures out of waste wood to sell as souvenirs. Having seen a lot of mementos being sold to soldiers by local inhabitants in other parts of Namibia and South Africa, HS was convinced that Caprivians did not possess the knowledge to manufacture similar figures. To provide them with this, he organised a "white carver" from South Africa to come to the Eastern Caprivi in 1974 to "teach" the local population how to produce supposedly 'traditional' wooden carvings, which could then be sold to military personnel.[196] According to HS, this programme was a success. In 1975 he organised a 'Green Day' in celebration of the Eastern Caprivi's nature, on which he awarded a prize to the "most talented carver". He also purchased the winner's carvings, but it remains unclear whether any further carvings were sold to anyone else.

HS's memories of his time as a forester in the Caprivi reveal the significance which the apartheid state attached to spatial surveying and the sending of botanical specimens to South African scientific institutions. Furthermore, his actions demonstrate common practices employed by South African 'experts' in relation to the local population as well as these experts' multi-layered entanglement with the SADF.

In general, South Africa saw significant potential for timber production in the Caprivi and invested into the research of the region's forests. While the eucalyptus did not leave behind an enduring legacy in the Caprivi, its introduction still serves as a telling case study for the broader topic of South African environmental policies in remote areas. In these

---

[195] HS, 10.03.2014, George.
[196] HS, 10.03.2014, George.

peripheral regions, a number of imperatives competed for attention: local fauna and flora had to be conserved; white-owned farms had to be protected from invasive weeds; and the demand from mines for timber had to be supplied. Moreover, at least in northern Namibia, all of these endeavours had to be realised in accordance with the wishes of the military if they were to be successfully concluded. Unlike with the introduction of eucalyptus, South Africa's protection of the Caprivi's indigenous forests had a more direct impact on the region and continues to affect the lives of local inhabitants to the present day, especially in the form of subsequently established 'community forests'.

Summarising Environmental Interventions in the Context of War

An analysis of the Caprivi's geographical and political context from the 1960s to the 1980s requires a nuanced understanding of environmental science and its interventions into Caprivian nature. There are three chief areas of consideration in this regard. Firstly, environmental measures served the South African occupation authorities as a key means to convince Caprivians of their goodwill or to at least promise locals some sort of future economic prosperity. Moreover, they offered the apartheid state the opportunity to portray itself as a 'bringer of development' and to present its signature segregationist policies of 'separate development' and homeland 'self-reliance' as viable. Secondly, environmental interventions produced an abundance of information on the Caprivi's natural environment. This not only benefitted environmental research, but also served as a crucial military-strategic resource in the SADF's fight against armed resistance. Thirdly, government interventions intensified as global awareness of the need to protect nature grew. The South African authorities thus laid the foundations for broader nature conservation projects, which continue to have a powerful impact upon the ordering of space in the region today.

As the information generated in the forestry and fishery surveys, in the fight against *Salvinia*, and during military reconnaissance operations proliferated, Caprivian nature and geography became increasingly familiar, documented and mapped. This new knowledge revived long dormant visions within the apartheid state for tourism and nature conservation in the Caprivi, according to which large sections of the region would be reserved for game parks and wildlife refuges. As Jaidev Singh and Henk van Houtum argued for the British colonial period in South Africa, nature conservation shares common roots with scientific forestry. In both of these fields, it has been assumed that the reservation of large conservation areas was not only important for the protection of fauna and flora, but also for the 'development' of local industries and settlements.[197] The interconnected networks of military personnel, environmental researchers and civil servants played a crucial role in the unfolding of such nature conservation projects in the Caprivi. These will form the focus of the following chapter.

---

[197] Singh, J. and H. van Houtum (2002), Post-colonial nature conservation in Southern Africa: same emperors, new clothes? *GeoJournal*, 58: 253–263 (here 254).

4 Wildlife and War (1975-1990)

Enduring lines of conflict between inhabitants, chiefs and the various governing authorities developed over the management of nature in the Caprivi from the beginning of South African rule in the region. These were most evident in relation to hunting regulations, access to natural recourses, and the protection of forests and rivers. It was also through these disputes that key questions of authority and governance were contested. From at least the 1960s onwards, South Africa exercised its power over the Caprivi through a combination of military force, economic development strategies, and environmental knowledge production. All of these policies came together in the late 1970s and the 1980s in the research and protection of what was increasingly seen as the Caprivi's most valuable asset, its 'charismatic' wildlife.[1]

The growing focus on wildlife conservation in the Caprivi in the late 1970s emerged as the wildlife population in the region diminished rapidly. This was caused predominantly by the SADF's presence in the area. The civil and military authorities in the Caprivi, however, sought to take advantage of this situation to present themselves as the would-be saviours of local fauna. This message was imparted in a number of ways, including via the production of ecological knowledge in the form of academic research or surveys as well as through more direct propaganda. The authorities' mounting interest in wildlife conservation also gave rise to an increase in the demand for labour. Game guards were introduced in the area from the mid-1970s, while SADF personnel became more frequently involved in matters concerning wildlife.

Unique to the Caprivi was the high military strategic value which it held for its South African occupiers and the significant influence which the military, police, and intelligence services could thus exert over the territory's civil administration and its nature conservation division. Three aspects of the militarisation of the Caprivi went hand in hand with wildlife conservation. Firstly, the SADF is today considered to have been the primary cause for the reduction of wildlife numbers in the area during the 1970s. Secondly, military reconnaissance and wildlife protection officials shared a joint interest in increasing their knowledge of the environmental features of the region. The SADF was thus happy to offer its support to the civil administration's endeavours in wildlife conservation by surveying the wildlife. Thirdly, the SADF sustained a narrative of promoting wildlife conservation within its

---

[1] The term 'charismatic wildlife' is often used for large wildlife which are favourites of trophy hunters and safari tourists. This includes the 'Big Five' of lion, elephant, rhinoceros, buffalo and leopard, but can also refer to rare species which can only be found in specific areas, such as the lechwe antelope in the Caprivi.

own bases. This allowed the SADF to portray itself as safeguarding the beautiful Caprivian natural environment from the threat of alleged 'communists' and 'terrorists', while providing legitimacy for some of its military activities in the region.

Unlike for development projects in the areas of fishery and forestry, which the South African authorities saw as a win-win situation which would bring with it both profit and the goodwill of the local population, many South African officials saw a political risk in the protection of wildlife. As DP, one of the first South African game wardens in the Caprivi, emphasised, nature conservation was unlikely to have been seen by local inhabitants as a source of income in the 1970s. Instead, he argued, it would more plausibly have turned Caprivians against the SADF, because inhabitants would see conservation measures as restricting their access to wildlife. As he observed, "[n]o one was prepared to upset the local situation by declaring protected areas as long as the Caprivians were willing to fight SWAPO".[2] Despite the authorities' fears that wildlife conservation could lead to resistance among subjects who had otherwise proven loyal to South Africa, the protection of wildlife became a central aim for the South African authorities in the Caprivi from the mid-1970s and especially in the 1980s. By the time Namibia became independent, the authorities in the Eastern Caprivi had proclaimed two national parks, established new wildlife conservation legislation, and drawn up plans for the growth of tourism in the area.

The Diminishing Wildlife Populations in the Caprivi

From the Protection of Huntable Game to the Preservation of Endangered Species

As with forestry and fishery, questions relating to wildlife conservation arose over the duration of South Africa's occupation. A central goal of colonial – and probably also pre-colonial – wildlife protection strategies had been to maintain game populations at a high enough level for them to sustain their rate of reproduction. In this way, a steady 'supply' of huntable wildlife could be guaranteed. In the Caprivi, this understanding of wildlife conservation went back to at least the mid-nineteenth century, when only chiefs were permitted to hunt on so-called 'kings' land'.[3] This urge to protect wildlife for hunting reasons – sometimes in combination with veterinarian concerns – later led colonial administrations in

---

[2] DP, 28.02.2014, e-mail.
[3] Such clearly defined areas in which only the members of the ruling elite (chiefs, kings or queens) were allowed to hunt seem to have already existed in pre-colonial times and are documented from at least the mid-nineteenth century onwards. On so-called 'traditional' hunting in Namibia from a legal perspective, see: Hintz (2003): 16–28. For an example of how hunting and wildlife management were represented in ethnographic accounts of the Kavango and the Western Caprivi, see: Fisch (1994). On the role of hunting in Kaoko, see: Bollig et al. (2016).

Southern and East Africa to proclaim the first national parks at the beginning of the twentieth century.[4]

As I described in above, the Caprivi was the site of colonial attempts to establish a national park in 1937, when a plan to convert the entire Western Caprivi into a wildlife protection area to be "cleared of people and stock" first emerged.[5] After the Second World War, alongside ideas of preserving wildlife as a resource for hunting, an increasing awareness of the economic potential of (safari) tourism developed globally. This led to the proclamation of many more national parks in Southern Africa.[6] The opening of the Chobe National Park in 1954 along Botswana's border with the Caprivi was of particular importance for the Caprivi.[7] Although the park led repeatedly to conflicts with Botswana, it also engendered instances of cross-border co-operation, such as in the case of *Salvinia* eradication.[8]

Nature conservation strategies in line with today's understanding of the concept were only introduced into the Caprivi in the mid-1970s. These addressed the systematic preservation, protection, or restoration of the natural environment – including natural ecosystems, vegetation, and wildlife – often through the proclamation of nature conservation areas.[9] South Africa's increasing interest in wildlife protection in the Caprivi in the 1970s –

---

[4] In 1907 the German colonial administration proclaimed Game Reserve 2 – which later became Etosha National Park – because it feared the extinction of most local game due to overhunting (Dieckman 2007: 74–77). In South Africa, the Sabie Game Reserve was founded in 1898 and upgraded into the Kruger National Park in 1926 (Carruthers 1995). In Tanzania, plans to establish game reserves emerged in the 1920s, with an area which later became known as the Serengeti being proclaimed as a game reserve in 1921 (Neumann, R. (1995), Ways of Seeing Africa: Colonial Recasting of African Society and Landscape in Serengeti National Park, *Cultural Geographies*, 2(2): 149–169).

[5] However, as Boden and Taylor argued, this was mainly for veterinarian reasons, see: Taylor (2012): 65 and Boden (2005). According to one document, a plan to turn the Eastern Caprivi into a game reserve already existed in 1929, but no other evidence could be found to support this claim. NAN, SWAA, A503/4, Caprivi Zipfel: Handing over to the South West African Administration. 26 October 1929, p. 10.

[6] See Chapter 2 for my discussion of the particular example of the Western Caprivi, which was proclaimed a game park in 1964 but then declared a closed military zone in 1965.

[7] For a historical overview of Botswana's wildlife protection policies before 1953, see: Mutwira, R. (1989), Southern Rhodesian Wildlife Policy (1890–1953): A Question of Condoning Game Slaughter? *Journal of Southern African Studies*, 15(2): 250–262. See also the case study of the Moremi National Park: Bolaane, M. (2005), Chiefs, hunters and adventurers: the foundation of the Okavango/Moremi National Park, Botswana. *Journal of Historical Geography*, 31: 241–259.

[8] There were two main disputes which arose from the establishment of the Chobe National Park on Botswana's border with the Caprivi. Firstly, protected predators, such as lions, crossed the border and became a threat to cattle farmers on the Namibian side of the river. Secondly, Caprivians entered the park to hunt illegally. Reports and correspondence relating to such incidents can be found for the 1960s to the 1980s, e.g. in NAN, CAF, 6/19/8, Poaching. Similar disputes have arisen in post-independence Namibia, see Chapter 5.

[9] Park, C. and M. Allaby (2007), *Oxford Dictionary of Environment & Conservation*. Oxford: University of Oxford Press, p. 283.

a policy which ran the risk of alienating hitherto loyal subjects – might be connected to a concurrent growing global awareness of the imperative to protect the environment. With the growing international condemnatory pressure on South Africa to withdraw from Namibia, the global prestige which could be gained through the protection of wildlife represented an attractive prize for Pretoria.

Although the chronology of the emergence of environmentalism is contested, most scholars agree that its influence rose dramatically in the 1970s.[10] A series of events in the early 1970s was crucial in this regard. The first Earth Day was celebrated by millions of people across the United States in 1970.[11] Greenpeace was founded in 1971, while one year later the Club of Rome published its highly influential book on 'The Limits to Growth'.[12] An important series of environmental conferences also commenced in 1972 with the hosting of the United Nations Conference on the Human Environment in Stockholm.[13] Of particular significance for my study are the Convention on International Trade in Endangered Species (CITES), which was signed in 1973, and the 1979 Convention on the Conservation of Migratory Species of Wild Animals (the so-called Bonn Convention), which were both concerned with the protection of big wildlife.[14] That the two treaties were ratified by the otherwise internationally ostracised South Africa was not surprising, as the country saw itself as exemplary in its policies to protect wildlife and was indeed regarded internationally as a role model for conservation in Africa.[15]

The SADF and the Shooting of Wildlife

South Africa's aspirations to be seen as a pioneer in the field of wildlife protection stood in stark contrast to the situation on the ground in the peripheries of South African power, where the SADF became heavily involved in the trade of ivory and rhino horn in the 1970s.[16] As all of my interviewees confirmed, the massive decline in wildlife numbers be-

---

[10] For a focused discussion on the history of environmentalism, see: Armeirio, M. and L. Sedrez, (eds.) (2014), *A History of Environmentalism. Local Struggles, Global Histories*. London and New York: Bloomsbury, p. 9–11.

[11] Earth Day was introduced by the United Nations Educational, Scientific and Cultural Organisation (UNESCO) as an international day of action in support of environmental protection and has since been celebrated annually in over 190 countries worldwide.

[12] Meadows et al. (1972).

[13] Armeirio et al. (2014): 9–11. This conference was followed by a number of world summits on environmental and climate issues, among them Rio de Janeiro (1992 and 2012), Kyoto (1997), Johannesburg (2002), Nairobi (2006), Copenhagen (2009), Paris (2015) and Bonn (2017).

[14] Cioc, M. (2009), *The Game of Conservation: International Treaties to Protect the World's Migratory Animals*. Athens OH: Ohio University Press, p. 57.

[15] See e.g.: Carruthers (1995) and Rangarajan M. (2003), Parks, Politics and History: Conservation Dilemmas in Africa. *Conservation and Society*, 1(1): 77–98.

[16] Ellis, S. (1994), Of Elephants and Men: Politics and Nature Conservation in South Africa. *Journal*

gan in the Caprivi in the same decade.[17] Although the means to control wildlife had long been contested, game had hitherto flourished in the region. From the mid-1970s both the South African rulers and ordinary Caprivians started to fear the loss of all wildlife.[18] Decades later, most of my interviewees remained convinced that the South African military and police were primarily responsible for this decline through their indiscriminate and large-scale hunting and capturing of animals. However, as I will show, this reason was seldom identified in contemporary official accounts. Blame was instead reserved for changing flood patterns as well as the growing human population in the Caprivi and their hunting, herding and agricultural activities.

SS, who later became a game guard and now works for the Ministry of Environment and Tourism (MET) in Katima Mulilo, remembered that, as a teenager growing up in the Caprivi in the 1970s, he saw "these big South African army trucks filled with nothing but lechwes [antelopes]. Some of them were killed and some could have been captured by them [SADF]; some of our animals are in the Kruger National Park now."[19] He recalled how the police received new rifles in 1976 and thereafter how "those people really made destruction; they were shooting like you could not believe, those police officers".[20] SADF and SAP personnel also hunted destructively; according to SS, they even shot animals to test their new weapons. He remembered how "if you saw a helicopter passing, they would shoot and you would just go and pick up the meat".[21] The indiscriminate hunting of wildlife by SADF officers is also vividly recalled by those who worked for the Caprivi' administration or the SADF at the time. The former chief RM remembered that "South Africa had a lot of guns and a lot of big trucks that they used to poach with".[22] Two South African officials, BW and HS, both recalled a number of incidents in which they caught other South African officials hunting illegally.[23]

The hunting activities of the South African security forces can be grouped into different categories, including the high-level involvement of the SADF as an institution in the global

---

of Southern African Studies, 20(1): 53–69.

[17] E.g.: SS, 15.05.2014, Katima Mulilo; BW, 10.03.2014, Sedgefield; TC, 11.05.2014, Mutjiku; AC, 21.05.2014, Kongola, BM, 21.05.2014, Sibinda; SM, 27.04.2014, Windhoek.

[18] On elephants, see: Chase, M.J. and C.R. Griffin (2009), Elephants caught in the middle: impacts of war, fences and people on elephant distribution and abundance in the Caprivi Strip, Namibia. *African Journal of Ecology*, 47(2): 223–233 and Kumleben, M.A. (ed.) (1996), *Inquiry into the Alleged Smuggling of and Illegal Trade in Ivory and Rhinoceros Horn in South Africa: Report*. Durban, p. 28.

[19] BM, 02.10.2012, Katima Mulilo.
[20] SS, 15.05.2014, Katima Mulilo.
[21] SS, 15.05.2014, Katima Mulilo.
[22] RM, 29.05.2014, Chinchimane.
[23] BW, 10.03.2014, Sedgefield.

trade in ivory and rhinoceros horn, 'leisure' hunting for tusks and other personal trophies by military and police personnel, and the capturing of live animals for transfer to South Africa's national parks. In relation to high-level institutional involvement, Stephen Ellis and others uncovered the SADF's deep entanglements in international ivory and rhinoceros horn trafficking from Southern Africa.[24] Ellis demonstrated how South African counterinsurgency forces were involved in smuggling ivory and rhinoceros horn out of various war zones in Southern Africa to sell in Asia, and he revealed how leading nature conservation organisations, including the World Wide Fund for Nature (WWF) International, provided cover for this illicit trade.[25] The profits made from this trafficking were allegedly split between South Africa's military intelligence services, conservation groups and the traffickers themselves.[26] Ellis went on to argue that trafficking in ivory and rhinoceros horn was not only seen to offer an income for the apartheid state and its security organs, but also formed a part of South Africa's policies to destabilise its neighbours.[27] South African intermediaries imported raw rhinoceros horn and ivory from Angola, Zimbabwe and Mozambique and then re-exported this to Asia. They thereby not only supported organised poaching syndicates in neighbouring countries, but also opened up trafficking routes for other goods, such as drugs and weapons.[28]

Jan Breytenbach, the South African colonel who headed various special units in the Caprivi, confirmed that ivory was smuggled out of the region.[29] Unsurprisingly, however, he passed on the blame to the Military Intelligence Divsion (MID) for this poaching. As intelligence officials were not trained soldiers, but merely "civvies put in uniforms", Breytenbach argued that they had no special relationship to nature. He was adamant that "fighting soldiers" like himself would never trade in ivory because "we have lived in the bush our whole lives, we learn to have a respect for the bush and have a love for the bush and the animals in it."[30] According to Breytenbach, however, this love for nature did not extend to the SAAF,

---

[24] Ellis (1994).
[25] From 1975 untill 1993, WWF International was headed by the South African economist and businessman Charles de Haes, who had close connections to the upper echelons of apartheid South Africa's financial and political elite. He was recommended for this position by Anton Rupert, one of the richest South African businessmen and a member of the *Afrikaner Broederbond* until at least 1974 (Ellis 1994: 53–69). Rupert later co-founded the Peace Park Foundation, see Chapter 5.
[26] Ellis (1994): 54, 63–64.
[27] Ellis (1994): 57.
[28] Ellis (1994): 57.
[29] Reeve, R. and S. Ellis (1995), An Insider's Account of the South African Security Forces' Role in the Ivory Trade. *Journal of Contemporary African Studies*, 13(2): 227–243 and Kumleben (1996): 484.
[30] Quoted in: Reeve et al. (1995): 26.

which was accused of flying out the illicit haul of tusks and horns. In 1996 the Commission of Inquiry into the Alleged Smugglings and Illegal Trade of Ivory and Rhinoceros Horn in South Africa (commonly known as the Kumleben Report) concluded that the SAAF was directly involved in the smuggling of both resources. This was said to have occurred not only from Angola, but also from within Namibia, at the very least between 1978 and 1980.[31]

Thereafter, a commercial front company known as *Frama Inter-trading Ltd.* took over the transport of the tusks and horns. This was facilitated by an arrangement with the SADF and the police forces in Namibia, according to which the company's transports would not be inspected.[32] This command extended to civil nature conservation officials, who were ordered by higher-ranking authorities in Windhoek and Pretoria to let Frama trucks pass through their checks even if they found ivory among the loads.[33] Furthermore, while the Kumleben Report concurred with Breytenbach's claim that the MID had been primarily responsible for the ivory trade, it did not exclude the possibility that other SADF officials might have taken part in the smuggling or in the hunting of elephants and rhinoceroses.[34] Of particular interest for this study is Kumleben's fifth finding, which concluded that the involvement of the SADF and *Frama* in the ivory trade would have served as an invitation to other servicemen and civilians in Namibia to participate in this lucrative business.[35]

The frequency with which animals were shot and traded in the Caprivi is also reflected in many of the memories of my interviewees. HS claimed that Otto Graupner, who served as the nature conservation officer in the Eastern Caprivi in the mid-1970s, "didn't do much because there was just too much to do. Because there was a lot of illegal hunting, still, not only by the army and the air force but also by the local people. Black, white, everybody was helping".[36] SS remembered that it was also common for soldiers to shoot game from low-flying planes, "just to kill them".[37]

'Leisure' hunting and the live capture of wild animals was a common practice for numerous low-ranking SADF staff in the Caprivi.[38] For many Caprivians at the time, the shooting and capturing of wild animals by common soldiers was a very dominant feature of South

---

[31] Kumleben (1996): 129.
[32] *Frama* was established by the MID with the purpose of supplying UNITA with weapons and other military supplies. See: Naylor, R.T. (2008), *Patriots and Profiteers: Economic Warfare, Embargo Busting and State-Sponsored Crime.* Montreal and Kingston: McGill-Queen's University Press, p. 177.
[33] Polla Swart, 10.06.2014, Windhoek. See also Kumleben (1996): 125–129.
[34] Kumleben (1996): 128–129.
[35] Kumleben (1996): 125–129.
[36] HS, 10.03.2014, George.
[37] SS, 02.10.2012, Katima Mulilo.
[38] E.g.: AC, 21.05.2014, Kongola.

Africa's occupation. Inhabitants of the small Zambezi River island of Impalila recalled in an interview in 2014 that during the period in which the South African military base was situated on the island (1972–1989), most of the wild animals disappeared.[39] This observation is noteworthy, since large game had generally been absent from the island and small antelope and monkeys had predominated. This loss of small wildlife on Impalila suggests that hunting on the island was not primarily undertaken to supply the international ivory and horn trade, but was instead carried out by low-ranking soldiers who sought suitably-sized wildlife to take home to South Africa as pets or small trophies.

In 1977 J.K. Thompson, the director of the Cape Province's Department of Nature and Environmental Conservation, sent an angry letter to the director of State Veterinary Services in Pretoria, complaining about "the importation of wild animals from border military areas".[40] He reiterated that it was not allowed to import animals to the Cape Province even if the soldiers obtained an export permit from the region of origin, as animals brought from border areas "might easily introduce human or animal disease".[41] In this regard, he referred to the case of an export permit which had been awarded by an official in Katima Mulilo to a soldier who sought to take a monkey back to Cape Town. In a forwarded letter to the CAF in Katima Mulilo, the state Veterinarian in Pretoria re-emphasised that none of the veterinarians doing military service in the Caprivi were "entitled to issue any movement permits for animals or animal products from Caprivi".[42] Although the law clearly did not permit the export of animals from the Caprivi, the transfer of Caprivian fauna to South Africa nevertheless took place. The export of wildlife form the Caprivi was not only done illicitly by South African soldiers, but also officially by conservationists seeking to enlarge wildlife populations in national parks. A community leader in the Western Caprivi remembered that "they [the South Africans] even took zebras, some giraffes and transported them to the Kruger Park and the Etosha Park, along with some rhinos".[43]

Who Was to Blame?

Unlike the memories of my interviewees, contemporary governmental records did not ascribe the reasons for the decrease in wildlife in the Caprivi to the hunting activities of

---

[39] Members of the Impalila conservancy, 23.06.2014, Impalila.
[40] NAN, CAF 6/19/2, Thompson to the Director of Veterinary Services Pretoria, Importation of Wild Animals, 02 May 1977.
[41] NAN, CAF 6/19/2, Thompson to the Director of Veterinary Services Pretoria, Importation of Wild Animals, 02 May 1977. This claim must be understood within the context of the broader veterinarian policies and laws applied in the northern territories of Namibia, see: Miescher (2012a).
[42] NAN, CAF, 6/19/2, Director of Veterinary Services Pretoria to Bezuidenhout, Importation of Wild Animals, 11 May 1977.
[43] TC, 11.05.2014, Mutjiku.

military personnel or the export of live animals. Instead, South African officials blamed the decline on Caprivians. A report written in 1970 by the South African conservation expert K. Kettlitz, who had visited the Caprivi in order to make wildlife protection recommendations, clearly indicated the reasons which the South African government claimed to be responsible for the loss of wildlife. Kettlitz urged Pretoria to take measures to stop the decline in wildlife numbers before the local human population started to take off, as he predicted it soon would. He argued that it would be important to "help" Caprivians to introduce more productive agricultural methods so that expanding land use patterns would not destroy wildlife habitats.[44] Similarly, Jacobus du Plessis Bothma, a South African professor of biology and an advisor to the SADF, succinctly expressed South Africa's official stance on the loss of wildlife in the region.[45] After a visit to the Caprivi in 1982, he declared his disappointment at how few animals he had seen. Nevertheless, he argued that the low wildlife numbers were a result of past land-use patterns and seemed convinced that these had begun to change for the better after the SADF had moved into the area.[46]

The condemning of the local Caprivian population as the main threat to wildlife did not mean that there were no reports about servicemen or administrative personnel who illegally shot game. A widely-reported case occurred in 1971, when four white privates and three administrative officials were caught hunting an elephant in the Western Caprivi.[47] But such incidents were mostly presented as isolated examples of misconduct by a few ill-behaved individuals and not as a genuine cause for the diminishing numbers of wildlife. Furthermore, white people – especially those in high-ranking positions – who were caught violating hunting regulations were often not charged at all or only had to pay a negligible fine, as was the case in the above example.[48]

The decline in wildlife numbers in the Caprivi during the Namibian War of Liberation, along with a shift in international conservation paradigms away from the protection of huntable game towards the preservation of precious nature, led the South African government to adjust its wildlife conservation policies in the 1970s. Accordingly, emphasis was

---

[44] NAN, LKM, 21/1/2, Beskerming van Wild: Oostelike Caprivi Zipfel, 9 December 1970, p. 10–11.
[45] Bothma was in charge of advising the SADF on conservation issues. In this and other positions, he was also involved in conservation surveys in the Kaoko and other parts of Namibia and South Africa. He published widely on wildlife ranching and also co-authored popular books on wildlife and nature, see e.g.: Hall-Martin, C. Walker and J. du P. Bothma (1988), *Kaoko: The Last Wilderness*. Johannesburg: Southern Book.
[46] Nature Conservation in the Caprivi: SADF Battles to Save our Heritage, *Paratus*, 11, 1982, p. 11.
[47] E.g.: NAN, NAR 12/1, Chief Director Pretorius to Colonel Jacobs, Onwettige Jag van Wild in Wes-Caprivi, 25 October 1971.
[48] NAN, NAR 12/1, Regering van Kavango, Justisie: Onwettige jag van wild deur beamptes 18 Oktober 71.

now placed on a holistic promotion of nature conservation, but the South African authorities continued to show no appetite for acknowledging their own role in the decline of wildlife in the region.

Saving Wildlife?

South Africa's reactions to the diminishing numbers of Caprivian wildlife in the 1970s were a response to the supposed culpability of local people and a few errant white individuals. Crucially, this response had to be recognisable as such so that it could serve as a benevolent justification for the SADF's presence in the Caprivi and its military activities in the region. Ever closer co-operation thus evolved between the Eastern Caprivi's civil administration and the SADF. Together, they emphasised the gathering of detailed knowledge and research on local wildlife. The civil administration also introduced stricter hunting and conservation laws, before eventually establishing hunting reserves and national parks in the late 1980s. All of these measures required a rise in nature conservation personnel, not only in administrative positions, but particularly in the field.

The Recruitment of Game Guards

From 1972 or 1973, one of South Africa's first reactions to the threat of wildlife extinction in the Caprivi was to recruit local game guards. These guards took over wildlife-related responsibilities from the police. CC, one of the first game guards to be appointed, remembered that before he and his colleagues took over "the workers or the policemen rather were dealing with the law enforcement in helping protect the animals. By the time we joined in 1973 those people went to retirement, and some workers joined us and some joined other ministries."[49]

Game guards occupied a crucial role as the feet on the ground in the struggle to protect wildlife in the Caprivi. However, as archival records relating to their daily lives are rare, the following section is based heavily on interviews with former game guards. As many game guards spent their entire careers working in nature conservation in the Caprivi, they proved to be a highly valuable source of knowledge on the subject and opened up a range of different perspectives on various developments within the field. Three game guards are of particular interest due to the specific temporal and geographical contexts in which they worked.

---

[49] CC, 02.11.2015, Windhoek.

CC was born in the Eastern Caprivi shortly after the Second World War.⁵⁰ He lived in his home village in the eastern floodplains of the Caprivi until he was appointed as a game guard in 1972 or 1973. Initially he worked in his home area, but was soon transferred to the western regions of the Caprivi, where he was mainly on duty in the vicinity of what would become the Mudumu National Park. With the establishment of the park in 1990, CC was transferred to its head office, where he worked in various capacities until 2004.⁵¹

BN grew up near Sangwali in the southern Caprivi. Having previously worked as an unskilled agricultural labourer, he entered the field of nature conservation in 1979. He was initially stationed as a game guard, mainly around the subsequent Nkasa Lupala National Park.⁵² He then worked for different offices responsible for nature conservation in the Eastern Caprivi for nearly thirty years, including for the first Namibian Anti-Poaching Unit (APO) established after independence. In 2002 he was promoted to the role of a game ranger for the Caprivi Regional Service and opted to transfer to the eastern floodplains, where he felt it was easier to keep out of family and village disputes. He continues to advise the MET in court cases against poachers.⁵³

SS was born in the eastern floodplains, close to the border with Botswana, in the early 1960s. He became a game guard in 1986, mainly working for the law enforcement unit in the vicinity of the later Nkasa Lupala and Mudumu National Parks. In 1998 or 1999 he enrolled in a further education programme at the recently-established Southern African Wildlife College in the Kruger National Park in South Africa. He subsequently became a high-ranking official at the MET office in Katima Mulilo, where he was put in charge of communal conservancies in the Zambezi Region.⁵⁴

The term 'game guard' was used in Namibia and elsewhere in Southern Africa from at least the early twentieth century, although not in a consistent manner. In the Caprivi, game guards were known by various names at different times and places. In the Western Caprivi, the authorities introduced 'Bushman guards' in as early as 1947, with the aim not only to 'protect' the so-called 'Bushmen' from other groups and to generally maintain law and order, but also to protect game. ⁵⁵ 'Bushman guards' were also employed in other areas of Namibia, especially in and around Etosha.⁵⁶ They reached their highest number – sixteen

---

⁵⁰ CC doubed the official documents which state that he was born in 1949 and assumed that he must have been older when he started in the field of nature conservation in 1974.
⁵¹ CC, 02.11.2015, Windhoek.
⁵² Nkasa Lupala (often written as Nkasa Rupara) National Park was founded in 1990 under the name of Mamili National Park, before being renamed in 2013 (see also Chapter 5).
⁵³ BN, 17.05.2014, near Sangwali.
⁵⁴ SS, 02.10.2012 and 15.05.2014, Katima Mulilo.
⁵⁵ Taylor (2012): 67 and Gordon et al. (1992): 162.
⁵⁶ Dieckman (2007): 186–204 and Miescher (2012a): 176.

in the entire Kavango Region (including the Western Caprivi) – in 1962, but were still remembered by many of my interviewees in the Western Caprivi who also referred to them as game guards.[57]

In contrast, the term 'game guard' was not mentioned in the Nature Conservation Ordinance of 1927, which still applied in Namibia in the 1970s, nor in any of the various new Nature Conservation Acts drafted in the early 1970s by the Eastern Caprivi Legislative Council.[58] According to the planned new Nature Conservation Act of 1976, the only two positions which were to be introduced were 'field officers' and 'honorary nature conservators'.[59] Field officers were to have been appointed by the homeland government and given wide-ranging powers to enforce the new act. This would have included, among others, the right to search any land, vehicles or camps, to seize evidence, to "destroy" dogs, and, perhaps most importantly, the right to arrest and detain any individual suspected of wildlife-related crimes.[60] The honorary nature conservators were envisaged to be appointed after consultation with the traditional authorities to support traditional leaders in the implementation of the new legislation.[61] Neither role corresponds to the responsibilities assigned to the first game guards when they started their work in the Eastern Caprivi in 1972 or 1973. Game guards did not have as much power as was envisioned for 'field officers', nor did they work as honorary advisors for the traditional authorities.

Only in 1974 did a governmental report define the kind of work which the former game guards whom I interviewed remembered performing in the Eastern Caprivi. In this 'Final Draft for Nature Conservation Planning and Development in the Eastern Caprivi', it was proposed to create posts for "nature conservation officers". These "should be native Caprivians, and should have basic training in nature conservation philosophy and methods". [62] They were also to be responsible for "patrolling and supervision of game reserves; for law enforcement and problem animal control in game reserves and controlled

---

[57] Gordon et al. (1992): 162. And Interviews with AC, 21.05.2014, Kongola and TC, 11.05.2014, Mutjiku.
[58] E.g.: NAN, CAF, 1/3/1_2, Eastern Caprivi Legislative Council Draft Enactment, 1973 or NAN, CAF, 6/19, Republic of South Africa, Eastern Caprivi Legislative Council, Eastern Caprivi Nature Conservation Enactment. Draft Enactment, 1973.
[59] These two roles were derived from the South West African Nature Conservation Regulations gazetted in 1959, see: South West African Administration (ed.) (1969), Duties and Powers of Nature Conservators and Honorary Nature Conservators, *Official Gazette*, 2952, 03 January 1969. Windhoek: Government Printer, p. 31–32.
[60] NAN, CAF, 1/3/1_2, Eastern Caprivi Legislative Council Draft Enactment, 1973, p. 16–17.
[61] NAN, CAF 6/19, Republic of South Africa, Eastern Caprivi Legislative Council. Eastern Caprivi Nature Conservation Enactment. Draft Enactment, 1973, p. 22.
[62] NAN, CAF, 6/19/7, Final Draft for Nature Conservation Planning and Development in the Eastern Caprivi, 1974.

hunting areas" as well as for "law enforcement and data collection in areas outside game reserves".[63]

It is not clear how many game guards were employed in total in the Eastern Caprivi in the 1970s and early 1980s. What is known, however, is that after 1974 there were at least three pairs of game guards on duty at a time, with each team deployed in a different area.[64] Generally, game guards remembered their working conditions as having been very tough. They were forced to cope with numerous hardships in the field. Often stationed away from their families in an area which they did not know, they were only permitted to return to Katima Mulilo once a month to collect their wages. There were no possibilities to communicate with their families and they often received no more than the very basic supplies required to perform their work.[65]

The game guards' responsibilities can be grouped into three main areas – research or surveys, law enforcement, and public awareness – which all constituted key pillars of nature conservation in the Caprivi.[66] Although these responsibilities were regarded as separate and were sometimes performed by specialised game guards, there was usually no clear-cut division of labour between them. Former game guards recalled that they were active in all three areas and identified two other variables which impacted decisively upon their work: firstly, whether they worked inside a clearly-defined conservation area or "in the villages"; and secondly, whether they were employed in their home region or elsewhere.

The former game guards agreed that the particular combination of working within "the villages" and in the vicinity of where they lived as being the toughest situation. Their role was to visit villages to convince locals not to shoot game. BN remembered that until the late 1980s the relationship between most Caprivians and the game guards was very poor. As he recalled, "[i]t was not easy because people were used to eat [game] meat. To tell people, and even the chief, to stop eating meat and things like that was an insult". If game guards told the villagers that they could be arrested for eating meat, "they looked at you as if you were not normal".[67] CC was even more candid, recalling that "communities hated us very much". For him, game guards "really provoked" local residents by effectively telling them that they could no longer shoot game and would thus need to eat their cattle instead. Often game

---

[63] NAN, CAF, 6/19/7, Final Draft for Nature Conservation Planning and Development in the Eastern Caprivi, 1974, p. 6.
[64] CC and BN each worked in separate teams of two, while both maintained that at least one further team existed.
[65] CC, 02.11.2015, Windhoek and BN, 17.05.2014, near Sangwali.
[66] NAN, CAF, 6/19/7, Final Draft for Nature Conservation Planning and Development in the Eastern Caprivi, 1974, p. 3.
[67] BN, 17.05.2014, near Sangwali.

guards were chased away from villages and only rarely were treated to something to eat or a place to stay.[68]

The vehemence of the hate and anger directed towards game guards is surprising, because it is doubtful that their presence would ever have evoked sufficient fear to prevent villagers, and especially their chiefs, from hunting wildlife. The game guards were all young men, usually did not come from influential families, and were not properly armed.[69] In interviews with a former chief, who served from 1971 to 1987, and other elderly residents of the region, none could even recall the existence of any hunting restrictions, even though the new hunting laws had been imposed in the 1970s. According to the former chief, "when people wanted to go and hunt, they would just come and inform me [...] so the hunting would be done orderly."[70] A former *Induma* (village head) from Ihaha in the far east of the Caprivi remembered that it was still very common to hunt animals, including even elephants and lions, along the Chobe River in the 1970s and that "local hunters" only respected the hunting laws of their respective traditional authorities, remaining oblivious to any hunting laws imposed by the South African authorities.[71] At the time of my interview with him, he was unaware that a hunting reserve had been proclaimed along the Namibian side of the Chobe River in the 1960s.

This suggests that, at least for some villagers, there must have been other reasons to hate game guards than the fear of being denied access to game meat. Game guards were one of the few representatives of the South African civil administration whom rural residents in the Caprivi would have encountered. South African authority was generally channelled indirectly through chiefs and headmen. Regardless of their limited power, game guards would thus also have been perceived as agents of the apartheid state. CC touched on this when he described how he and his colleagues had been chased away from villages. As he recalled, "they told you: 'Go tell your government to collect the animals, go with them! We don't want you here!'"[72] Especially given the increasing recruitment of Caprivians for South Africa's paramilitary *Koevoet* unit from 1979, the game guards became ever more often seen as a potentially treacherous agent of occupation.[73]

The relatively low impact of the game guards' presence on hunting practices in the villages did not mean that wildlife protection had no effects on rural life in the Eastern Caprivi

---

[68] CC, 02.11.2015, Windhoek.
[69] Normally the game guards were unarmed, sometimes they had access to simple hunting rifles or shotguns (CC, 02.11.2015, Windhoek).
[70] RM, 29.05.2014, Linyanti.
[71] AM, 10.09.2015, Ihaha.
[72] CC, 02.11.2015, Windhoek.
[73] DP, 28.02.2014, e-mail.

in the 1970s. If they became aware of anyone who was contravening game laws, game guards were tasked with informing their superiors in Katima Mulilo so that "the whites from Katima could go behind the poachers".[74] They could also inform the SADF if military personnel were seen hunting illegally and did sometimes discover soldiers engaging in such misconduct.[75] More importantly, co-operation with the SADF and the police allowed game guards to become more effective in exercising their authority. Joint patrols were conducted, while in turn the SADF would sometimes request support from game guards if they caught a poacher.[76]

The nature of the game guards' work changed during the 1980s, when the first nature conservation areas were being planned. As their duties began to shift away from the villages and into the proposed conservation areas, game guards were tasked with setting up regional conservation offices within the envisioned conservation areas. At first, the offices were nothing more than simple camps where the game guards were obliged to stay. Moreover, they were no longer allowed to go into the villages during their shift and were fined if they did so.[77] CC remembered that the station which he helped to build in Mudumu was "deep in the forest".[78] He and his colleagues were

> dropped there on the station, supplied with a rucksack, blankets, tents, water and mealie meal [corn porridge]. Then you go into the bush and sleep under the tree. These patrols went on for four days, then you came back to the station, then you went on patrol again.[79]

SS even recalled that game guards would sometimes be dropped off at a station in the bush and then forced to walk back home to Katima Mulilo. As he remembered, "[c]oming back to Katima Mulilo could take three months, walking through the bush, in all corners of the area you got to control".[80]

During the 1970s and 1980s, game guards were crucial for the collection of zoological data which was later used to define which areas and animal species were to be singled

---

[74] BN, 17.05.2014, near Sangwali. However, according to BN, game guards did not always report such cases, sometimes for fear of retribution, sometimes as a result of inefficient means of communication with Katima Mulilo.
[75] SS, 15.05.2014, Katima Mulilo; CC, 02.11.2015, Windhoek and RM, 29.05.2014, Chinchimane.
[76] BN, 17.05.2014, near Sangwali.
[77] CC, 02.11.2015, Windhoek. It remains unclear why game guards were no longer allowed to enter the villages. However, given the militarised nature of the area, it is most likely that there were military-strategic and security reasons for this new rule which were intended to prevent interaction between game guards and local inhabitants.
[78] CC, 02.11.2015, Windhoek.
[79] CC, 02.11.2015, Windhoek.
[80] SS, 15.05.2014, Katima Mulilo.

out for protection. Many former game guards recalled this work favourably in comparison to their awareness-raising and law enforcement responsibilities. Although collecting specimens or counting animals in the bush was remembered as being hard, lonely and painful labour, game guards appreciated being spared tense interactions with village residents. CC described how the role mainly required game guards to "recognise the areas where animals were found and report what was found to the office".[81] To do this, they patrolled large sections of the area by foot, mostly in teams of two. The information which they gathered also proved to be valuable when the boundaries of the national parks were defined in the late 1980s.

All the interviewed former game guards described their work as interesting and most chose to continue in the role for the majority of their careers. Nevertheless, all agreed that they were faced with very harsh working conditions, met with antagonism from local communities, and received little support from their superiors in Katima Mulilo. According to the interviewees, this only changed after Namibia's independence in 1990. Thereafter, as BN explained, "the human rights started to work and they could no longer just drop you somewhere with no transport and nothing".[82] BN also regarded the modern weapons which were brought into the Caprivi in the 1990s by former PLAN fighters as helpful for countering poachers more effectively. Moreover, SS and CC both explained that tensions between nature conservation authorities, the police and traditional authorities eased after 1990, thereby opening up space for new approaches to nature conservation.

Producing Reports, Surveys and Maps for Nature Conservation

Alongside the employment of game guards, a second aspect of South Africa's wildlife protection policy in the Caprivi was the production of reports, surveys and maps to serve the purposes of nature conservation. These became an important basis for the establishment of the first nature conservation areas in the region towards the end of the 1980s.

The constitution of knowledge systems – including knowledge produced through the 'systematisation' of nature and based on scientific research, naming and mapping – was one of the key elements of imperial power in the nineteenth and early twentieth centuries.[83] In the Caprivi, this power/knowledge axis became visible once again in the interplay between environmental research, mapping and the militarisation of the region. This enduring alli-

---

[81] CC, 02.11.2015, Windhoek.
[82] BN, 17.05.2014, near Sangwali.
[83] On various aspects of the interplay between nature and imperialism, see e.g. the edited volumes: Beinart et al (2007) and Griffiths et al. (1997). On naming, see: Carter, P. (1987), *The Road to Botany Bay. An Exploration of Landscape and Histroy*. London: Faber and Faber, particularly p. 1–34. On mapping as a means of imperial control and conquest, see: Etherington (2007).

ance remained effective until at least Namibia's independence in 1990 and may, in some regards, persist into the present.

The fundamental importance that South African officials ascribed to the surveying and research of Caprivian nature mirrored the SADF's concern to understand a space which had endured as a war zone since the 1960s. Seen from the perspective of the SADF, helping the civil authorities to produce knowledge on nature and cooperating with it in other aspects of nature conservation became a further channel to exert military power. By acting together in what were supposedly the best interests of Caprivian nature, the civil and military authorities could also join forces to present the South African occupation as a benevolent endeavour which was ultimately for the benefit of the local population and their natural environment.

Though the different ruling authorities in the Caprivi all concerned themselves with the region's wildlife, whether through hunting activities or regulations, imprecise plans for nature conservation areas, or in conflict or co-operation with neighbouring territories in relation to the movement of wildlife, a lack of the scientific data necessary for effective nature and wildlife conservation strategies endured until the late 1960s.[84] For other areas of South Africa which later became homelands, the acquisition of environmental knowledge had already become a South African priority by the late 1950s.[85] However, it was only during the public hearings of the Odendaal Commission in 1963 when the surveying and control of animal movements – alongside the introduction of game reserves and closed seasons for hunting – was suggested as means of developing the Eastern Caprivi.[86] Although forestry and other fields of development did attract surveys and further research soon after the Odendaal hearings, it nevertheless took another ten years before the first experts in wildlife and nature conservation were sent to the territory.[87] Prior to this, a scientific survey on nature conservation, the Tinely Report, had only been conducted for the Western Caprivi.[88]

---

[84] Although there were no prior ecological surveys conducted for the Eastern Caprivi, various miscellaneous information on wildlife was gathered earlier, e.g.: Wilhelm, J.H. (1933), Das Wild des Okavangogebietes und des Caprivizipfels, *Journal of the South West Africa Scientific Society*, 6: 51–74.

[85] Carruthers, J. (2008), "Wilding the farm or farming the wild"? The evolution of scientific game ranching in South Africa from the 1960s to the present. *Transactions of the Royal Society of South Africa*, 63(2):160–181 (here 165–166).

[86] As suggested, for example, by Jack Ashwin, the manager of the Witwatersrand Native Labour Association post near Katima Mulilo (NASA, KC SWA, 72/35, Minutes of the public hearings, February 1963, p. 21).

[87] NAN, ARCAT, BB2598, Breitenbach, F. (1968), Long-term Plan of Forestry Development in the Eastern Caprivi Zipfel, George.

[88] NAN, ARCAT, BB0478, Tinley, K.L. (1966), Western Caprivi Conservation Area, South West Africa: A Proposal of Natural Land Resource Land Use, August 1966.

One of the earliest scientific reports on nature conservation in the Eastern Caprivi was the above-mentioned 1970 report by K. Kettlitz of the Nature Conservation Branch of the Transvaal Provincial Administration.[89] Kettlitz travelled through the Eastern Caprivi for two weeks, using land transport as well as routine surveillance flights in a South African Police helicopter. In his report, Kettlitz concluded that the territory's growing population posed the main threat to wildlife, but also noted that hunting by whites could become an additional risk factor.[90] His report emphasised that conservation was important for reasons of both local and national political relevance. In view of the impending establishment of a 'self-governing' Eastern Caprivi homeland, from when nature conservation would be, at least formally, a Caprivian responsibility, Kettlitz called for South Africa to provide all possible means of support for the new homeland's conservation division. This should be done in a very diplomatic, non-coercive manner, he recommended, by demonstrating to Caprivians how they themselves would profit from the protection of wildlife. He then listed possible benefits of wildlife conservation and discussed these in relation to applicability for the Eastern Caprivi.[91]

Kettlitz described the potential aesthetic and scientific advantages of wildlife protection as less relevant to "the Bantu", who, he argued, would not have the capacity to appreciate or understand them. He then listed further possible benefits of conservation, including religious, spiritual, educational, cultural and political values, but concluded with the general remark that "[t]he Bantu of East Caprivi do not understand and carry no interest in these values".[92] In his opinion, the only means to appeal to locals to assist in the protection of Caprivian wildlife lay in underlining its economic potential, particularly in the contexts of controlled tourism and hunting. This, Kettlitz proposed, could be achieved by promising to channel a percentage of the money spent in the Caprivi by tourists or on the meat of hunted animals to local communities. He thus anticipated a trend which would become heavily influential in nature conservation policy around the world in the early 1970s. After a decades-long search, this profit-orientated approach to wildlife conservation finally offered the ruling authorities in the Eastern Caprivi a viable option for 'developing' the territory.

Kettlitz emphasised this opportunity in a letter which he sent to the Department for Bantu Administration in Pretoria to accompany his report. In the letter, he summarised the

---

[89] NAN, LKM, 21/1/2, Beskerming van Wild: Oostelike Caprivi Zipfel, 3 December 1970. Like the above-mentioned Bothma, Kettlitz also worked for different government departments in the planned homelands while conducting scholarly research on wildlife and hunting, see e.g.: Kettlitz, K. (1962), Game on farms, *Fauna and Flora*, 13: 19–24.
[90] NAN, LKM, 21/1/2, Beskerming van Wild: Oostelike Caprivi Zipfel, 3 December 1970, p. 10.
[91] NAN, LKM, 21/1/2, Beskerming van Wild: Oostelike Caprivi Zipfel, 3 December 1970.
[92] NAN, LKM, 21/1/2, Beskerming van Wild: Oostelike Caprivi Zipfel, 3 December 1970, p. 11 (Translation of the Afrikaans original by the author).

most urgent nature conservation aims in the Caprivi and identified what he saw as the only way to realise these:

> Lechwes are not only of invaluable worth for the Bantu tribes of the Caprivi, but the Caprivi is also the only place in the Republic where this species occurs. This means that if we let the lechwe go extinct in the Caprivi, it would certainly provoke serious domestic and international responses. Because of the Republic's prestige in the field of nature conservation, we can hardly afford this. In the long term, the protection of lechwes can only occur on the basis of scientific knowledge. Therefore, I urge you to insist that this wildlife species is studied properly.[93]

He continued by requesting sufficient funds and personnel to undertake such surveys and he promised to search for suitable candidates.[94]

The quote draws attention to several reasons which underlay South Africa's growing interest in the research and protection of the rare lechwe as well as Caprivian wildlife in general. Firstly, Kettlitz reinforced the common perception that Caprivian flora and fauna was completely different from that found in the rest of South African territory. Secondly, he highlighted how important the protection of wildlife species, particularly those in the occupied territory of Namibia, was to sustain South Africa's international reputation as a leader in the field of nature conservation. Thirdly, he linked nature conservation to South Africa's stated goal of supporting local people in safeguarding anything which the occupying authorities defined as important for their economic development.

Kettlitz's proposals for investment in nature conservation in the Eastern Caprivi gained the attention of his superiors in Pretoria. In 1973 the biologists BW and Otto Graupner were transferred from the Transvaal Provincial Administration's Department of Nature Conservation to the Eastern Caprivi. Both already worked in the field of nature conservation in the Transvaal. In the Eastern Caprivi, BW focussed mainly on fisheries research and Graupner on wildlife management, but both worked closely together.[95] According to BW, they had been deployed to the Eastern Caprivi because the apartheid state saw the need for systematic research, surveys, and protection of nature in the region.[96] Because of the ongoing war there and the Caprivi's military-strategic importance, the two biologists were likely to have been closely screened to ensure their loyalty to the apartheid state.[97]

---

[93] NAN, LKM, 21/1/2, Kettlitz to Bantu Administration, Beskerming van Wild: Oostelike Caprivi Zipfel, 9 December 1970 (Translation of the Afrikaans original by the author).

[94] NAN, LKM, 21/1/2, Kettlitz to Bantu Administration, Beskerming van Wild: Oostelike Caprivi Zipfel, 9 December 1970.

[95] BW, 03.05.2013, e-mail.

[96] BW, 10.03.2014, Sedgefield.

[97] According to the historian David Anderson, such background screenings for civil servants were common practice in apartheid South Africa, particularly for those awaiting transfer to strategi-

One of the first tasks which they undertook was to produce a report on the state of nature conservation in the area and to recommend further measures in this regard. In their 1974 report on "Nature Conservation Planning and Development", the two conservationists emphasised why they regarded nature conservation as imperative.[98] They argued that nature should be protected in the Eastern Caprivi for various reasons, of which most can be seen as economic aims. BW and Graupner saw the flora and fauna of the Caprivi as a renewable resource which could unlock significant economic potential, not only for South Africa, but also to create jobs locally. They then declared that the protection of nature was important because "it forms part of the land".[99] This referral to being "of the land" might suggest that the two conservationists sought to highlight the point that though nature conservation had been practiced long before the arrival of 'Europeans' in the area, it should now be advanced by South African experts in a scientific manner. In the rest of the report, they repeatedly underlined the importance of using scientific knowledge to protect flora and fauna. "Research", BW and Graupner observed, "is necessary to collect information on the natural wildlife resources of the territory, so that these resources may be wisely managed".[100] They also saw it as particularly important in the Caprivi to conduct "regular censuses of animal populations, determination of movement patters of game and the causes of such movements, vegetation surveys [and the] ecology of important game species".[101]

The notion of wildlife as an economic resource was cited in the report as a central motivation for its research and protection. Moreover, it was also assumed that the economic development which would accompany wildlife conservation would also offer Caprivians the opportunity to earn an income. In order to realise this potential, BW and Graupner repeatedly emphasised that further investment in conservation research was essential: "Research is expensive and requires highly trained personnel; in the early stages, it may thus be advisable to have research projects undertaken by members of other departments, e.g. Transvaal Nature Conservation Division."[102]

---

cally sensitive regions (personal conversation with David Anderson).

[98] NAN, CAF, 6/19/7, Final Draft for Nature Conservation Planning and Development in the Eastern Caprivi, 1974.

[99] NAN, CAF, 6/19/7, Final Draft for Nature Conservation Planning and Development in the Eastern Caprivi, 1974. p. 1.

[100] NAN, CAF, 6/19/7, Final Draft for Nature Conservation Planning and Development in the Eastern Caprivi, 1974. p. 6.

[101] NAN, CAF, 6/19/7, Final Draft for Nature Conservation Planning and Development in the Eastern Caprivi, 1974, p. 8.

[102] NAN, CAF 6/19/7, Final Draft for Nature Conservation Planning and Development in the Eastern Caprivi, 1974, p. 4.

Their appeal for more support seems to have been heard. Shortly after the report was submitted, more conservation experts from the Transvaal Nature Conservation Division were transferred to the Eastern Caprivi and a budget was drawn up to employ game guards. The CAF is said to have even managed to acquire funds from the government of South Africa for a speedboat to assist with its ichthyological research. However, even more so than the Department of Bantu Administration in Pretoria, it was the SADF which came to provide the staunchest support for the surveying and research of Caprivian flora and fauna. Unsurprisingly the SADF also shared a strong interest in the results thereof.

Military Surveillance and Wildlife Protection

The SADF and the civil nature conservationists both shared a common interest in getting to know the Caprivi in precise detail. For example, natural features such as dense bush or swamps appear prominently on military maps of the area.[103] As one former member of the SAAF explained: "Knowing nature was and still is essential to win a war. Particularly in the Bush War, the bush was the only thing we shared with our enemies, for both of us, nature was enemy and ally."[104] While the fight against a hostile and at times brutal natural environment is a common trope in soldier memories of war, in the context of the Namibian War of Liberation nature has also been remembered as beautiful, vulnerable, and a key ally in the search for prime spots to launch attacks or take cover.[105] In his book which compared memories of South African and United States soldiers, Gary Baines observed that Namibian nature and terrain has been remembered by combatants as "both enemy and friend".[106] However, in order to fully harness its benefits and gain a strategic advantage over the enemy, Namibian nature first had to be researched and mapped in detail. The techniques which it thus employed to expand relevant spatial knowledge were identified as a strength of the SADF by a former PLAN fighter, who believed that "without knowing Caprivi's natural oddities, SADF would not have found us at all. But they had the techniques."[107] Indeed, across time and space, warfare and nature conservation have not only shared a long history

---

[103] Maps found in the archive of the South African Air Force Museum, Cape Town (no archival numbers).
[104] NN, 12.03.2014, Cape Town. Bush War was a commonly used term for the Namibian War of Liberation.
[105] For a typical description of warfare in and against a hostile nature, see e.g.: Marlantes, K. (2009), *Matterhorn*. Berkeley: El Leon Literary Arts. For a description of nature by a member of the SADF who was stationed in Northern Namibia, see: Breytenbach (1997).
[106] Baines, G. (2014), South Africa's 'Border War': Contested Narratives and Conflicting Memories. London: Bloomsbury, p. 42.
[107] CK, 09.05.2014, Ondangwa.

of common scientific cause, but also the same imperatives of keeping territory tightly controlled and clean of invaders.[108]

The SADF's second interest in nature conservation corresponded perfectly with the civil authorities' desire to buy Caprivian loyalty through 'development'. This interest derived from the SADF's strategy of 'non-combatant' warfare, as evidenced in particular in its 'Winning the Heart and Minds Campaign' (WHAM) and Civic Action Programme (CAP). Paul Dobson, a civic action teacher who was later imprisoned for desertion, and the peace activist Gavin Evans listed the main goals of these campaigns at the End Conscription Campaign Peace Festival held in South Africa in 1977:

> The Civic Action Programme is the principle instrument of this 'hearts and minds' campaign. The programme's motivation being, in essence, to win over the local black populace in whatever region of its operation, through actions designed, amongst others: a) to present the army as a 'friend' and 'protector', b) to alleviate, as far as possible within the given parameters, the people's socio-economic circumstances, so c) giving this 'target' (the people) 'something to defend'. d) to identify South Africa's 'real enemy', namely the ANC and SWAPO, and the threat both organisations pose.[109]

Lieneke Eloff de Visser has shown how the WHAM and CAP campaigns as well as other similar programmes were strongly based on two publications by a senior United States and South African army veteran respectively, in which they set out the basics for winning so-called counter-revolutionary wars and pinpointed the necessity of winning "the sympathy and support of the people upon whom the insurgents depend."[110] However, in practice, Eloff de Visser argued, the SADF, the police (and later *Koevoet*), and the civil administration authorities lacked a unity of purpose within the operational areas in northern Namibia, especially in the former Ovamboland. While the SADF attempted to establish 'good relations' with the local population in order to obtain information on SWAPO insurgents, the police sought to acquire intelligence through fear tactics and torture, especially via its paramilitary

---

[108] There is a growing literature on the shared epistemological, linguistic and material features evident in the control of both alien plants and people, particularly migrants. Most prominently, see: Comaroff et al. (2001). For a more recent account, see: Lidström, S., S. West, T. Katzschner, M.I. Pérez-Ramos and H. Twidle (2015), Invasive Narratives and the Inverse of Slow Violence: Alien Species in Science and Society, *Environmental Humanities*, 7(1): 1–40. On the example of aquatic plants, see: Murray, S. (2005), Working for Water's 'AlienBusters': Material and Metaphoric Campaigns Against 'Alien Invaders', *Critical Arts* 19(1–2).

[109] Historical Papers Research Archives, University of the Witwatersrand (HPRA), AG1977, End Conscription Campaign Peace Festival, Gavin Evans and Paul Dobson, Hearts and Minds, p. 8.

[110] Eloff de Visser (2011): 85–86; McCuen, J.J. (1969), *The Art of Counter-Revolutionary War: The Strategy of Counter-insurgency*. London: Faber; Fraser, C.A. (1964), Lessons learnt from past Revolutionary Wars, (unpublished manuscript, Pretoria).

wing, *Koevoet*.¹¹¹ Although this double-sided exercising of power could be understood as a carrot and stick approach of terror combined with protection, Eloff de Visser posited that similar differences in strategy were evident among the various branches of South African authority in the Caprivi. There, she argued, the CAP "undermined" the efforts of the weak civil administration to provide basic services; if it became clear that the few available public services were primarily provided by the SADF, it would be difficult to sustain the apartheid state's narrative of having created 'self-governing' homelands which would continue to function after the withdrawal of the SADF.¹¹² Ultimately, the imbalance in power between the civil administration and the SADF highlighted once again that the supposed development projects initiated by the South African government and the homeland's own government would remain ineffectual and subordinate to military aims and interests.

It remains unclear from the archival records and my interviews to what extent South African CAP members were involved in surveying and researching Caprivian nature. Nevertheless, they did 'support' the CAF, which was also responsible for wildlife and nature conservation in the territory, until at least 1981.¹¹³ Only then did the representatives of the wildlife division requested the SADF to withdraw its civic action support and declare themselves "capable of performing [their duties] without assistance from the army".¹¹⁴

Along with the 'support' provided by CAP officials, the SADF also promoted its own internal nature conservation programmes and regulations from the mid-1970s. According to EB, a major who served at the Environmental Coordination Office of the South African National Defence Force, the SADF drew up its own nature conservation policies in the 1970s after media reports in South Africa which accused it of destroying nature, and wildlife in particular, in its operational areas.¹¹⁵ In 1978 the SADF published an article in its own journal, *Paratus*, which declared that:

> In accordance with the current concern expressed by a large spectrum of the South African population for the preservation of our natural environment, the SADF has instituted far-reaching measures aimed at restoring and maintaining the essential but precarious balance between fauna and flora in those areas occupied by the SA Defence Force.¹¹⁶

---

[111] Eloff de Visser (2011): 91–94.
[112] Eloff de Visser (2011): 90–91.
[113] JL, 18.05.2014, Malengalenga.
[114] NAN, CAF, 1/1, Withdrawal of Civic Action Members of the South African Army, 8 May 1981.
[115] EB, 20.06.2014, Pretoria.
[116] Nature Conservation in the SA Defence Force, *Paratus*, August 1978, p. 34. This proposal was not so much aimed at maintaining a "balance between fauna and flora", but at establishing a means of tracking the conservation of endangered wildlife and plants as well as keeping "indigenous fauna and flora" protected from 'foreign' vegetation and game.

In accordance with these aims, Magnus Malan, the chief of the SADF, issued a nature conservation directive in 1976. This was to be adopted by all of the different branches within the SADF and was endorsed by the four South African provincial administrations, the SWA Administration, and the South African Department of Nature Conservation.[117] The directive called for the use of soldiers who were "qualified in fields related to conservation" to draw up proposals for nature conservation. They would thus be tasked with using "their knowledge [to] evaluate the various areas in terms of such variables as topography, geology, available water, potential for the introduction of fauna and flora in relation to existing biocontent, fire hazards and problems related to the control of poaching".[118] In particular, the latter point – the protection of wildlife and the fight against wildlife crimes – and the closely-related issue of the translocation of animals were discussed in numerous other articles in *Paratus* over subsequent years.[119] EB recognised that the SADF's protection of and research into wildlife was not undertaken out of an intrinsic concern for preserving nature, but, at least in Namibia, for two other reasons; namely, as part of the WHAM strategy and as a means of military reconnaissance.[120] Another reason for the SADF's growing 'interest' in nature and wildlife protection might be seen in the possibilities which conservation afforded to the organisation to present itself in a more positive light to the 'white' South African public, which was growing increasingly sceptical of the country's destructive wars in Namibia and Angola. Given that the SADF adopted nature conservation policies for these extrinsic reasons, it is perhaps less surprising that it was simultaneously involved in the illicit hunting and trading of wildlife in and from the Caprivi and elsewhere in Southern Africa.

The general directive adopted by the SADF in 1976 was followed by a more detailed policy directive in 1978.[121]. Its content supports EB's assertion that environmental research for the purposes of nature conservation was also important for military reconnaissance. The directive gave clear instructions that the SADF was to invest more into the scientific research of nature for purposes of conservation, criticising how "over the years the SA Defence Force has endeavoured, to protect fauna and flora as far as possible, without the ap-

---

[117] Nature Conservation in the SA Defence Force, *Paratus*, August 1978, p. 35.
[118] Nature Conservation in the SA Defence Force, *Paratus*, August 1978, p. 35.
[119] E.g.: 'SAW hou wild gesond en gelukkig op LMB Hoedspruit', *Paratus*, April 1980, p. 36; 'Nature Conservation and the SADF: Preserving our natural riches', *Paratus*, July 1980, p. 14–15; 'Die SAW is ook 'n troste bewaker van die natuur', *Paratus*, August 1980, p. 18–19; Nature Conservation in the Caprivi – SADF battles to save our heritage, *Paratus*, November 1982, p. 10–11; 'Hoedspruit haven of peace for wildlife', *Paratus*, June 1984.
[120] EB, 20.06.2014, Pretoria.
[121] NAN, CAF, 6/20/1, Nature Conservation in the SADF, SA Policy Directive, 4 January 1978. This directive was also sent to the civil administration in the Eastern Caprivi.

plication of scientific nature conservation measures".[122] To promote a change in approach, the directive instructed that all military personnel with an interest in nature conservation or an educational background relevant to the field should be supported in gaining more knowledge about the natural environment of the geographical areas in which they served. As key measures to protect game, the directive ordered that the SADF should keep track of all animals which were shot by the SADF and reduce these numbers to a minimum, as well as regularly conduct game counts and surveys, all in consultation with the respective departments of nature conservation in the organisation's various operational areas.

Mutual Practices of the Civil Administration and the SADF

In the Caprivi, two main research practices were employed by both the CAF and the SADF; namely, road track or cutline censuses and aerial photography. For the SADF, both practices were mainly used to conduct regular military surveillance, while nature conservation officials often utilised the data to map planned nature conservation areas. The results of these surveys were often detailed charts and maps of the region's natural features.

Mapping was a central practice for the South African occupation authorities in the 1970s and 1980s and became an effective means to exert spatial power.[123] As I argued above, the control of *Salvinia Molesta* as well as the commodification of Caprivian forests went hand in hand with the collection of spatial data and the production of maps. In relation to conservation discourse and practice in the Caprivi in the 1970s, mapping, as "a specific set of power-knowledge claims", served as a powerful vehicle for "defining and claiming space" and played a crucial role in both military and ecological surveillance.[124]

Road Track Censuses

A technique practiced in Namibia by both conservationists and the military to count and track the movements of wildlife and people were the so-called road track censuses or cutline counts. Cut-lines, or *kaplyne* in Afrikaans, had existed in Namibia since at least German colonial times, when they were initially created to control cattle movements for veterinarian reasons or to inhibit the spread of bushfires.[125] Later they proved to be of high military-strategic value for South Africa in its war in northern Namibia. From the late 1960s onwards, South African police and border control units intensified their efforts to cut lines of about three to ten metres in width through the bush vegetation along Namibia's northern border

---

[122] NAN, CAF, 6/20/1, Nature Conservation in the SADF, SA Policy Directive, 4 January 1978.
[123] Etherington (2007): 1–10.
[124] Crampton et al. (2006): 12; Wood (2006): 26.
[125] Miescher, G. (2009), Keeping the threats out: The Red Line and the War Zone (unpublished paper, University of Western Cape).

with Zambia and Angola.[126] The border could thus be more easily patrolled and controlled from trucks so as to prevent the clandestine movement of people and goods through the dense bush. With the intensification of the war in the 1970s, the SADF extended this network of cut-lines deeper into Namibian territory. This allowed SADF staff to use the lines to move around the bush faster and patrol the entire operational area more effectively.[127]

An ex-SADF soldier recalled in his personal account of the Namibian War of Liberation that a key function of the cut-lines was to render it possible for the SADF to track the footprints of enemy fighters:

> Running in lines from east to west were kaplyne. These were long sandy 'roads' stretching for miles, which were impossible to cross [without leaving traces]. They lay in a band between the border and just north of the farming areas, like Tsumeb, and often ran between farming fences. The army used a buffalo to drag a tree so that the kaplyne were swept clear daily and we could check for fresh spoor.[128]

The cut-lines were also very valuable for the civil authorities responsible for nature conservation. The cut-lines afforded game guards and conservation officials easier access to the bush, which was especially helpful when counting animals. The movement of wildlife was traced in exactly the same way as the SADF attempted to track down enemy combatants. Conservation officers and their game guards would clear and grate the cut-lines in the evenings. The following morning, with the help of so-called 'Bushmen Trackers', tracks which animals had left behind in the sand could be identified and counted.[129] The results of these counts were visually depicted on maps and statistically analysed in detailed charts.[130] This was a labour-intensive method, but it allowed for systematic research on animal movement patterns.

Aerial Photography and Mapping
A second practice which was used by the SADF as well as nature conservationists in the Caprivi was aerial photography. From its beginnings in the early twentieth century, aerial photography was promoted by armed forces across the world as a means to overcome the

---

[126] HS, 10.03.2014, George.
[127] A rough map of the most important cut-lines in the Eastern Caprivi was drawn by Ben van der Waal in 1976: NAN, CAF, 49/6/19–5, Road Track Census Map, 1976. There were also cut-lines in the Western Caprivi, but these could not be used by the civil administration because its officials had no access to the area (SM, 27.04.2014, Windhoek).
[128] Thompson (2006): 118. See also: Miescher (2009): 1.
[129] HS, 10.03.2014, George and BW, 10.03.2014, Sedgefield.
[130] NAN, CAF, 6/19/5 Road track census counting sheets, 1976 and NAN, CAF, 49/6/19–5, Road track census map, 1976.

inaccuracy of military maps.[131] In a Southern African context, the Anglo-Boer War (1899–1902) made it especially clear to British military strategists that accurate and detailed maps were essential for winning a war and served as a catalyst for the British military to undertake systematic mapping efforts.[132] Soon after the end of the Anglo-Boer war, mapping and survey units, supported by scouts, were introduced throughout the British Armed Forces to improve on the very basic cartographic data which had hitherto been available from combat zones. In Southern Africa, aerial photography became a common technique in military reconnaissance as well as cartography during the First World War.[133] However, South Africa's nascent Union Defence Force (UDF), which still relied heavily on British support at the time, fought its South West African Campaign (1914–1915) largely on the basis of conventional reconnaissance undertaken by scouts.[134] It was only during the Second World War that the UDF's survey companies became famous for the support which they provided to British and US American troops in Europe by producing accurate military maps from aerial photographs.[135]

When the South African Police and subsequently the SADF increased their presence in northern Namibia from the late 1960s, they still had to rely on very basic maps. The only relatively detailed map of Namibia which was available at the time was the so-called 'farm map'. This was actually a set of maps which charted all privately-owned farms in Namibia, but the entire area to the north of the Red Line, where no private farms existed, only appeared in the form of contours.[136] To overcome this inadequate mapping, the SADF began to invest in improving the cartographic coverage of territory between the Red Line and Namibia's northern border, and later extended its efforts to map parts of southern Angola.[137] This work was mainly undertaken by three survey squadrons responsible for gathering geo-

---

[131] Jacobs, A. and H. Smit (2004), Topographic Mapping Support in the South Africa Military During the 20th Century, *Scientia Militaria*, 32(1): 32–50 (here 32).

[132] The Boer forces seemed to have relied more on the personal knowledge of the areas where they fought which most of their combatants possessed (Jacobs et al. (2004): 36).

[133] Hodson, Y and A. Gordon (1997), *An illustrated history of 250 Years of Military Survey*. Tolworth: Military Survey Defence Agency, p. 15–16.

[134] Jacobs et al. (2004): 36.

[135] On the history of the South African Air Force, see also: Dedering, T. (2015), Air Power in South Africa, 1914–1939. *Journal of Southern African Studies*, 41(3): 451–465.

[136] For a general history of cartography in Namibia, see: Moser, J. (2007), Untersuchungen zur Kartographiegeschichte von Namibia: Die Entwicklung des Karten- und Vermessungswesens von den Anfängen bis zur Unabhängigkeit 1990 (PhD thesis, University of Dresden) and the short article: Moser, J. (2008), Untersuchungen zur Kartographiegeschichte von Namibia: Die Entwicklung des Karten- und Vermessungswesens von den Anfängen bis zur Unabhängigkeit 1990. *Cartographica Helvetica: Fachzeitschrift für Kartengeschichte*, 38: 41–43. See also: Leser (1982) and Miescher (2012b): 777.

[137] Leser (1982).

graphical data and producing corresponding maps. Especially in the early 1980s, but also to a less frequent extent in the 1970s, field-mapping officers were deployed to all large military camps in M'pacha, Rundu and Oshakati to "annotate, update, reproduce, and supply maps as needed by the territorial forces".[138] Map production was assisted by the SAAF, which provided survey flights and high-resolution aerial photographs. On the ground, field-mapping officers were supported by terrain evaluation specialists, who were often civilians. For example, a preliminary terrain survey in southern Angola was conducted by Hendrik Johannes von Moltitz Harmse, a geologist from Potchefstroom University (now North-West University) in co-operation with Denzil Edwards from the South African National Botanical Institute.[139] Together, they proved that it was possible to obtain useful geographical and ecological information on a combat zone outside of the state's boundaries.[140] Their report also laid the foundations for the establishment of a specialised military geographical unit which was based at Potchefstroom University and was responsible for conducting terrain evaluations in northern Namibia and southern Angola.[141]

The maps which were produced on the basis of the newly acquired geographical data obtained through aerial photography and territorial surveys were the first detailed maps of northern Namibia and were used for military and civilian purposes. One of the earliest of these maps was the so-called 'Chinery's map', a map for pilots which documented northern Namibia, including the Caprivi, as well as southern Angola and neighbouring parts of Botswana and Zambia.[142] It was published in 1978 and combined sections from several smaller detailed survey maps.[143] The survey maps depicted natural features and were still being used by the civil administration's nature conservationists and foresters as late as the mid-1980s.[144]

The civil authorities in the Eastern Caprivi utilised aerial photography to count wildlife and draw maps of their distribution. Aerial surveys were conducted by the South African Air Force, particularly during periods with lower levels of military activity.[145] The flights were made in a Mirage IIIR2Z aircraft which was fitted with a specially-mounted aerial re-

---

[138] Jacobs et al. (2004): 47.
[139] Jacobs et al. (2004): 47.
[140] In 1975 or 1976, the SADF also succeeded in stealing a set of maps from the MPLA in Angola to use as a basis for their own maps. According to rumour, however, the maps which were produced from this data never reached the operational area, having instead gone missing in Grootfontein (Jacobs et al. (2004): 46).
[141] Jacobs et al. (2004): 47.
[142] Named after Ed Chinery, who served for the SAAF in the Namibian Liberation War.
[143] Liebenberg et al. (2010). Inner cover.
[144] BW, 10.03.2014, Sedgefield and PS, 10.06.2014, Windhoek.
[145] DP, 28.02.2014, e-mail; BW, 10.03.2014, Sedgefield, SM, 27.04.2014, Windhoek.

connaissance platform. A former SAAF member explained in an interview that the control stick of this particular fighter aircraft had two buttons: "Left bomb, right picture".[146] The Mirage IIR2Z was the fastest fighter jet the SAAF had in its possession. It was involved in reconnaissance flights into Angola, but also in attacks on military and refugee camps, such as the Cassinga Massacre in 1978.[147] The photographs which it took were not only used by the SADF's aerial photograph interpreter to extract geographical and cartographical information and identify built objects and natural features, but also by ecologists and conservationists to gather information on wildlife and vegetation. Other aircraft which were employed for animal counts were the Cessna 185 and the Allouette helicopter. These aircraft would be flown by SAAF pilots and staffed with a nature conservation expert and one or two counters, whose role it was to count animals from the air, mostly without taking any photographs.[148]

In 1976, based on the data obtained from the aerial surveys, the road track censuses, and the manual counts by game guards, a South African nature conservation officer in the Caprivi sketched a map of potential nature conservation and hunting areas in the Eastern Caprivi by adding the proposed reserves to the same hand-drawn maps which he had earlier produced himself to use for the *Salvinia molesta* monitoring campaign (Figure 1).[149] He remembered that: "We did not have any support and drew our own maps. I actually hand-drew a map of my study [area] from aerial photos I got from the Air Force".[150] According to the conservation officer, cartographic facilities only became more readily available in the 1990s for non-military uses in "remote areas" such as the Caprivi.[151]

In a report which was sent to officials in Pretoria and the Eastern Caprivi along with the map of the proposed reserves, it was recommended that the first step towards the goal of proclaiming nature conservation areas should be to conduct a further "assessment of present status of wildlife in the area and of present hunting pressure".[152] The boundaries of the nature conservation areas which were proposed were based mainly on what were considered to be the natural distribution patterns and movements of animals.

The conservationist's stated goal was to proclaim nature reserves which would ensure that "all habitat types in Caprivi" would be conserved, thereby "preserv[ing] a representation

---

[146] CT, 26.03.2014, Cape Town.
[147] Kjolberg, J.-O., *The Dassault Mirage III in South African Service*, www.mirage4fs.com/slides15.html [accessed 20.07.2006] on the Cassinga Massacre, e.g.: Williams (2015): 30–61.
[148] NAN, CAF, 6/19/7, Aerial Census of Wildlife in the Eastern Caprivi During August 1980, 1980, p. 2.
[149] NAN, CAF, 6/19/5, Proposed Nature Reserves Caprivi, Map by Ben C.W. van der Waal, 1976.
[150] BW, 03.05.2013.
[151] BW, 03.05.2013.
[152] NASA, BAO 20/271, Nature Reserve Planning for Caprivi, 1976.

of the available habitats and wildlife".[153] However, DP, a South African game warden who was stationed in the Eastern Caprivi at the time, held a different memory of how suitable wildlife protection areas were decided upon. According to him, "[o]ur protected areas were entirely based on the traditional hunting areas of local chiefs" and therefore did not represent a cross-range of habitat types.[154]

While the surveying of wildlife was carried out at a rapid pace, the conservation areas proposed on the 1976 sketch map did not materialise in the form in which it was recommended. However, the proposals did become a spatial blueprint for subsequent conservation plans, and the map later served as a basis for the demarcation of the national parks which were established in the eastern parts of the Eastern Caprivi after the responsibility for nature conservation in the territory was transferred to Windhoek in 1980.[155]

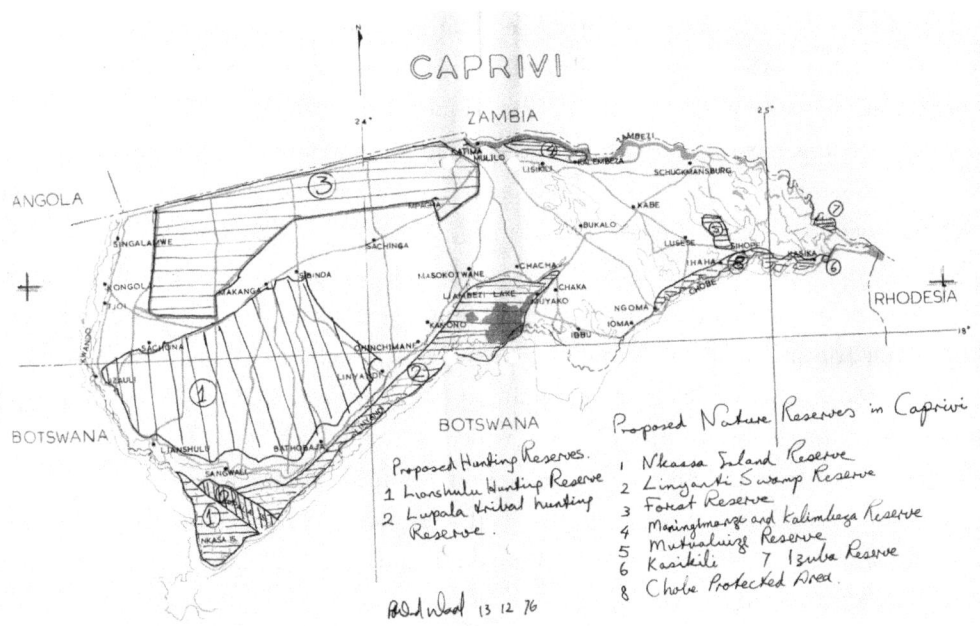

Fig. 1: Proposed Nature Reserves Caprivi, Map by Ben C.W. van der Waal, 1976. NAN, CAF, 6/19/5

---

[153] NAN, CAF, 6/19/5, Nature Conservation Work Programme, 1976/1977, p. 2 and NASA, BAO 20/271, Nature Reserve Planning for Caprivi, 1976.
[154] DP, 28.02.2014. As I will show the following section, the notion of 'chief's land' was raised again when the demarcation of the first conservation areas began on the ground.
[155] PS, 03.08.2012, Windhoek.

The Proclamation of National Parks in the 1980s

Politics and War in the 1980s

In the last decade of South Africa's occupation, Namibia's political-administrative structure became increasingly complex and the war in the north of the territory intensified. In 1977, after years of intense domestic and international pressure and protests, South Africa abolished the post of Administrator of South-West Africa. The new position of Administrator-General, still appointed by the South African government, was assigned more governmental authority within Namibia and given the main task of preparing for the creation of an independent, but still white minority-ruled – or at least racially organized – Namibia.[156] The first Administrator-General, Justice M. Steyn, ended some aspects of 'petty apartheid', such as the legislation which prohibited inter-racial marriage, and softened elements of the pass and labour laws; for example, the forced deportation of unemployed Africans from urban areas ceased, but black Namibian still required permission to work in towns and cities.[157] Nevertheless, the most important arms of government remained under direct South African control, including, most significantly, the police and military forces. Internal elections for a Constituent Assembly in 1978 were boycotted by SWAPO and not recognised internationally.[158] They were won by the Democratic Turnhalle Alliance (DTA), a white-dominated political grouping of representatives from different 'population groups'.[159] This DTA-government was in power until its collapse in 1983; in 1985 it was replaced by a similar experiment, the interim Transitional Government of National Unity. Both governments were meant to sustain South Africa's ambition of maintaining its power over Namibia by establishing a pro-forma or internally independent state which was still ruled by a white minority and whose powers remained subject to the veto of the Administrator-General.[160]

Without going into the complex details of the many different administrative bodies in Namibia in the 1980s and their respective relationships to South Africa, two aspects of the period are worth noting in relation to the contemporary political context of the Caprivi.[161] Firstly, the DTA drafted a constitution for a system of rule which was based

---

[156] Wallace (2011): 291–292.
[157] Wallace (2011): 287.
[158] SWAPO boycotted the election after South Africa refused to allow the UN to organise or supervise the poll and did not agree to the release of politicians who were still imprisoned under the so-called Terrorism Act. See: Mashuna, T. (2015), The 1978 Election in Namibia. In J. Silvester (ed.), *Reviewing Resistance in Namibian History*. Windhoek: UNAM Press, p. 178 –191 (here 186).
[159] After the elections, Namibia was increasingly called 'SWA/Namibia'.
[160] Wallace (2011): 291–302.
[161] For a detailed overview of Namibia's political-administrative system, see: Du Pisani, A. (2000), State and Society under South African Rule. In C. Keulder (ed.), *State, Society and Democracy: A*

on a three-tier system of government with a federal structure and responsibilities divided between central, ethnic, and local authorities made up of elected representatives. The second tier, represented by each of the eleven ethnic administrations of the homelands, would possess authority over all members of the designated ethnic groups, even if they were not resident in their respective ethnic areas. This revised political-administrative system should thus be understood as constituting "a reinvention of the Bantustan policy [...] rather than its abandonment".[162]

Secondly, South Africa's attempts to 'namibianise' their security forces in Namibia led to the foundation of SWATF in 1980 and SWAPOL in 1981. While both still fell within their respective South African chains of command, their upper ranks consisted primarily of white Namibians.[163] Also since the late 1970s, so-called local battalions were established for the different 'ethnic' groups of northern Namibia. Most famous were the 101 Battalion, consisting of Oshivambo-speaking soldiers, and the 201 Battalion, which was mainly made up of so-called 'Bushmen soldiers' and was based at Omega in the Western Caprivi. Although the SADF had started to employ Khwe- and Ju-speakers as trackers in 1974, 201 Battalion was its first unit almost exclusively comprising Khwe- and !Kung-speaking soldiers.[164] Working for the SADF was often a coping strategy for them to compensate for the loss of income from agriculture and cattle which they incurred as a result of the severe drought of 1980/81.[165]

The most notorious unit of the local security forces was *Koevoet*, a counter-insurgency unit within the South West African Police which was founded in 1979 and mainly consisted of white South African commanders and black Namibian fighters. Their excessively violent campaign against SWAPO and PLAN, their willingness to engage in brutal forms of torture, and their indiscriminate use of violence against civilians rendered them responsible for most of the harm suffered by the civilian population in northern Namibia in the 1980s.[166] The already-mentioned 32 'Buffalo' Battalion, which was founded in the mid-1970s, was a similarly brutal special unit within the SADF. Particularly active in the 1980s, it largely comprised former FNLA fighters from Angola and was founded and commanded by the

---

Reader in Namibian Politics. Windhoek: Macmillan Education: 49–76 (here 68–74).

[162] Wallace (2011): 287.

[163] See Chapter 3 on the discussions around the exact dates of the establishment of the units. No Namibian citizenship existed until 1990; for the pre-independence period, the noun 'Namibian' thus refers to residents of Namibia. For the general sake of consistency and because SWATF still fell within the structures of the SADF, I continue to use the term 'SADF' in this chapter. See also: Du Pisani (2000): 61.

[164] Taylor (2012): 73.

[165] Wallace (2011): 294.

[166] Wallace (2011): 296.

aforementioned Jan Breytenbach, who earned fame for his books on warfare and the Caprivian wildlife.[167]

The war on both sides of the Namibia-Angola border became more direct and violent in the 1980s, leading to the death of thousands of civilians in northern Namibia and to hundreds of thousands of civilian casualties in southern Angola.[168] This intensification of the war had its roots in the internal developments in Namibia discussed above, but also in the changing global political climate of the late Cold War era. New right-wing governments came to power in the United States (1981) and the United Kingdom (1979) which both regarded apartheid South Africa as a bastion against the spread of communism in Africa. The Western Bloc's now more stridently anti-communist stance was also reinforced at a Southern African regional level by P.W. Botha's rise to the Prime Minister of South Africa in 1978. As a hawkish former defence minister, Botha was prepared to apply whatever force was necessary to sustain white hegemony in South Africa and Namibia.[169] By the end of the 1970s, he had introduced his infamous 'total strategy' to achieve this goal. This consisted of a range of measures, from conventional military interventions in neighbouring countries and counter-insurgency measures against the anti-apartheid and Namibian liberation movements to, among others, the assassination of political enemies, car bombings, and armed raids in townships.[170]

The second half of the 1980s saw a rise in domestic protests in Namibia, particularly by recently-established student and women's organisations, which further served to undermine South Africa's continued occupation. [171] In August 1988 the Protocol of Geneva was signed, which led to the ultimate agreement by which Cuban and South African troops would be

---

[167] Subjective histories of Battalion 32 are told in many popular books, mostly written by former members of the unit. See e.g.: Nortje, P. (2003), *32 Battalion: The Inside Story of South Africa's Elite Fighting Unit*. Cape Town: Zebra Press; for Jan Breytenbach's own memoirs, see: Breytenbach, J. (2014), *The Birth and Growth of 32 Battalion from Former Enemies and Terrorists into Decorated Soldiers*. Pretoria: Protea Book House. A critical and detailed historical account of Battalion 32 has yet to be published.

[168] On civilian casualty figures for Namibia, see e.g.: Akawa, M. and J. Silvester (2007), 'Their Blood Waters our Freedom, Naming the Dead: Civilian Causalities in the Liberation Struggle', *The Namibian*, 24.08.2007. Based on newspaper reports, Akawa and Silvester estimated that at least 1,268 civilians died in the war in Namibia in the period from 1979 to 1989, probably much more. Dale (2014: 13) posited a total war death count in Namibia of between 12,000 and 25,000 individuals, including combatants, with most deaths occurring in the 1980s. A report by the UN estimated that over 300,000 children were killed in the war in southern Angola in the period from 1980 to 1989 alone (Wallace 2011: 300).

[169] Du Pisani (2000): 68–74.

[170] For an overview of the 'total strategy' or 'total onslaught' in South Africa, see e.g.: Coleman, M. (1998), *A Crime Against Humanity: Analysing the Repression of the Apartheid State*. Cape Town: Mayibuye History Series. On Namibia, see e.g.: Silvester et al. (2014).

[171] Wallace (2011): 305.

withdrawn from Angola and South Africa's occupation of Namibia would be terminated (Brazaville Protocol, 13 December 1988). In February 1989, the United Nations Transition Assistance Group (UNTAG) was deployed to Namibia to oversee the country's transition to independence. After a final large attack on PLAN guerrillas in April 1989, the SADF finally withdrew from Namibia, *Koevoet* was demobilised, and most exiled Namibians returned home. Parliamentary elections were held in December 1989. These were won convincingly by SWAPO with a 57% share of the vote, ahead of the DTA (28%) and a number of smaller parties. On 21 March 1990, Namibia declared its independence. This was followed by the implementation of the new national constitution.[172]

The End of the Eastern Caprivi Homeland

Unlike in the rest of northern Namibia, the war in the Eastern Caprivi was not significantly fiercer in the 1980s than in earlier years. After Angola's independence in 1975 and SWAPO's internal troubles in Zambia in 1976, the main theatre of war gradually shifted westwards from the Caprivi, especially after SWAPO transferred its headquarters from Lusaka to Luanda in 1979.[173] A further reason for the milder military activity in the Caprivi might have been South Africa's reaction to PLAN's mortar and rocket assault on Katima Mulilo in 1978, which was prepared from Zambia and killed at least ten South African civic service members.[174] This attack is also described as leading to a shift in South Africa's military strategy towards Zambia. Pretoria now sought to 'persuade' Lusaka to cease support for liberation organisations by 'luring' it with promises of economic co-operation.[175] Nevertheless, the SADF remained conspicuous in the Eastern Caprivi, while the Western Caprivi continued to be a closed military zone.

The most important administrative change in the Eastern Caprivi in the early 1980s was the discontinuation of the South Africa-administered Eastern Caprivi homeland in 1980. After forty-one years of more or less indirect rule from Pretoria, authority for the territory, as one of the eleven new ethnic second-tier administrations, was transferred back to the SWA/Namibian government in Windhoek. The new second-tier authority in the Eastern Caprivi consisted of an Executive Committee and a so-called Administration for Caprivians, with both split according to the Eastern Caprivi's two recognised ethnic groups into parallel

---

[172] Wallace (2011): 306–307.
[173] Eloff de Visser (2013). In 1976 internal disputes within SWAPO between the organisation's leaders and PLAN fighters led the Zambian Defence Force to imprison many PLAN members at the request of SWAPO cadres in Lusaka. On these conflicts, see: Williams, C.A. (2011), Ordering the Nation: SWAPO in Zambia, 1974–1976. *Journal of Southern African Studies*, 37(4): 693–713. See also: Williams (2015).
[174] Kangumu (2011): 156–158.
[175] Eloff de Visser (2013).

structures which were headed by the groups' respective chiefs. While the Administration for Caprivians oversaw most areas of governance – including land distribution, health care, schooling, social services, agriculture, forestry, and culture – other areas became the responsibility of the central government in Windhoek. These included some aspects of public health and epidemiology, water supply, transport, and nature conservation. The fact that agriculture and forestry remained the responsibility of the Administration for Caprivians, while nature conservation was run from Windhoek indicates the importance and strategic significance which was attached to conservation in the 1980s.[176]

Most of my Caprivian interviewees did not recall any change in the way in which they were governed after this transfer of power. Nevertheless, as occurred after previous transfers of governmental authority in the Caprivi, the administrative changes were accompanied by a series of reports and surveys. The most extensive of these was the 'Eastern Caprivi Regional Development Strategy', an over 200-page report compiled by a group of 'experts' from South Africa in 1983.[177] It was based on several months of fieldwork and included a detailed description of the Eastern Caprivi's political, social and economic state as well as recommendations for its further economic development. The territory's most significant areas of economic potential were identified as lying in agriculture, forestry, fishing and, nature conservation and tourism.[178] This report is one of the very few administrative documents from the 1980s which concerns the Caprivi and is currently available; many other records relating to the Administration for Caprivians seem to have failed to have found their way into the archives. Furthermore, the few publications on Caprivian history do not cover the 1980s in detail.[179] In the following section, I will consequently rely primarily on the interviews which I conducted with individuals who played a role in the proclamation of the Eastern Caprivi's two national parks in 1990.

Promoting Nature Conservation and Tourism as the Caprivi's Future

The political-administrative restructuring in 1980 had the effect that many government officials were no longer based in or deployed from Pretoria, but Windhoek. As a result, a transfer of authority in the field of nature conservation took place from the Katima Mulilo-based CAF, for which BW and DP worked, to the SWA/Namibia Directorate of Nature Con-

---

[176] Van der Vegte, J.H., C.W. Forster and W.B. Forse (1983), Eastern Caprivi Regional Development Strategy. (Unpublished Government Document: Windhoek), p. 11–15.
[177] Van der Vegte et al. (1983).
[178] Van der Vegte et al. (1983): 80–198.
[179] E.g.: Kangumu (2011). In his otherwise extensive account of the history of the Caprivi, Kangumu only discusses the 1980s in a few scattered sentences (e.g. p. 124–127), in which he argues rather vaguely that a shift from tribal to political participation occurred after 1980.

servation and Recreation Resorts headed by Polla Swart. He was a trained biologist who worked in different roles within the field of Namibian nature conservation from the 1960s until his retirement in 1996.[180] In 1980, the year in which he took over the responsibility for nature conservation in the Caprivi, he conducted a small survey on conservation in the Eastern Caprivi and recommended further steps to be taken towards the proclamation of game parks in the territory.[181] In his proposals, he referred directly to the conservation areas which Ben Van der Waal had proposed in 1976 and largely concurred that they should form a basis for further planning.[182] However, he also stated that more research was needed before the reserves could be proclaimed and that it would be important to first discuss the proposals with botanists, mammalogists and ornithologists as well as anthropologists.[183] This emphasis on a rigorously scientific approach to nature conservation was central to Swart's approach to conservation throughout his fifty-year career. He had obtained a Master's degree in biology from the University of Stellenbosch and, together with his predecessor, B.J.G. de la Bat, edited *Madoqua*, a Namibian scientific journal for conservation research.[184] Swart repeatedly underlined the importance of scientific research for the success of Namibian conservation and proudly remembered that up to ten scientists had worked for the directorate in the 1970s.[185]

The research which he proposed to plan for the establishment of conservation areas in the Caprivi was not completed before independence, but he did oversee one further detailed aerial animal count. This was undertaken by three wildlife experts and supported by the SAAF, which supplied pilots and equipment.[186] BW suggested at the time that annual animal censuses should henceforth have been undertaken, but there is no evidence which indicates if these were ever conducted.

Data collected in the 1980 animal count also informed the already-cited Eastern Caprivi Regional Development Strategy Report's recommendations on nature conservation and

---

[180] See also the interview conducted with him in *Getaway* magazine in 1989: Polla Swart, *Getaway*, May 1989: 34–39.

[181] NASA, BAO, 20/271, Swart, P., Natuurbewaring: Voorlofige Verslag, 1980. Although the directorate had no direct influence over nature conservation in the Eastern Caprivi before 1980, Swart emphasised that he had been in constant exchange with its officials even prior to 1980. Officially, Swart's department was also responsible for nature conservation in the Western Caprivi, but he was only permitted to work there after Namibia's independence in 1990 (PS, 10.06.2014, Windhoek).

[182] NAN, CAF, 6/19/5, Proposed Nature Reserves Caprivi, Map by Ben C.W. van der Waal, 1976.

[183] NASA, BAO, 20/271, Swart, P., Natuurbewaring: Voorlofige Verslag, 1980.

[184] Madoqua – Journal of Nature Conservation Research in South West Africa (1969–1997).

[185] PS, 10.06.2014 and 03.08.2012, Windhoek.

[186] NAN, CAF, 6/19/7, Aerial Census of Wildlife in the Eastern Caprivi during August 1980, 1980.

tourism.[187] The authors of the report, J.H. van der Vegte, C.W. Forster and W.B. Forse, seem to have been aware of global shifts in wildlife conservation practice. As they emphasised, it was crucial to see conservation as important, "not in isolation, i.e. for preservation of unique flora and fauna, but also for its importance to agriculture, forestry and natural resource utilisation". Nevertheless, they continued to present wildlife preservation as the most lucrative form of conservation and argued that conservation "should not be placed in opposition to rural development, but should be part of the development process".[188]

As Kettowitz and van der Waal had proposed in the 1970s, van der Vegte and his colleagues recommended the proclamation of conservation areas as a means not only to protect fauna, but also as a possible source of income for nearby residents.[189] They identified two areas where the proposed parks could be proclaimed, both of which had already been drawn on van der Waal's map: the Nkasa-Rupara islands in the extreme south of the Eastern Caprivi and the Mudumu reserve in the east of Eastern Caprivi. The former, van der Vegte argued, was uninhabited, difficult to reach and based on the "hunting grounds for the Mafwe Chief", who, they predicted, would soon have no more game to hunt if the area remained unprotected.[190] The second proposed area, the Mudumu, was recommended mainly for touristic reasons; it lay near to the main road between Katima Mulilo and Windhoek, already possessed a small guest camp in the village of Lianshulu, and would offer the village population jobs in the reserve. The report argued that both proposed national parks constituted a unique habitat for some game and would also protect animals which were rare in other parts of Namibia. Nevertheless, the authors of the report insisted on two provisions which, as I will show below, would become the subject of much negotiation and dispute in subsequent years. Firstly, the authors demanded that the national parks should not be "taken away from the Caprivi as potential production area" and that Caprivians should still be allowed to make some use of them as an economic resource. Secondly, their proclamation should be "subject to acceptance by the Chiefs and *Khutas* and that these areas will be managed for the benefit of the people".[191]

In the report, the establishment of nature conservation areas was primarily advocated as a strategy to promote the touristic potential of the Eastern Caprivi. Van der Vegte and his colleagues acknowledged that the region was "risky" for investment in tourism because of

---

[187] Van der Vegte et al. (1983): 150–158 and 175–188.
[188] Both quotes: Van der Vegte et al. (1983): 150.
[189] Van der Vegte et al. (1983): 153. It was not possible to obtain statistics relating to tourists arrivals in the region before independence, but the ongoing war at the time, the lack of transport facilities, the rudimentary infrastructure and complicated permit regulations all point towards a very low number of tourists.
[190] Van der Vegte et al. (1983): 154.
[191] Van der Vegte et al. (1983): 155–156.

the ongoing war, Namibia's uncertain political future, and the perception of the Caprivi as "one of Africa's strife and war torn areas". However, this did not prevent them from proposing a detailed four-phase programme for the development of tourism in the Caprivi. This, they recommended, should be principally the responsibility of the Department of Nature Conservation in Windhoek, because at "present Caprivians have neither the skills nor the finance to develop, manage or conserve the region's attractions". Nevertheless, locals should be given "the potential to provide some services that could be demanded by the tourists", such as offering *Mokolo* (dugout canoe) trips or selling fish.[192]

Proclaiming the Nkasa-Lupala (Mamili) and Mudumu National Parks

One of the very last acts of the South African-controlled white minority government in Namibia was to proclaim the Nkasa-Lupala (Mamili) National Park and the Mudumu National Park on first of March 1990, a few weeks before the country's independence.[193] The developments leading to the proclamations illustrate how the plans for nature conservation areas, which had been discussed for decades, were in the end hurriedly implemented to ensure that the national parks were established before independence. The proclamation of the two parks should thus not only be seen as a consequence of the many surveys, plans and strategies which had been produced since the middle of the century, but also as laying the foundations for developments in conservation and tourism in the post-independence era.

In the lead-up to the proclamation of the Mudumu National Park, the population of the village of Nakatwa near Lianshulu was forcibly removed.[194] This decision led to a series of disputes and conflicts between the evicted residents and the relevant regional authorities as well as the SWA/Namibian and post-independence national governments.[195] While most of my interviewees who lived in the Caprivi knew about the removals in Lianshulu, there

---

[192] Van der Vegte et al. (1983): 179–180.
[193] Administrator-General for the Territory of South West Africa (ed.) (1990), AG 18, *Official Gazette*, 5904, 1 March 1990. Windhoek, p. 3. The first park was initially called the 'Mamili National Park' in honour of the Mafwe chief, Mamili. When the Mayeye group split from the Mafwe *Khuta* in 1992, many 'Mayeye' were no longer prepared to have their land named after the chief of the Mafwe *Khuta*, which they perceived as having long 'colonised' their land. The park was thus renamed as the Nkasa-Lupala National Park in 2013, sometime also spelled Nkasa-Rupara. The Mudumu National Park often appeared in documents as Mdumu National Park.
[194] It is unclear how many people were evicted. Also uncertain is the name and nature of this settlement, with some interviewees referring to it as the village of "Nakatwa", while others spoke of it as merely "some parts" of Lianshulu.
[195] JL, 18.05.2014, Malengalenga and PL, 13.05.2014, Katima Mulilo. See also: Integrated Rural Development and Nature Conservation (IRDNC) (ed.) (2011), *Lessons from the Field*. Windhoek: IRDNC: 64–68.

is hardly any evidence of them in written documents.[196] One reason for this near-silence in the written record might be that the removals happened during a time of military conflict, when, against the backdrop of even worse atrocities, the eviction of a few dozen people would not have made the headlines. Furthermore, forced removals were a common practice in apartheid South Africa and Namibia, with many occurring in much more heavily populated centres than those in the remote and rural Caprivi.

PL, who grew up in Nakatwa and later served as a high-ranking official in the Eastern Caprivi government before becoming a politician in independent Namibia, today heads a group of activists who demand the downsizing of the Mudumu National Park to a size which would allow the former inhabitants of Nakatwa to return to their original homes.[197] A second activist in this group is JL, a headman in Malengalenga, who was involved in the negotiations over the park's boundaries in the 1980s as an official in the Administration for Caprivians.[198] RM, the chief of the Mafwe from 1971 to 1987, initially led the *Khuta*'s negotiations with the Nature Conservation Directorate in Windhoek over the boundaries of the two parks.[199] His counterpart representing the Namibian administration was PS, who, as its director of Nature Conservation, spent several weeks in the Caprivi in 1989 and 1990 to negotiate and execute the eventual proclamation of the two national parks.[200]

The exact chronology leading up to the ultimate establishment of the two parks remains unclear. Nkasa-Lupala had already been proposed on Van der Waal's 1976 map as a nature (Nkasa) and hunting (Lupala) reserve within boundaries which largely corresponded to those of today.[201] Mudumu appeared on the map as part of a much larger proposed Lianshulu Hunting Reserve. Both national parks appeared in more or less their current form in the Eastern Caprivi Regional Development Strategy of 1983, alongside the remark that the "boundaries are subject to confirmation".[202] At this stage, the residents who were subsequently evicted from the Lianshulu area appear to still have been living in their homes, while plans to develop the village into a tourist centre still stood.[203] The year in which the Nakatwa removals took place is no longer certain. PL was unsure of the exact year, but

---

[196] Only after Namibia's independence the removals were mentioned in some media articles and reports, see e.g.: IRDNC (2011) 64–68 and Mayeyi Traditional Authority calls for Extension Mudumu National Park borders, *Namibian Broadcasting Coperation (NBC)*, 2011, www.nbc.na/news/mayeyi-traditional-authority-calls-extension-mudumu-national-park-borders.511 [accessed: 02.02.2017].
[197] PL, 13.05.2014, Katima Mulilo.
[198] JL, 18.05.2014, Malengalenga.
[199] RM, 29.05.2014, Linyanti.
[200] PS, 10.06.2014 and 03.08.2012, Windhoek.
[201] NAN, CAF, 6/19/5, Proposed Nature Reserves Caprivi, Map by Ben C.W. van der Waal, 1976.
[202] Van der Vegte et al. (1983): Appendix Fig. 10.1.
[203] Van der Vegte et al. (1983): 155.

mentioned 1982 as a possibility, while JL claimed that they must have occurred in 1985.[204] Work on the establishment of the two national parks began in the first half of the 1980s. During this time, game guards were sent to the parks to build camps within their proposed boundaries.[205] By no later than 1984, a nature conservation law enforcement unit was active within the current boundaries of what would become the Mudumu National Park.[206] RM remembered that both parks were established – but not yet officially proclaimed – during his chieftainship, which ended in 1987. He recalled that "Mudumu, Mamili and Lupala game parks were established when I was chief. Therefore houses [camps] were built on Nkasa and Lupala [islands]. Lupala belonged to the chief, I protected Lupala and the nature conservation protected the others."[207] According to Mamili, only nature conservation officials and game guards were allowed to enter the Nkasa-Lupala reserve without his permission. This may suggest that access to at least the area of the Nkasa-Lupala reserve was controlled to some degree from the early 1980s.

To understand the implications of the proclamation of the national parks and the forced removals to Lianshulu, it is important to put the focus on people who lived in the vicinity of the parks. Many of them identified themselves as belonging to the Mayayi ethnic group and not to the Mafwe, whose chief had ruled the residents of the area since the German colonial era.[208] They would thus not have accepted RM as their chief, nor as their legitimate representative in the consultations with Windhoek regarding the boundaries of the proposed national parks. Instead, they would have felt, as PL put it, as if they had been "doubly colonised – by South Africa and by the Mafwe chief".[209]

The evictions from Nakatwa took place years before the Mudumu National Park was officially proclaimed, but were clearly linked to its establishment. PL, who lived in Katima Mulilo at the time, remembered:

> All people from [Nakatwa nearby] Lianshulu village were forced to remove. One day in 1982 they [officials from the Directorate of Nature Conservation] just came with big lorries, they threatened to burn down the village, they were promised water and schools but they just dumped them under a tree and they had to walk for three kilometres to find water. There was no food, nothing. It was painful and serious, up to now we are fighting the government to remove the park.[210]

---

[204] JL, 18.05.2014, Malengalenga and PL, 13.05.2014, Katima Mulilo. A second set of evictions seem to have taken place immediately after the park's proclamation in 1990. See IRDNC (2011): 63.
[205] CC, 02.11.2015, Windhoek.
[206] SS, 15.05.2014, Katima Mulilo.
[207] RM, 29.05.2014, Chinchimane.
[208] Kangumu (2011): 41. Only after independence the Namibian Government recognised the chief of the Mayeyi as a traditional authority.
[209] PL, 13.05.2014, Katima Mulilo.
[210] PL, 13.05.2014, Katima Mulilo.

PL recalled that evicted residents were promised a new village with houses, running water and a school, but the evictees were forced to survive on the land of others. PS did not recall any removals, but emphasised his many visits to "the chiefs" and the close co-operation which he claimed to have sought with local inhabitants while the boundaries of the parks were being defined.

> I had already started to negotiate with the people from Eastern Caprivi, before 1980 […], but it was only talks. We had a lot of talks with the people to try and establish the game parks like the present one Mudumu and Nkasa we also tried to tell them about the advantages of having that kind conservation things but it was difficult to convince them. After 1980, we started again with it and eventually we made agreements to establish the Mudumu National Park and the Nkasa National Park. And they were proclaimed just before independence.[211]

PS mentioned repeatedly that he had "really good relations with the big chiefs from Eastern Caprivi, Mamili and Liswani [sic]. We had a lot of meetings with them."[212] These "good relations" were also confirmed by Mamili, who in his then capacity as a chief recalled having worked very closely together with nature conservation officials. He did concede, however, that the latter had the final say when it came to hunting and conservation regulations:

> You would not just hunt as a chief but you also get authorisation from the government office and you would tell them that you want to go hunt in that particular place and they would indicate in the permit whether you are allowed to go hunt.[213]

Mamili then went on to recall how "the South African government gathered the chiefs together and told them to protect the animals, it was like it was an order from the South African government on animal protection". Nevertheless, he insisted that "people wanted to protect the animals" and that wildlife conservation was always "a co-operation between the chiefs, the people, and the government".[214]

Unsurprisingly, people living close to the parks who considered themselves to be of 'Mayeye' ethnicity and did not recognise RM as their legitimate chief held a different view on the matter. The current 'Mayeye' chief was adamant in my interview with him in 2014 that "no Mayeye was ever asked about the park".[215] He argued that "Mayeye people" continued to suffer from the effects of parks which were proclaimed by "South African nature

---

[211] PS, 10.06.2014 Windhoek.
[212] PS, 10.06.2014 Windhoek. PS is probably referring to Chief Joshua Moraliswani (1945–1996) here. Chief Kisko Liswani was only installed after PS's retirement.
[213] RM, 29.05.2014, Chinchimane.
[214] RM, 29.05.2014, Chinchimane.
[215] BS, 14.05.2014, Sangwali. In 1992 the Namibian government recognized the 'Mayeye' traditional authoritiy.

conservation officials who did not know anything about nature conservation".[216] JL, who was party to the negotiations over the park's boundaries as a representative of the second-tier Administration for Caprivians, concurred with BS's assessment. He could not recall that nature conservation officials had held any meetings with residents of the immediate vicinity without members of the 'Mafwe' *Khuta* being present.[217] PL went even further, claiming that the "national parks were made forcefully without the people" and that "they [nature conservation officials] only consulted with the traditional authorities of the Mafwe", who were happy to "give away the land of the Mayeye".[218]

PS remembered likewise that "there was a lot of opposition; there were all these people that were not happy with all what the government was doing in their land". However, he remained convinced that they would ultimately come to understand that his plans would benefit them. According to PS, he spent weeks "in the bush" talking to opponents of the planned parks until they believed that the authorities "are not going to take away the land from them" and that the parks were "for their best interest".[219]

After the consultations regarding the two parks' boundaries as well as the eviction of residents from within this area, the precise demarcation of the boundaries began. PS recalled that: "When we discussed the last meeting that we had for the boundaries of Mudumu game reserve, we stayed there for three weeks with the local people in the bush and we walked along the boundaries to show them where we thought the boundaries had to be. We had always tried to keep them involved."[220] RM retained similar memories of these "three weeks":

> When they [the officials from Windhoek] went to demarcate the boundary, they camped at Mabanga, on the tar road that leads to Windhoek. They moved from that area trying to demarcate the boundaries of the park and they used the South African government transport.[221]

The party, according to RM, consisted of one "white guy from nature conservation [probably PS]", while the rest were "local people who knew the area well".[222] The locals would have been responsible for physically demarcating the boundary on the ground. PS also mentioned that professional cartographers formed part of the group. He remembered that after the completion of the demarcation process, conservation officials had "more or less

---

[216] BS, 14.05.2014, Sangwali.
[217] JL, 18.05.2014, Malengalenga.
[218] PL, 13.05.2014, Katima Mulilo.
[219] PS, 10.06.2014, Windhoek.
[220] PS, 10.06.2014, Windhoek.
[221] RM, 29.05.2014, Chinchimane.
[222] RM, 29.05.2014, Chinchimane.

the finalised agreement with them [local people], so we then pushed the proclamation a little bit".[223] PS and other officials were determined to push through the proclamations before independence because they were "afraid that it would take a long time for them [the post-independence government] to proceed with the system".[224] A further reason for the rapid passing of the proclamations was offered by JL. According to him, the SWA/Namibia government proclaimed a much larger total area than that to which the administration in the Eastern Caprivi had initially agreed. He believed that Windhoek had thus sought to rush through the proclamation process before independence because it feared that there would be legal recourse open to the affected communities in an independent Namibia which could compel the renegotiation of the boundaries to conform to the size which had been initially agreed upon by all sides.[225]

Towards Post-colonial Wildlife Conservation

The strategy adopted by departing colonial regimes to proclaim conservation areas shortly before independence is familiar from other contexts, including the Massai Mara National Park in Kenya (proclaimed in 1961), Kafue National Park in Zambia (c. 1959) or Amber Mountain National Park in Madagascar (1958). Such proclamations can be understood as an attempt to claim space or otherwise "affect, influence, or control people and assert control over a geographic area", a process also known as 'territorialisation'.[226] A cogent example thereof can be found in the demarcation and proclamation of protected areas in the Caprivi by the departing South African occupying power seeking to secure for itself an enduring influence which would survive the termination of its institutional authority in the region.

During the final years of its occupation of Namibia, a number of different strategies presented themselves as possibilities for South Africa to claim this long-lasting influence in the Caprivi. In the late 1970s and early 1980s, the authorities in the Caprivi sought to apply coercive means to achieve this goal, as evident in the increased SADF presence in the Caprivi. However, as I showed in this chapter, the rulers also invoked additional, non-coercive methods to exert control over the Caprivi and, in particular, its proposed con-

---

[223] PS, 10.06.2014, Windhoek.
[224] PS, 10.06.2014, Windhoek.
[225] JL, 18.05.2014, Malengalenga. Developments in nature conservation in the Caprivi in the post-independence era showed that these fears were misplaced (Chapter 5).
[226] Sack, R. (1986), *Human territoriality: Its theory and history*. Cambridge: Cambridge University Press, p. 19. See also: Bassett, T. and D. Gautier (2014), Regulation by Territorialization: The Political Ecology of Conservation & Development Territories, *EchoGeo*, 29(4): 1–7.

servation areas. These approaches included extending the promise of economic profit to Caprivian residents and involving local chiefs in the creation of the conservation areas.[227] These laid a foundation for the nature conservation strategies adopted in the Caprivi in the post-independence era.

South Africa's different strategies of maintaining control over the Caprivi evolved in the interplay between military power, the promise of economic development, and the protection of wildlife. It was in this process that the newly-emerging paradigms of community- and market-based conservation encountered enduring apartheid policies of separate development and supposedly self-governing ethnic authorities under the control of chiefs. Within this context, a basis was laid for subsequent nature conservation projects in the area.

Nature conservation was a field through which central aspects of governance in the Caprivi were both revealed and contested. Although the practice of nature conservation corresponded neatly with South Africa's strategies for exercising control in the region, it also became a key vehicle through which individuals and communities could express dissatisfaction to the South African occupation. Many of the early advocates of community-based resource management, an approach which gained influence in Namibian conservation policy in the late 1980s, were people who, at least according to their own memories, saw the strengthening of communities through wildlife protection as a means to resist the South African occupation or at least mitigate some of its effects.[228] As I will show in the following chapter, some of these activists later joined forces with former officials in the SADF and other important persons within the apartheid system to advocate for further nature conservation and wildlife protection policies in post-independence Namibia.

Memories of the negotiations which led to the evictions in and around Lianshulu, the demarcation of the boundaries of the national parks, and the parks' eventual proclamations remain complex and contested. These memories demonstrate that policy promises such as 'community-based' or 'in close co-operation with the local population' can be rather empty when applied to nature conservation. In the case of the two national parks discussed in this

---

[227] In relation to East Asia, Nancy Peluso also described how strategies of territorialization can function through non-coercive means, such as by incorporating promises of economic development or community involvement into conservation strategies: Peluso, N. (1993), Coercing Conservation? The politics of state resource control. *Global Environmental Change*, 3(2), p. 199–217.

[228] Owen-Smith, G. (2010), *An Arid Eden: A Personal Account of Conservation in the Kaokoveld*. Jeppestown: Jonathan Ball, p. 74–77. In his autobiography, Owen-Smith, a long-serving and celebrated nature conservationist in North-Western Namibia, described the difficulties of working as a representative of the apartheid state with local inhabitants in the territory. He went on to proudly recount how he had stood up for the views of Helen Suzman's Progressive Party while socialising with hardline officials from the Department of Bantu Administration. According to Owen-Smith, a security file was opened on him after this incident.

chapter, attitudes towards nature conservation in the Caprivi are still shaped by Caprivians' perceptions of unfair treatment in and exclusion from the negotiations. While PL was generally in favour of nature and wildlife conservation, he still observed a "South African attitude" in the way in which many nature conservationists have continued to go about their work in the Caprivi since independence.[229] JL became very critical of his own work in the field of nature conservation and developed a "deep mistrust" towards the stated goals of community conservancy projects.[230]

As I will show in the following chapter, the framing of nature conservation proposals as 'community-based' became a central concern of environmental policy in Namibia in the 1990s and 2000s. However, it is not only in relation to community-based tourism that Namibian independence in 1990 should be understood as a less than clean break from the past. The legacies of discourses, practices and personnel from the region's colonial and apartheid past continue to impact upon present-day nature conservation initiatives. It is crucial to analyse these continuities – and the discontinuities – in order to understand recent conservation politics in the region.

---

[229] PL, 13.05.2014, Katima Mulilo.
[230] JL, 18.05.2014, Malengalenga.

5 Nature and Peace?

Namibia's independence brought with it major changes in the lives of people living in the Caprivi, as well as in its governance and economy. Indeed, the end of South African rule and the installation of a new, democratic political system must be seen as a watershed moment in both Namibian and Caprivian history. However, the changes which occurred in 1990 were not complete, and the legacy of nearly one hundred years of colonial and apartheid rule could not be erased simply by introducing a new system of governance. Scholars of Southern African humanities, social sciences and history have argued that it is hardly possible to research or even understand Southern Africa's present without taking into account its twentieth-century past. For them, Namibian and South African history did not end in 1990 or 1994.[1] Nevertheless, many historical studies conclude at these landmark years, while social sciences often understand 'post-apartheid' or 'post-independence' as the most useful temporal category of analysis in Southern African studies.[2]

Researching and writing recent Caprivian history and tracing the main fractures which emerged in the region in the early 1990s poses a series of methodological challenges, from the inaccessibility of much archival material due to legal restrictions to the at times confusingly large and diverse array of other available information, grey literature and (expert) opinion. Nevertheless, employing the historiographic methods of qualitative and non-representative interviews still allows for a fruitful discussion of current discourses, arguments and interpretations of the pasts and presents of people impacted by conservation. As such, this chapter does not purport to take the place of much needed socio-ecological or economic micro-studies of recent conservation initiatives in the region; what it aims to do instead is to put the Caprivi's apartheid history, its post-independence history and the most recent developments in nature conservation in dialogue with each other and write them into a broader discussion on Southern African conservation politics over the course of the last two decades.[3]

---

[1] For a general overview, see e.g.: Lalu (2009), Sitze (2013); in relation to history and the archive: Stoler (2009); in relation to cities and architecture: Shepherd, N. and Murray, N. (2007), Introduction: Space, Memory and Identity in the Post-Apartheid City. In: Murray, N., N. Shepherd and M. Hall (ed.), *Desire Lines: Space, Memory and Identity in the Post-Apartheid City*. New York: Routledge, p. 1–18;

[2] See also, e.g.: Cobley, A. (2001), Does Social History Have a Future? The Ending of Apartheid and Recent Trends, South African Historiography. *Journal of Southern African Studies*, 27(3): 613–625.

[3] See also Harvey (2005) and Moore (2016).

Accordingly, this chapter takes the ecological, economic and military complex which I elaborated in the previous chapters as a starting point to reflect on the continuing interplays between nature conservation, development, cartography, borders and violence in the Caprivi today. After Namibian independence in 1990, nature conservation in the area underwent numerous important changes, but nevertheless retained and readjusted many practices from its pre-independence past.[4] If Clapperton Chakanetsa Mavhunga was right when he stated bluntly that "[t]he problem with the national park or game reserve in Africa is that it is a colonial relict struggling to adjust to a postcolonial reality", one would expect to find continuities – of the discursive variety at the very least – from conservation's colonial past within its postcolonial, capitalist present.[5] I will explore these continuities, but also illustrate the disruptions which have occurred, with reference to two post-independence initiatives in nature conservation which have had a significant impact on the Caprivi: communal conservancies and transfrontier conservation areas (TFCAs).[6] Strikingly, three key historical features of nature conservation in the region which I have identified in this study are also evident in more recent conservation initiatives: namely, the underlying influence of narratives of (economic) development; the (re)production of power relations through mapping and ecological research; and conservation's entanglement with practices of warfare and military reconnaissance. Discussing these three fields enables us to understand the ways in which communal conservancies and TFCAs apply and reinforce ideas of development and continue to employ practices of mapping and bordering similar to those used in the pre-independence era. At the same time, it reveals the role which both initiatives play in increasingly militarised and violent forms of nature conservation in Southern Africa in general and in the Caprivi in particular. It is thus imperative to examine the two initiatives

---

[4] Singh et al. (2002)
[5] Mavhunga, C.C. (2014), *Transient Workspaces: Technologies of Everyday Innovation in Zimbabwe.* Cambridge: MIT Press, p. 5.
[6] A Transfrontier Conservation Area (TFCA) is defined in the Southern African Development Community's (SADC) *Protocol on Wildlife Conservation and Law Enforcement* as a component of a larger ecological region which straddles the boundaries of two or more countries and encompasses one or more protected areas as well as multiple use resource areas (South African Development Community SADC (ed.) (1999), *Protocol on Wildlife Conservation and Law Enforcement*. Maputo: SADC Publications, p. 4). TFCAs are often called 'Peace Parks' in the media or for promotional purposes. For an overview of the terminology, see: Ali, S.H. (2007), Introduction: A Natural Connection between Ecology and Peace? In S.H. Ali (ed.), *Peace Parks: Conservation and Conflict Resolution*. Cambridge: MIT Press, p. 1–18 (here 6–7). I will use the two terms interchangeably. Communal Conservancies are defined by the Namibian Association of Community Based Natural Resource Management Support Organisations (NACSO) as "self-governing entities, run by their members, with fixed boundaries that are agreed with adjacent conservancies, communities or land owners" (www.nacso.org.na/conservancies [accessed 01.01.2017]). In the Caprivi, the TFCA encompasses also all the community conservancies.

within their local Caprivian as well as their wider (Southern) African historical contexts. As I have shown, these were repeatedly marked by authoritarian control and repression in rural areas in the name of 'science', '(separate) development', and 'modernity'.[7]

In the following section, I will first outline Caprivi's fractured history after independence, showing how – unlike in many other parts of Namibia – the country's democratic transition in 1990 did not bring peace and stability to the region. However, the region did seem to provide a promising opportunity for introducing communal conservancies and TFCAs. I will then situate these two initiatives in relation to pre-independence narratives of 'bringing development' to the region and more recent promises of economic development through market-based conservation approaches. Thereafter, I will discuss a further salient feature of TFCAs – shared, to a lesser extent, by communal conservancies – namely, their role in the re-mapping of large sections of Southern Africa, again reflecting discourses and practices which were already common in the 1970s and 1980s.[8] In recent times, private companies and NGOs have collected cartographic survey data and produced maps for both initiatives. In the Caprivi and along its borders, as in many other regions of Southern Africa, the processes of economic development and peace-making are still deeply interwoven with elements of securitisation, border control and violence.[9]

The Caprivi after Independence

Conflicts in the Post-independence Era

While Namibia's transition from an occupied territory of apartheid South Africa into an independent, democratic and capitalist state generally occurred without significant incident, many serious incidents which threatened the peace in post-independence Namibia occurred in the Caprivi. After Namibia gained its formal independence on 21 March 1990, it took only a few months before a new, progressive constitution came into effect.[10] This was based on the primacy of human rights and a non-discriminatory policy towards questions of sex,

---

[7] Dzingirai, V. (2003), New Scramble for the African Countryside. *Development and Change*, 34(2): 243–263 (here 245).

[8] See e.g. the edited volume: Ramutsindela, M. (ed.) (2014), *Cartographies of Nature: How Nature Conservation Animates Borders*. Newcastle upon Tyne: Cambridge Scholars Publishing. Although the conservancies and the TFCAs both emphasise the protection of fauna and flora as the main goal of their mapping activities, they have adopted different cartographic methods.

[9] For an overview of the interconnections between violence and nature conservation, see e.g.: Duffy, R. (2010), *Nature Crime: How We're Getting Conservation Wrong*. New Haven and London: Yale University Press.

[10] Wallace (2011): 309. The Constituent Assembly had already drafted and adopted the new constitution in 1989.

race, colour, ethnic origin, and religion as well as social and economic status.[11] Most former PLAN fighters were integrated into the newly-founded Namibian Defence Force (NDF) or the Namibian Police Force, while a stable and largely peaceful and democratic political system was established. In the Caprivi, however, the 1990s was a turbulent period, during which many of the fault lines beneath the surface of independent Namibia's apparent success story were exposed by conflicts and disputes between various traditional authorities, the marginalisation of the Western Caprivi, the emergence of a Caprivi secessionist movement, and the spill over from the Angolan Civil War.

Shortly after independence, the Caprivi stated to witness clashes between different ethnically-defined groups. For example, long-simmering tensions between the Masubia and the Mafwe Traditional Authorities turned violent. The two authorities had been officially recognised since the German colonial era and were important for South Africa in the implementation of its policies of indirect rule and homeland politics. The Masubia Royal House Declaration, which was issued in 1991 and claimed 'indigenous' rights over the entire Caprivi for the 'Masubia', was a key driver of the renewed outbreak of conflict between the two traditional authorities which led to the killing of several individuals, including teachers from one group working in areas which were considered to belong to the other authority.[12] The central state reacted by negotiating a peace agreement in May 1993 which required, among other terms, that "there should be a mutual recognition of each other's area of jurisdiction based on tribal districts".[13] For Kangumu, these attempts by Windhoek to solve the dispute by proposing a physical boundary between the respective 'tribal districts' were similar to those of earlier colonial administrations, which had failed to understand that ethnicity was not spatially definable and that clear boundaries could thus not be drawn between "tribal groups".[14] The boundaries hence remain contested and disputes have not ceased since the signing of the agreement.[15]

---

[11] Wallace (2011): 309–310. Although Namibia's new constitution has been domestically and internationally celebrated as progressive and fair, scholars have observed a discrepancy between its aims as a document and the way in which it has been applied in society (Melber, H. (2014), *Understanding Namibia: The Trials of Independence*. London: Hurst: 13–19). See also: Erasmus, G. (2010), The Constitution: Its Impact on Namibian Statehood and Politics. In C. Keulder (ed.), *State, Society and Democracy: A Reader in Namibian Politics*. Windhoek: Macmillan Education: 77–105.

[12] Kangumu (2011): 188 The conflict goes back at least as far as the designation and recognition of the two groups by the German colonial administration in the early years of the twentieth century. For a detailed historical study on the conflict, see: Kangumu (2011).

[13] Quoted in: Kangumu (2011): 184.

[14] Kangumu (2011): 186.

[15] For an overview of the skirmishes which took place between the two traditional authorities in 2016, see: Mongudhi, T. (2016), Tribalism dominates agenda 2017, *The Namibian*, 20.06.2016, p. 1–2.

Soon after independence, the Mayeyi Traditional Authority broke away from the Mafwe Traditional Authority and was recognised by the Namibian state as a traditional authority in its own right in 1993.[16] A further split from the Mafwe Traditional Authority occurred in 2004, when the Namibian state recognised the Mashi Traditional Authority as the Caprivi's fourth traditional authority.[17]

The withdrawal of the SADF from Namibia by 1990 also had a major impact on life in the Western Caprivi. Its population had decreased in the first half of the twentieth century, especially after the 1930s when its inhabitants were no longer permitted to keep cattle. Cattle farmers duly had to leave the area, leaving behind only those people whose livelihood did not depend on cattle, mainly the so-called 'Khwe'.[18] From the 1970s, many 'Khwe' men were hired by the SADF as trackers or soldiers or to work in the military bases. With the end of the South African occupation, they lost their livelihoods.[19] The SADF gave its former employees in the Western Caprivi the option of resettling in South Africa. While about 370 families chose to move there, about 5,000 people remained in the Western Caprivi.[20] Julie Taylor described the years which followed for those who stayed as marked by "impoverishment and exclusion".[21] Not only did they lose their relatively well-paid jobs, but they were also seen by many fellow Namibians as traitors for having fought for, or at least benefitted from, the SADF. A 'Khwe' headman, remembered in an interview how the governor of the Kavango Region had accused him openly of having "tracked for the whites, holding white people's arms to make sure that SWAPO people died".[22]

This feeling of being actively discriminated against by the government was fuelled when the Namibian state rejected an application in 2001 by a group of Khwe-speaking people for an officially recognised chieftaincy, arguing that the Western Caprivi belonged historically to the Mbukushu Traditional Authority.[23] This same reasoning may have underlain the

---

[16] Kangumu (2011): 184. See also Chapter 4.
[17] See also: Hipondoka, M. (2008), Mapping Areas of Officially Recognized Traditional Authorities and Land Board Jurisdictions. Windhoek: Ministry of Lands and Resettlement.
[18] Taylor (2012): 62.
[19] Boden (2003): 88. For more details, see: Van Wyk, A.S. (2014), The Militarisation of the Platfontein San (!Xun and Khwe): The Initial Years 1966–1974. *The Journal for Transdisciplinary Research in Southern Africa*, 10(3): 133–151.
[20] Referring to a NGO report from 2005, Taylor wrote that 80% of those who remained could be labelled as 'Khwe', although ethnic divisions are not as precise as such specific figures suggest (Taylor 2012: 81).
[21] Taylor (2012): 81.
[22] TC, 11.05.2014, Mutjiku.
[23] Boden (2003): 88. The Mbkushu Traditional Authority, based in Andara to the west of the Caprivi, controls the Mukwe District in the western Caprivi. The Mashi Traditional Authority, the Mayeyi Traditional Authority and the Mafwe Traditional Authority all claim authority over large parts of the western Caprivi.

partition of the Western Caprivi into the Caprivi Region (today: Zambezi Region) and the Kavango Region (today: Kavango East) in 1998. Many inhabitants of the western Caprivi perceived this subdivision as a governmental measure to further weaken their position against the claims of the neighbouring Traditional Authorities.[24]

A third state initiative which inhabitants of the western Caprivi often perceived as being directed against them was the reintroduction of nature conservation regulations in the Caprivi Game Park in the early 1990s, decades after the area had been turned into a closed military zone.[25] Following the withdrawal of the SADF, many people in the Western Caprivi had no choice but to survive by gathering wild fruits and hunting small animals. During the South African occupation, these subsistence strategies had been largely tolerated; now, in the post-independence era, they came into conflict with the state's stricter enforcement of park regulations. As TC recalled, the "South Africans did colonise us, but they did not restrict us from going to get our food in the land. Unlike now, now this has gotten worse".[26] The sense among local inhabitants that they were being neglected or even actively hindered from participation in any form of economic development grew even stronger when the Namibian state merged the Caprivi Game Park with the neighbouring Mahango National Park to create the Bwabwata National Park in 2007, effectively rendering its earlier promises to deproclaim parts of the park meaningless.[27]

The estimated few thousand residents who remain in the western Caprivi today are the only people in Namibia who live within the boundaries of a national park.[28] As a result, they are prevented from founding their own communal conservancies, through which they could otherwise have gained at least a semblance of control over their land's natural resources.[29] Although the success of the conservancy concept was questioned by many community leaders in the western Caprivi, most would still regard having their own conservancies as an opportunity to at least regain the feeling of being "normal citizens, like everybody else."[30] The government, however, followed a different approach and gave permission to other conservancies located beyond the park's boundaries to set up their own tourist camps within the park.[31] In lieu of a conservancy, the park's residents were given the mere opportu-

---

[24] TC, 11.05.2014, Mutjiku and AC, 21.05.2014, Kongola. See also: Boden (2004) and Taylor (2012).
[25] Boden (2004), Taylor (2012), TC, 11.05.2014, Mutjiku.
[26] TC, 11.05.2014, Mutjiku.
[27] Taylor (2012): 74.
[28] With the exception of some small villages along the Kuiseb river as well as some national park employees who live within the park where they work, for example at the Okaukuejo settlement in the Etosha National Park.
[29] See the following subchapter for a definition and discussion of communal conservancies.
[30] TC, 11.05.2014, Mutjiku.
[31] These include, for example, a camping area on the western shore of the Kwando River which is

nity of setting up an association to receive, from the Ministry of Environment and Tourism (MET), a percentage of the profits gained through trophy hunting.[32] Tellingly, at the time of my field research in 2014, most residents of the western Caprivi depended on food aid from the state.[33]

Caprivi Secessionism and the Angolan Civil War

The most serious threats to peace and security in post-independence Namibia were the attacks carried out by the secessionist Caprivi Liberation Army (CLA) on Katima Mulilo in August 1999, the severe response to these from the Namibian Defence Force, and the spillover of the civil war in Angola into the Caprivi.[34] The CLA's attacks on state and military installations in Katima Mulilo on the morning of 2 August 1999 were the culmination of its attempt to bring about the secession of the Caprivi from Namibia. This aim had been formulated since the mid-1990s and was shared by the United Democratic Party (UDP), which was led by a former acting vice-president of SWAPO, Mishake Albert Muyongo.[35] During the attacks, eight soldiers and policemen, as well as five separatists were killed before the NDF managed to regain control of the situation on the same day.[36] Shortly before the attacks,

---

jointly run by the Mayuni Conservancy and the Mashi Traditional Authority. A luxury lodge has also stood at this spot since 2015 which claims to partner with the "Mashi chief" in an attempt to create "sustainable communities" (www.africanmonarchlodges.com/our-involvement [accessed 01.01.2017]).

[32] Boden (2003): 95.

[33] This occurred primarily through the so-called San Feeding Programme of the Office of the Prime Minister, see: www.sandevelopment.gov.na/san-feeding-programme.htm [31.12.2017]. AK, 30.05.2014, Omega I. More recent data was not available for the western Caprivi, but, according to a newspaper report in 2017, around 700,000 people in Namibia were partly dependent on government food relief programmes. Among the most affected groups were the so-called San communities in the western Caprivi (Shaanika, H. (2017), 700 000 rely on drought relief, *New Era*, 20.01.2017).

[34] A broad academic literature exists on the Caprivi secessionist movement. Shortly after the 1999 attacks, Maria Fisch published a short book in which she defended the aims of the secessionist movement with reference to the region's history (Fisch 1999). This argument was questioned by Bennett Kangumu, e.g. in: Kangumu (2011): 237–262 and Zeller (2007). From a political scientist's perspective, see also: Melber, H. (2009), One Namibia, One Nation? The Caprivi as Contested Territory. *Journal of Contemporary African Studies*, 27(4): 463–481. Based on anthropological methods, see: Guijarro, E.M. (2013), An Independent Caprivi: A Madness of a Few, a Partial Collective Yearning or a Realistic Possibility? Citizen Perspectives on Caprivian Secession. *Journal of Southern African Studies*, 39(2): 337–352.

[35] The UDP was founded by Muyongo in 1985 as the successor party of CANU. In the 1994 Namibian general election, Muyongo ran as the DTA's presidential candidate and won a 23 per cent share of the vote. After the attacks by the CLA, which is commonly regarded as the UDP's armed wing, the DTA suspended the UDP and its leadership from the alliance. In 2006 the UDP was banned nationally.

[36] Kangumu (2011): 237.

many residents, especially from the already-marginalised Khwe-speaking population in the Western Caprivi, had fled to Botswana, fearing the government's harsh response to the secessionist movement. Immediately after the attacks, many more left Namibia, while over a hundred alleged secessionists were arrested in the Caprivi and imprisoned in Grootfontein and Windhoek.[37] The leadership of the UDP, meanwhile, managed to flee and received asylum in Denmark.[38]

The secessionists' arguments for an independent Caprivi are based on two main assertions. Firstly, they made the historical claim that the Caprivi was never part of German South West Africa, as defined in the colonial treaties of the nineteenth-century. Furthermore, it was claimed that the CANU and the SWAPO had agreed at the time of their merger in 1964 that all Caprivians would be given the chance to decide on whether they wanted to be part of a future independent Namibia or to form a Caprivian state of their own.[39] The secessionists' second argument was developmental or economic. They posited that because of the SWAPO government's record of "tribalism and nepotism", the Caprivi would remain neglected and economically marginalised as long as it continued to be part of Namibia.[40]

Kangumu provided two further possible explanations for the rise of a secessionist movement in the Caprivi. Firstly, he showed that the development of the movement was closely

---

[37] The accused were detained, some for as long as sixteen years, before their cases were heard. The trial eventually commenced in 2002 and only ended in 2015, by which time twenty-two of the detainees had died in prison. In 2003, forty-four were acquitted or released after only being found guilty of minor offences, as were a further forty-seven in 2015. Ultimately, only thirty of the detainees were found guilty of high treason, murder or attempted murder. The treatment of the prisoners and their long detention without trial was strongly condemned by Namibian and international human rights organisations. (Menges, W. (2015), 30 guilty in treason trial, *The Namibian*, 15.09.2015, p. 1 and Amnesty International (ed.) (2016), *Amnesty International Report 2015/2016: The State of the World's Human Rights*. London: Amnesty International, p. 265–266.) Many of the refugees in Botswana, along with their children who were born in the Dukwe refugee camp, remain in the camp and refuseed to go back to Namibia, even though the United Nations High Commissioner for Refugees (UNHCR) and the Namibian government have both promised to assist them after their return to Namibia.

[38] This included Mishake Muyongo, and the then chief of the Mafwe Traditional Authority, Boniface Mamili. See also: Lilemba, J.L. and Y.H. Matemba (2015), Reclaiming indigenous knowledge in Namibia's post-colonial curriculum: the case of the Mafwe people. In K. Chinsembu (ed.), *Indigenous Knowledge in Namibia*. Windhoek: UNAM Press: 283–309.

[39] For an overview of the historical arguments espoused by the exiled members of the secessionist movement, see their own account of the Caprivi's history on the webpage of the exiled UDP, which is now based in Copenhagen: History: Caprivi Zipfel. The Controversial Strip, Part I–III www.caprivifreedom.com/history [15.08.2016]. See also: Fisch (1999).

[40] See e.g.: Guijarro (2013): 346. In relation to the alleged underdevelopment of the Caprivi, it is important to understand, as this study has shown, that the region had been a main focus for South African investments in infrastructure and economic development during the occupation. When these ceased after Namibia's independence, many Caprivians were left with a feeling that they were now being neglected by the government (Kangumu 2011: 262).

linked to the political career of its figurehead, Muyongo, and deeply imbedded in the internal politics of the Caprivi, especially in the rivalries and disputes between the Mafwe and Masubia traditional authorities. Kangumu thus proposed understanding the movement as an extreme form of "negotiation of the Namibian nation in local terms" with a "blend of ethnicity and nationalism".[41] He thereby interpreted the Caprivi secessionist movement as the most overt example of the extent to which questions of ethnicity and nationalism have remained fundamental to political disputes in Namibia. Secondly, he acknowledged that there was a historical component to the movement's claims, but located this in the last two decades of the South African occupation and not in the nineteenth century or the early years of the armed struggle.

This latter point is also relevant in relation to the Caprivi's role in the Angolan Civil War, which lasted until 2002. As Bennet Kangumu has shown, when South Africa realised in the 1980s that it might not be able to keep Namibia under its permanent control, Pretoria developed plans to support the creation of an independent Caprivian state by the name of 'Itenge'.[42] This was envisaged as a 'friendly' South African satellite through which the apartheid state could secure its threatened interests in the region.[43] If such a plan did in fact exist, it was never realised; however, a more easily executable means to achieve a similar goal might have been for South Africa to support Muyongo in building up a rebel group to disrupt the 1989 Namibian parliamentary election and thereby destabilise the country.[44] Even if the origins of the CLA may indeed have lain in this sort of covert support from the dying apartheid state, hard evidence for this claim is yet to emerge. South Africa had, however, already resorted to similar destabilisation tactics by sponsoring UNITA in Angola and the Resistência Nacional Moçambicana (RENAMO) in Mozambique.[45]

Particularly in the aftermath of the attacks on Katima Mulilo, the Namibian government expressed concerns about alleged co-operation between the UNITA and the CLA. These concerns were based on the suspicion that the CLA had been receiving military training in UNITA camps in southern Angola since at least the mid-1990s, if not already during the time of the South African occupation.[46] Partly for this reason, Namibia consented to the Angolan military using the Caprivi as a base from which to attack UNITA camps in 2000. In response to this deal, UNITA repeatedly attacked civilians in the Caprivi, especially in the

---

[41] Kangumu (2011): 238. This assessment has been partially questioned by Guijarro, who showed that the 'ethnic divide' between the secessionists and those who want the Caprivi to remain a part of Namibia is not as clear as has often been assumed (Guijarro 2013: 350).
[42] Kangumu (2011): 244–266. See also: Flint (2003).
[43] Flint (2003): 420.
[44] Kangumu (2011): 244.
[45] Ellis (1994), Isaacman et al. (2015): 553–557.
[46] Boden (2003).

western Caprivi, killing over one hundred people in 2000.[47] UNITA's incursion, as well as the fear of being held responsible by the NDF for supporting the CLA, again forced many civilians, especially from the Western Caprivi, to flee to Botswana. Others were arrested or supposedly disappeared from or died in NDF detention.[48]

It is not within the scope of this book to elaborate further on this period of conflict in the Caprivi, which lasted chiefly from 1998 until the end of the Angolan Civil War in 2002. However, what is important to repeat is that, for many Caprivians, lasting peace only arrived in 2002 – if indeed it has, with hundreds of Caprivians still languishing in refugee camps in Botswana, in exile in other countries, or in Namibian prisons. Furthermore, according to Julie Taylor and many of my informants, harassment and violence still characterise politics in the western Caprivi, while the political situation in the Eastern Caprivi has generally remained tense.[49]

Communal Conservancies and Peace Parks

The Caprivi has been central to the development of community-based nature conservation and transfrontier conservation areas. One of the first communal conservancies to be established in Namibia is located in the Caprivi, while the entire region has been incorporated into the Kavango Zambezi Transfrontier Conservation Area (KAZA TFCA), otherwise known as the KAZA Peace Park or simply KAZA.[50]

The creation of communal conservancies and TFCAs reflect wider Southern African, if not global, trends in nature conservation and demonstrate the field's entanglements with notions of economic development, security-orientated surveillance and the production of spatial knowledge. As such, the Caprivi's communal conservancies and the KAZA TFCA must be understood within the historical context of the close interconnections between nature, environmental research, development and warfare in the region during the South African occupation and its aftermath.

---

[47] Taylor (2012): 99.
[48] Taylor (2012): 99.
[49] For example, AK mentioned the NDF's eviction of a small village in the western Caprivi in 2010, supposedly because of its inhabitants' support for the secessionist cause (AK, 30.05.2014, Omega I). According to many informants and from my own experiences, police intelligence's control of political activism remains firm throughout the Caprivi. See also: Taylor (2012).
[50] In most promotional material and press articles as well as in the interviews which I conducted, the KAZA Transfrontier Conservation Area was referred to as the KAZA Peace Park. VS of the KAZA TFCA head office in Kasane insisted on using the term 'area'. For him, the term 'park' is too easily associated with "the idea of a closed, strongly controlled and uninhabited national park" (VS, 27.07.2011, Kasane). On the terminology of nature conservation areas, see: Ali (2007): 6–7. I will use 'KAZA TFCA' and 'KAZA Peace Park' interchangeably, often referring to the area simply as 'KAZA'.

The interplay between ideas of development, military practices and technologies, and environmental knowledge production provided an important spatial basis for the ordering and delimitation of various nature conservation spaces within the Caprivi. As such, these areas have been constituted and maintained through a mix of practices which has blurred the distinctions between the imperatives of conservation, development and security.

Communal Conservancies

One of the earliest conservancies to be established in Namibia was the Salambala Conservancy, located in the Zambezi Region, in 1998.[51] By 2016, fourteen further conservancies had been created in the Zambezi Region. Together, these covered about a third of the total area of the region and were home to about 31,000 inhabitants at the time.[52]

With the passing of Namibia's Nature Conservation Amendment Act of 1996 (No. 5 of 1996), "communities" located on communal land could apply to the Ministry of Environment and Tourism to acquire usage rights in relation to wildlife and tourism within a geographically defined area.[53] This opportunity was seen by the Namibian state as an extension of the property rights over wildlife which were accorded to white owners of private farms in the late 1960s.[54] These rights had been granted on the assumption that the commodification and privatised conservation of wildlife would provide farmers with an opportunity to earn a profit through hunting, the sale of live game, and tourism.[55] The then government of Namibia had regarded the introduction of this legislation as a success, because many cattle farmers had started to switch to game farming and tourism, thereby boosting the profits of the tourism industry and bringing about an increase in the number of economically useful wildlife on private farms.[56]

As the Ministry of Environment and Tourism emphasised with reference to the granting of ownership rights over wildlife in a policy document in 1995, "[t]he discrimination of the past needs to be redressed, and people living on communal land need to be afforded the

---

[51] The first conservancy to be established in Namibia was the Nyae Nyae Conservancy, located in the Otjozondjupa Region, in 1997. There are no conservancies in western Caprivi.
[52] www.nacso.org.na/conservancies [01.01.2016]. There are also three community forest areas which are run on similar principles to the conservancies. However, all residents of the community forests are members of their respective projects, while in the conservancies not all residents are members.
[53] Jones, B. (2010), The Evaluation of Namibia's Communal Conservancies. In F. Nelson (ed.), *Community Rights, Conservation and Contested Land: The Politics of Natural Resource Governance in Africa*. London and Washington DC: Earthscan: 106–120 (here 106–107).
[54] E.g.: CB, 23.08.2012, Windhoek. See also: Jones (2010): 108. Other sources indicate that this law was only introduced in 1975, see: Owen-Smith (2010): 540.
[55] CB, 23.08.2012, Windhoek.
[56] CB, 23.08.2012, Windhoek.

same rights as were conferred on commercial farmers".[57] However, communal areas differed markedly from private farms in that no individual property rights existed for the land. The ownership of wildlife could thus not be transferred to individual landowners. This challenge of awarding ownership rights over wildlife to people who were not foreseen to obtain land titles was circumnavigated by the introduction of communal conservancies, by which the Nature Conservation Amendment Act of 1996 awarded "communities" usage rights for natural resources found on communal land.[58] Communities could only gain these rights by forming a conservancy, namely "a local common property resource management institution which has a defined membership, defined area of land and a governing constitution".[59]

According to the act, any group of people living on communal land can apply to the Ministry of Environment and Tourism to establish a conservancy. A conservancy will be awarded if it has:

a) an elected representative committee
b) agreed on a legal constitution regarding the management and utilization of game
c) has the ability to manage funds
d) provides a method for the equitable distribution of income from the wildlife and tourism
e) has a defined membership
f) has defined boundaries and
g) the area is not leased or proclaimed as national park or game reserve.[60]

Within a recognised conservancy, the conservancy committee can allow residents to hunt wildlife, for subsistence according to the general hunting laws. It can also allow people to carry out trophy hunting within quotas set by the state and sell hunting permits to private

---

[57] Quoted in: Jones (2010): 113.
[58] Land relations and property rights in northern Namibia are more complex than the clear differentiation between freehold, privately-owned land and communal land would suggest. Romie Vonkie Nghitevelekwa described communal land as "a complex and contested terrain comprising of different social actors, who manoeuvre and struggle to control and use land" (Nghitevelekwa, R.V. (2016), Land relations and property rights in central-north Namibia's communal lands. In M. Ramutsindela, G. Miescher and M. Boehi (eds.), *The Politics of Nature and Science in Southern Africa*. Basel: Basler Afrika Bibliographien, p. 209). Most importantly, she described how individual property rights to land are only one of many possible means of access to land and resources (228). See also: Jones (2010): 117.
[59] The distinction between being a member of a 'community' and being a member of a conservancy remains often unclear. According to IRDNC, residents of areas which form part of conservancies do not have to become members of their respective conservancy. In reality, it would appear that generally all residents become conservancy members when they turn eighteen (Personal comments by IRDNC personnel). However, Jones (2010) included all inhabitants of a conservancy in 'the community', irrespective of whether they were members of the former or not.
[60] Jones (2010): 107–8.

trophy hunters. The sale and purchase of live game animals as well as the negotiation of contracts with private investors for commercial tourism projects is also permitted.[61] All income from these activities goes to the conservancies, which are free to decide on how to spend it.

There are two main reasons for the swift reform of nature conservation in Namibia in the 1990s and the conservancies' right to fully retain the income which they earn. The first, as Nelson and Agrawal argued, is mainly a result of the low tax revenue which the state earned from wildlife and tourism in communal lands in comparison to what it received from national parks and privately-owned game farms and reserves.[62] This stood in stark contrast to neighbouring countries such as Zambia, where the wildlife sector in communal areas provided the state with the majority of its gross income in the field of tourism.[63] The Namibian state therefore did not stand to lose much income by giving the conservancies full rights to revenue earned through wildlife.[64]

The second reason for the rapid and thorough implementation of a community-based approach to nature conservation in post-independence Namibia was the opening up of the country for international tourism and foreign investment after 1990. It was in this changing economic and political context that ideas of promoting nature conservation and nature-based tourism as the solution for rural development took hold in Namibia. New in this approach was that the government believed it no longer needed to rely on a state-centred approach to achieve this goal, but could allow itself to fall back on the powers of the market. In the words of the Zimbabwean social scientist Vupenyu Dzingirai:

> [a]fter many years of violent and militaristic methods of wildlife conservation the state has finally joined hands with private business. These two parties [...] actively invite 'tribesmen' and poachers to put down their spears and be part of what they and many others call community conservation.[65]

---

[61] Jones (2010): 108.
[62] Nelson, F. and A. Agrawal (2008), Patronage or Participation? Community-based Natural Resource Management Reform in sub-Saharan Africa. *Development and Change* 39(4): 557–585.
[63] Nelson et al. (2008). See also: Gibson, C.C. (1999), *Politicians and Poachers*. Cambridge: Cambridge University Press.
[64] Jones (2010): 108. In 1993, before legal provision was made for the establishment of conservancies, the Caprivi made roughly NAD 600,000 (approximately USD 160,000 at the exchange rate of the day) revenue from trophy hunting, the most for any communal area. In comparison, the country's total revenue from the wildlife sector came to an approximate amount of USD 16 million during the same year. See: Yaron, G., T. Healy, and C. Tapscott (1993), *The Economics of Living with Wildlife in Namibia: Report for the World Bank*. Washington DC.
[65] Dzingirai (2003): 243.

Continuing in this scornful tone, Dzingirai went on to identify some central critiques of community-based approaches, including the delegation of state responsibilities to private companies, the definition of "communities" as "tribesmen" rooted to their natural environment within geographically and institutionally fixed ethnic structures, and the continuation of violent and colonial forms of wildlife conservation by other means.[66] As I have shown, all of the points raised by Dzingirai's critique had also antecedents in pre-independence Caprivi.

Peace Parks

The second key feature of Namibia's post-independence nature conservation policy – and that of the Caprivi in particular – are transfrontier conservation areas. According to the definition provided by the International Union for Conservation of Nature and Natural Resources (IUCN), this term applies to a protected area "that straddles one or more borders between states, sub-national units such as provinces or regions, autonomous areas and/or areas beyond the limits of national sovereignty".[67] The first transfrontier park was established in 1932 with the opening of the Waterton Lakes Glacier International Peace Park on both sides of the USA-Canada border.[68] In South Africa, the idea of creating transfrontier conservation areas was taken up by the billionaire Anton Rupert, who had been president of the WWF South Africa in the 1970s and 1980s. Together with Bernhard von Lippe-Biesterfeld, prince of the Netherlands and founding president of the WWF, and Nelson Mandela, Rupert founded the Peace Park Foundation (PPF) in 1997.[69] By the early 2000s, the organisation had become highly influential among conservation circles in Southern Africa. The PPF focusses predominantly on supporting the establishment of protected areas which cross state borders. However, unlike some earlier transfrontier areas such as Waterton, the peace parks which have emerged to span the borders of many southern African countries were not only seen as nature conservation areas, but as representing the "confluence of several mutually reinforcing interests, mainly those of biodiversity conservation, economic development, cultural integrity and regional peace and security".[70] The PPF, which portrays itself in its slogan as offering "the global solution", has enjoyed the support of many prominent figures, including the head of states of South Africa, Namibia, Botswana, Angola and Zimba-

---

[66] Dzingirai (2003).
[67] Quoted by: Sandwith, T., C. Shine, L. Hamilton, and D. Sheppard (2001), *Transboundary Protected Areas for Peace and Cooperation*. Gland: IUCN.
[68] Ali (2007): 2.
[69] Duffy (2006): 97–98.
[70] Hammill, A. and C. Besançon (2007), Measuring Peace Park Performance: Definitions and Experiences. In Ali, S.H. (ed.), *Peace Parks, Conservation and Conflict Resolution*. Cambridge MA: MIT Press: 23–40 (here 25).

bwe.[71] Marja Spierenburg and Harry Wels described the illustrious group of South African and international donors who finance the PPF's activities as "conservative philanthropists, royalty and business elites".[72] Although the extent of the direct influence of transfrontier conservation areas on grassroots socio-economic conditions in Southern Africa is disputed, their discursive impact has been striking. In recent years, the peace parks have been the subject of widespread international media coverage, while the PPF as well as some individual TFCAs have won important conservation awards.[73]

The KAZA Peace Park, whose area covers the entire Caprivi and incorporates the region's national parks, conservancies and urban areas alike, is one of eighteen peace parks which have been established or conceptualised in Southern and East Africa since 1997.[74] The aims of the KAZA TFCA, as they appear in its treaty of establishment, were to create a conservation area roughly equivalent to the size of France (approximately 520,000 km^2) which would cover territory in five different states (Angola, Botswana, Namibia, Zambia and Zimbabwe).[75] The project was officially announced in 2006, when the five countries and the Southern African Development Community (SADC) concluded a Memorandum of Understanding (MoU). It was then launched on 15 March 2012, when the five ministers responsible for environment, wildlife and tourism of the five partner states hosted "various stakeholders" in Katima Mulilo and unveiled the KAZA TFCA Treaty.[76]

---

[71] The PPF is also backed financially by Club 21, a trust of donors representing, among others, leading global luxury brand, mining and oil companies, such as Richemont, De Beers or Total. Other members of the Club 21 include the Edmond de Rothschild Foundation and the WWF. For a complete list of the PPF's donors, see: http://www.peaceparks.org/story.php?pid=1&mid=4 [accessed 22.01.2017].

[72] Spierenburg, M. and H. Wels (2009), Conservative Philanthropists, Royalty and Business Elites. *Antipode*, 42(3): 647–670. For a general discussion on philanthropic funding of nature conservation in Southern Africa, see also: Ramutsindela, M., M. Spierenburg, and H. Wels (2011), *Sponsoring Nature: Environmental Philanthropy for Conservation*, London: Earthscan/Routledge.

[73] Peace parks have been the subject of articles or reports in international media publications or networks such as *National Geographic, The Guardian, New York Times, Japan Times, BBC, CNN, Al-Jazeera, France 1, n-tv* and *Deutsche Welle* as well as across newspapers and television stations in Southern Africa.

[74] For a visual overview, see the PPF's map by the: www.peaceparks.org/story.php?pid=100&mid=19 [15.08.2016]

[75] www.kavangozambezi.org/about-us [accessed 01.03.2017].

[76] www.peaceparks.org/tfca.php?pid=27&mid=1008 [accessed 30.01.2017].

Narratives of Development

Conservation, Development, and the Commodification of Nature

The commodification of nature has been central to the approach towards conservation which was adopted in the Caprivi during the South African occupation and has been intensified after independence. The term 'commodification of nature' denotes methods of rendering natural objects and entities as well as nature-related practices tradable, usually by ascribing them with 'economic values'.[77] At the heart of such approaches is the assumption that everything can "in principle be treated as a commodity".[78] According to David Harvey, this extends to property rights over "processes, things, and social relations, [so] that a price can be put on them, and that they can be traded subject to legal contract".[79] In this way, an "increasing amount of life's facets become embedded in competitive markets and subject to trade in monetary terms".[80] In the case of the Caprivi, many of these tradable facets of life related to the region's natural environment and practices of nature conservation, trophy hunting and tourism.

The notion that nature could be protected by converting its parts, such as charismatic wildlife, into a tradable commodity was not unheard of in the Caprivi. Nature conservation in the region had often been portrayed as a developmental intervention for the well-being of its population. For example, the South African occupation authorities had considered the promise of small-scale profits for the local population as a means to encourage them to protect animals. As I discussed earlier, the South African official K. Kettlitz emphasised in a report published in 1970 that the protection of Caprivian wildlife would be important for the economic development of the region. Furthermore, he considered providing Caprivians with a means to profit from conservation as the only viable strategy to successfully further game preservation in the area. Some two decades before the official introduction of market-based community conservation strategies in the Caprivi, Kettlitz thus proposed monetary incentives as a means to encourage locals to protect wildlife. In this regard, he recommended that some of the money spent in the Caprivi by tourists, as well as the meat of animals killed by trophy hunters, should be distributed amongst the local population.[81]

---

[77] Büscher (2013) and Castree, N. (2003), Commodifying What Nature? *Progress in Human Geography*, 27(3): 273–297.
[78] Harvey, D. (2005), *A Brief History of Neoliberalism*. Oxford: Oxford University Press, p. 165 and Büscher 2013: 34.
[79] Harvey (2005): 165.
[80] Büscher (2013): 13.
[81] NAN, LKM, 21/1/2, Beskerming van Wild: Oostelike Caprivi Zipfel, 9 December 1970: 11–12.

In the same vein, the authors of the Eastern Caprivi Development Plan argued in 1983 that safari and hunting tourism could be of significant benefit for locals.[82] However, within the institutionally racist and undemocratic context of South African occupation, the authors could be open about what they regarded as the considerable limitations of the possible involvement of Caprivians. They wrote that "individual Caprivians have neither the skill nor the finance to develop, manage or conserve Caprivi's natural attractions", but could be relied upon to offer simple tourist services, such as log-boat tours or the sale of fish.[83]

The idea that the rural population could be urged to protect wildlife by promising them a share of the profits of its commodification reflected a general trend in nature conservation in the 1970s.[84] The vision of using market mechanisms – namely, the distribution of resources according to monetary demand and supply – to achieve conservation gained strength in the 1980s, when the concept of the 'sustainable utilisation' of wildlife and ecosystems came into focus.[85] In 1980, when the IUCN, the United Nations Environment Programme, and the WWF jointly published their 'World Conservation Strategy', they 'officially' set their sights on aligning the goals of conservation with those of economic development.[86] As such, the credo of the global left-wing, anti-capitalist environmentalist movement of the 1960s and 1970s that the goals of corporations were incompatible with those of nature conservation was replaced by the idea that a 'sustainable' economy was the only way to preserve nature.[87]

However, the extent to which the repeatedly invoked policy of using nature conservation to further local development in the Caprivi in the 1970s and 1980s was linked to these global developments is doubtful. While South African conservation circles were aware of international trends in the field, Pretoria's nature conservation policies in the Caprivi must still be understood in relation to the apartheid policy of 'separate development' and self-governing homelands. Furthermore, apartheid conservation policy was still influenced by

---

[82] Van der Vegte et al. (1983): 150–158 and 175–188.
[83] Van der Vegte et al. (1983): 180.
[84] Armeirio et al. (2014).
[85] MacDonald, K.I. (2011), The Devil is in the (Bio)diversity. In D. Brockington and R. Duffy (eds.), *Capitalism and Conservation.* Malden MA and Oxford: Wiley Blackwell: 44–81 (here 48).
[86] Adams and Hutton (2007): 147–183 and International Union for Conservation of Nature and Natural Resources (ed.) (1980), *World Conservation Strategy – Living Resource Conservation for Sustainable Development.* Gland.
[87] Brockington, D. and R. Duffy (2011), Introduction: Capitalism and Conservation: The Production and Reproduction of Biodiversity Conservation. In D. Brockington and R. Duffy (eds.), *Capitalism and Conservation.* Malden MA and Oxford: Wiley Blackwell: 1–17 (here 2). For texts by left-wing, anti-capitalist environmentalists, see e.g.: Roberts, A. (1979), *The Self-Managing Environment.* London: Allison & Busby or O'Connor, J. (1988), Capitalism, nature, socialism: a theoretical introduction. *Capitalism Nature Socialism*, 1(1): 11–38.

enduring elitist notions of nature conservation, according to which rich elites promoted the protection of specific wildlife species for their own hunting and safari pleasure.[88]

In order to recognise what the commodification of nature in post-apartheid Southern Africa entails, it is crucial to understand recent developments in nature conservation within the wider political context of neoliberalism, which has shaped governmental policy in many parts of the subcontinent since at least the 1990s.[89] The labelling of these recent developments in conservation as 'neoliberal' or as part of a trend towards the 'neoliberalisation' of nature has been a source of much debate in critical geography, history, sociology and ecology in the early twenty-first century.[90] Though it has also become a widely accepted prism through which to understand recent conservation trends in Southern Africa, the term 'neoliberalism' has been very broadly applied, and definitions have varied significantly.[91]

In order to account for the historical and socio-economic context of particular conservation efforts, it is crucial to understand 'neoliberalism' as a process of 'neoliberalisation'.[92] I follow Jaime Peck, who posited that, because clearer definitions of neoliberalism are simply not possible, "concretely grounded accounts of the process must be chiselled out of the interstices of state/market configurations".[93] This definition allows for a departure from a highly contested, yet often relatively static model. It also presents the opportunity to understand

---

[88] As described in the case of the Arusha National Park in Tanzania by: Neumann, R.P. (1998), *Imposing Wilderness: Struggles over Livelihood and Nature Preservation*. Berkeley: University of California Press or for the colonial era in Kenya by: Steinhart (2006).

[89] On neoliberal politics in South Africa since 1990, see e.g.: Bond, P. (2005), *Elite Transition: From Apartheid to Neoliberalism in South Africa*. Pietermaritzburg: University of KwaZulu-Natal Press.

[90] There is a vast body of literature discussing the interplay between neoliberalism and nature (conservation) globally. See e.g.: articles by Castree (2003), Castree (2008), Castree (2011) or Haynen et al. (2007), Igoe, J. and Brockington, D. (2007), Neoliberal Conservation: A Brief Introduction, *Conservation & Society*, 5(4): 432–449. Within a southern African context, see e.g.: Büscher (2013), Ramutsindela (2007), Ramutsindela and Shabangu (2013).

[91] See e.g.: Saad-Filho, A. and D. Johnston (2005), Introduction. In: A. Saad-Filho and D. Johnston (eds.), *Neoliberalism: A Critical Reader*. London: Pluto: 1–6 (here 2–3). Saad-Filho and Johnston argued that there is no clear definition for the term 'neoliberal', while David Harvey provided a very broad definition: "Neoliberalism is in the first instance a theory of political economic practices that proposes that human well-being can best be advanced by liberating individual entrepreneurial freedoms and skills within an institutional framework characterized by strong private property rights, free markets and free trade. The role of the state is to create and preserve an institutional framework appropriate to such practices [...]. It must also set up those military, defence, police and legal structures and functions required to secure private property rights and to guarantee, by force if need be, the proper functioning of markets. Furthermore, if markets do not exist (in areas such as land, water, education, health care, social security, or environmental pollution) then they must be created, by state action if necessary" (Harvey 2005: 2).

[92] Peck, J. (2010), *Constructions of Neoliberal Reason*. Oxford: Oxford University Press, p. 19. See also: Castree (2010); Büscher (2013): 12.

[93] Peck (2010): 15–16.

specific initiatives which impact upon the Caprivi today within the context of concrete local and regional histories, as undertaken in this book.[94]

While the historical aspects of neoliberalisation processes represent a promising avenue for further analysis, this approach calls for a thorough understanding of the specific socio-economic and political contexts of the various conservation initiatives. Such analysis would contribute to a better understanding of the role which nature conservation has played in creating a badly paid workforce or even a rural proletariat, as has been discussed recently in the field of critical conservation studies.[95]

The master narrative about the history of (communal) wildlife management in Africa which is commonly cited as a justification for the privatisation or decentralisation of resource management, especially wildlife protection, claims that the colonial state centralised control of and monopolised access to land, resources and wildlife which had "previously been controlled by more localized institutions".[96] Independent post-colonial nation-states then took over these monopolies in order to "drive modernization processes and control patronage recourses".[97] However, attempts at modernisation failed as a result of corruption, patronage or other endogenous reasons.[98] According to this view, the state's control of natural recourses only served to present a barrier to local people's abilities to profit directly from their environment by placing their services on the global market.[99] The withdrawal of the state from the management of natural resources was propelled by the rise of international neoliberalism, in particular in the form of structural adjustment programmes instituted by the International Monetary Fund (IMF) and World Bank. These compelled many highly-

---

[94] Nonetheless, it is also crucial to observe that there are some central features of neoliberalisation which appear to be only peripheral to neoliberal nature conservation, such as processes of financialisation. See: Harvey (2005): 33 and Brockington et al. (2011): 12.

[95] See e.g.: Mosimane A. W. and J.A. Silva, (2014), Boundary Making in Conservancies: The Namibian Experience. In: M. Ramutsindela, M. (ed.), *Cartographies of Nature: How Nature Conservation Animates Borders*. Newcastle upon Tyne: Cambridge Scholars Publishing: 83–111 and Sidikoff, G. (2009), The low-wage conservationist: Biodiversity and perversity of value in Madagascar. *American Anthropologist* 11(4): 443–455. See also: Spierenburg, M. and S. Brooks (2014), Private Game Farming and its Social Consequences in Post-Apartheid South Africa: Contestations over Wildlife, Property and Agrarian Futures. *Journal of Contemporary African Studies*, 32(2): 151–172. This is particularly relevant to Namibia, where Gordon and Douglas observed a similar historical trend towards the creation of 'San' people as a rural proletariat during the South African occupation. See: Gordon et. al (1992).

[96] Nelson, F. (2010), Introduction: The Politics of Natural Resource Governance in Africa. In F. Nelson (ed.), *Community Rights, Conservation and Contested Land: The Politics of Natural Resource Governance in Africa*. London and Washington DC: Earthscan: 3–31 (here: 3).

[97] Nelson (2010): 3.

[98] Chabal, P. and J.-P. Daloz (1999), *Africa Works: Disorder as Political Instrument*. Oxford: James Currey and Ake, C. (1996), *Democracy and Development in Africa*. Washington: Brookings.

[99] Nelson (2010): 2.

indebted countries to privatise and decentralise state assets and functions in the late 1970s and 1980s.[100] It was during this period that in Namibia and South Africa wildlife ownership was transferred from the white-minority state to white landowners, leading to "increases of both the number of animals and the economic productivity of wildlife as a form of land use".[101]

As I have shown, this narrative is not fully applicable to the historical context of the former South African-occupied areas of northern Namibia, such as the Caprivi. Under South African rule, the process of protecting Caprivian nature through pricing it and turning it into a tradable commodity was undertaken in combination with coercive measures. After independence and within the confines of a new constitutional order, alternative means had to be found to encourage Caprivians to seek a profit through nature conservation-related activities. The solution was seen by the government and the involved NGOs to lie in the dynamics of the market itself, which, it was presumed, would force "its participants to discipline themselves to do what is required to remain competitive in selling their product".[102] It was supposed that a predominantly rural population like that in the Caprivi would be driven away from subsistence hunting or agriculture towards economically more promising fields, such as tourism or controlled trophy hunting. In the following section, I will return to the two major initiatives in Caprivian nature conservation in the post-independence neoliberal economy and contextualise these in relation to narratives of 'development'.

Communal Conservancies and Narratives of Development in the Caprivi

Despite criticism that the profits gained from natural resources and wildlife management in communal areas often remain insignificant, Namibia's conservancy approach has been portrayed domestically and internationally as a success.[103] To assess the degree to which the promised positive economic effects have been experienced in the Caprivi, in-depth, critical socio-economic analyses at a regional, village or even family level would be needed. Such research is yet to be conducted for most of the conservancies in the Caprivi.[104] In their 2012

---

[100] On such programmes and their impact on poor countries, see, e.g. Brown, E., B. Milward, G. Mohan, A.B. Zack-Williams (eds.) (2000), *Structural Adjustment: Theory, Practice and Impacts*. London: Routledge.
[101] Nelson (2010): 9.
[102] Büscher (2013): 13.
[103] Jones (2010): 108.
[104] The most thorough study on the economics and issues relating to land rights of conservancies in the Caprivi remains a study undertaken for the Legal Assistance Centre in Windhoek, which focused mainly on the Salambala Conservancy but also provided reasonably detailed information on the other conservancies in the region. Harring, S.L. and W. Odendaal (2012), *"God stopped making land!": Land Rights, Conflict and Law in Namibia's Caprivi Region*. Windhoek: LAC. See also: Mosimane, A. (2003), Caprivi Region Conservancies Management Profiles: Mashi, Impalila,

report, Sidney Harring and Willem Odendaal focused on the Salambala conservancy, reaching the conclusion that the general economic impact of conservancies on Namibia's rural population is "clearly mixed".[105] While conservancies undoubtedly provide a "major infusion of cash into communal villages", the authors also emphasised that a closer examination of these cash flows yielded "much more mixed" results.[106] In particular, this is because only a small number of conservancies in Namibia make most of the profit in the sector, and even the most profitable conservancies are usually still highly dependent on a few trophy hunters or commercial tourism investors. Other research on the economic impact of conservancies in Namibia shows a similarly unequal picture. Most of the academic research which investigated the socio-economic impact of conservancies at a community level observed an overall positive effect.[107] However, the few studies which examined conservancies' socio-economic impact on individuals or households noted negligible benefits, no effect at all, or even a generally negative impact.[108] Even when conservancies do earn some income, this does not necessarily reach all its members, let alone all its inhabitants.[109] The biggest proportion of the conservancies' income is generally distributed as wages to conservancy employees. A smaller amount is invested into tourism infrastructure and other so-called community projects. Most jobs in the conservancies are low-income positions, with the average wage for a community game guard in Namibia being NAD 1,000 (USD 77) per month.[110]

An influential actor in community conservation in the Zambezi Region has been Integrated Rural Development and Nature Conservation (IRDNC). This Namibian NGO supports conservancies in a variety of ways, including through the education of game guards, women empowerment projects, mapping projects, networking, and by providing legal assistance. It

---

Kasika, Wuparo, Mayuni, Salambala and Kwandu. (Unpublished MRCC Research Report, Windhoek, University of Namibia).

[105] Harring et al. (2012): 18.

[106] Harring et al. (2012): 18.

[107] E.g.: Naidoo, R., G. Stuart-Hill, L.C. Weaver, J. Tagg, A. Davis and A. Davidson (2011), Effect of diversity of large wildlife species on financial benefits to local communities in northwest Namibia. *Environment Resource Economy*, 48: 321–335.

[108] Riehl, B., H. Zerriffi and R. Naidoo (2016), Effects of Community-Based Natural Resource Management on Household Welfare in Namibia. *PLoS ONE* 10(5): e0125531.

[109] In 2014, an estimated total population of 175,000 people were living in 78 communal conservancies throughout Namibia. The combined income of all conservancies was given as NAD 38 million (ca. USD 2.9 million) in the same year, most of which was generated through trophy hunting. This would amount to a total annual income of about NAD 220 (USD 17) per conservancy resident, if equally shared among every inhabitant. See: www.irdnc.org.na/our-impact.html [15.04.2016].

[110] www.irdnc.org.na/our-impact.html [15.04.2016]. The average wage for unskilled workers in the agriculture, fishery and forestry sectors in 2014 was NAD 2,100 per month. (Namibia Statistics Agency (2015), *Namibia Labour Force Survey 2014*. Windhoek: Namibia Statistics Agency). The community game guards do not normally work full-time.

was founded in the 1980s in north-western Namibia, where it played a major role in saving the black rhinoceros from extinction by co-operating closely with "community leaders".[111] After the implementation of the new nature conservation legislation in 1996, the organisation became active in supporting the newly-established conservancies in what it calls "the three most remote corners of the country"[112]: the Kunene, Zambezi and Kavango East Regions. In this task, it worked closely with a network of private donors, fellow NGOs and state institutions under the umbrella of the Namibian Association of Community Based Natural Resource Management Support Organisations (NACSO).

Prominently placed on the IRDNC's website is a quote ascribed to George Mutwa, son of the former chief of the traditional authority which controls the land on which the Salambala Conservancy is located. Mutwa purportedly stated that "[w]ildlife is gold";[113] for the IRDNC, this signifies that the "[u]tilization of wildlife is necessary in developing Africa – if wild animals bring no benefits people won't conserve them".[114] This reasoning reflects many of the points made in this book about how conservationists have discounted the possibility that 'people', namely Africans, could have an intrinsic interest in protecting wildlife. At the same time, it identifies the promise of (an often minimal) profit as the only means to encourage rural Africans to protect wildlife.

As such, the IRDNC's understanding of wildlife conservation not only displays aspects of the conservation discourse of the past, but also embodies many of the critiques which scholars of critical conservation studies have advanced over the last decade. These critiques encompass two major, often interrelated, arguments. The first understands recent conservation measures as a continuation of colonial practices,[115] while the second identifies a major qualitative shift in more recent projects towards the commodification or neo-liberalisation of nature.[116] Evidence of continuities with colonialism is apparent in the IRDNC's (at least rhetorical) reduction of the rural African population in Namibia to a homogeneous community which must be shown the path to development. This reinforces earlier colonial and apartheid representations of a 'native problem' which could be solved by the 'development'

---

[111] For an insider's view of the history and development of the IRDNC, see the extensive autobiography by its co-founder, Garth Owen-Smith: Owen-Smith (2010).
[112] Homepage IRDNC, www.irdnc.org.na/history.html [30.04.2016].
[113] Homepage IRDNC, www.irdnc.org.na [30.04.2016].
[114] http://www.irdnc.org.na/what-we-do.html [30.04.2016].
[115] Adams, W.M. and M. Mulligan (2003), *Decolonizing Nature: Strategies for Conservation in a Postcolonial Era*. London and Sterling: Earthscan Publications: 9; Singh et al. (2002): 253–263, Brockington and Igoe (2006), Neumann (1998).
[116] Barrett, G., S. Brooks, J. Josefsson, N. Zulu (2013), Starting the Conservation: Land Issues and Critical Conservation Studies in Post-Colonial Africa. *Journal of Contemporary African Studies*, 31(3): 336–344 (here 337).

of the so-called native population in rural areas. Furthermore, it draws on a colonial narrative which called for the "saving [of] Africa from the Africans".[117] Grounds for the second critique can be seen in the IRDNC's proposed solution of incorporating the mechanisms of markets into nature conservation. Nature conservation areas are thereby no longer conceptualised as spaces which should be sealed off from economic forces, but as commodities in their own right which are key to the economic development of rural areas.[118] In the view of the government and many NGOs, community-based nature conservation thus increasingly became rural areas' main, if not only, asset which was worthy of further support and subsidisation.

Although a belief in the positive impact of the conservancies was widely expressed in the Caprivi too, I also came across critical voices expressed by several trade unionists, politicians and other individuals.[119] Unlike the supporters of conservancies, they either did not consent to me recording their interviews or did not agree to formal interviews for fear of the severe repercussions of speaking out, ranging from physical threats and defamation to loss of business.[120] These critical voices contradicted the dominant narrative which portrayed conservancies as a means of assisting people to regain ownership rights and control over their land and its natural resources. They often addressed the inequality which exists between a local elite which collaborates with NGOs and international conservation groups and the marginalised majority of village residents living within or next to the conservancies. A symptom of this disparity, they pointed out, was that the management of the conservancies was often more interested in wildlife protection than supporting the local population, an accusation which had been repeated over the course of the last century in relation to the management of wildlife in the area.

One critic of the conservancies who was prepared to discuss his concerns with me was PL, a former official within the Eastern Caprivi homeland administration who became a politician in the post-independence regional government. According to him, "the conservancies are fine and the idea behind is not bad, but there are still some rules that are not community-focused but more animal- or wildlife-focused." As a reason for this, he identified the "mentality" of the people in charge for conservancies, who had not learnt to listen to the general population in the Caprivi and still acted in the manner of the former South African administrators. For PL, this attitude underpinned existing power structures; as he claimed,

---

[117] E.g.: Adams et al. (2003) and Brockington et al. (2006).
[118] Barrett et al. (2013): 338.
[119] PL, 13.05.2014, Katima Mulilo; MS, 29.06.2014, Katima Mulilo; PN, 17.08.2012, Windhoek.
[120] www.irdnc.org.na/what-we-do.html [30.04.2016].

the advocates of the conservancies "only talk to the chiefs", who themselves stand to gain the most from the conservancies.[121]

PL's main criticism, however, lay in what he saw as the underlying logic of the conservancies. While conservancies have been unable to make sufficient profit to support their populations, their existence has increasingly reduced the opportunities for their residents to exploit other potential sources of income, such as commercial farming. For PL, "proper economic development" in the Caprivi was no longer possible as state compensation for the yield or livestock losses which farmers suffered as a result of the growing numbers of wildlife often amounted to less than a farmer's actual expenses.[122]

In order to conceptualise these contestations over the communal conservancies, it is helpful to return to the framework of neoliberal conservation discussed above, especially given that underlying narratives of and positive assumptions about development had a long history in the region. After independence, two mechanisms of Namibia's conservancy policy supported the extension of neoliberal development practices into communal lands, in the process provoking discord and contestation.[123] First, the designated communities were tasked with facilitating their own 'socio-economic development' through the investment of the income which they derived from conservation.[124] The result has been that local poverty alleviation and other state services have become increasingly reliant on revenue from a global, capitalist tourism market. In order to align themselves with these new imperatives and gain an income, residents have been compelled to become either labourers or providers of the stereotypical resources and services of their environment (hunting and safari tourism) or their 'culture' (ethno-tourism). Community-based resource management strategies have thus pushed rural dwellers into becoming custodians of a specific, historically constructed 'rural' way of life catering to the consumption patterns and desires of a global, urban elite of hunters and tourists.[125] This role resembles elements of the 1983 Eastern Caprivi Strategic Development Plan, in which "individual Caprivians" were proposed as badly-paid service providers and unskilled labourers for an emerging tourism market.[126]

The second mechanism through which conservancies have reinforced neoliberal policies has been through the growing incorporation of local residents into a formal labour market,

---

[121] All quotes: PL, 13.05.2014, Katima Mulilo.
[122] PL, 13.05.2014, Katima Mulilo.
[123] Mosimane et al. (2014): 85.
[124] As an example, Mosimane and Silva noted that the conservancies, as opposed to the state, have become increasingly responsible for paying farmers compensation for livestock loss by wildlife. Mosimane et al. (2014): 85.
[125] See also: Brockington et al. (2011), Mosimane et al. (2014). On hunting: Bollig et al. (2016), 70–74.
[126] Van der Vegte et al. (1983): 180.

mostly in poorly-paid positions in lodges or for the conservancies themselves, often as game guards. Not only are people who work for a conservancy or in the tourism industry consequently ever more unable to provide much-needed labour on family farms, but these farms also increasingly suffer from the negative consequences of conservation, including the reduction of grazing land and cropland and corresponding livestock and crop loss.[127]

Though it is not within the scope of this study to assess whether incorporation into the global tourism market as well as the state's focus on promoting the economic self-reliance of "communities" helped some individuals or groups to improve their living standards, statistics on conservancy income do show that most communal conservancies, like many earlier conservation initiatives, have not yet contributed significantly to the reduction of rural poverty in the Caprivi.[128] Indeed, there are indications that suggest that conservancies are having a similar effect to other neoliberal projects, which, as David Harvey has argued, have helped to "restore and maintain class power and privilege".[129] Although they may offer a potential path to economic growth, communal conservancies carry with them the danger of perpetuating the exploitation of the rural population for cheap labour at the same time as they offer the rich luxury services at a cheap price. This system is upheld, however, by the eventual profits and riches which conservancies constantly promise their residents. Conservancies thus "perpetuate existing structural inequalities in the global economy, whereby large multinational tourism operations are poised to capture more financial benefits than local residents".[130] This is also evident in the central role which conservancies have played in the privatisation of rural development. As the Namibian state has increasingly renounced its responsibilities in the area of rural development and transferred its powers to private actors, the conservancies have been quick to partner with global investors in the tourism industry and related sectors to take over state functions, such as the reimbursement of lost cattle or even poverty reduction schemes.

In conclusion, the communal conservancy programme has been one of a number of initiatives which make up the history of market expansion and increasing rural dependence on low-paid labour contracts in the Caprivi. Moreover, through their role in the commodification and neoliberalisation of Caprivian nature, conservancies paved the way for an even more ambitious neoliberal nature conservation intervention, the KAZA Transfrontier Conservation Area or Peace Park.

---

[127] Mosimane et al. (2014): 85.
[128] Riehl et al. (2015).
[129] Harvey (2005): 119–120.
[130] Mosimane (2014): 85.

Peace Parks and Narratives of Development

While the communal conservancies' contribution to the neoliberalisation and privatisation of nature conservation and rural development in Namibia is contested, it is more broadly acknowledged by scholars that transfrontier conservation areas are archetypal for neoliberal nature conservation.[131] In one sense, this is striking; peace parks' top-down approach, which contrasts with the supposedly grassroots approach of the conservancies, is somewhat atypical for neoliberal policies, which are usually guided by ideas of individual responsibility and self-exploitation. However, even with its top-down approach, the peace park concept fits comfortably into the general tenets of the neoliberalisation of nature conservation and rural development, particularly through its effective combining of strategies of consensus, anti-politics and marketing.[132] As such, the PPF was increasingly successful in promoting its slogan of peace parks as "the global solution" to many of the problems relating to the economic development of rural and peripheral regions.

In order to contextualize the TFCA's powerful influence upon development discourses in Southern Africa, it is important to examine the views of people living within the boundaries of the projects. Unlike the conservancies, which are well-known among the Caprivi's rural inhabitants, awareness of KAZA appeared to be much lower when I commenced my research in 2012. This observation might be due to the notion of economic development to which KAZA subscribes, which operates largely on a discursive level as a powerful vision presenting itself as universally valid for the entire Southern African region, if not for the whole world.[133]

In 2011, days before the KAZA treaty was signed, I struggled to find any opinions on it at all in the region.[134] The only people who were aware of the planned peace park were tourism entrepreneurs, high-ranking conservation officers and representatives of NGOs. They all praised KAZA as "a great opportunity for investments" and for "unleashing the potential for further tourism", and therefore as a "chance for the local population's development".[135] While

---

[131] Büscher (2013). See also: Ramutsindela, M. (2007), *Transfrontier Conservation in Africa: At the Confluence of Capital, Politics and Nature.* Wallingford and Boston MA: CABI; Ramutsindela et al. (2013), Duffy, R. (2011), Peace Parks and Global Politics: The Paradoxes and Challenges of Global Governance. In S.H. Ali (ed.), *Peace Parks: Conservation and Conflict Resolution.* Cambridge: MIT Press: 55–68.

[132] Büscher (2013).

[133] Büscher (2013): 80, Duffy, R. (2006). The potential and pitfalls of global environmental governance: the politics of transfrontier conservation areas in Southern Africa. *Political Geography* 25: 89–112 (here 92).

[134] This is particularly striking, as planning for KAZA had already begun in 2003 and a first Memorandum of Understanding was signed in 2006.

[135] The quotes above are from MP, 23.07.2011, Kayaru; CW, 26.07.2011, Katima Mulilo and KS, 26.07.2011, Katima Mulilo.

the sentiments expressed in the first two quotes were not unexpected from persons who stood to profit from nature conservation and tourism, the question of the project's potential benefit for 'the local population' is worth examining. While the few individuals who knew about KAZA constantly alluded to its potential for an as yet undefined 'local population', the very people to whom this might have referred remained completely unaware of the initiative. Even some of the game guards who worked in the MET camps in the various national parks in the Caprivi had, as late as 2011, not yet heard of KAZA.[136]

Given the initially low level of public awareness about KAZA in the region, it was striking to hear how the local tourism and conservation elite frequently referred to 'the local population' and its significance for the KAZA project. At the same time, however, the owner of one of the largest local tourism businesses in the Caprivi declared that KAZA would be a "very good initiative" if it contributed to the easing of visa regulations for travellers moving between the participating countries; but, she added, this envisioned free movement of people should apply only to tourists if the measure was not to be a disaster for all parties. She concluded by stating that, for KAZA and other TFCAs, "the problems are the people".[137] In the same vein, an influent conservationist in Katima Mulilo argued that, although KAZA would help rural residents to obtain an income, inhabitants should still be convinced to move out of some of the parks' territories, where "they [would otherwise] remain poor and have a negative impact on the fragile nature".[138]

Although in the Caprivi those who stood to gain the most from KAZA had some knowledge of the project, in other areas of the park, especially in Angola, awareness seemed to be even lower. During my visit in 2012 to the University of Lubango, the closest university to KAZA's Angolan section, I could not find anyone who was involved in any way in the planning of the park or who was willing or even able to comment on it. Furthermore, it was not possible to travel to the Angolan section of the park without an official invitation or without being on an organised tour.

This lack of popular awareness of KAZA, even in its immediate vicinity, supports the assumption that when the PPF and its local advocates spoke of 'the economic development of the local population', they had only a specific group of people in mind for a very circumscribed role, namely those who would make up the future labour force for the tourism industry and associated sectors.[139] Here again, as in the case of the conservancies, it is worth

---

[136] This was despite the fact that, at the time, there were already maps of KAZA on the walls of most of the MET camps and offices in the Caprivi.
[137] KS, 26.07.2011, Katima Mulilo.
[138] CW, 26.07.2011, Katima Mulilo.
[139] Ndidzulafhi Sinthumule made a similar argument in relation to the Greater Mapungubwe Peace Park in South Africa and Botswana. Moreover, he showed that the multiple land-use strategy pro-

recalling the Eastern Caprivi Strategic Development Plan of 1983, in which local residents were proposed as providers of low-skill services to the tourism industry; they could be encouraged to offer their labour, so it was thought, by the prospect of earning a small income.[140] However, in contrast to the tightly state-controlled economy of pre-independence Namibia, private companies and influential NGOs, such as the Peace Park Foundation, are now entrusted with opening up such opportunities for the 'local population'. As the PPF declares: "In order to capitalise on the rapid growth of tourism worldwide, ecotourism destinations in Africa – and southern Africa specifically – need professional staff and the necessary infrastructure to cater for those who come to experience Africa's natural wonders."[141] To this end, the PPF invites "unemployed people from impoverished rural backgrounds" to do a one-year course at either the 'SA College for Tourism' or at the 'Tracker Academy', which are both run by the PPF and financed by international donors and private tourism companies.[142]

By 2014/2015, awareness of KAZA had risen in the Caprivi. KAZA was now relatively well-known and informal discussions often revealed the high expectations which many Caprivians placed in the peace park. The majority of the people to whom I talked hoped that KAZA would attract more tourists and, consequently, more income for themselves and their families. Even most of the management and advocates of the conservancies – some of whom had still been sceptical of KAZA in 2012, perhaps out of fear of having their influence diluted within such a large-scale project – were largely in favour of the project by 2014.[143] Expectations of the benefits which KAZA would bring had also become wide-ranging. The head of the Mayeyi Traditional Authority, for example, hoped that an immediate by-product of KAZA would be for him to receive financial assistance to cover transport costs

---

moted by the park furthered its goal of gaining access to extra land, but led to losses of income and land for other groups: Sinthumule, N.I. (2016): Multiple-land use practices in transfrontier conservation areas: the case of Greater Mapungubwe straddling Botswana, South Africa and Zimbabwe. *Bulletin of Geography: Socio–economic Series*, 34: 103–115.

[140] Van der Vegte et al. (1983): 180.
[141] www.peaceparks.org/college.php [15.08.2016].
[142] www.peaceparks.org/college.php [15.08.2016].
[143] There has been surprisingly little research hitherto conducted on the relationship between communal conservancies and transfrontier conservation areas, exceptions are: Ramutsindela, M. and I. Sinthumule (2017), Property and Difference in Nature Conservation. *Geographical Review*, 107(3): 415–432 and Ramutsindela, M. (2009), Transfrontier Conservation and Local Communities. In J. Saarinen, F. Becker, H. Manwa and D. Wilson (eds.), *Sustainable Tourism in Southern Africa: Local Communities and Natural Resources in Transition*. Bristol: Channel View, p. 169–188. The KAZA management in the Caprivi insisted on its willingness to support and include the communal conservancies in its planning through the furthering of cross-border co-operation between conservancies. Communal conservancy leaders were generally supportive of the KAZA project in 2014/2015, although they were still unclear about KAZA's exact implications for the conservancies.

for meetings with fellow traditional leaders in Botswana and Angola.[144] He also hoped that a five-star lodge would eventually be built within his jurisdiction which could be reached by helicopter from Livingstone in Zambia and could thus accommodate tourists during floods. The director of the Livingstone Museum, meanwhile, hoped that KAZA would make it easier for school classes from Zimbabwe and Namibia to visit the museum.[145] He also hoped that co-operation with neighbouring countries would be strengthened and that Livingstone, as "the only city in the KAZA that offers more than wildlife", might become a centre for arts and culture as well as tourism. This was also a reference to the city of Livingstone's earlier plans to promote itself as a southern Zambian cultural hub as well as to its former role as a regional transport and communication centre.[146]

By 2014, more and more people appeared to have become aware of KAZA and its promises of 'economic development', often seeming to believe in these wholeheartedly. However, few had already benefited directly from the project themselves.[147] While there has been a general boom in tourism in the Caprivi over the previous decade, especially for luxury lodges, it remains to be assessed to what extent this has been the result of KAZA or of an inevitable upswing after the tourism sector stagnated during the Caprivi's various crises and conflicts in the 1990s and early 2000s.[148] Even more importantly, the question of whether and to what degree KAZA is bringing 'economic development' and positively impacting the lives of ordinary Caprivians must still be answered; the above observations only serve to show how KAZA's advocates, particularly the PPF, have managed to convince many local people of their vision.

Such successful attempts to convince people of the potential for economic development and profit are not new to the region, but, as Bram Büscher argued, today's TFCAs should be understood within more general paradigms of neoliberal conservation.[149] Although TFCA's residents have divergent and even conflicting interests, these can all be met by the promises of the peace park's promoters, which purports not to be a 'political project', but a "global solution" to which all people can subscribe. As Büscher explains for the Maloti-Drakensberg Peace Park, TFCAs promote themselves as technical, apolitical solutions to the problems of

---

[144] BS, 14.05.2014, Sangwali.
[145] VK, 27.09.2012, Livingstone.
[146] Archives of the Livingstone Museum (LM), 1/5/11_1–10 Correspondence with Ministry of Tourism (and Natural Resources), 1966–1990. Livingstone was also a central hub for the Caprivi's administration until Zambia's independence in 1964.
[147] See also: Ramutsindela (2009).
[148] At least six new lodges opened in the Caprivi in the period from 2011 to 2017, most of which cater for luxury tourists.
[149] Büscher (2013): 80.

the world.[150] Although highly political in their interventions into both international politics and local land-use strategies, peace parks proclaim themselves as a means of overcoming both the restrictions of political borders and the conflicts inevitable in negotiations between parties with competing interests.[151] Under the slogan that "nature has no boundaries", the PPF has, according to its chief executive officer, attempted to transcend "man-made" or "political borders" in order to support the "neutral definition of eco-systems".[152]

In order to sustain this narrative and to overcome the inherent contradiction of being, at its core, a political actor with supposedly neutral and apolitical aims, the PPF has attempted to promote large-scale projects.[153] Peace parks – and, in particular, KAZA, with its enormous size in a politically complex transnational setting spanning over five countries – have succeeded in convincing ordinary people, investors and politicians alike to believe in them as a blueprint for economic development which transcends the challenges and conflicts of everyday politics. The PPF and partner NGOs are open about this and related goals, as the remarks by the PPF chief executive suggest. In the same interview, he went on to state that the sheer size of the park is important, as in tourism "bigger is better".[154] In a short promotional text by WWF Germany, a financial sponsor of the KAZA project, the organisation writes of the park as a "mixture of a conservation area and an employer" and formulates the hope that its employees, the game guards, will pass on to their children the "dream of one day also wearing the uniform of the game guards and getting paid for it."[155]

All in all, KAZA has so far had few immediate or visible effects on the lives of most of the over two million people living within its boundaries. Nevertheless, it has succeeded in creating a vision of itself as a neutral, technical and apolitical "model of meaning to which people should attach their fortunes".[156] However, although very handsomely portrayed as sustainable and community-based, the rural development which KAZA has to offer to its residents is clearly based on the assumption that they will become game guards and other labourers who should pass on their fascination for low-wage work to future generations. This again serves to perpetuate the existing power structure which separates large-scale global investors, international tourists and a local elite, on the one hand, from a cheap rural labour

---

[150] Büscher (2013): 80. There are interesting parallels here with earlier large-scale 'projects' envisioned to bring development to the region, such as those projects outlined in the Odendaal Plan (see Chapter 3).
[151] See also: Ferguson (1990).
[152] WM, 11.07.2011, Stellenbosch.
[153] Büscher (2013): 80.
[154] WM, 11.07.2011, Stellenbosch.
[155] www.wwf.de/themen-projekte/projektregionen/kavango-zambesi-kaza/zustand-und-bedeutung [02.08.2016]. Own translation from the German original.
[156] Büscher (2013): 80.

force on the other. Nevertheless, presented, as is typical for neoliberal projects, as an apolitical solution for the benefit of all, KAZA is difficult to resist for poor rural residents, to whom it often appears to represent their only chance of a better future.[157]

Mapping and Bordering in Conservancies and Peace Parks

A second line of continuity in nature conservation in the Caprivi is formed by ecological research and mapping, which have remained key practices in the field since independence. Conservancies and the KAZA Peace Park have utilised both practices, especially mapping, which in turn have impacted upon the region's internal and external borders and spatial configuration. This book underlines the importance of understanding conservation and related practices of controlling nature, such as mapping, as the product of sets of human relationships rather than as a science based on 'exact' principles.[158] I have also shown that it is in the interplay between the exercising of power and the production of knowledge that such relationships were constituted and contested. As Singh and Houtum argued, "conservation [...] was produced as a disciplinary tool for the expansion of state control through the domain of public lands and enhanced rule-making and was supported by actors and agents responsible for the production and dissemination of conservation knowledge".[159] The production of maps and other forms of (environmental) knowledge becomes particularly revealing in a post-colonial setting, where power relations are often no longer as transparent as they were, for example, in the Caprivi under South African occupation.

In the following, I will discuss how the communal conservancies and the KAZA Peace Park have continued to influence and reshape the Caprivi's complex pattern of borders and boundaries. I will do so by examining two processes of bordering, both of which have been reinforced by conservationists' mapping activities in the region.[160] The first is cartographic processes of bordering, such as the mapping of land-use areas within communal conservancies or the delimitation of KAZA's external boundaries. This form of spatial planning is often based on so-called (socio-)ecological surveys, which are similar to the reports and development plans compiled by South African officials during the occupation. Closely linked to cartographic bordering or spatial planning for conservation is a second bordering process. This can be described as societal bordering, by which people are usually separated

---
[157] Harvey (2005): 2.
[158] See also: Singh et al. (2002): 254 and Harvey (2005): 165.
[159] Singh et al. (2002): 254.
[160] Ramutsindela, M. (2014), Ecology, Borders and Society. In M. Ramutsindela (ed.), *Cartographies of Nature: How Nature Conservation Animates Borders*. Newcastle upon Tyne: Cambridge Scholars Publishing: 1–16 (here 3).

according to their rights and abilities to access land and resources. For Maano Ramutsindela, this process involves dividing "privileged locals" from the "unprivileged other" on the lower rungs of a global hierarchy which is headed by the "privileged global other", who can access resources from afar.[161]

The Caprivi, as it exists in its post-colonial present, remains interwoven by a complex web of borders and boundaries. This study shows the crucial role which nature conservation has played in establishing this particular spatial structure, not only as manifested on the ground, but also in its representation on maps. Ramutsindela has urged scholars to pay more attention to borders and processes of bordering in nature conservation and has called for a greater focus on how "multiple borders are (re)constituted on a single site, and how this process unfolds in projects involving various aspects of nature".[162] For Harris and Hazen, meanwhile, mapping for conservation is "a complex of interrelated spatial and territorial strategies common to contemporary conservation practice".[163] To understand such strategies and how they interrelate with political and geographical borders, a deeper understanding of local historical context – as I provided for the Caprivi in the previous chapters of this book – as well as a departure from a narrow definition of borders as the external boundaries of nation-states is required. In order to realise the latter, different forms of internal border must be identified and, more fundamentally, the ways in which borders have been conceptualised in academic research must be reconsidered.

The Function of Borders in the Caprivi

On a drive in a car from Rundu, to the west of the Caprivi to the Botswanan town of Kasane, just to the east of the Caprivi, at least one international border, one regional border, two veterinary borders, five national park borders and a time zone border will be crossed. In the process, the same car will be registered repeatedly, passports will be shown, fees paid, shoes disinfected, forms filled in and further orders issued. Other borders will be crossed which may remain unnoticed, including linguistic borders; borders of former kingdoms, chiefdoms or other past administrative entities; land-use borders; communal conservancies borders; and municipal borders. None of these borders has remained static, as I have shown, and all have changed, shifted and been contested over time. Besides these political, cultural and socio-economic borders, physical barriers such as rivers, fences and swamps will also be overcome.

---

[161] Ramutsindela (2014): 3.
[162] Ramutsindela (2014): 3.
[163] Harris, L. and H. Hazen (2006), Power of Maps: (Counter)mapping for Conservation, *ACME: An International E-Journal for Critical Geographies,* 4(1): 99–130 (here 101).

Historiographies, especially those relating to Africa, remain often fixated, however, with international borders.[164] Africa's international borders have been a much-contested and -researched topic for scholars from a variety of disciplines over the course of recent decades. In 1972, Saadia Touval argued that presenting the national borders of recently-independent African states as wholly imposed by the former colonial powers downplayed the role of Africans in the definition, acceptance, and perpetuation of the borders.[165] For Anthony I. Asiwaju, international borders in Africa are obviously arbitrary, were imposed by external powers, and tore apart "culture areas or ethnic groups", as evident in Southern Africa with for example the "partition" of the "Tswana", the "Ova Herero" and the "Khoisan Basarwa"; however, he went on to argue that, at a micro-sociological level, "partitioned Africans have nevertheless tended in their normal activities to ignore the boundaries as dividing lines and to carry on social relations across them more or less as in the days before the partition".[166]

Since the 1990s, academic debates have shifted from the question of whether international borders exist in the minds and affect the daily lives of people living in borderlands to the question of *how* they exist and *how* they are used. From these discussions, the idea of borders as conduits or as economic opportunity has emerged.[167] In his book on a group living on both sides of the Ghana-Togo border, Paul Nugent combined these various ideas to show that, although international borders in Africa may generally have had a divisive impact, the interests shared by people across the Ghana-Togo border ensured that this was not "sufficient to override the forces conspiring towards maintenance of the border".[168] As such, the local impact of the border diminished in relation to the extent powerful people on both sides profited from continued interaction.

In the following years, in view of the growing trend towards globalisation and international cooperation, scholars began to question whether international borders retained any analytic value at all. While some saw other borders, such as ‚cultural' borders, as more relevant, others argued that all types of borders were losing their relevance amid the high

---

[164] For an overview of African border studies, see e.g.: the 2010 special issue of the *Journal of Borderland Studies*, especially: Coplan, D. (2010), Introduction: From empiricism to theory in African border studies. *Journal of Borderland Studies,* 25(2): 1–5. See also the edited volume: Engel, U. and P. Nugent (eds.) (2010), *Respacing Africa*. Amsterdam: Brill.
[165] See: Touval, S. (1972), *The Boundary Politics of Independent Africa*. Cambridge MA: Harvard University Press, p. 3–17.
[166] Asiwaju, A.I. (1985), The Conceptual Framework. In: A.I. Asiwaju (ed.), *Partitioned Africans: Ethnic Relations Across Africa's International Boundaries, 1884–1984*. London: Hurst & Co: 1–18 (here 3).
[167] See e.g.: Nugent, P. and A.I. Asiwaju (eds.) (1996), *African Boundaries: barriers, conduits and opportunities*. London: Cassell/Pinter.
[168] Nugent, P. (2003), *Smugglers, Secessionists and Loyal Citizens of the Ghana-Togo Frontier: The Lie of the Borderlands Since 1914*. Athens: Ohio University Press, p. 274.

mobility of people, goods and ideas in a globalising world.[169] However, as global political trends in the last decade have shown, international borders do not appear to have lost any of their significance, but to have instead been reordered and reinforced under new circumstances.[170]

In the Caprivi, where no point is more than thirty kilometres away from an international border, these borders have exerted a significant influence on local life since they were first defined. For many Caprivians, the delimitation and control of these boundaries represented one of the most overt forms of colonial oppression.[171] In the second half of the twentieth century, the desire to control Namibia's external borders – particularly its northern border with Angola and Zambia – was also partly responsible for South Africa's growing interest in the Caprivi. Indeed, the long-running war affecting the region was commonly known in South Africa as the 'Border War'. Although the border provided Namibian refugees and liberation movement fighters with opportunities to cross into the relative safe havens of Zambia and Angola, it also offered a launch-pad for South Africa to carry out attacks to destabilise Namibia's northern neighbours and support SADF allies in the Angolan Civil War.

Crucial to the function of borders is mapping, not only in the case of international borders, as described above, but especially when internal boundaries, such as those between different land-use or conservation areas, are considered. The definition of these boundaries requires comprehensive surveying and mapping.[172] As I described for the period of South African occupation, cartographic and ecological surveys thus represented a central concern for the South African administration and military in the Caprivi. The detailed surveys and maps of the region's natural features which resulted from these endeavours informed subsequent plans for nature conservation and still constitute a decisive factor for the organisation of the Caprivi's contemporary spatial structure.[173] This indicates that mapping has never simply been a reflection of what exists, but also always serves specific interests and thus contains the potential to shape the future. As Denis Wood has argued, "because these interests select what from the vast storehouse of knowledge [...] the map will represent, these

---

[169] See: Appadurai (1996). 337–349. On 'cultural borders' see: Kolossov, V. (2005), Border Studies: Changing Perspectives and Theoretical Approaches. *Geopolitics*, 10(4): 1–27 (here 12–13).

[170] As it is for example described for the European Union's new focus on its external borders. See: Van Houtum, H. (2010), Human Blacklisting: The Global Apartheid of the EU's External Border Regime. *Environment and Planning D: Society and Space,* 28: 957–976.

[171] For example, AC recalled that the residents of his village only realised that they were living under colonial rule when, in the late 1950s, the border between the Caprivi and Angola became more strictly controlled. AC, 21.05.2014, Kongola.

[172] Ramutsindela (2014), Sinthumule, N.I. (2016), more generally see also: Singh et al. (2002): 253–263.

[173] See also the discussion on the legacy of apartheid spatial patterns in contemporary South African cities, e.g.: Shepherd et al. (2007).

interests are embodied in the map as presences and absences".[174] By drawing some (new) borders onto a map and excluding others, mapmakers create new spaces. The assumption of critical cartography "that maps *make* reality as much as they represent it" is thus crucial in situating recently established nature conservation areas within the Caprivi's complex border histories and networks.[175] In the following, I will examine mapping undertaken by the conservancies and KAZA respectively.

Cartographic Processes of Conservation

> On communal land there were no fences – and without defined borders, which community should be allowed to benefit from migratory game? For this reason, the boundaries of 'communal area conservancies' would have to be negotiated between neighbours, but instead of fences a GPS could be used to record the agreed reference points on a map.[176]

This is how Garth Owen-Smith, a well-known Namibian conservationist who has been active in the field for decades, remembers the discussions regarding the planning of communal conservancy boundaries in the 1990s. While proper fencing was one of the preconditions for white farmers to acquire property rights over the wildlife on their farms under South African occupation, the building of new fences was not seen as a viable option for communal land after independence.[177] Nevertheless, as Owen-Smith's statement highlights, to give 'communities' property rights over wildlife required communal areas to be spatially defined in some way. This process was duly regulated in the Nature Conservation Act of 1996, which defined boundaries as one of the basic requirements for a conservancy to be recognised by the government. As the legislation stipulated, a "conservancy has defined boundaries agreed by neighbouring communities".[178]

The vaguely defined concept of 'neighbouring communities', in particular, carried with it the potential for conflict. As the distribution and administration of land in Namibia's communal areas remains mostly in the hands of traditional authorities, the delimitation of a conservancy's boundaries must usually meet with the consent of the chiefs of 'neighbouring communities', whose decisions may not necessarily reflect the democratic will of their

---

[174] Wood (1992): 1.
[175] Crampton et al. (2006): 15.
[176] Owen-Smith (2010): 541.
[177] Mosimane et al. (2014) and CW, 26.07.2011, Katima Mulilo. The state saw fencing as working against the very idea of communal land and feared that it would lead to disputes among rural land users. However, there is an increasing tendency to fence off sections of communal land all over Northern Namibia. See: Nghitevelekwa (2016).
[178] Jones (2010): 109.

communities.¹⁷⁹ This process also assumes that clearly demarcated boundaries between the various traditional authorities exist, which is not the case in the Caprivi.¹⁸⁰

Secondly, the mapping of fixed boundaries around the conservancies makes it more difficult for conservancy residents to refuse membership of the conservancy in which they live. Moreover, non-members must still cope with the effects of the spatial definition of conservancy boundaries and designated conservancy land-use patterns. This option for residents to decline to become a member of the conservancies is often cited to counter criticism that conservancies reinforce colonial notions of ethnicity, which defined Africans through their membership of a community and failed to acknowledge their agency as individuals.¹⁸¹ Nevertheless, conservancy boundaries are often based on the supposedly traditional administrative boundaries of traditional authorities. These enduring boundaries, which were mostly established under colonial rule, were normally not clearly demarcated, but are often very familiar to people living in the area.

In order to map the boundaries of conservancies, their borders must first be clearly demarcated. ML of the NACSO office in Windhoek, confirmed that this process of boundary formation makes up most of the consulting work which her organisation performs for the conservancies. She identified the definition of conservancy boundaries as an opportunity to "emancipate" local communities and give them a voice.¹⁸² This view is shared by Mosimane and Silva, who argued that "local residents" often took advantage of boundary-making to "empower themselves" and sometimes found ways "to reinforce their claim to territories in the name of conservation".¹⁸³ While they agree that most of the conservancies are based on pre-existing, often colonial, spatial configurations, they also posit that conservancy boundary-making can assist rural residents to "create new social spaces, establish new ethnic groups, reaffirm loyalties with traditional authorities, and better position themselves to control specific economic development strategies".¹⁸⁴ An example of the establishment of "new groups" arises in relation to the Mayuni Conservancy, which I will come back to later.

With the establishment of the KAZA Peace Park, a new and powerful actor in the re-mapping of the Caprivi emerged in the early twenty-first century. A closer examination of the mapping and bordering practices employed by the PPF and the KAZA shows that the

---

[179] Nghitevelekwa (2016).
[180] Kangumu (2011): 172–176.
[181] For a critique of the conservancy concept's understanding of the notion of 'community', see: Mosimane et al. (2014): 90–91. See also: Singh et al. (2002).
[182] ML, Windhoek, 29.04.2014.
[183] Mosimane et al. (2014): 106. On such acts as strategies of territorialisation, see also: Bassett et al. (2014).
[184] Mosimane et al. (2014): 105.

organisation perceives mapping and other forms of spatial modelling, such as geographic information systems (GIS), as crucial for conservation. For CB, a GIS expert at the PPF, "everything is spatially driven" in conservation and all research data is looked at "in space".[185] He underlined the power which the PPF ascribes to spatial practices when he warned against publicising maps prematurely; as he noted, "you do not want to create false expectations" because "you just put down boundaries on maps".[186] He thus recognised that even boundaries which are only defined on maps have the power to at least create expectations, if not space as such.

However, the language employed by the PPF in their promotional material suggests that the organisation considers mapping to be about more than just providing information or creating expectations, but also about "securing space".[187] Tellingly, this was the title of a page which appeared on the PPF website until 2006 and linked directly to maps of the planned TFCAs.[188] The foundation has produced a great variety of maps of the KAZA area since the first plans for the KAZA Peace Park emerged.[189] As the PPF itself attributes significant real-world effects to the maps which it produces, visual aspects of its mapping practices should be studied in greater detail. This is also especially relevant given the history of cartography in the Caprivi, where the securing and control of space through mapping and conservation formed a key motivation for earlier cartographic interventions in the region. For example, it was – among others – this incentive which led the SADF and the civil administration in the Eastern Caprivi to partner with each other in the 1970s and 1980s to produce maps of the Caprivi and southern Angola.

Societal Implications of Mapping for Conservation

Alongside these spatial impacts of mapping for conservation, a second noteworthy feature of post-independence conservation cartography in the Caprivi is the effect it has had on the daily lives of local residents. George Barrett has called for an understanding of mapping for conservation as it relates to patterns of inclusion and exclusion.[190] Spatial modelling and cartography help to render land-use patterns and wildlife distributions visible and, as

---

[185] CB, 22.04.2014, Stellenbosch.
[186] CB, 22.04.2014, Stellenbosch.
[187] Spierenburg, M. and H. Wels (2006), "Securing Space": Mapping and Fencing in Transfrontier Conservation in Southern Africa. *Space and Culture*, 9(3): 294–312 (here 298).
[188] Spierenburg et al (2006): 298. The page on "Securing Space", which was available on the PPF's website in 2006, can be accessed through the following internet archive: https://web.archive.org/web/20060128122532/http://www.peaceparks.org:80/.
[189] For a general account of the PPF's role in mapping TFCAs, see: Spierenburg et al (2006). The PPF's chief executive officer is also supposedly a GIS expert. CB, 22.04.2014, Stellenbosch.
[190] Barrett et al (2013): 339.

such, reinforce a distinction between those who are deemed to be acceptable land users and those who are not, by 'scientifically' presenting certain patterns of land use as less harmful to the environment than others.[191] As Brosius and Russell argued, this has allowed for the reinvigoration of the colonial depiction of Africans as being solely interested in exploiting their land's resources and possessing no intrinsic interest whatsoever in its conservation.[192] Therefore, through processes of mapping, nature conservation not only informs ways to "devise and manage […] boundaries between nature and society", but also imposes and sustains boundaries within society.[193] By doing so, communal conservancies as well as transfrontier conservation areas have created new spaces and opportunities for global capital and privileged 'local' elites at the same time as they risk circumscribing most rural Africans within narrow ethnic identities.[194]

The power which the mapping of conservancies can impart to specific groups can be observed in the example of the Mayuni Conservancy, to the south of the Caprivian village of Kongola which was gazetted in 1999. The conservancy was initially proposed by a then sub-chief of the Mafwe Traditional Authorities, Joseph Mayuni, shortly after the new nature conservation legislation was passed in 1996. As the conservancy's boundaries were being finalised, a dispute broke out with the rest of the Mafwe traditional authority. Mayuni was thus compelled to accept the reduction of the conservancy's territory to the area under his jurisdiction as a sub-chief, the only proposal to which the Mafwe Traditional Authority was willing to agree. During the same time, Mayuni also applied to the Namibian state for recognition as a chief.[195] In an interview in 2014, he confirmed that the establishment of the conservancy had been helpful to realise his goal of leaving the Mafwe Khuta to form his own Mashi Traditional Authority.[196] When the traditional authority was recognised in 2004 with Mayuni as its chief, its boundaries were taken from those of the Mayuni Conservancy. This case suggests that the conservancy was also proposed and mapped for other reasons than

---

[191] Barrett et al. (2015): 137. See also: Ramutsindela (2014): 3.
[192] Brosius, J.P. and D. Russell (2003), Conservation from Above: An Anthropological Perspective on Transboundary Protected Areas and Ecoregional Planning. In U.M. Goodale, M.J. Stern, C. Margoluis; A.G. Lanfer and M. Fladeland (eds.), *Transboundary Protected Areas: The Viability of Regional Conservation Strategies*. Binghampton: Food Production Press: 39–65 (here 48–51). See also: Sinthumule (2016).
[193] Bryan, S. (2012), Contested boundaries, contested places: the Natura 2000 Network in Ireland. *Journal of Rural Studies*, 28(1): 80–94 (here 80). Ramutsindela (2014): 4.
[194] See also: Spierenburg, M., C. Steenkamp and H. Wels (2008), Enclosing the Local for the Global Commons: Community Land Rights in the Great Limpopo Transfrontier Conservation Area. *Conservation and Society*, 6(1): 87–97 and Hughes, D.M. (2006), *From Enslavement to Environmentalism: Politics on a Southern African Frontier*. Seattle: University of Washington Press. On the financial backing of the Peace Park Foundation, see: Spierenburg (2010).
[195] Mosimane et al. (2014): 96–99.
[196] JM, 28.05.2014, Choi.

the protection of wildlife and its potential to deliver tourism revenue and investment. Mayuni and his supporters also used the conservancy to redefine the boundaries between the two traditional authorities, and, perhaps most importantly, to support his aim of establishing a new traditional authority under his own leadership. Ultimately, the delimitation of the conservancy's boundary served not only to divide local residents between its territory and that of the neighbouring areas that only later became conservancies, but also to define under the authority of which of the two chiefs they would live.

However, conservancies are not only a key determinant in the definition of external boundaries, but also help to fix land-use patterns which had previously been much more flexible, often in a manner which corresponds to the interests of profit. In my interview with Joseph Mayuni, he repeatedly underlined his willingness to protect wildlife for monetary purposes. As he declared, "[w]hen I see an elephant I do not see its meat anymore, I see the 200,000 Namibian dollars we can make by selling the hunting licence".[197] Such a profit-orientated approach to conservancies, as Mosimane and Silva showed for the Uibasen Conservancy in the Kunene Region, impacts upon the internal organisation of land-use patterns within conservancies, whereby particular land uses are assigned acreage in proportion to the size of the potential profit which it is estimated that they can make.[198] Within the contemporary economic context, hunting tends to be favoured with the largest amount of land in most conservancies. Moreover, as land uses and their designated land users are no longer open to interpretation and discussion but are fixed in the conservancies' land-use maps, these spatial configurations quickly become entrenched.

GIS data collection in conservancies and the mapping of conservancies – processes in the Caprivi which are both supported by NGOs such as the IRDNC and are often utilised to determine the internal land-use patterns of conservancies – are often portrayed by NGOs and some scholars as counter- or community mapping.[199] Derived from an influential article by Nancy Peluso, the term counter-mapping purports to contest or undermine more hegemonic spatial ordering, such as mapping undertaken by the state.[200] In relation to environmental mapping, Peluso described how forest users in Indonesia had been commissioned to produce forest maps which counter mapping undertaken by the state that had undermined their access to and interests among local forest resources. In the same manner, Taylor argued that residents in the Bwabwata National Park have utilised mapping of the land on which they live to "debate claims to land and territory".[201] She further argued that from

---

[197] JM, 28.05.2014, Choi.
[198] Mosimane et al. (2014): 103–105 and Sinthumule (2016).
[199] E.g. in relation to the Western Caprivi, see: Taylor (2008) and Taylor (2012).
[200] Peluso (1995): 383–406.
[201] Taylor (2008): 1768.

the perspective of "some San activists, the mapping of San knowledge is about re-claiming histories that have been marginalised, if not made virtually invisible, by colonialism and apartheid".[202] Mapping has thus been seen as a powerful and, in certain contexts, empowering tool also in "socio-political rather than environmental causes", as the case of the Mayuni Conservancy illustrated.[203]

However, the mapping of remote areas, particularly if undertaken by so-called local people, can also be seen from a more Foucauldian perspective as an extension of governmentality into the most isolated regions. According to this view, the mapping of the conservancies would support the state and its partner NGOs and transnational corporations in rendering remote spaces – along with their inhabitants and resources – more 'legible' and easier to control.[204] Therefore, as Taylor showed for mapping in the Western Caprivi and Mosimane and Silva for boundary-making in the conservancies, what is termed as community- or counter-mapping may be a practice used to contest existing power-structures in certain situations, but it can also be used by powerful public- and private-sector actors to extend their control over remote areas, as the subsequent example of KAZA highlights.[205] What is yet to be achieved in relation to the Caprivi is a more radical counter-mapping which serves as a practice "that fundamentally questions the assumptions or biases of cartographic conventions, that challenges predominant power effects of mapping, or that engages in mapping in ways that upset power relations".[206] Proponents of community-mapping initiatives have thus often failed to recognise that the mapping of conservancies and other conservation areas in the Caprivi has remained locked within the narrow frameworks of neoliberal nature conservation and the commodification of conservation as well as discourses of ethnicity and rural identity, all of which draw from the long history of environmental and ecological research and mapping in the region.[207]

At least on a discursive level, mapping practices also play a pivotal role for the Peace Park Foundation, particularly for those relating to the definition of KAZA's internal and external boundaries. Because the PPF purports to promote regional peace through the overcoming of international borders and close transfrontier cooperation in nature and wildlife conservation, it is crucial to examine how the organisation engages with international boundaries and to recognise that for the PPF, mapping primarily represents a powerful tool for promot-

---

[202] Taylor (2008): 1767.
[203] Taylor (2008): 1774.
[204] See: Ferguson (1990).
[205] Taylor 2008: 1768 and Mosimane et al. (2014).
[206] Harris et al (2006): 99–130
[207] On apartheid South Africa's mapping of land-use patterns in the homelands and the legacies thereof, see: McCusker, B. and M. Ramudzuli (2007), Apartheid spatial engineering and land use change in Mankweng, South Africa: 1963–2001. *The Geographical Journal*, 173(1): 56–74.

ing the vision of a ‚boundless', peaceful nature conservation area in order to attract both foreign investment and international tourists.[208]

As discussed above, scholarly work on international borders, particularly those of former colonies, can be grouped around three main perspectives: borders as constraints or barriers; borders as economic opportunities; and borders as irrelevant in a globalised world.[209] All of these viewpoints can be identified in the Peace Park concept. Firstly, international borders are seen as a barrier, not only for the free movement of wildlife, but also for socio-economic development in regions often perceived as peripheral. As the name 'peace park' suggests, the overcoming of international borders is seen as furthering peace, an assumption which presumes that international borders are a potential cause of conflict. Secondly, the establishment of cross-border conservation areas are presented as an opportunity for the development of local economies. Furthermore, peace parks invoke their transborder nature as a marketing tool to attract tourists and foreign investors and donors. In this sense, international borders are seen as an economic resource. Finally, with its universal vision of a ‚boundless' Africa, and its support for the introduction of single tourist visas covering participating countries, the peace park concept advocates a notion of international borders as irrelevant in a globalised world.[210]

The Caprivi's past and present illustrate that the overcoming of international borders is not sufficient to realise the PPF's stated goal of creating ‚boundless' areas. The Caprivi has seen many of its internal borders changing their function and location several times over the course of the last century, often leading to disputes and contestations. Although KAZA's backers repeatedly stress that all such borders must be softened, they themselves have been heavily involved in the drawing of new lines across the map. Moreover, KAZA's power brokers play a decisive role in deciding which borders are to be softened for whom. While tourists benefit from such policies, as the example of the KAZA visa

---

[208] The PPF's CEO emphasised that the overriding vision of the PPF is to create "boundless spaces". The name 'Transfrontier Conservation Area' itself engages with notions of borders and space. On how TFCAs claim space, see: Spierenburg (2006): 294–312. This article provides a short history of the use of maps and fences in wildlife conservation and how this changed with the rise of TFCAs. Much more thoroughly researched than KAZA in this regard is the Great Limpopo Transfrontier Park, see: Lunstrum (2010): 129–143.

[209] For a summary of these arguments, see: Feyissa, D. and M.V. Hoehne (2010), State Borders and Borderlands as Resources. In D. Feyissa and M.V. Hoehne (eds.): *Borders and Borderlands as Resources in the Horn of Africa*. Suffolk: James Currey: 1–26.

[210] A so-called 'KAZA visa' was introduced in 2015 which allowed tourists to obtain a single visa for Zambia and Zimbabwe. Shortly after its introduction, the visa scheme was terminated, but was reintroduced by March 2017. The PPF is still advocating for a visa which would permit tourists to visit all five participating countries. However, especially in relation to Angola, this seems unlikely to be introduced soon.

shows, locals living along the borders remain as restricted in their movements as before.[211] It is this (re-)creation of borders – often referred to as bordering processes – which must be critically addressed.

To understand how KAZA has impacted processes of bordering in the region, it is instructive to look at how the park's external boundaries have been defined. These boundaries, which have shifted repeatedly in recent years, have been consistently drawn and redrawn onto maps to reflect any changes. The visual insistence on newly-created outlines is juxtaposed by the erosion of internal boundaries within KAZA, including international borders. In many of these cartographic representations, the park is highlighted by a uniform colour, while areas beyond its boundaries are presented only schematically. On schematic maps on its website, KAZA is promoted as a visually equal space alongside the territories of the five participating countries.[212]

This overt cartographic depiction of the park's external boundaries appears to contradict the PPF's vision of a 'boundless Africa'. However, their emphatic representation on the map contrasts with the relative insignificance of KAZA's external boundaries on the ground. According to the PPF's CEO, the Peace Park's external borders were still vague at the time of its founding and, at least initially, were not planned to become clearly demarcated, controlled or fenced off. He claimed that they were drafted according to natural ecosystem boundaries or the outer flanks of the annual migration paths of elephants, before being carefully negotiated with "local decision-makers".[213] A further consideration, he added, was that the park's boundaries were intended to connect KAZA with already-existing conservation areas in order to create corridors for game.

Hence, although they are very loosely defined on the ground and their exact function in the five participating countries remains uncertain, KAZA's external boundaries feature very prominently in the park's visual representation (Figure 3).[214] As Henk van Houtum argued for the European Union's external borders, such a constant and powerful cartographic

---

[211] An extreme example of this restriction is the island of Impalila in the Zambezi River. The island belongs to Namibia, but can only be reached from Botswana or Zambia for most of the year. In order to reach their regional capital, Katima Mulilo, Impalila islanders must usually obtain a Namibian exit stamp on the island, an entry stamp for Botswana in Kasane, an exit stamp at the Botswanan border with Namibia in Ngoma, and another entry stamp for Namibia on the other side. Because there is no border post on the Zambian side of the river, it is not permitted to cross into the country directly from Impalila. To enter Zambia legally, another detour via Botswana would be required.
[212] http://www.kavangozambezi.org/contact-us [accessed 02.03.2017].
[213] WM, 11.07.2011, Stellenbosch.
[214] On the newest verstion of the PPF's homepage (2018) this visual representation changed, it shows the KAZA with defused outlines: http://www.peaceparks.org/story.php?pid=1008&mid=1073 [accessed 15.02.2018].

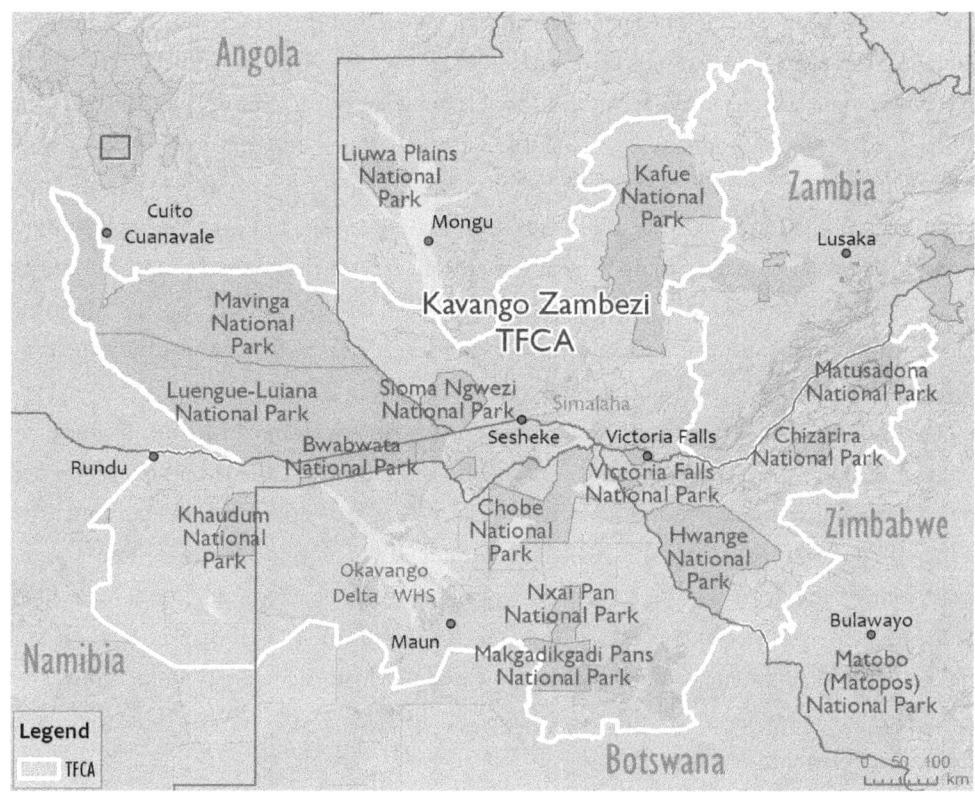

Fig. 2: Map of the Kavango Zambezi Transfrontier Conservation Area. Updated version provided by PPF.

invocation of boundaries implies "the continuous (search for the) legitimisation and justification of the location and demarcation of a border, which is seen as a manifestation of one's own claimed, distinct, and exclusive territory/identity/sovereignty".[215] However, it is not only through the definition of an external border by which KAZA's backers make their claim to space, but also, in van Houtum's words again, by ensuring that "all possible social and spatial dynamics that might occur are given meaning and a vision by looking through the eyes of the self-defined territory/identity/sovereignty."[216]

At the same time as its external borders are being drawn, new scientific maps of the KAZA TFCA are being developed as a cartographic basis for so-called Integrated Development Plans (IDPs) to be used for land-use planning within KAZA's territory. The KAZA

---

[215] Van Houtum (2010): 959.
[216] Van Houtum (2010): 959. Similar arguments have been made in relation to South African homeland politics. On the importance of internal boundaries or external borders in the creation of a 'Caprivi identity', see Kangumu (2011), 172–176 or Zeller (2015) respectively.

secretariat in Kasane has so far developed an IDP for each of the park's five country-sectors as well as one 'Master Integrated Development Plan', which serves as summary of the five IDPs.[217] Based on various surveys and geographic analyses of the area's socio-economic conditions, the IDPs are intended to recommend land-use patterns and provide "potential investors and donors with a priority framework for developments within KAZA".[218] According to CB, the IDPs constitute a central spatial undertaking for KAZA, but "at this stage is [an] all paper-based exercise based on top-level interventions".[219] He then noted the importance of GIS and mapping projects for conservation in general, acknowledging that the definition of land-use patterns and the park's external boundaries has occurred through a top-down approach to mapping focussed on spatial fixing.

One example which illustrates how mapping for conservation can turn into more concrete forms of boundary-making are the so-called elephant or wildlife corridors. These pathways are intended to allow elephants to roam freely across international borders. Their location is determined on the basis of data produced by high-tech tracking tools and in aerial surveys which tracks the movements of elephants. For example, Elephants without Borders (EWB), a NGO which conducts elephant surveys for KAZA, noted that its "research is revealing that elephants are using old pathways, and historical corridors to exploit 'new lands'", thereby allowing elephants from overpopulated areas in Botswana to move to areas where fewer elephants are found.[220]

Historical elephant migration routes, of course, do not stop at international borders. The idea of transborder corridors is thus central to the vision of peace parks and strongly endorsed by KAZA. Based on the surveys of EWB and other organisations, elephant corridors were mapped and established. However, it soon became clear that the supposed historical corridors did not take into account the fact that human beings now lived and farmed on the routes which elephants might have used in the past. As a solution, the PPF raised more than EUR 500,000 through crowd-founding projects to fence in some of KAZA's elephant corridors. As the organisation declared in the project outline, the envisioned thirty-six kilometres of fencing "will effectively serve as a visual demarcation between the wildlife area and the open area, preventing settlement by people and encouraging animal movement

---

[217] KAZA Secretariat (ed.) (2015), *KAZA TFCA Master Integrated Development Plan*. Kasane. The IDPs for the Zambian and Zimbabwean sections of KAZA can be downloaded at: www.kavangozambezi.org/publications-protocols-?page=1 [accessed 03.03.2017]. On the socio-economic impact of such forms of spatial land-use planning, see also: Sinthumule (2016).
[218] KAZA Secretariat (2015): ix.
[219] CB, 22.04.2014, Stellenbosch.
[220] www.elephantswithoutborders.org/tracking.php [18.02.2017]. By the PPF's own estimates, there are currently about 150,000 elephants living in northern Botswana, 50,000 in Zimbabwe and 16,000 in the Caprivi, with an annual elephant population growth rate of 5% across KAZA.

from the overpopulated areas in the South, through to Kafue National Park [Zambia] in the north".[221] While wildlife fences are described as a 'visual demarcation', for people who live in the vicinity the presence of the fences is very real and the subject of much dispute.[222] Furthermore, even where no fences are built, the creation of wildlife corridors can drastically affect the lives of people living within them. In 2014, for example, the Namibian state took the decision to henceforth pay less compensation for wildlife-related stock or crop loss to farmers living within demarcated elephant corridors. This was intended to act as an incentive to convince farmers to move out of the corridors so that elephants could be left to roam freely through them and across borders.[223]

For the reasons discussed, and despite their visions of a 'boundless nature', KAZA and, to a certain degree, the communal conservancies have tended to seek the consolidation of borders, whether in the form of land-use borders or boundaries which divide the people who profit from wildlife from those who are expelled in the name of wildlife conservation.

Nature and Violence

Besides 'economic development' and 'mapping and researching', a third thematic complex has been and continues to be closely associated with nature conservation in the Caprivi; namely, the way in which conservation, on the one hand, and warfare, violence and security, on the other, have been entangled and mutually reinforcing. Like the other two interrelationships, this pattern did not cease with Namibia's independence, the end of the civil war in Angola, or the establishment of the Peace Park. Unlike in most parts of Namibia, armed unrest, (state) violence, and even aspects of open war did not come to an end in the Caprivi in 1990. Indeed, even after the end of the Angolan Civil War in 2002, the Caprivi has still witnessed human deaths at the hands of security forces. Over the last decade, at least thirty people have been killed on or near the border between Botswana and Namibia's Zambezi Region. They were shot dead by the Botswana Defence Force (BDF) for being suspected poachers.[224] Some were, however, unarmed and not in possession of any wildlife products. When asked about Botswana's nature conservation policies, MI, a conservationist and leading figure in the BDF's anti-poaching unit, declared:

---

[221] www.pifworld.com/nl/projects/gFCv4CC-OP8/the-elephant-corridor/about [18.08.2016].
[222] AC, 21.05.2014, Kongola.
[223] Personal comment by an employee of the Ministry of Environment and Tourism (MET).
[224] Mongudhi, T., J. Konopo and N. Ntibinyane (2016): 'Deadly borders...30 Namibians killed through Botswana's shoot-to-kill policy', *The Namibian*, 09.03.2016.

Botswana's president [Ian Khama] as a trained soldier has a no bullshit tactic. We have laws and we enforce those laws. If you don't obey the law you can die. If you go to a national park with a gun you commit a violent crime, and the president as a soldier he will use violence against you. We shot three guys at the border to Namibia.[225]

The Botswanan president's brother, Tshekedi Khama II, endorsed this view with the statement that: "Poaching is a culture; we have to kill the supply to starve the culture. That is one of the reasons why, in Botswana, with our anti-poaching unit, we don't necessarily interrogate the poacher."[226]

Militarised Conservation

The shooting of alleged poachers on the Namibia-Botswana border and the above quotes by two leading conservationists reflect a global development in recent nature conservation practices which has been especially evident in Southern Africa, namely the militarisation of nature conservation. This strategy is presented as necessary to police and prosecute wildlife-related crime in what is portrayed by its supporters as a "war against poachers".[227] Although the extent of militarisation and the use of force in anti-poaching strategies has risen dramatically in the last decade globally, militarised conservation tactics are not new in East and Southern Africa, as the so-called wildlife wars of the 1980s illustrate. One of the first of these 'wars' occurred in Kenya, where the state accused bandits from Somalia of crossing the border between the two countries to hunt down Kenya's elephant population. A brutal state response under the country's then director of Wildlife Services, Richard Leakey, followed.[228] In the late 1980s, the Zimbabwean president, Robert Mugabe, introduced a shoot-to-kill policy to counter rhinoceros poachers. This was soon followed by the so-called Rhino Wars of the Zambezi Valley, during which, as the Zimbabwe Defence Force (ZDF) proudly announced, it had killed more poachers than black rhinoceroses were shot that

---

[225] MI, 03.10.2015, Basel.
[226] Quoted in Mongudhi et al. (2016). Parenthetically, Tshekedi Khama served as Botswana's Minister for Environment and Wildlife and is also a shareholder of an arms procurement company which provides the BDF with arms and ammunition, as well a co-owner of several luxury tourism businesses. See also: Ditlhase, Y., (2012), Khama Inc: All the president's family, friends and close colleagues, *Mail & Guardian*, 02.11.2012.
[227] See on Kenya and Indonesia: Peluso (1993), on Latin America: Ybarra, M. (2012), Taming the jungle, saving the Maya Forest: Sedimented counter-insurgency practices in contemporary Guatemalan conservation, *Journal of Peasant Studies*, 39(2): 479–502, for a global perspective, see: Fairhead, J. (2001), International Dimensions of Conflict Over Natural and Environmental Resources. In: N. Peluso and M. Watts (eds.), *Violent environments*. Cornell University Press: 213–236, on Southern Africa: Lunstrum (2014) and Duffy, R (2016), War, by conservation. *Geoforum*, 69(2): 238–248 (here 238).
[228] For his own account of the period, see: Leakey, R. (2001), *Wildlife Wars. My Battle to Save Kenya's Elephants*. London: PAN.

year. Most of the victims were shot from helicopter gunships while crossing into Zimbabwe from Zambia.[229]

During apartheid rule in the Caprivi, the militarisation of nature conservation did not only take the form of military force against alleged poachers. There were many further ways in which nature conservation officials and the SADF partnered with or depended on each other. Although military violence during this period was not explicitly directed against alleged poachers, nature conservation in the Caprivi remained rooted in the militarisation of the region in many respects. In this regard, some of the conservation practices employed during the South African occupation can be thought of as forerunners to more recent strategies revealed by the concepts of 'green militarization' and 'green violence'.

Elizabeth Lunstrum coined the term 'green militarization' to describe "the use of military and paramilitary (military-like) actors, techniques, technologies, and partnerships in the pursuit of conservation".[230] Büscher and Ramutsindela expanded upon this with their concept of 'green violence', which incorporates both the "material and non-material aspects of violence and the manner in which violence takes social and linguistic form".[231] 'Green violence' thus describes a context in which the practices and aims of nature conservation and warfare overlap, similar to the case in the Caprivi during the Namibian War of Liberation. This parallel is even more visible in Rosaleen Duffy's more radical claim that nature conservation can often become a means of war itself. According to this view, nature conservation no longer resorts to military techniques in order to protect biodiversity, but as a means to of exerting control over 'remote' areas of geostrategic significance, as for example within the context of the global War on Terror.[232] In the case of the Horn of Africa, Duffy posited that "nature (wildlife) is remade to extend and deepen the powers of states engaged in the War on Terror in areas where they currently have limited reach".[233] Furthermore, she described how nature conservation is increasingly making use of the latest military and counter-insurgency technologies used by governments and private security companies for the same goal of controlling people and territory. These include, for example, armed drones or camera traps with automated sensors which "transmit alerts of gunfire, vehicle movement, and human presence".[234]

---

[229] Duffy (2020): 104.
[230] Lunstrum (2014): 817.
[231] Büscher et al. (2016): 4.
[232] Duffy (2016).
[233] Duffy (2016): 240.
[234] Duffy (2016): 245. On joint technologies used in the Caprivi by both the SADF and the civil administration in the Caprivi under during South African rule, see also Chapter 4.

Scholarly conceptions of violence and militarisation in the field of nature conservation are mostly based on recent developments in democratic states such as South Africa, Namibia or Mozambique. The notion that nature conservation in the Caprivi was also militarised during the time of the earlier military occupation might be less surprising, but in many regards the merging of military technologies, personnel and practices with those of nature conservation which occurred during this period served to set the basis for the more recent militarisation of conservation in the region. As such, nature conservation in in the contemporary democratic states of Southern Africa is not only vested in its militarised past, but is still interwoven with militarised practices. The spatial practices applied in conservation in the Caprivi today are largely based on those used during the mapping and surveying missions which conservationists undertook in co-operation with the SADF during the South African occupation. Furthermore, SADF military techniques such as road track censuses continue to be employed by conservationists in the Caprivi, while many of the former SADF personnel who were based in the region stayed on in the Caprivi to work in the field of nature conservation after independence.[235]

Although the application of violent methods to combat suspected poachers is not as dominant a feature of nature conservation in Namibia as it is in Botswana and other Southern African countries, militaristic approaches to conservation in the Caprivi did not cease in 1990.[236] This particularly in regards to the strict enforcement of shoot-to-kill policies targeting poachers on its international borders, as described above, but ironically also extend to the practices of the KAZA Peace Park.

Peace Parks?

Over the last decade, a disturbingly high number of rhinoceroses have been illegally hunted in Southern Africa. In 2014 in South Africa alone, this figure peaked at over 1200 dead animals, with most of the killings having occurred in the Kruger National Park within the Great Limpopo TFCA.[237] The numbers have remained high, with over one thousand rhinoceroses illegally killed in South Africa every year since.[238] While exact data for KAZA is not avail-

---

[235] They included, most famously, Jan Breytenbach, the former commander of the SADF's Buffalo Battalion. See, for example, his personal account of his 'fight' to save Caprivian wildlife: Breytenbach (1997).

[236] Botswana employs large sections of the country's military forces to combat wildlife crimes; Zambia also permits law enforcement units to shoot suspected poachers; and South Africa's nature conservation strategies are marked by the growing influence of private security companies.

[237] https://www.savetherhino.org/rhino_info/poaching_statistics [accessed: 02.01.2018].

[238] https://www.savetherhino.org/rhino_info/poaching_statistics [accessed: 02.01.2018]. Data for Namibia is more difficult to obtain, but it is estimated that around 80 rhinoceroses have been illegally shot in the country every year since 2015 (http://www.poachingfacts.com/poaching-statistics/

able, media reports also suggest that rising numbers of rhinoceroses and elephants have been poached within the Namibian section of the park.[239]

These figures have shaken the peace park concept to its core. In response, in an attempt to ensure the protection of charismatic species, a key aim at the heart of the peace park vision, conservation efforts have become increasingly violent.[240] Büscher and Ramutsindela argued that these measures were spearheaded by the South African government and the Peace Park Foundation and demanded by a more and more vocal – usually white – section of the Southern African public. The result has been an increasing willingness on the part of the relevant actors to employ violent means to combat anything which could possibly threaten their common vision of the peaceful and profitable co-existence of wildlife with humans. In relation to the Kruger National Park, also part of a TFCA, Büscher and Ramutsindela offered two reasons as to why many of the relevant power brokers do not recognise the contradiction of using violence to sustain so-called peace parks. Firstly, as peace parks are presented as a 'global solution', their advocates fail to take into account the specific and often violent histories of many of the regions in which they are located.[241] Secondly, poachers are increasingly placed into a discursive 'space of exception', in which their right to fair treatment or even their right to life is no longer acknowledged.[242] Violent anti-poaching measures are thereby represented as legitimate tactics in a "just war" in which the use of violence against a loosely defined 'enemy' is legitimised and normalised.[243] This war is increasingly fought not only by conventional militaries, but also by private security companies, such as Maisha Consulting, which has also participated in counter-insurgency measures in Afghanistan and Iraq.[244]

Most of these observations are also applicable to the KAZA, although not all apply to the Caprivi. While the official conservation policies of Zambia, Botswana and Zimbabwe have relied heavily on violent practices for many years, nature conservation in Namibia was until very recently less militarised.[245] However, in the case of the Western Caprivi, where the

---

rhino-poaching-statistics [accessed: 02.01.2018]).

[239] Jason, L. (2017), Cops seize 13 elephant tusks in Bwabwata. *New Era*, 12.01.2017.

[240] Büscher et al. (2016): 2.

[241] Büscher et al. (2016): 2.

[242] Büscher et al. (2016): 3.

[243] Lunstrum (2014): 819.

[244] Duffy (2016): 244. It is also important to consider that alongside the rise in militarised anti-poaching practices in Southern Africa, incidents of collusion between state officials and international poaching syndicates also appear to be increasing. In South Africa, for example, the then State Security Minister, David Mahlobo, was accused of colluding with a rhinoceros horn trafficker. See: Ngubeni, N. (2016), Reports: SA state security minister linked to rhino horn trafficker, *EWN*, 23.12.2016.

[245] However, as recent occurrences have shown, Namibia appears to be gradually turning towards

MET is directly responsible for the rule of law, reports of violence against alleged poachers are becoming increasingly common. In the first months of 2017, for example, at least four people were shot dead by the Namibian Police Force for allegedly violating hunting laws.[246] Many of my interviewees also reported less overt forms of state violence, such as the building of fences to keep the local population out of the park's 'core conservation areas'.[247] Officially, however, Namibia did not apply military force against poachers prior to 2017 and has in many instances openly criticised its neighbours for excessive use of force.[248] Two possible reasons stand out for this approach. Firstly, Namibia still permits trophy hunting; this may have made it more difficult for the country to push poachers into a discursive 'state of exception' while, at the same time, welcoming hunters from all over the world. Secondly, Namibia's non-coercive community-based conservancy model is seen as highly successful and has been praised internationally as an exemplary case in the field of conservation. To replace this approach or even to allow militarised forms of conservation to take hold in nearby areas might have been seen by the state as potentially harmful for Namibia's global reputation as a leader in the field of community-based tourism and conservation.

Nevertheless, Namibia – and, especially, the Caprivi – have still provided examples of 'green violence'. This not only takes the form of the increasing police brutality against suspected poachers, but, significantly in this regard, also involves a fourth set of actors which are becoming more and more influential in the field of conservation in Namibia, namely private security companies which offer their services to the state and conservation NGOs.[249] As Büscher and Ramutsindela showed for South Africa, ever-louder demands for stricter anti-poaching laws from concerned sections of the public and conservation NGOs play an influential role in driving harsh state responses. Indeed, a growing community of concerned individuals and NGOs is urging the Namibian state to take up arms against poachers; some have even taken matters into their own hands.

---

    more militarised methods of nature conservation (see Chapter 6).

[246] Muyamba, J. (2017), Police exchange fire with poachers in Bwabwata. *New Era*, 14.03.2017.

[247] E.g.: AC, 21.05.2014, Kongola.

[248] As the Namibian government did, for example, in the above-mentioned case of the suspected Namibian poachers who were shot near Botswana's border with Namibia. Tjihenuna, T. (2015) 'Government condemns Botswana for shooting Namibians', *The Namibian*, 07.10.2015. However, in 2016 there were rumors that the NDF was training a special secret nature conservation law enforcement unit in the Western Caprivi. Although I could not find any evidence for this claim, it came up repeatedly in many of my informal discussions and in some interviews.

[249] Lunstrum (2014). On the co-operation between private (security) companies, French and British military experts, and nature conservation organisations in Namibia, see: Smit, E. (2015), Private sector takes up arms to save the rhino, *The Namibian Sun*, 23.07.2015.

In January 2016, a farmer near Okahandja in central Namibia shot at four people who had illegally hunted a kudu on his farm, killing one.[250] The farmer was arrested and charged with murder; his trial has been postponed several times and the verdict is yet to be announced.[251] The reactions to this incident mirror trends which Büscher and Ramutsindela identified for South Africa.[252] In comments on online news websites, on Facebook, and in online forums, readers expressed their solidarity with the farmer and 'dehumanised' the alleged poachers. One group which did so was an organisation with the cynical name, Wildlife at Risk International (or, WAR international).[253] In many of their and similar groups' social media accounts, comments were left in support of the farmer's action and calls were made for others to follow his lead. One comment proposed "no jail, simply kill them, blood for blood".[254] Even in the readers' comments section of a leading national daily newspaper, *The Namibian*, another commenter wrote: "That's the way to go, shoot to kill any poacher in your private farm. Do the same in Etosha [National Park] too please."[255]

This open dehumanisation of alleged poachers was also apparent in my interviews and informal discussions in the Caprivi, particularly in the case of people who worked in the conservation and wildlife industries and who saw themselves as warriors in a just struggle against poachers. In this regard, they appeared to be no longer particularly concerned with protecting their business interests, but by the opportunity to become a sort of 'war hero'. This heroising of nature conservationists is also evident in many recently published popular memoirs, such as those by Jan Breytenbach or Garth Owen-Smith, in which the authors describe their 'battles' to save wildlife.[256]

Summarizing Narratives of Violence and Development

Trapped by this supposedly ethical crusade are residents in or near conservation areas, who are often left with no choice but to decide between fulfilling the role in nature conservation's 'global solution' which others have assigned to them or falling into a 'state of exception'.[257] JM of the Mashi Traditional Authority, who successfully applied to establish a conservancy and is well known for supporting nature conservation, noted this in an inter-

---

[250] Suspected poacher shot and killed on Farm Otukaruno, *The Namibian*, 28.01.2016
[251] The farmer was granted bail in July 2017. Judgment is expected to be delivered in January 2018.
[252] Büscher et al. (2016): 19–20.
[253] www.war-international.org [accessed: 03.03.2017].
[254] www.facebook.com/WAR-Wildlife-At-Risk-International-195153390619509 [accessed: 03.03.2017].
[255] www.namibian.com.na/index.php?page=archive-read&id=146713 [accessed: 03.03.2017].
[256] Owen-Smith (2014), Breytenbach (1997).
[257] Büscher et al. (2016).

view, complaining that "there is no option, they support us as long as we conserve wildlife, but what about agriculture? Who supports us there?"[258] In this respect, he recalled how he had unsuccessfully attempted to obtain a fenced-in agricultural plot. He also expressed his concern that young men in rural areas would only be willing to either work in nature conservation or to become poachers, with both options promising a better life than agriculture. As he argued, there were no viable alternatives to these two choices and, with not enough jobs available in the conservation sector, many local residents would be forced to become illegal hunters.[259] PY, a controversial Namibian human rights activist, was even more radical in his criticism, making the extreme statement that nature conservation as practiced in Southern Africa merely represents "a hidden way to clear spaces from people. No longer in a physical way, but through creating areas in which people live who were bereft of their humanity."[260] For him, the 'state of exception' which Büscher and Ramutsindela identified in relation to the perception of alleged poachers in Southern Africa has been extended to all people living in conservation areas.[261]

PY's statement would not reflect the views of a broader Namibian public. Nevertheless, irrespective of where exactly one draws the frontlines in the debate, it remains clear that nature conservation in the Caprivi, as in Southern Africa in general, continues to be not only vested in histories of violence and war, but still represents a set of practices, interests and individuals inextricably linked to violence. Bearing this in mind, Vupenyu Dzingirai's claim, cited at the beginning of this chapter, must be refined. It is no longer sufficient to maintain that after "many years of violent and militaristic methods of wildlife conservation", these practices have now been replaced by a partnership between the state and private business which "invit[es] 'tribesmen' and poachers to put downs their spears".[262] Instead, private business has joined hands with the state to further an approach which resembles those of previous regimes in the Caprivi: the practising of nature conservation via (military) force and particularly the promising of profit.

---

[258] JM, 28.05.2014, Choi.
[259] JM, 28.05.2014, Choi.
[260] PY, 17.08.2012, Windhoek.
[261] Büscher et al. (2016): 20.
[262] Dzingirai (2003): 243.

6 Conclusion

This study has investigated three principal trajectories. Firstly, it illustrated how the historiographical engagement with Namibia's northern territories – and in particular the Caprivi, a seemingly peripheral region under South African control – can contribute to a better understanding of the apartheid state's policies and practices. Secondly, it elaborated on how these policies and practices altered and evolved over time and how they were constituted, and reconstituted, in relation to nature conservation in the Caprivi. Thirdly, it demonstrated that some of the features of South Africa's rule over the region have endured or re-emerged in the post-independence era.

One of the major conclusions of this study is that the imperatives of nature conservation, militarisation and development have been intricately entwined in the Caprivi. This entanglement stems from their interlinked past, a history which continues to leave its impact on the region today. I have shown how, alongside military occupation, research on local nature as well as the exploitation and conservation of the natural environment became a central means for apartheid South Africa to expand its power over northern Namibia. The South African authorities' surveying and mapping endeavours in the Caprivi – whether in search of potentially profitable raw materials and other economic resources, for military or geopolitical reasons, or for purposes of wildlife conservation – showed that the seemingly competing aims of economic development or modernisation, natural science or nature conservation, and militarisation necessitated close mutual ties which, in turn, engendered multi-layered forms of interaction. This historical perspective offers crucial insights which can inform the often intense contemporary political and scholarly debates on neoliberal nature conservation, communal conservancies and transfrontier conservation areas. Moreover, as the two most important post-independence nature conservation initiatives in the Caprivi, conservancies and the Kavango-Zambezi Transfrontier Conservation Area (KAZA TFCA) can reveal the many ways in which conservation-development-military entanglements continue to shape space and society in the region today.

As I posited in the introduction, this study thus offers an argument against conceptual confines, whether in the form of rigid analytical boundaries between supposedly separate spheres of politics, such as economic development, nature conservation and military power; circumscribed historical eras, like the apartheid and post-apartheid periods; or neatly defined political-geographical-historiographical entities, such as Namibia and South Africa. To understand past and present nature conservation initiatives and policies in the Caprivi – or, indeed, more generally in Southern Africa – it is thus crucial to reappraise the relevance of conceptual boundaries and emphasise the search for continuities and entanglements across different concepts and paradigms. By the same token, to untangle this study's findings in the form of a neat conclusion would be to risk undermining my overall position that they should be seen as being interlinked. Nevertheless, for the sake of clarity, I will recapitulate some of my most important arguments, before opening the discussion for some relevant questions beyond the immediate scope of my research.

My study lies at the intersection of two important theoretical debates; the first concerns the place of development discourse in South African policy at the supposed peripheries of the apartheid state, including in the homelands and in Namibia; the second tackles the extent to which military practices, nature conservation, and the production of ecological and environmental knowledge served Pretoria as mutually reinforcing means to exert its control over these supposedly remote regions. Both debates are closely interrelated, ongoing, and relevant for the post-apartheid Caprivi.

While the Caprivi was long represented by the South African colonial authorities in the region as being 'beyond the last frontier', it was entangled within the respective Southern African political networks of the British Empire and its South African occupier. I illustrated that the first decades of South African rule over the Caprivi were not defined by mere "administrative neglect", as suggested by Bennett Kangumu, but that this period was marked by the sort of ambivalent administration typical of many colonial contexts of indirect rule.[1] South Africa's policies towards the Caprivi reflected a general tendency among colonial regimes in indirectly-ruled territories all over colonial Africa of attempting to appropriate natural resources at the lowest possible administrative cost. In the case of the Caprivi, at least until the 1950s, no economic resources of significant value or benefit for South Africa were found, but the many reports and surveys which were undertaken by the South African administration indicate that the occupying authorities were on the lookout for opportunities for economic development and exploitation. Even when no potential could be identified, the information which was gathered on the region was important for creating a context in which governance could be extended and subsequent economic opportunities detected and exploited. In so doing, the South African authorities could sustain the narrative of modernisation and economic development with which it sought to win the loyalty of local inhabitants and, in particular, of the chiefs.

The focus which the South African administration placed on this narrative as a means to justify its rule shifted over time. In systems of indirect rule, development has typically been presented as a colonial intervention to uplift or civilise dependent locals. However, in

---

[1] Kangumu (2011): 72.

the Caprivi in the 1960s, the development narrative was increasingly presented as a hegemonic vision for a future in which colonial suppression would be a politically legitimate and economically productive tool to enable development. The Odendaal Report (1963), which set out the basis for the introduction of South Africa's homeland and separate development policies in Namibia, contributed significantly to promoting this new approach. Increasing international and internal pressure on South Africa to end its occupation of Namibia led Pretoria to seek strategies to legitimise its rule, for example by presenting South African occupation as an enabling factor for local development, while the same strategy was useful to secure the continued loyalty of locals. One important means of combining these two aims was the creation of supposedly self-reliant and self-governing homelands.

For the South African authorities in the Caprivi from the 1960s, the natural environment provided an opportunity to implement such a strategy based on a development narrative. It was in the fields of forestry, fishery and, in particular, wildlife conservation that key features of South African governance were applied, negotiated and contested. Not only did the dual protection and utilisation of the region's natural resources allow the administration to project the image that it was enabling local people to secure a livelihood, but the research on nature which it undertook corresponded neatly with the military aims of the SADF, which was fighting a brutal war in, from and near the Caprivi during the same period.

Constant references to potential profit or economic development have been central to nature conservation programmes in the Caprivi since independence. The logic of market-based conservation has allowed a diverse range of conservation concepts to develop – spanning from the community-based model of the communal conservancies to large-scale top-down projects such as the KAZA TFCA – which run parallel, or sometimes even in cooperation, with each other.

A second key outcome of this study are the close links which it has revealed between military practices, science and mapping, and nature conservation in the Caprivi. All served South Africa to extend and exert its power and control in the Caprivi, converging in the late 1970s and 1980s in the research and protection of what was increasingly seen as the region's most valuable asset, wildlife. South Africa's interest in wildlife conservation in the Caprivi increased from the mid-1970s, reaching a peak in the 1980s, at a time when the country was also intensifying its military endeavours in northern Namibia and southern Angola. This book has examined how ecological and environmental surveys and other forms of natural scientific research in the Caprivi also served the SADF's overarching military and strategic agenda in the area, which was focussed on sustaining South Africa's military intervention in Angola as well as its fight against the Namibian liberation movement in Zambia and Angola and within the Caprivi.

Practices of surveying, surveillance, and environmental research were used by both the SADF and the civil administration to control the region's nature and its people. For example, cut-lines and aerial photography had both military-strategic and conservation applications, from tracking and controlling the movements of enemy fighters and locating their potential hiding places to collecting data on wildlife and the natural environment which informed conservation proposals. Furthermore, the SADF's rhetorical focus on nature conservation allowed the apartheid state to present the South African military presence in northern Namibia to the white South African public as a benevolent endeavour for the good of people and animals in the area. This also provided a useful propaganda tool for South Africa from the 1970s, when the country sought to overcome its pariah image by increasingly presenting itself internationally as a global pioneer in the field of conservation.

In the 1980s, based on the data collected through entangled practices of environmental research and military surveillance, plans for nature conservation areas were (re-)drawn in the Caprivi. For their implementation and in the name of conservation, residents were evicted from their homes and space was rearranged, not only according to military imperatives, as in the Western Caprivi, but also in line with the aims of the civil administration and the traditional authorities. The proclamation of the Nkasa Lupala and Mudumu National Parks only weeks before Namibia's independence was a manifestation of these interwoven interests shared by the military, the 'chiefs' and the civil administration. Furthermore, by proclaiming the two conservation areas shortly before its withdrawal from Namibia, the apartheid state also laid a spatial basis for post-independence conservation in the Caprivi.

I have shown that when the South African authorities established the two national parks, they did not solely rely on coercive means such as forced removals. Instead, these were combined with non-coercive approaches, including promising local inhabitants a small share of the potential profits which were to be gained from nature conservation and by maintaining the impression that communities were involved in the planning of conservation areas through the involvement of chiefs in these discussions.

Although Namibia's – and with it the Caprivi's – political context changed dramatically with the coming of Namibian independence, there was no clean break in terms of either policy or practice in the field of nature conservation after 1990. Instead, the current status quo of market-orientated conservation enacted via decentralised or community-based approaches has a long history in the region. Moreover, as recent anti-poaching measures have shown, military and police influence within conservation remains significant.

The findings of this study raised a series of questions just beyond its scope which are worth recalling here. As I have demonstrated, the height of apartheid South Africa's homeland policies in the late 1970s – a time when the Caprivi became a fully-fledged, pseudo-independent homeland – coincided with a shift in global approaches towards nature conservation. In line with emerging neoliberal trends towards decentralisation and market-based development, global conservation policy began to place its faith in market mechanisms while seeking to involve ever more non-state actors such as 'the community'. By researching conservation policy in the Caprivi in the late 1970s and 1980s, it soon became clear how unproblematically new community-based and market-oriented approaches functioned alongside apartheid structures of homeland and 'separate development' governance. My findings revealed that contemporary South African reports constantly referred to the involvement of communities and their chiefs in all discussions on conservation. Apartheid rhetoric also proved its flexibility in the Caprivi. While the common racist assertion that 'black' people were unable to understand monetary systems and could not cope with money had been invoked by South African officials in numerous contexts, a different narrative emerged in the context of Caprivian nature conservation from as early as the 1970s. This claimed that the only principles which black people would understand were those derived from the quest for economic profit. In order to protect wildlife, local people would thus have to gain a share of any wildlife-related revenues, an assumption which was also at the heart of the market-based conservation models which gained global momentum in the same period.

The seamlessness with which early neoliberal as well as late-apartheid homeland and separate development policies worked in parallel, if not hand in hand, would be a stimulating avenue for further research, including in relation to other spheres of governance or on a broader, more comparative scale. This latter approach, for example, could be of particular value for understanding apartheid history from a post-apartheid perspective or in transcending the overly narrow conception of apartheid as a chronologically- and geographically-contained occurrence.

A second set of themes which arise from this study is concerned with the broad question of the role which human society has been playing within larger natural systems. This study has exposed the manner in which nature conservation in the Caprivi has perpetuated – and, in many ways, continues to perpetuate – unequal power structures which allow a global elite to profit at the expense of impoverished local inhabitants, all for the sake of preserving what this self-same elite takes upon itself to define as worth saving: charismatic wildlife in a supposedly unspoiled 'African' landscape. In this context, even supposedly benevolent initiatives are often based on or risk reinforcing narrow colonial notions of ethnicity or systemically unequal capitalist structures and rarely achieve emancipatory goals. Nevertheless, finding a means of establishing a just and equitable co-existence between humans and other parts of nature is rightly one of the most pressing concerns facing humanity. Indeed, as many scholars and activists have pointed out, a peaceful and equitable global human society is barely conceivable as long as humans continue to exploit, abuse and enslave animals and ecosystems.[2]

Departing from my own area of expertise here, I see it as imperative – not only for historical research, but even more so from a wider social and political perspective – to bring 'nature' back into the discussion on human-nature relations. For example, in this study it proved to be very fruitful to challenge the commonly accepted geographical and temporal boundaries of apartheid. Transcending these boundaries in turn calls for the rethinking of other boundaries which inhibit a full understanding of the topic of society and nature, and its relationship, in the Caprivi, but also generally. The disciplinary boundaries within which this thesis is situated must also be transcended. Namely, this would require a thorough (re-)investigation of Caprivian natural history, including a re-examination of the interplay between nature, history and society, from a broader transdisciplinary perspective. As such, the interrelations between nature and society – as well as the boundaries which divide them – would need to be reconceptualised together with and within the particular historical, political, socio-economic and environmental context of the Caprivi.

This process would also entail a rethinking of this study's context that departs from ideas of boundaries which uphold an overly strict dichotomy between human society and nature as well as between the natural sciences and the humanities. This would allow for a repositioning of human society within the realm of nature and a concomitant return to the assumption that nature has intrinsic value and a right to exist in, of and for itself rather than for the material benefit of humans. Further it could challenge the assumptions of neoliberal nature conservation, which see animals and natural environments merely as objects of capital value for a global elite or as means of subsistence for poor rural populations. Not only would such a change in perspective ensure that people living in regions such as the Caprivi would no longer be reduced to their function within a system of capitalist extraction, but it would also open up new opportunities for creating a fairer society which would embrace humans and the rest of nature on a more equal and less extractive basis decoupled from nature conservation's long association with colonialism, oppression, violence and economic exploitation. As such, this would allow for more meaningful theoretical and political engagement with questions of animal rights and how human societies relate to their non-human natural environments which may ultimately suggest ways to include non-humans within visions of an equitable and less violent future.

---

[2] Over recent decades, an intense scholarly and political debate has taken place over such questions and their legal, moral, economic, environmental, sociological, historical and ethological implications. It is not possible to provide a detailed overview of this debate here, but my thinking was informed, for example, by Nilbert (2002), Torres (2007) and Harraway (2015). A recent overview can be found in Moore (2016).

Recent tourism and conservation trends in Namibia, however, would suggest that the realisation of this vision remains a distant dream. According to the latest statistics on tourism in Namibia, tourist arrivals and levels of international investment in the sector continue to rise; nevertheless, it remains questionable under which conditions the poor in the Caprivi will benefit from this boom, if at all.[3] As I have argued, evidence largely suggests that market-based nature conservation serves primarily – at least if looked at it on systemic level – to perpetuate inequalities between a global urban tourism elite and the cheap rural labour force who ensure that the former can live out their dreams of an unspoilt and wild 'Africa'. While the impact of market-based conservation on biodiversity and local economies is still the subject of much debate, it seems unquestionable that along with the rising economic value attached to wildlife – whether as objects for tourism, legal trophy hunting, or the global illicit ivory and rhinoceros horn trade – violence is also on the rise as a means to protect wildlife or acquire wildlife products. This violence is increasingly aimed at suspected poachers. On the last day of 2016, Namibia's Minister for Environment and Tourism, Pohamba Shifeta, sent a text message to Namibian media outlets, confirming the deadly shooting of three suspected poachers in the Bwabwata National Park:

> We have taken a serious decision, as I announced three weeks ago, to invoke the Criminal Procedures Act for self-defense whenever poachers fire at our units. Poachers shooting at anti-poaching units will regret having done so if they ever survive the firepower of our well-trained special units.[4]

While details of what occurred during this particular incident are not yet clear, it appears evident that wildlife-related violence has been on the rise in Namibia in late 2016 and early 2017.[5] At least one of the arrested suspects was reported to have been carrying an AK-47 assault rifle. At the same time, the incident was described by the media as the first time that Namibian anti-poaching units had used lethal force against suspected poachers. Indeed, Shifeta declared that the state would continue to take the fight to poachers, increasingly with the help of the Namibian Defence Force:

> We vowed to show [the alleged poachers] that there is an authority. We have also started to deploy the special unit of the NDF (Namibia Defence Force) in Bwabwata National Park.[6]

---

[3] World Travel and Tourism Council (ed.) (2017), *Travel & Tourism Economic Impact 2016 Namibia*, London.
[4] Anti-Poaching unit gun down three, *New Era*, 04.01.2017, frontpage.
[5] In the first months of 2017, more shoot-outs between anti-poaching units and suspected poachers were reported in the Bwabwata National Park. See: Muyamba (2017).
[6] Anti-Poaching unit gun down three, *New Era*, 04.01.2017, frontpage.

Over fifty years since the Western Caprivi Game Park (today, the Bwabwata National Park) was declared a closed military zone by the South African occupation authorities, it is now the independent Namibian state which has deployed its military to the area to protect what it sees as one of the country's biggest asset: wildlife. Wildlife conservation has become such a lucrative source of income for the global tourism industry that the Namibian state is willing to apply militarised and violent measures in order to protect the economic value of its wildlife and sustain what it regards as the magic bullet for the growth of its tourism sector, its future rural development, and the preservation of wildlife: market-orientated and community-based conservation.

From a strictly economic perspective, these measures appear to be working. In the Caprivi, new lodges open frequently in conservancies, more conservancies are being planned, KAZA is attracting a growing degree of investment and more and more tourists to the region, and in Katima Mulilo, the region's biggest town, tourism infrastructure is burgeoning. Some Caprivians will undoubtedly benefit from this rapid growth in the tourism sector, but many will remain trapped in a system which has long endured in the region, a system in which influential elites advocate the protection of some animals and local socio-economic development, but only to the extent to which these measures support their own privileges and maintain the power structures from which these are derived.

Abbreviations

APO	Namibian Anti-Poaching Unit
BDF	Botswana Defence Force
BSAC	British South Africa Company
CAF	Caprivi Department of Agriculture and Forestry
CANU	Caprivi National Union
CAP	Civic Action Programme
CITES	Convention on International Trade in Endangered Species
CLA	Caprivi Liberation Army
DTA	Democratic Turnhalle Alliance
ECZ	Eastern Caprivi Zipfel
EWB	Elephants without Borders
GIS	Geographic Information Systems
HNP	Herenigde Nasionale Party
IDP	Integrated Development Plan
IMF	International Monetary Fund
IRDNC	Integrated Rural Development and Nature Conservation
IUCN	International Union for Conservation of Nature and Natural Resources
KAZA TFCA	Kavango Zambezi Transfrontier Conservation Area
MET	Ministry of Environment and Tourism (Namibia)
MID	Military Intelligence Division (SADF)
MoU	Memorandum of Understanding
MPLA	Movimento Popular de Libertação de Angola
NASCO	Namibian Association of Community Based Natural Resource Management
NDF	Namibian Defence Force
NGO	Non-Governmental Organisation
NP	Nasionale Party
OPC	Ovambo People's Congress
OPO	Ovamboland People's Organization
PLAN	People's Liberation Army of Namibia
PPF	Peace Park Foundation
RENAMO	Resistência Nacional Moçambicana
SADC	Southern African Development Community
SADF	South African Defence Force
SAP	South African Police
SWAPO	South West African People's Organization
SWAPOL	South West African Police
SWATF	South West African Territory Forces
TFCA	Transfrontier Conservation Area
UDF	South African Union Defence Force
UDP	United Democratic Party
UN	United Nations Organisation
UNIP	United National Independence Party (Zambia)
UNITA	União Nacional para a Independência Total de Angola
UNTAG	United Nations Transition Assistance Group
WAR	Wildlife at Risk International
WHAM	Winning the Hearts and Minds
WNLA	Witwatersrand Native Labour Association
WWF	World Wide Fund for Nature
ZDF	Zimbabwe Defence Force

Sources

Interviews

AC, 21.05.2014   Kongola, interview conducted by the author, taped
AK, 30.05.2014   Omega I, interview conducted by the author
AM, 10.09.2015   Ihaha, interview conducted by Lieneke Eloff de Visser and the author, taped. Interpreter: Benjamin Mabuku
BM, 02.10.2012   Katima Mulilo, interview conducted by the author
BM, 21.05.2014   Sibinda, interview conducted by the author, taped
BN, 17.05.2014   near Sangwali, interview conducted by the author, taped
BS, 14.05.2014   Sangwali, interview conducted by the author
BW, 03.05.2013   interview by e-mail, conducted by the author
BW, 10.03.2014   Sedgefield, interview conducted by the author, taped
CB, 22.04.2014   Stellenbosch, interview conducted by the author, taped
CB, 23.08.2012   Windhoek, interview conducted by the author, taped
CC, 02.11.2015   Windhoek, interview conducted by the author and Bennett Kangumu, taped
CG, 08.04.2014   Cape Town, interview conducted by the author, taped
CK, 09.05.2014   Ondangwa, interview conducted by the author
CS, 15.08.2012   Windhoek, interview conducted by the author, taped
CT, 26.03.2014   Cape Town, interview conducted by the author
CW, 26.07.2011   Katima Mulilo, interview conducted by the author, taped
DP, 28.02.2014   interview by e-mail conducted by the author
EB, 20.06.2014   Pretoria, interview conducted by the author, taped
HS, 10.03.2014   George, interview conducted by the author, taped
JL, 18.05.2014   Malengalenga, interview conducted by the author and Silva Lieberherr
JM, 28.05.2014   Choi, interview conducted by the author. Interpreter: Beaven Munali
KS, 26.07.2011   Katima Mulilo, interview conducted by the author, taped
Members of the Impalila conservancy, 23.06.2014, Impalila, group interview conducted by the author, taped
MI, 03.10.2015   Basel, interview conducted by the author and James Merron, taped
ML, 29.04.2014   Windhoek, interview conducted by the author, taped
MP, 23.07.2011   Kayaru, interview conducted by the author
MS, 29.06.2014   Katima Mulilo, interview conducted by the author, taped
NN, 12.03.2014   Cape Town, interview conducted by the author
PL, 13.05.2014   Katima Mulilo, interview conducted by the author, taped
PR, 21.04.2014   Napier, interview conducted by the author, taped
PS, 03.08.2012   Windhoek, interview conducted by the author, taped
PS, 10.06.2014   Windhoek, interview conducted by the author, taped
PY, 17.08.2012   Windhoek, interview conducted by the author, taped
RM, 29.05.2014   Chinchimane, interview conducted by the author, taped. Interpreter: RM Junior
SM, 27.04.2014   Windhoek, interview conducted by the author, taped
SS, 02.10.2012   Katima Mulilo, interview conducted by the author
SS, 15.05.2014   Katima Mulilo, interview conducted by the author, taped
TC, 11.05.2014   Mutjiku, interview conducted by the author, taped
VK, 27.09.2012   Livingstone, interview conducted by the author, taped
VS, 27.07.2011   Kasane, interview conducted by the author
WM, 11.07.2011 Stellenbosch, interview conducted by the author, taped

National Archives of Namibia (NAN)
Administration for Caprivians (ACS)
5/3/2   Opleiding: Natuurbewaring
Accessions (A)
A.871   Documents on the History of Eastern Caprivi (Boundary Dispute Masubiya / Mafwe)
Kavango Administration (AKA)
1/5/1   Landbou und Bosbou
Caprivi Agriculture and Forestry (CAF)
1/1   Tribal Authorities: Policy, Decisions and Institutions
1/3/1–2   Legislation and Regulation: Draft Revision and Amendment
2/10/1   Office Administration and Auxiliary Services: Staff Main File (whites)
6/18/15/1   Agricultural Matters: Salvinia Spray Project
6/18/15/2   Agricultural Matters: Weed Control
6/19   Policy Decisions, Instructions and Law
6/19/2   Policy Decisions, Instructions and Law: Beskerming van Fauna en Flora
6/19/2/2   Policy Decisions, Instructions and Law: Problem Herbivore
6/19/5   Beskerming van Fauna en Flora
6/19/7   Nature Conservation: development and utilization
6/20/1   Policy Decisions, Instructions, Trip Reports
South West African Administration (SWAA)
A503/1   Caprivi Strip Administration
A503/4   Eastern Caprivi Reports
A503/5   Boundaries
A205/21   Protection of Nature: Flora and Fauna
A503/25   Control of Western Caprivi
Magistrate Katima Mulilo (LKM)
N1/15/2–9   Native Affairs
21/1/2   Dierbeskerming en Natuurbewaring: Fauna & Flora
Native Commissioner Rundu (NAR)
12/1   Jag
Nature Conservation and Tourism South West Africa Administration (NTB)
22/2/1–3   Beleidskommissie FRANK
Unpublished Holdings of the Library of the Archive (ARCAT)
BB2598   F. Breitenbach (1968), Long-term Plan of Forestry Development in the Eastern Caprivi Zipfel
BB0478   K.L. Tinley (1966), Western Caprivi Conservation Area, South West Africa: A Proposal of Natural Land Resource Land Use

National Archives of South Africa (NASA)
Secretary of Native Affairs (NTS)
463/400/1   Caprivi Zipfel Annual Reports
Commission Reports (KC)
SWA 2/6   Commission of Enquiry into the Affairs of South West Africa: Ancillary Documents
SWA 72/35   Commission of Enquiry into the Affairs of South West Africa: Minutes of the Public Hearings
Prime Minister's Office (PM)
72/EM2/70/2   References: Commission of Enquiry into the Affairs of South West Africa

Departments of Bantu Administration and Development, Co-operation and Development, Plural Relations and Development Aid (BAO)
20/271   Landbou Natuurbewaring Caprivi

Other Collections
Archives of the Livingstone Museum (LM)
1/5/11_1–10   Correspondence with Ministry of Tourism (and Natural Resources)
South African National Defence Force Documentation Centre (SANDFDOC)
Historical Papers Research Archives, University of the Witwatersrand (HPRA)
Archives of the South African Air Force Museum Ysterplaat

Webpages
(The exact URLs with complete paths and dates of access for the relevant subpages can be found in the footnotes.)

www.africanmonarchlodges.com
www.archive.org
www.caprivifreedom.com
www.elephantswithoutborders.org
www.facebook.com
www.irdnc.org.na
www.iucn.org
www.kavangozambezi.org
www.namibian.com.na
www.nacso.org.na
www.nacso.org.na
www.peaceparks.org
www.pifworld.com
www.poachingfacts.com
www.sandevelopment.gov.na
www.savetherhino.org
www.war-international.org
www.wikipedia.org
www.wwf.de

Bibliography

Adams, W.M. and M. Mulligan (2003), *Decolonizing Nature: Strategies for Conservation in a Post-colonial Era.* London and Sterling: Earthscan Publications.
Adams, W.M. and J. Hutton (2007), People, Parks and Poverty: Political Ecology and Biodiversity Conservation, *Conservation and Society*, 5: 147–183.
Administrator-General for the Territory of South West Africa (ed.) (1990), AG 18, *Official Gazette*, 5904, 1 March 1990. Windhoek.
Akawa, M. and J. Silvester (2007), 'Their Blood Waters our Freedom': Naming the Dead: Civilian Causalities in the Liberation Struggle, *The Namibian*, 24.08.2007.
Ake, C. (1996), *Democracy and Development in Africa.* Washington: Brookings.
Akweenda, S. (1997), *International Law and the Protection of Namibia's Territorial Integrity. Boundaries and Territorial Claims.* The Hague: Klewer Law International.
Ally, S. and A. Lissoni (eds.) (2018), *New Histories of South Africa's Apartheid-Era Bantustans.* New York: Routledge.
Ali, S.H. (2007), Introduction: A Natural Connection between Ecology and Peace? In S.H. Ali (ed.), Peace Parks: *Conservation and Conflict Resolution.* Cambridge: MIT Press: 1–18.
Amnesty International (ed.) (2016), *Amnesty International Report 2015/2016: The State of the World's Human Rights.* London: Amnesty International.
Anderson, D.M. and R. Grove (eds.) (1987), *Conservation in Africa: People, Policies and Practice.* Cambridge: Cambridge University Press.
Anderson, D.M. and D.H. Johnson (1988), *The Ecology of Survival: Case Studies from Northeast African History.* Boulder: Westview.
Anti-Poaching unit gun down three, *New Era*, 04.01.2017, frontpage.
Appadurai, A. (1996), *Modernity at Large: Cultural Dimensions of Globalization.* Minneapolis: University of Minnesota Press.
Armeirio, M. and L. Sedrez, (eds.) (2014), *A History of Environmentalism. Local Struggles, Global Histories.* London and New York: Bloomsbury.
Ashforth, A. (1990), *Politics of Official Discourse in Twentieth-Century South Africa.* Oxford: Clarendon Press.
Asiwaju, A.I. (1985), The Conceptual Framework. In: A.I. Asiwaju (ed.), *Partitioned Africans: Ethnic Relations Across Africa's International Boundaries, 1884–1984.* London: Hurst & Co: 1–18.
Baines, G. (2014), *South Africa's 'Border War': Contested Narratives and Conflicting Memories.* London: Bloomsbury.
Barrett, G., S. Brooks, J. Josefsson and N. Zulu (2013), Starting the Conversation: Land Issues and Critical Conservation Studies in Post-Colonial Africa, *Journal of Contemporary African Studies*, 31(3): 336–344.
Barrett, G., S. Brooks, J. Josefsson and N. Zulu (eds.) (2015), *The Changing Face of Land and Conservation.* New York: Routledge.
Barton, G. (2002), *Empire Forestry and the Origins of Environmentalism.* Cambridge: Cambridge University Press.
Bassett, T. and D. Gautier (2014), Regulation by Territorialization: The Political Ecology of Conservation & Development Territories, *EchoGeo*, 29(4): 1–7.
Beinart, W., P. Delius and S. Trapido (eds.) (1986), *Putting a plough in the ground: Accumulation and Dispossession in rural South Africa, 1850–1930.* Johannesburg: Ravan.
Beinart, W. and C. Bundy (1987). *Hidden Struggles in Rural South Africa: Politics and Popular Movements in the Transkei and Eastern Cape, 1890–1930.* London: James Currey.
Beinart, W. and J. McGregor (2003), *Introduction.* In W. Beinart and J. McGregor (eds.), *Social History and African Environments.* Athens: Ohio University Press.

Beinart, W. and J. McGregor (eds.) (2003), *Social History and African Environments*. Athens: Ohio University Press.

Beinart, W. and L. Hughes (eds.) (2007), *Environment and Empire*. Oxford: Oxford University Press.

Beinart, W., K. Brown, and D. Gilfoyle (2009), Experts and Expertise in Colonial Africa Reconsidered: Science and the Interpenetration of Knowledge, *Africa Affairs* 108(432): 413–433.

Bennett, B.M. (2010), The El Dorado of Forestry: The Eucalyptus in India, South Africa, and Thailand, 1850–2000, *International Review of Social History*, 55(18): 25–50.

Bennett, B.M. (2011a), A Global History of Australian Trees, *Journal of the History of Biology*, 44: 125–145.

Bennett, B.M. (2011b), Naturalising Australian Trees in South Africa: Climate, Exotics and Experimentation, *Journal of Southern African Studies*, 37(2): 265–280.

Bennett, B.M. and J.M. Hodge (eds.) (2011), *Science and Empire: Knowledge and Networks of Science Across the British Empire, 1800–1970*. New York: Palgrave Macmillan.

Bertrand, A. (1899), *The Kingdom of the Barotsi, Upper Zambezia: A Voyage of Exploration in Africa*. London: T Fisher Unwin.

Biko, S. (1987). *I Write what I Like: A Selection of His Writings* (first published 1978). Johannesburg: Heinemann.

Biwa, M. (2012), 'Weaving the past with threads of memory': narratives and commemorations of the colonial war in southern Namibia. (PhD thesis: University of the Western Cape).

Bley, H. (1968), *Kolonialherrschaft und Sozialstruktur in Deutsch-Südwestafrika 1894–1914*. Hamburg: Leibniz Verlag.

Boden, G. (2004), Prozesse sozialen Wandels vor dem Hintergrund staatlicher Eingriffe: Eine Fallstudie zu den Khwe in West Caprivi/Namibia. (PhD Thesis: University of Cologne).

Böhlke-Itzen, J. (2004), *Kolonialschuld und Entschädigung: Der deutsche Völkermord an den Herero 1904–1907*. Frankfurt am Main: Brandes und Apsel.

Bolaane, M. (2005), Chiefs, hunters and adventurers: the foundation of the Okavango/Moremi National Park, Botswana. *Journal of Historical Geography*, 31: 241–259.

Bolaane, M. (2013), *Chiefs, Hunters and San in the Creation of the Moremi Game Reserve, Okavango Delta: Multiracial Interactions and Initiatives, 1956–1979*. Osaka: National Museum of Ethnology.

Bollig, M. (1998a), Power and Trade in Precolonial and Early Colonial Kaokoland 1860s–1940s. In P. Hayes, J. Silvester, M. Wallace and W. Hartmann (eds.), *Namibia under South African Rule: Mobility and Containment, 1915–46*. Oxford, Windhoek and Athens OH: James Currey, Out of Africa and Ohio University Press: 175–194.

Bollig, M. (1998b), The Colonial Encapsulation of the North-Western Namibian Pastoral Economy, *Africa: Journal of the International African Institute*, 68(4): 506–536.

Bollig, M. (2005), *Risk Management in a Hazardous Environment. A Comparative Study of Two Pastoral Societies*. New York: Springer.

Bollig, M. (2009), Visions of Landscape: An Introduction. In M. Bollig and O. Bubenzer (eds.), *African Landscapes: Interdisciplinary Approaches*. New York: Springer: 1–40.

Bollig, M. (2013), Conserving the Margins of Empire: Knowledge Production, Visions and Practices of Species Protection in North-Western Namibia. (Unpublished paper presented at the South African Empire Workshop, Basel).

Bollig, M. and E. Olwage (2016), The Political Ecology of Hunting in Namibia's Kaokoveld: From Dorsland Trekkers' Elephant Hunts to Trophy Hunting in Contemporary Conservancies. *Journal of Contemporary African Studies*, 34: 61–79.

Bond, P. (2005), *Elite Transition: From Apartheid to Neoliberalism in South Africa*. Second edition. Pietermaritzburg: University of KwaZulu-Natal Press.
Braverman, I. (2008), "The Tree Is the Enemy Soldier": A Sociolegal Making of War Landscapes in the Occupied West Bank. *Law & Society Review,* 42(3): 449–482.
Brenzinger, M. (2003), *The Khwe History: A Struggle for Recognition: Report to the Legal Assistance Centre, Windhoek*. University of Cologne: Institute for African Studies.
Breytenbach, J. (1997): *Eden's exile: One Soldier's Fight for Paradise*. Cape Town: Queillerie Publishers.
Breytenbach, J. (2014), *The Birth and Growth of 32 Battalion from Former Enemies and Terrorists into Decorated Soldiers*. Pretoria: Protea Book House.
Brockington, D. and J. Igoe (2006), Eviction for Conservation: A Global Overview. *Conservation and Society,* 4(3): 424–470.
Brockington, D. and R. Duffy (2011), Introduction: Capitalism and Conservation: The Production and Reproduction of Biodiversity Conservation. In D. Brockington and R. Duffy (eds.), *Capitalism and Conservation*. Malden MA and Oxford: Wiley Blackwell: 1–17.
Brosius, J.P. and D. Russell (2003), Conservation from Above: An Anthropological Perspective on Transboundary Protected Areas and Ecoregional Planning. In U.M. Goodale, M.J. Stern, C. Margoluis; A.G. Lanfer and M. Fladeland (eds.), *Transboundary Protected Areas: The Viability of Regional Conservation Strategies*. Binghamton: Food Production Press: 39–65.
Brown, E., B. Milward, G. Mohan, A.B. Zack-Williams (eds.) (2000), *Structural Adjustment: Theory, Practice and Impacts*. London: Routledge.
Brown, J. (2016), *The Road to Soweto: Resistance and the Uprising of 16 June 1976*. Johannesburg: Jacana.
Brubaker, R. and F. Cooper (2000), Beyond „Identity". *Theory and Society*, 29: 1–47.
Bruchmann, R. (2000), *Caprivi, An African Flashpoint: An Illustrated History of Namibia's Tropical Region Where Four Countries Meet*. Northcliff: self-published.
Bryan, S. (2012), Contested boundaries, contested places: the Natura 2000 Network in Ireland. *Journal of Rural Studies*, 28(1): 80–94.
Bryant, R.L. (1998), Power, knowledge and political ecology in the third world: a review, *Progress in Physical Geography*, 22(1): 79–94.
Bundy, C. (1987), Land and Liberation, Popular Rural Protest and the National Liberation Movements in South Africa 1920–1960. In S. Marks and S. Trapido (eds.), *The Politics of Race, Class and Nationalism in Twentieth Century South Africa*. London and New York: Longman: 254–286.
Bureau of Political-Military Affairs (ed.) (2009), *United States Government Counterinsurgency Guide*. Washington.
Büscher, B. (2013), *Transforming the Frontier. Peace Parks and the Politics of Neoliberal Conservation in Southern Africa*. Durham and London: Duke University Press.
Büscher, B. and M. Ramutsindela (2016), Green Violence, Rhino Poaching and the War to Save Southern Africa's Peace Parks. *African Affairs*, 115(458): 1–22.
Carruthers, J. (1995), *The Kruger National Park: A Social and Political History*. Pietermaritzburg: University of Natal Press.
Carruthers, J. (2008), "Wilding the farm or farming the wild"? The evolution of scientific game ranching in South Africa from the 1960s to the present. *Transactions of the Royal Society of South Africa*, 63(2): 160–181.
Carter, P. (1987), *The Road to Botany Bay. An Exploration of Landscape and History*. London: Faber and Faber.
Castree, N. (2003), Commodifying What Nature? *Progress in Human Geography*, 27(3): 273–297.

Castree, N. (2008), Neo-liberalisation of Nature I and II. *Environment and Planning*, A40(1): 153–173.
Castree, N. (2010), Neoliberalism and the Biophysical Environment 2: Theorising the Neoliberalisation of Nature. *Geography Compass*, 4(12): 1734–1746.
Chabal, P. and J.-P. Daloz (1999), *Africa Works: Disorder as Political Instrument*. Oxford: James Currey.
Chapman, J. (1868), *Travels in the interior of South Africa*. London: Bell and Daldy.
Chase, M.J. and C.R. Griffin (2009), Elephants caught in the middle: impacts of war, fences and people on elephant distribution and abundance in the Caprivi Strip, Namibia. *African Journal of Ecology*, 47(2): 223–233.
Cioc, M. (2009), *The Game of Conservation: International Treaties to Protect the World's Migratory Animals*. Athens OH: Ohio University Press.
Cobley, A. (2001), Does Social History Have a Future? The Ending of Apartheid and Recent Trends, South African Historiography. *Journal of Southern African Studies*, 27(3): 613–625.
Cohen, D.W., S.F. Miescher and L. White (2001), Introduction: Voices, Words, and Historiography. In: L. White, S. Miescher and D.W. Cohen (eds.), *African Words, African Voices. Critical Practices in Oral History*. Bloomington: Indiana University Press: 1–27.
Coleman, M. (1998), *A Crime Against Humanity: Analysing the Repression of the Apartheid State*. Cape Town: Mayibuye History Series.
Comaroff, J. and J.L. Comaroff (2001), Naturing the Nation: Aliens, Apocalypse and the Postcolonial State. *Journal of Southern African Studies*, 27(3): 627–51.
Cooper, F. (1997a), Review Reviewed Work: Citizen and Subject: Contemporary Africa and the Legacy of Late Colonialism by Mahmood Mamdani. *International Labor and Working-Class History*, 52: 156–160.
Cooper, F. (1997b), Modernizing Bureaucrats, Backward Africans and the Development Concept. In F. Cooper and R. Packard (eds.), *International Development and the Social Sciences*. Berkeley: University of California Press: 64–92.
Coplan, D. (2010), Introduction: From empiricism to theory in African border studies. *Journal of Borderland Studies*, 25(2): 1–5.
Coron, W., G. Miles and J. Gitlin, (1992), Becoming West: Toward a New Meaning for Western History. In G. Miles, J. Gitlin (eds.), *Under an Open Sky: Rethinking America's Western Past*. New York: W.W. Norton.
Cousins, B., M.T. Hoffman, N. Allsopp, R.F. Rohde (2007), A synthesis of sociological and biological perspectives on sustainable land use in Namaqualand. *Journal of Arid Environments*, 70(4): 834–846.
Crampton, J.W. (2001), Maps as Social Constructions. Power, Communication and Visualization. *Progress in Human Geography*, 25(2): 235–252.
Crampton, J.W. and J. Krygier (2006), An Introduction to Critical Geography. *An International E-Journal for Critical Geographies (ACME)*, 4(1): 11–33.
Crosby, A. W. (1972), *The Columbian Exchange: Biological and Cultural Consequences of 1492*. Westport: Greenwood.
Crosby, A. W. (1986), Ecological Imperialism: The Biological Expansion of Europe, 900–1900. New York: Cambridge University Press.
Crutzen, P.J. and E.F. Stoermer (2000), The Anthropocene, *Global Change Newsletter*, 41: 17–18.
D'Amato, A. (1966), The Bantustan Proposals for South-West Africa. *Journal of Modern African Studies*, 4(2): 177–192.
Dably, S. (2009), Security and environmental change. Cambridge: Polity.

Dale, R. (1993), Melding War and Politics in Namibia: South Africa's Counterinsurgency Campaign, 1966–1989. *Armed Forces & Society*, 20(1): 7–24.

Dale, R. (2014), *The Namibian War of Independence, 1966–1989: Diplomatic, Economic and Military Campaigns*. Jefferson: McFarland and Company.

De Waal, A. (1989), *Famine That Kills: Darfur, Sudan, 1984–1985*. New York: Oxford University Press.

De Wet, C.J. (1995), *Moving Together, Drifting Apart: Betterment Planning and Villagisation in a South African Homeland*. Johannesburg: Witwatersrand University Press.

Dedering, T. (2015), Air Power in South Africa, 1914–1939. *Journal of Southern African Studies*, 41(3): 451–465.

Deleuze, G. and F. Guattari (1987), *A Thousand Plateaus*. Minneapolis: University of Minnesota Press.

Diamond, J. (1997), *Guns, germs and steel. The fates of human societies*. New York: Norton.

Diamond, J. (2004), *Collapse: How Societies Choose to Fail or Succeed*. New York: Viking.

Die SAW is ook 'n troste bewaker van die natuur. *Paratus*, August 1980: 18–19.

Dieckmann, U. (2007), Hai‖om in the Etosha Region: A history of colonial settlement, ethnicity and nature conservation. Basel: Basler Afrika Bibliographien.

Ditlhase, Y., (2012), Khama Inc: All the president's family, friends and close colleagues, *Mail & Guardian*, 02.11.2012.

Dobell, L. (2000), *Swapo's Struggle for Namibia, 1960–1991: War by Other Means*. Basel: P. Schlettwein Publishing.

Dobler, G. (2014), *Traders and Trade in colonial Ovamboland, 1925–1990: Elite Formation and the Politics of Consumption under Indirect Rule and Apartheid*. Basel: Basler Afrika Bibliographien.

Dowler, L. (2012), Gender, militarization and sovereignty. *Geography Compass*, 6 (8): 490–99.

Drechsler, H. (1966), *Südwestafrika unter deutscher Kolonialherrschaft*. Stuttgart: Steiner.

Du Pisani, A. (1986), *SWA/Namibia: The Politics of Change and Continuity*. Johannesburg: Jonathan Ball.

Du Pisani, A. (2000), State and Society under South African Rule. In C. Keulder (ed.), *State, Society and Democracy: A Reader in Namibian Politics*. Windhoek: Macmillan Education: 49–76.

Du Toit, A. (2010), The Owl of Minerva and the Ironic Fate of the Progressive Praxis of Radical Historiography in Post-apartheid South Africa. *History and Theory*, 49: 266–280.

Duffy, R. (2006), The potential and pitfalls of global environmental governance: the politics of transfrontier conservation areas in Southern Africa. *Political Geography* 25: 89–112.

Duffy, R. (2010), *Nature Crime: How We're Getting Conservation Wrong*. New Haven and London: Yale University Press.

Duffy, R. (2011), Peace Parks and Global Politics: The Paradoxes and Challenges of Global Governance. In Ali, S.H. (ed.), *Peace Parks: Conservation and Conflict Resolution*. Cambridge: MIT Press: 55–68.

Duffy, R (2016), War, by conservation. *Geoforum*, 69(2): 238–248.

Dzingirai, V. (2003), New Scramble for the African Countryside. *Development and Change*, 34(2): 243–263.

Eckl, A. (2000), What Happened to Kavango's Early Colonial History? The Colonial Production of Kavango Land and Peoples, 1891–1951. (Unpublished paper, Windhoek).

Ehrlich, P.R. (1968), *The Population Bomb*. New York: Ballantine Books.

Ellis, S. (1994), Of Elephants and Men: Politics and Nature Conservation in South Africa. *Journal of Southern African Studies*, 20(1): 53–69.

Eloff de Visser, L. (2011), Winning Hearts and Minds in the Namibian Border War. *Scientia Militaria*, 39(1): 85–100.

Eloff de Visser, L. (2013), South Africa's Achilles' Heel: The Strategic Significance of the Eastern Caprivi of Namibia'. (Unpublished paper presented at the South African Empire Workshop, Basel).

Emmett, A. (1988), Popular Resistance in Namibia. In B. Wood (ed.), *Namibia 1884–1984: Readings on Namibia's History and Society*. London: Namibia Support Committee: 224–258.

Engel, U. and P. Nugent (eds.) (2010), *Respacing Africa*. Amsterdam: Brill.

Erasmus, G. (2010), The Constitution: Its Impact on Namibian Statehood and Politics. In C. Keulder (ed.), *State, Society and Democracy: A Reader in Namibian Politics*. Windhoek: Macmillan Education: 77–105.

Erichsen, Caspar W. (2005), *The Angels of Death Has Descended Violently Among Them*. Leiden: African Studies Centre.

Erkkilä, A. and H. Siikonen, (1992), *Forestry in Namibia 1850–1990*. Joensuu: University of Joensuu.

Erkkilä, A. (2001), *Living on the Land: Change in Forest Cover in North-Central Namibia 1943–1996*. Joensuu: University of Joensuu.

Escobar, A. (1999), After Nature: Steps to an Antiessentialist Political Ecology. *Current Anthropology*, 40(1): 1–30.

Esselborn, S. (2004), Koloniale Landschaft und industrielle Landwirtschaft: Das Groundnut Scheme. In F. Uekötter (ed.), Ökologische Erinnerungsorte. Göttingen: V&R: 219–250.

Etherington, N. (2007), Introduction. In N. Etherington (ed.), *Mapping Colonial Conquest: Australia and Southern Africa*. Crawley: University of Western Australia Press.

Etherington, N. (ed.) (2007), *Mapping Colonial Conquest: Australia and Southern Africa*. Crawley: University of Western Australia Press.

Fairhead, J. (2001), International Dimensions of Conflict Over Natural and Environmental Resources. In N. Peluso and M. Watts (eds.), *Violent environments*. Ithaca: Cornell University Press: 213–236.

Fairhead, J. and M. Leach (2003), *Science, Society and Power: Environmental Knowledge and Policy in West Africa and the Caribbean*. Cambridge: Cambridge University Press.

Fanon, F. (1963), *The Wretched of Earth* (translation of the French original of 1961). New York: Grove.

Ferguson, J. (1990), *The Anti-Politics Machine: 'Development', Depoliticization and Bureaucratic Power in Lesotho*. Minneapolis: University of Minnesota Press.

Feyissa, D. and M.V. Hoehne (2010), State Borders and Borderlands as Resources. In D. Feyissa and M.V. Hoehne (eds.): *Borders and Borderlands as Resources in the Horn of Africa*. Suffolk: James Currey: 1–26.

First, R. (1963), *South West Africa*. Baltimore: Penguin.

Fisch, M. (1994), *The World of Traditional Hunters along the Kavango River*. Windhoek: Macmillan Education Namibia Publishers.

Fisch, M. (1996), *Der Caprivizipfel während der deutschen Zeit, 1890–1914*. Cologne: Rüdiger Köppe.

Fisch, M. (1999), *The Secessionist Movement in the Caprivi: A Historical Perspective*. Windhoek: Namibia Scientific Society.

Fleisch, A., W.J.G. Möhlig (2002), *The Kavango Peoples in the Past. Local Historiographies from Northern Namibia*. Cologne: Rüdiger Köppe.

Flint, L. (2003), State-Building in Central Southern Africa: Citizenship and Subjectivity in Barotseland and Caprivi. *International Journal of African Historical Studies*, 36(2): 393–428.

Fontain, J. (2015), *Remaking Mutirikwi: Landscape, Water and Belonging in Southern Zimbabwe*. London: James Currey.
Ford, J. (1971), *The Role of the Trypanosomiases in African Ecology: A Study of the Tsetse Fly Problem*. London: Clarendon.
Foucault, M. (1975), *Surveiller et punir: Naissance de la prison*. Paris: Gallimard.
Frankel, P.H. (1984), *Pretoria's Preatorians: Civil-Military Relations in South Africa*. Cambridge: University of Cambridge Press.
Fraser, C.A. (1964), Lessons learnt from past Revolutionary Wars (unpublished manuscript, Pretoria).
Gallo, E. (2014), Civilisation and empire: A challenging nexus. *Human Figurations*, 3(1).
Geldenhuys, C. (1977), Woodland Management Plan for the Nakabunze Reserve, Eastern Caprivi (unpublished report, George).
Geldenhuys, C. (1990), *Woodland Management Plan for the Nakabunze Reserve, Eastern Caprivi, translation of the Africans original of 1977*. Pretoria: Department of Water Affairs and Forestry.
Geldenhuys, C. (1997), Sustainable Harvesting of Timber from Woodlands in Southern Africa: Challenges for the Future. *The Southern African Forestry Journal*, 178(1): 59–72.
Gewald, J.-B. (2013), Beyond the Last Frontier: Major Trollope and the Eastern Caprivi Zipfel. In M. de Bruijn and R. van Dijk (eds.), *The Social Life of Connectivity in Africa*. Basingstoke: Palgrave: 81–93.
Gibson, C.C. (1999), *Politicians and Poachers*. Cambridge: Cambridge University Press.
Gilomee, H. (2009), A Note on Bantu Education, 1953–1970. *South African Journal of Economics*, 77(1): 190–198.
Giraut, F., S. Guyot and M. Houssay-Holzschuch (2005), La Nature, les Territoires et le Politique en Afrique du Sud. *Annales. Histoire, Sciences Sociales*, 60(4): 695–717.
Gissibl, B. (2016), *The Nature of German Imperialism: Conservation and the Politics of Wildlife in colonial East Africa*. New York: Berghahn.
Glacken, J.C. (1967), *Traces on the Rhodian Shore: Nature and Culture in Western Thought from Ancient Times to the End of the Eighteenth Century*. Berkeley: University of California Press.
Goldblatt, I. (1971), *History of South West Africa from the Beginnings of the Nineteenth Century*. Cape Town: Juta & Co.
Gordon, R.J. (1977), *Mines, Masters and Migrants: Life in a Namibian Mine Compound*. Johannesburg: Ravan.
Gordon, R.J. and S. Douglas (1992), *The Bushmen Myth: The Making of a Namibian Underclass*. Oxford: Westview.
Gordon, R.J. (2005), The Making of Modern Namibia: A Tale of Anthropological Ineptitude? *Kleio*, 37(1): 26–49.
Gore, A. (2006), *An Inconvenient Truth: The Planetary Emergency of Global Warming and What we can do about it*. New York: Rodale.
Green, L. (1952), *Lords of the Last Frontier: The Story of South West Africa and its People of all Races*. Cape Town: H.B. Timmins.
Griffiths, T. and L. Robin (eds.) (1997), *Ecology and Empire: Environmental History of Settler Societies*. Edinburgh: Keele University Press.
Guijarro, E.M. (2013), An Independent Caprivi: A Madness of a Few, a Partial Collective Yearning or a Realistic Possibility? Citizen Perspectives on Caprivian Secession. *Journal of Southern African Studies*, 39(2): 337–352.
Hall-Martin, C. Walker and J.P. Bothma (1988), *Kaoko: The Last Wilderness*. Johannesburg: Southern Book.

Hamilton, C., B. Mbenga and R. Ross (2010), The production of preindustrial South African History. In C. Hamilton, B. Mbenga and R. Ross, (eds.): *The Cambridge History of South Africa*, Volume 1, from early times to 1885. Cambridge: Cambridge University Press.
Hamilton, C., V. Harris, G. Reid (2002), Introduction. In: C. Hamilton, V. Harris, J. Taylor, M. Pickover, G. Reid and R. Saleh (eds.), *Refiguring the Archive*. Dordrecht: Kluwer.
Hamilton, C., V. Harris, J. Taylor, M. Pickover, G. Reid and R. Saleh (eds.) (2002), *Refiguring the Archive*. Dordrecht: Kluwer.
Hammill, A. and C. Besançon (2007), Measuring Peace Park Performance: Definitions and Experiences. In Ali, S.H. (ed.), *Peace Parks, Conservation and Conflict Resolution*. Cambridge: MIT Press: 23–40.
Haraway, D. (2015), Anthropocene, Capitalocene, Plantationocene, Chthulucene. *Environmental Humanities*, 6(1): 159–165.
Harcourt, W. and I.L. Nelson (eds.) (2015), *Practising Feminist Political Ecologies: Moving Beyond the 'Green Economy'*. London: Zed Books.
Haricombe, L.J. (1995), *Out in the Cold: Academic Boycotts and the Isolation of South Africa*. Ann Arbor: Information Resources Press.
Harley, J.B. (1989), Deconstructing the Map. *Cartorgaphica*, 26(2): 1–20.
Harley, J.B. (1990), Cartography, Ethics and Social Theory. *Cartographica*, 27(2): 1–23.
Harries, P. (2007), *Butterflies and Barbarians: Swiss Missionaries and Systems of Knowledge in South-East Africa*. Athens: Ohio University Press.
Harring, S.L. and W. Odendaal (2012), *"God stopped making land!": Land Rights, Conflict and Law in Namibia's Caprivi Region*. Windhoek: LAC.
Harris, L. and H. Hazen (2006), Power of Maps: (Counter)mapping for Conservation. *An International E-Journal for Critical Geographies (ACME)*, 4(1): 99–130.
Harvey, D. (2005), *A Brief History of Neoliberalism*. Oxford: Oxford University Press.
Hayes, P. (1992), A *History of Ovambo* of Namibia, 1880–1935. (PhD theses: University of Cambridge).
Hayes, P., J. Silvester, M. Wallace, W. Hartmann (eds.) (1998), *Namibia Under South African Rule: Mobility and Containment, 1915–1946*. Oxford: James Currey.
Hayes, P. (2000), Camera Africa: Indirect Rule and Landscape Photographs of Kaoko. In G. Miescher und D. Henrichsen (eds.), *New Notes on Kaoko*. Basel: Basler Afrika Bibliographien: 48–76.
Hayes, P. (2010), Bush of Ghosts. In J. Liebenberg and P. Hayes (eds.), *Bush of Ghosts: Life and War in Namibia 1986–1990*. Cape Town: Umuzi: 27–113.
Haynen, N., J. McCarthy, W.S. Prudham, P. Robbins (2007), *Neoliberal Environments: False Promises and Unnatural Consequences*. London: Routledge.
Heinze, R. (2014), „It Recharged Our Batteries": Writing the History of the Voice of Namibia. *Journal of Namibian Studies*, 15: 25 – 62.
Henrichsen, D. (2000), Pilgrimages into Kaoko: Herrensafaris, 4x4s and Settler Illusions. In G. Miescher und D. Henrichsen (eds.), *New Notes on Kaoko*. Basel: Basler Afrika Bibliographien: 159–188.
Henrichsen, D., G. Miescher, C. Rassool, L. Rizzo (2015), Rethinking Empire in Southern Africa. *Journal for Southern African Studies*, 41(3): 431–435.
Herbst, J. I (2000), *States and Power in Africa: Comparative Lessons in Authority and Control*. Princeton: Princeton University Press.
Higginson, J. (1992), Liberating the Captives: Independent Watchtower as an Avatar of Colonial Revolt in Southern Africa and Katanga, 1908–1941. *Journal of Social History*, 4: 55–80.
Hinz, M.O. (2003), *Without Chiefs there would be no Game: Customary Law and Nature Conservation*. Windhoek: Out of Africa.

Hipondoka, M. (2008), *Mapping Areas of Officially Recognized Traditional Authorities and Land Board Jurisdictions.* Windhoek: Ministry of Lands and Resettlement.

History: Caprivi Zipfel. The Controversial Strip, Part I–III, www.caprivifreedom.com/history [15.08.2016].

Hodson, Y. and A. Gordon (1997), *An illustrated history of 250 Years of Military Survey.* Tolworth: Military Survey Defence Agency.

Hoedspruit haven of peace for wildlife, *Paratus,* June 1984: 14–15.

Holub, E. (1975), *Seven Years in South Africa: Facsimile Reproduction of the 1881 Edition.* Johannesburg: Africana Book Society.

Horrell, M. (1963), *A Survey into Race Relations in South Africa.* Johannesburg: South African Institute of Race Relations.

Hughes, D.M. (2006), *From Enslavement to Environmentalism: Politics on a Southern African Frontier.* Seattle: University of Washington Press.

Igoe, J. and Brockington, D. (2007), Neoliberal Conservation: A Brief Introduction, *Conservation & Society,* 5(4): 432–449.

Iliffe, J. (1979), *A Modern History of Tanganyika.* Cambridge: Cambridge University Press.

Integrated Rural Development and Nature Conservation (IRDNC) (ed.) (2011), *Lessons from the Field.* Windhoek: IRDNC.

International Union for Conservation of Nature and Natural Resources (ed.) (1980), *World Conservation Strategy – Living Resource Conservation for Sustainable Development.* Gland.

Isaacman A.F. and B.S. Isaacman (2013), *Dams, Displacement, and the Delusion of Development: Cahora Bassa and Its Legacies in Mozambique, 1965–2007.* Athens, OH: Ohio University Press.

Isaacman, A.F. and B.S. Isaacman (2015), Extending South Africa's Tentacles of Empire: The Deterritorialisation of Cahora Bassa Dam. *Journal of Southern African Studies,* 41(3): 541–560.

Jaarsveld, F.A. (1981), *Van Van Riebeeck tot P.W. Botha.* Johannesburg.

Jabavu, D.D.T. (1928), *The Segregation Fallacy and Other Papers.* Lovedale.

Jackson, A. (2001), Bechuanaland, the Caprivi Strip and the First World War. *War & Society,* 19(2): 109–142.

Jacobs, A. and H. Smit (2004), Topographic Mapping Support in the South Africa Military During the 20th Century. *Scientia Militaria,* 32(1): 32–50.

Jansen, J.D. (1995), Understanding social transition through the lens of curriculum policy: Namibia/South Africa. *Journal of Curriculum Studies,* 27(3): 245–261.

Jason, L. (2017), Cops seize 13 elephant tusks in Bwabwata. *New Era,* 12.01.2017.

Jensen, S. and O. Zenker (2015), Homelands as Frontiers: Apartheid's Loose Ends. *Journal for Southern African Studies,* 42(5): 937–952.

Jones, B. (2010), The Evaluation of Namibia's Communal Conservancies. In F. Nelson (ed.), *Community Rights, Conservation and Contested Land: The Politics of Natural Resource Governance in Africa.* London and Washington DC: Earthscan: 106–120.

Jones, R.T. and P.T. Mackey (2015), An Overview of Copper Smelting in Southern Africa. *Copper Cobalt Africa,* 2(8): 499–504.

Jonker, J. (2005), Excavating the legal Subject, *Griffith Law Review,* 14(2): 187–212.

Kangumu, B. (2011), *Contesting Caprivi: A History of Colonial Isolation and Regional Nationalism in Namibia.* Basel: Basler Afrika Bibliographien.

Katjavivi, P.H. (1988), *A History of Resistance in Namibia.* Paris: UNESCO.

KAZA Secretariat (ed.) (2015), *KAZA TFCA Master Integrated Development Plan.* Kasane.

Keese, A. (2010), Introduction. In A. Keese (ed.), *Ethnicity and the long-term perspective: The African Experience.* London: Peter Lang, p. 9–25.

Keet, J.D.M. (1947), *Caprivi Zipfel: Forestry and Allied Questions. Report to the Secretary of Native Affairs*. Pretoria.

Kettlitz, K. (1962), Game on farms, *Fauna and Flora*, 13: 19–24.

Khumalo, K. and W. Freimund (2014), Expanding Women's Choices through Employment? Community-Based Natural Resource Management and Women's Empowerment in Kwandu Conservancy, Namibia. *Society & Natural Resources*, 27(10): 1024–1039.

Kjekshus, H. (1977), *Ecology, Control and Economic Development in East African History: The Case of Tanganyika 1850–1950*. London, Heinemann.

Kjolberg, J.-O., *The Dassault Mirage III in South African Service*, www.mirage4fs.com/slides15.html [accessed 20.07.2006]

Kolossov, V. (2005), Border Studies: Changing Perspectives and Theoretical Approaches. *Geopolitics*, 10(4): 1–27.

Kössler, R. (2000), From Reserve to Homeland: Local Identities and South African Policy in Southern Namibia. *Journal of Southern African Studies*, 26(3): 447–462.

Kreike, E. (2004), War and the Environmental Effects of Displacement in Southern Africa, 1970s–1990s. In W. Moseley and B.I. Logan (eds.), *African Environment and Development: Rhetoric, Programme and Reality*. Aldershot: Ashgate: 90–110.

Kreike, E. (2013), *Environmental Infrastructure in African History: Examining the Myth of Natural Resource Management in Namibia*. New York: Cambridge University Press.

Kruger, C.E. (1984), History of the Caprivi Strip 1890–1984. (Unpublished manuscript).

Krüger, D.W. (1969), *The Making of a Nation: A History of the Union of South Africa, 1910 – 1961*. Johannesburg: Macmillan.

Krüger, G. (1992), Fallstudie Namibia. In: A. Harneit-Sievers (ed.), *Kriegsfolgen und Kriegsbewältigung in Afrika: Der Nigerianische Bürgerkrieg, 1967–1970*. Hannover: 221–242.

Krüger, G. and D. Henrichsen (1998), "We Have Been Captives Long Enough. We Want to be Free": Land, Uniforms and Politics in the History of Herero in the Interwar Period. In P. Hayes, J. Silvester, M. Wallace and W. Hartmann (eds.), *Namibia under South African Rule: Mobility and Containment, 1915–46*. Oxford, Windhoek and Athens OH: James Currey, Out of Africa and Ohio University Press: 149–174.

Krüger, G. (1999), *Kriegsbewältigung und Geschichtsbewusstsein: Realität, Deutung und Verarbeitung des deutschen Kolonialkriegs in Namibia 1904 – 1907*. Göttingen: Vandenhoeck und Ruprecht.

Krüger, G. (2009), *Schrift, Macht, Alltag: Lesen und Schreiben im kolonialen Südafrika*. Köln, Weimar, Wien: Böhlau-Verlag.

Kumleben, M.A. (ed.) (1996), *Inquiry into the Alleged Smuggling of and Illegal Trade in Ivory and Rhinoceros Horn in South Africa: Report*. Durban.

Lahman, M.K.E., K.L. Rodriguez, L. Moses, K.M. Griffin, M.B. Menoza and W. Yacoub (2015), A Rose by any other Name is still a Rose? Problematizing Pseudonyms in Research, *Qualitative Inquiry*, 21(5): 445–453.

Lalu, P. (2009), *The Deaths of Hintsa: Postapartheid South Africa and the Shape of Recurring Pasts*. Cape Town: HSRC.

Lalu, P. (2015), Empire and Nation. *Journal of Southern African Studies*, 41(3): 437–450.

Latour, B. (1993), *We have never been modern*. Cambridge: Harvard University Press.

Layes, C. and J. Saul (1995), *Namibia's Liberation Struggle: The Two-Edged Sword*. London: James Currey.

Le Roux, P. and M. Müller (2009), *Le Roux and Müller's Field Guide to the Trees and Shrubs of Namibia*. Windhoek: MacMillan Education.

Leach, M. and C. Green (1997), Gender and Environmental History: From Representation of Women and Nature to Gender Analysis of Ecology and Politics. *Environment and History* 3(3): 343–70.

Leakey, R. (2001), *Wildlife Wars. My Battle to Save Kenya's Elephants*. London: PAN.

Legassick, M.C. (1974), Legislation, Ideology, and Economy in Post-1948 South Africa. *Journal of Southern African Studies*, 1: 5–35.

Legassick, M.C. and H. Wolpe (1976), The Bantustans and Capital Accumulation in South Africa. *Review of African Political Economy*, 7: 87–107.

Legassick, M.C. (2010), *The Politics of a South African Frontier: The Griqua, the Sotho-Tswana, and the Missionaries, 1780–1840*. Basel: Basler Afrika Bibliographien.

Lenggenhager, L. (2009), Empty Landscapes, Wild Animals an Unspoiled People: Motifs in Namibian Tourism Advertising. In: G. Miescher, L. Rizzo and J. Silvester, *Posters in Action: On the History of Production, Circulation and Reception of Namibian Posters*. Basel: Basler Afrika Bibliographien, 31–44.

Lenggenhager, L. (2015), Nature, War and Development: South Africa's Caprivi Strip, 1960–1980. *Journal for Southern African Studies*, 41(3): 467–483.

Lenggenhager, L. (2016), Circulating nature: from north-eastern Namibia to South Africa and back, 1960–1990. In: M. Ramutsindela, G. Miescher and M. Boehi (eds.), *The Politic of Nature and Science in Southern Africa*. Basel: Basler Afrika Bibliographien: 87–105.

Leon, C.E. (2009), *Movement and Belonging: Lines, Places and Spaces of Travel*. New York: Peter Lang.

Leser, H. (1982), *Namibia, Südwestafrika: Kartographische Probleme der neuen topographischen Karten 1:50'000 und 1:250'000 und ihre Perspektiven für die Landesentwicklung*. Basel: Basler Afrika Bibliographien.

Lester, A. (2003), Historical Geographies of Southern Africa, *Journal of Southern African Studies*, 29(3): 595–613.

Lidström, S., S. West, T. Katzschner, M. I. Pérez-Ramos and H. Twidle (2015), Invasive Narratives and the Inverse of Slow Violence: Alien Species in Science and Society. *Environmental Humanities*, 7(1): 1–40.

Liebenberg, J. and P. Hayes (eds.) (2010), *Bush of Ghosts: Life and War in Namibia 1986–1990*. Cape Town: Umuzi.

Likuwa, K.L. (2015), Colonialism and the Development of the Contract Labour System in Kavango. In J. Silvester (ed.), *Reviewing Resistance in Namibian History*. Windhoek: UNAM Press: 105–126.

Lilemba, J.L. and Y.H. Matemba (2015), Reclaiming Indigenous Knowledge in Namibia's Post-colonial Curriculum: the Case of the Mafwe People. In K. Chinsembu (ed.), *Indigenous Knowledge in Namibia*. Windhoek: UNAM Press: 283–309.

Livingstone, D. (1857), *Missionary Travels and Researches in South Africa*. London: J. Murray.

Livingstone, D.N. (2003), *Putting Science in Its Place: Geographies of Scientific Knowledge*. Chicago: Chicago University Press.

Locher, F. (2009), Environmental History: The Origins, Stakes, and Perspectives of a New Site for Research. *Revue d'Histoire Moderne et Contemporaine*, 56(4): 7–38.

Lövbrand, E., S. Beck, J. Chilvers, T. Forsyth, J. Hedren, M. Hulme, R. Lidskog and Vasileiadou, E. (2015). Who speaks for the future of Earth? How critical social science can extend the conversation on the Anthropocene. *Global Environmental Change*, 32: 211–218.

Lunstrum, E. (2010), Reconstructing history, grounding claims to space: history, memory, and displacement in the Great Limpopo Transfrontier Park. *South African Geographical Journal*, 92(2): 129–143.

Lunstrum, E. (2014), Green Militarization: Anti-Poaching Efforts and the Spatial Contours of Kruger National Park. *Annals of the Association of American Geographers*, 104(4): 816–83.

MacDonald, K.I. (2011), The Devil is in the (Bio)diversity. In D. Brockington and R. Duffy (eds.), *Capitalism and Conservation*. Malden MA and Oxford: Wiley Blackwell: 44–81.

Macedo, D. (2011), De-Colonizing Indigenous Knowledge. In L.M. Semali and J. L. Kinchelo (eds.), *What is Indigenous Knowledge. Voices from the Academy*. New York: Routledge.

MacKenzie, J.M. (1988), *The Empire of Nature Hunting, Conservation and British Imperialism*. Manchester: Manchester University Press.

MacKenzie, J.M. (1997), Empire and the ecological apocalypse: The Historiography of the Imperial Environment. In T. Griffiths, L. Robin (eds.), *Ecology and Empire: Environmental History of Settler Societies*. Edinburgh: Keele University Press: 215–128.

Malm, A. (2016), *Fossil Capital: The Rise of Steam Power and the Roots of Global Warming*. London: Verso.

Mamdani, M. (1996), *Citizen and Subject: Contemporary Africa and the Legacy of Late Colonialism*. Princeton: Princeton University Press.

Mamdani, M. (1998), Is African studies to be turned into a new home for Bantu education at UCT? (Text of remarks at the Seminar on the Africa Core of the Foundation Course for the Faculty of Social Sciences and Humanities, University of Cape Town).

Maritz, C. (1996), The Subia and Fwe of Caprivi, *Africa Insight*, 26(2): 177–186.

Marks, S. (1972), Liberalism, Social Realities, and South African History, *Journal of Commonwealth Studies*, 10(3): 243–249.

Marlantes, K. (2009), *Matterhorn*. Berkeley: El Leon Literary Arts.

Mashuna, T. (2015), The 1978 Election in Namibia. In J. Silvester (ed.), *Reviewing Resistance in Namibian History*. Windhoek: UNAM Press, p. 178 –191.

Mavhunga, C.C. (2014), *Transient Workspaces: Technologies of Everyday Innovation in Zimbabwe*. Cambridge: MIT Press.

Mayeyi Traditional Authority calls for Extension Mudumu National Park borders, *Namibian Broadcasting Corporation (NBC)*, 2011, www.nbc.na/news/mayeyi-traditional-authority-calls-extension-mudumu-national-park-borders.511 [accessed: 02.02.2017]

Mbeki, G. (1964), *South Africa: The Peasants' Revolt*. Baltimore: Penguin Books.

McCracken, J. (1982), Experts and expertise in colonial Malawi. *African Affair*, 81(322): 101–16.

McCracken, J. (2012), *A history of Malawi, 1859–1966*. Woodbridge: James Currey.

McCuen, J.J. (1969), *The Art of Counter-Revolutionary War: The Strategy of Counter-insurgency*. London: Faber.

McCullers, M. (2012), Lines in the Sand: The Global Politics of Local Development in Apartheid Era Namibia, 1950–1980. (PhD thesis, Emory University).

McCusker, B. and M. Ramudzuli (2007), Apartheid spatial engineering and land use change in Mankweng, South Africa: 1963–2001. *The Geographical Journal*, 173(1): 56–74.

McKittrick, M. (1998), Generational Struggles and Social Mobility. In P. Hayes, J. Silvester, M. Wallace and W. Hartmann (eds.), *Namibia under South African Rule: Mobility and Containment, 1915–46*. Oxford, Windhoek and Athens OH: James Currey, Out of Africa and Ohio University Press: 241–262.

McKittrick, M. (2013), An Empire of Rivers: Climate Anxiety, Imperial Ambition, and the Hydropolitical Imagination in Southern Africa 1919–1950. (Unpublished paper presented at the South African Empire Workshop, Basel 2013).

McKittrick, M. (2015), An Empire of Rivers: The Scheme to Flood the Kalahari, 1919–1945. *Journal of Southern African Studies*, 41(3): 485–504.

McNeill, J.R. (2003), Observations on the Nature and Culture of Environmental History. *History and Theory*, 42(4): 5–43.

McNeill, J.R and E.S. Maudlin (eds.) (2014), *A Companion to Global Environmental History*. Chichester: Wiley-Blackwell.

Meadows, D.H., G. Meadows, J. Randers and W.W. Behrens (1972), *The Limits to Growth*. New York: Universe Books.

Melber, H. (2009), One Namibia, One Nation? The Caprivi as Contested Territory. *Journal of Contemporary African Studies*, 27(4): 463–481.

Melber, H. (2014), *Understanding Namibia: The Trials of Independence*. London: Hurst.

Menges, W. (2015), 30 guilty in treason trial, *The Namibian*, 15.09.2015.

Miescher, G. (2006), The Ovambo Reserve Otjeru (1911–1938), The Story of an African Community in Central Namibia. *BAB Working Paper*, 1.

Miescher, G. (2009), Keeping the threats out: The Red Line and the War Zone. (Unpublished paper, University of Western Cape).

Miescher, G. (2012a), *Namibia's Red Line. The history of a veterinary and settlement border*. New York: Palgrave.

Miescher, G. (2012b), Facing Barbarians: A Narrative of Spatial Segregation in Colonial Namibia. *Journal of Southern African Studies*, 38(4): 769–786.

Miescher, G. (2013), *Die Rote Linie: Geschichte der Veterinär- und Siedlungsgrenze in Namibia, 1890er–1960er Jahre*. Basel: Basler Afrika Bibliographien.

Mongudhi, T. (2016), Tribalism dominates agenda 2017, *The Namibian*, 20.06.2016: 1–2.

Mongudhi, T., J. Konopo and N. Ntibinyane (2016), Deadly borders…30 Namibians killed through Botswana's shoot-to-kill policy, *The Namibian*, 09.03.2016: 1.

Moore, J. W. (2016), Anthropocene or Capitalocene? Nature, History, and the Crisis of Capitalism. In J. W. Moore (ed.), *Anthropocene or Capitalocene? Nature, History, and the Crisis of Capitalism*. Oakland: PM Press: 1–13.

Moorsom, R. (1972), Underdevelopment, Contract Labour and Worker Consciousness in Namibia, 1915–72. *Journal of Southern African Studies*, 4(1): 52–87.

Moser, J. (2007), Untersuchungen zur Kartographiegeschichte von Namibia: Die Entwicklung des Karten- und Vermessungswesens von den Anfängen bis zur Unabhängigkeit 1990. (PhD thesis, University of Dresden).

Moser, J. (2008), Untersuchungen zur Kartographiegeschichte von Namibia: Die Entwicklung des Karten- und Vermessungswesens von den Anfängen bis zur Unabhängigkeit 1990. *Cartographica Helvetica: Fachzeitschrift für Kartengeschichte*, 38: 41–43.

Mosimane, A.W. (2003), Caprivi Region Conservancies Management Profiles: Mashi, Imapilia, Kasika, Wuparo, Mayuni, Salambala and Kwandu. (MRCC Research Report, Windhoek, University of Namibia).

Mosimane A.W. and J.A. Silva (2014), Boundary Making in Conservancies: The Namibian Experience. In M. Ramutsindela (ed.), *Cartographies of Nature: How Nature Conservation Animates Borders*. New Castle upon Tyne: Cambridge Scholars Publishing: 83–111.

Müller, A.J. (2014), *"The Inevitable Pipeline into Exile": Botswana's Role in the Namibian Liberation Struggle*. Basel: Basler Afrika Bibliographien.

Murray, S. (2005), Working for Water's 'Alien Busters': Material and Metaphoric Campaigns Against 'alien Invaders'. *Critical Arts* 19(1–2): doi: 10.1080/02560040585310091.

Mutwira, R. (1989), Southern Rhodesian Wildlife Policy (1890–1953): A Question of Condoning Game Slaughter? *Journal of Southern African Studies*, 15(2): 250–262.

Muyamba, J. (2017), Police exchange fire with poachers in Bwabwata. *New Era*, 14.03.2017.

Myers, J.C. (2008), *Indirect Rule in South Africa: Tradition, Modernity, and the Costuming of Political Power*. Rochester: University of Rochester Press.

Naidoo, R., G. Stuart-Hill, L.C. Weaver, J. Tagg, A. Davis and A. Davidson (2011), Effect of diversity of large wildlife species on financial benefits to local communities in northwest Namibia. *Environment Resource Economy*, 48: 321–335.

Namibia Statistics Agency (2015), *Namibia Labour Force Survey 2014*. Windhoek: Namibia Statistics Agency.

Nash, A. (1999), Dilemmas of the Left Academy: A Report on the 1998 Socialist Scholars Conference. *African Sociological Review*, 3(1): 168–198.
Nash, R. (1967), *Wilderness and the American Mind*. Yale: Yale University Press.
Nature Conservation in the Caprivi – SADF battles to save our heritage, *Paratus*, November 1982: 10–11.
Nature Conservation in the SA Defence Force, *Paratus*, August 1978: 34–37.
Naylor, R.T. (2008), *Patriots and Profiteers: Economic Warfare, Embargo Busting and State-Sponsored Crime*. Montreal and Kingston: McGill-Queen's University Press.
Nelson, F. (2010), Introduction: The Politics of Natural Resource Governance in Africa. In F. Nelson (ed.), *Community Rights, Conservation and Contested Land: The Politics of Natural Resource Governance in Africa*. London and Washington DC: Earthscan: 3–31.
Nelson, F. and A. Agrawal (2008), Patronage or Participation? Community-based Natural Resource Management Reform in sub-Saharan Africa. *Development and Change* 39(4): 557–585.
Neumann, R.P. (1995), Ways of Seeing Africa: Colonial Recasting of African Society and Landscape in Serengeti National Park. *Cultural Geographies*, 2(2): 149–169.
Neumann, R.P. (1998), *Imposing Wilderness: Struggles over Livelihood and Nature Preservation*. Berkeley: University of California Press.
Nghitevelekwa, R.V. (2016), Land relations and property rights in central-north Namibia's communal lands. In M. Ramutsindela, G. Miescher and M. Boehi (eds.), *The Politics of Nature and Science in Southern Africa*. Basel: Basler Afrika Bibliographien.
Ngubeni, N. (2016), Reports: SA state security minister linked to rhino horn trafficker, *EWN*, 23.12.2016.
Nieftagodien, N. (2014), *The Soweto Uprising*. Johannesburg: Jacana.
Nilbert, T. (2002), *Animal Rights/Human Rights: Entanglements of Oppression and Liberation*. Oxford: Rowman & Littlefield.
Nortje, P. (2003), *32 Battalion: The Inside Story of South Africa's Elite Fighting Unit*. Cape Town: Zebra Press.
Nugent, P. and A.I. Asiwaju (eds.) (1996), *African Boundaries: barriers, conduits and opportunities*. London: Cassell/Pinter.
Nugent, P. (2003), *Smugglers, Secessionists and Loyal Citizens of the Ghana-Togo Frontier: The Lie of the Borderlands Since 1914*. Athens: Ohio University Press.
O'Connor, J. (1988), Capitalism, nature, socialism a theoretical introduction. *Capitalism Nature Socialism*, 1(1): 11–38.
Olwig, K.R. (2003), Natives and Aliens in the National Landscape. *Landscape Research*, 28(1): 61–74.
Onselen, C. (1982), *Studies in the Social and Economic History of the Witwatersrand, 1886–1914*. Johannesburg: Longman.
Orth, I. (1999), Landrechte und Identität bei südafrikanischen Wildbeutern: Eine Fallstudie zu den Kxoe in West Caprivi (Namibia). (MA thesis, University of Cologne).
Osterhammel, J. (1998), Die Wiederkehr des Raums. *Neue Politische Literatur*, 43 (3): 374–397.
Owen-Smith, G. (2010), *An Arid Eden: A Personal Account of Conservation in the Kaokoveld*. Jeppestown: Jonathan Ball.
Park, C. and M. Allaby (2007), *Oxford Dictionary of Environment & Conservation*. Oxford: University of Oxford Press.
Peck, J. (2010), *Constructions of Neoliberal Reason*. Oxford: Oxford University Press.
Peluso, N. (1993), Coercing Conservation? The politics of state resource control. *Global Environmental Change*, 3(2): 199–217.

Peluso, N. (1995), Whose woods are these? Counter-mapping forest territories in Kalimantan, Indonesia. *Antipode,* 27(4): 383–406.

Pelzer, A.N. (ed.) (1966), *Verwoerd Speaks: Speeches 1948–1966.* Johannesburg: AFP Publishers.

Perkins, C. (2004), Cartography: Cultures of Mapping: Power in Practice. *Progress in Human Geography,* 28: 381–391.

Pieterse, N. (1995), *White on Black. Images of Africa and Blacks in Western Popular Culture.* New Haven: Yale University Press.

Plaatje, S. (1914), *Native Life in South Africa.* London: King and Son.

Polla Swart, *Getaway,* May 1989: 34–39.

Pretorius, J. (1975), The Fwe of the Eastern Caprivi Zipfel. (MA thesis, University of Stellenbosch).

Ramutsindela, M. (2007), *Transfrontier Conservation in Africa: At the Confluence of Capital, Politics and Nature.* Wallingford and Boston MA: CABI.

Ramutsindela, M. (2009), Transfrontier Conservation and local Communities. In J. Saarinen, F. Becker, H. Manwa and D. Wilson (eds.), *Sustainable Tourism in Southern Africa: Local Communities and Natural Resources in Transition.* Bristol: Channel View: 169–188.

Ramutsindela, M., M. Spierenburg, and H. Wels (2011), *Sponsoring Nature: Environmental Philanthropy for Conservation.* London: Earthscan/Routledge.

Ramutsindela, M. and M. Shabangu (2013), Conditioned by neoliberalism: a reassessment of land claim resolutions in the Kruger National Park. *Journal of Contemporary African Studies,* 31(3): 441–456.

Ramutsindela, M. (2014), Ecology, Borders and Society. In M. Ramutsindela (ed.), *Cartographies of Nature: How Nature Conservation Animates Borders.* Newcastle upon Tyne: Cambridge Scholars Publishing: 1–16.

Ramutsindela, M. (ed.) (2014), *Cartographies of Nature: How Nature Conservation Animates Borders.* Newcastle upon Tyne: Cambridge Scholars Publishing.

Ramutsindela, M. and I. Sinthumule (2017), Property and Difference in Nature Conservation. *Geographical Review,* 107(3): 415–432.

Rangarajan, M. (2003), Parks, Politics and History: Conservation Dilemmas in Africa. *Conservation and Society,* 1(1): 77–98.

Rassool, C. and L. Witz (1996), South Africa: A World in One Country: Moments in International Tourist Encounters with Wildlife, the Primitive and the Modern. *Cahiers d'Études Africaines,* 36(143): 335–371.

Rassool, C. (2010), Power, knowledge, and the politics of public pasts. *African Studies,* 69: 79–101.

Redding, S. (2006), *Sorcery and Sovereignty: Taxation, Power, and Rebellion in South Africa, 1880–1963.* Athens: Ohio University Press.

Reeve, R. and S. Ellis (1995), An Insider's Account of the South African Security Forces' Role in the Ivory Trade. *Journal of Contemporary African Studies,* 13(2): 227–243.

Republic of South Africa (ed.) (1964), *Report of the Commission of Enquiry into South West Africa Affairs, 1962–1963.* Pretoria: Government Printer.

Republic of South Africa (ed.) (1976), *Government Gazette,* 129(5022), 19.03.1976. Pretoria: Government Printer.

Resurreccion, B.P. and R. Elmhirst (2008), Gender, Environment and Natural Resource Management. New Dimensions, New Debates. In B.P. Resurreccion and R. Elmhirst, (eds.), *Gender and Natural Resource Management: Livelihoods, Mobility and Interventions.* London: Earthscan: 3–22.

Rhoodie, E. (1967), *South West: The Last Frontier in Africa.* Pretoria: Vortrekkerspres.

Riehl, B., H. Zerriffi and R. Naidoo (2016), Effects of Community-Based Natural Resource Management on Household Welfare in Namibia. *PLoS ONE* 10(5): e0125531.

Rizzo, L. (2012), *Gender and Colonialism: A History of Kaoko in North-Western Namibia, 1870s–1950s*. Basel: Basler Afrika Bibliographien.

Roberts, A. (1979), *The Self-Managing Environment*. London: Allison & Busby.

Rockström, J., W. Steffen, K. Noone, Å. Persson, F.S. Chapin, E. Lambin, T.M. Lenton, M. Scheffer, C. Folke, H. Schellnhuber, B. Nykvist, C.A. De Wit, T. Hughes, S. van der Leeuw, H. Rodhe, S. Sörlin, P.K. Snyder, R. Costanza, U. Svedin, M. Falkenmark, L. Karlberg, R. W. Corell, V.J. Fabry, J. Hansen, B. Walker, D. Liverman, K. Richardson, P. Crutzen, and J. Foley. (2009), Planetary Boundaries: Exploring the Safe Operating Space for Humanity. *Ecology and Society*, 14(2).

Rodney, W. (1972), *How Europe Underdeveloped Africa*. London: Bogle-L'Ouverture Publications.

Sack, R. (1986), *Human territoriality: Its theory and history*. Cambridge: Cambridge University Press.

Salia-Bao, K. (1991), *The Namibian Education System under the Colonialists*. Randburg: Hodder & Stoughton.

Sandwith, T., C. Shine, L. Hamilton and D. Sheppard (2001), *Transboundary Protected Areas for Peace and Cooperation*. Gland: IUCN.

Sasa, D. (2000), The Mayeyi Chieftainship. (Unpublished paper presented at the *Public History, Forgotten History* Conference in Windhoek).

SAW hou wild gesond en gelukkig op LMB Hoedspruit, *Paratus*, April 1980: 36.

Schlettwein, C.H.G. and Bethune, S. (1992), Aquatic weeds and their management in southern Africa: Biological control of Salvinia Molesta in the Eastern Caprivi. In: T. Matiza and H.N. Chabwela (eds.), *Wetland Conservation Conference for Southern Africa: Proceedings of the Southern African Development Coordination Conference held in Gaborone, Botswana, 3 – 5 June 1991*. Gland: IUCN: 173–188.

Sehani, M. (2000), The Mafwe/Mayuni Crisis: Rival Histories and the Assertion of Identity in the Caprivi. (Unpublished paper presented at the *Public History, Forgotten History* Conference in Windhoek).

Semali, L. M. and J.L. Kinchelo (eds.) (2011), *What is Indigenous Knowledge: Voices from the Academy*. New York: Routledge.

Shaanika, H. (2017), 700 000 rely on drought relief, *New Era*, 20.01.2017.

Shamukuni, D.M. (1972), The baSubiya. *Botswana Notes and Records*, 4: 161–184.

Shepherd, N. and Murray, N. (2007), Introduction: Space, Memory and Identity in the Post-Apartheid City. In: Murray, N., N. Shepherd and M. Hall (ed.), *Desire Lines: Space, Memory and Identity in the Post-Apartheid City*. New York: Routledge, 1–18.

Shigwedha, V.A. (2017), *The Aftermath of the Cassinga Massacre: Survivors, Deniers and Injustices*. Basel: Basler Afrika Bibliographien.

Shiva, V. (1988), *Staying Alive: Women, Ecology and Survival in India*, New Delhi: Zed Press.

Shiweda, N. (2011), *Omhedi: Displacement and Legitimacy in Oukwanyama Politics, Namibia, 1915–2010*. (PhD Thesis, University of the Western Cape).

Sidikoff, G. (2009), The low-wage conservationist: Biodiversity and perversity of value in Madagascar. *American Anthropologist* 11(4): 443–455.

Sillitoe, P. (ed. (2006), *Local Science vs. Global Science: Approaches to Indigenous Knowledge in International Development*. New York: Berghahn Books.

Silvester, J., M. Wallace and P. Hayes (1998), Trees Never Meet: Mobility and Containment, an Overview 1915–1946. In P. Hayes, J. Silvester, M. Wallace and W. Hartmann (eds.), *Namibia under South African Rule: Mobility and Containment, 1915–46*. Oxford, Windhoek and Athens OH: James Currey, Out of Africa and Ohio University Press: 3–50.

Silvester, J., M. Akawa, and N. Shiweda (2014), The Namibian Liberation Struggle. In A. J. Temu and J.N. Tembe (eds.), *Southern African Liberation Struggles: Contemporaneous Documents, 1950–1994: Volume 3.* Dar es Salaam: Mkuki Na Nyota: 119–205.

Silvester, J. (2015), Forging the Fifth Province. *Journal for Southern African Studies*, 41(3): 505–518.

Silvester, J. (ed.) (2016), *Reviewing Resistance in Namibian History*. Windhoek: UNAM Press.

Singh, J. and H. van Houtum (2002), Post-colonial nature conservation in Southern Africa: same emperors, new clothes? *GeoJournal*, 58: 253–263.

Sinthumule, N.I. (2016), Multiple-land use practices in transfrontier conservation areas: the case of Greater Mapungubwe straddling Botswana, South Africa and Zimbabwe. *Bulletin of Geography: Socio–economic Series*, 34: 103–115.

Sitze, A. (2013), *The Impossible Machine, A genealogy of the South African Truth and Reconciliation Commission*. Ann Arbor: Michigan University Press.

Smit, E. (2015), Private sector takes up arms to save the rhino, *The Namibian Sun*, 23.07.2015.

Smith, A.D. (1998), *Nationality and Modernity: A critical Survey of Recent Theories of Nations and Nationalism*. London and New York: Routledge.

South African Development Community SADC (ed.) (1999), *Protocol on Wildlife Conservation and Law Enforcement*. Maputo: SADC Publications.

South West Africa Administrator's Office (ed.) (1927), Ordinance No 5, *Official Gazette*, 233, 20 May 1927. Windhoek: Government Printer.

South West African Administration (ed.) (1969), Duties and Powers of Nature Conservators and Honorary Nature Conservators, *Official Gazette*, 2952, 03 January 1969. Windhoek: Government Printer.

Spierenburg, M. and H. Wels (2006), „Securing Space": Mapping and Fencing in Transfrontier Conservation in Southern Africa. *Space and Culture*, 9(3): 294–312.

Spierenburg, M., C. Steenkamp and H. Wels (2008), Enclosing the Local for the Global Commons: Community Land Rights in the Great Limpopo Transfrontier Conservation Area. *Conservation and Society*, 6(1): 87–97.

Spierenburg, M. and H. Wels (2009), Conservative Philanthropists, Royalty and Business Elites. *Antipode*, 42(3): 647–670.

Spierenburg, M. and S. Brooks (2014), Private Game Farming and its Social Consequences in Post-Apartheid South Africa: Contestations over Wildlife, Property and Agrarian Futures. *Journal of Contemporary African Studies*, 32(2): 151–172.

Steinhart, E.I. (2006), *Black Poachers, White Hunters. A social history of hunting in Colonial Kenya*. Oxford: James Currey.

Steward, A. (1963), *South West Africa: The Sacred Trust*. Johannesburg: da Gama Publications.

Stoler, A.L. (2009), *Along the Archival Grain: Epistemic Anxieties and Colonial Common Sense*. Oxfordshire: Princeton University Press.

Stolten, H. E. (ed.) (2007), *History Making and Present Day Politics: The Meaning of Collective Memory in South Africa*. Uppsala; Nordiska Afrikainstitutet.

Storey, W.K. (2008), *Guns, Race, Power in Colonial South Africa*. Cambridge: Cambridge University Press.

Streitwolf, K. (1911), *Der Caprivizipfel*. Berlin: Süsserott.

Sullivan, S. (2001), Gender, ethnographic myths & community-based conservation in a former Namibian 'Homeland'. In D.L Hodgson (ed.), *Rethinking pastoralism in Africa*. London: James Currey: 142–164.

Suspected poacher shot and killed on Farm Otukaruno, *The Namibian*, 28.01.2016.

Taylor, J.J. (2008), Naming the land: San Countermapping in Namibia's West Caprivi. *Geoforum*, 39: 1766–1775.

Taylor, J.J. (2012), *Naming the Land: San Identity and Community Conservation in Namibia's West Caprivi*. Basel: Basler Afrika Bibliographien.

Thompson, J.H. (2006), *An Unpopular War: From Afkak to Bosbefok: Voices of South African National Servicemen*. Cape Town: Zebra Press.

Thomson, L. and M. Wilson (eds.) (1969), *Oxford History of South Africa*, Vol. 1. Oxford: Oxford University Press.

Thomson, L. and M. Wilson (eds.) (1971), *Oxford History of South Africa*, Vol. 2. Oxford: Oxford University Press.

Tischler, J. (2013), *Light and Power for a Multiracial Nation. The Kariba Dam scheme in the Central African Federation*. Basingstoke: Palgrave Macmillan.

Tjihenuna, T. (2015), Government Condemns Botswana for Shooting Namibians. *The Namibian*, 07.10.2015.

Torres, B. (2007), *Making a Killing: The Political Economy of Animal Rights*. Oakland: AK.

Touval, S. (1972), *The Boundary Politics of Independent Africa*. Cambridge MA: Harvard University Press.

Tropp, J. (2006), *Natures of Colonial Change: Environmental Relations in the Making of the Transkei*. Athens: Ohio University Press.

Tsotsi, M.W. (1981), *From Chattel to Wage Slavery. A new approach to South African History*. Maseru: Lesotho Printing and Publishing Co.

Tucker, H. and B. Boonabaana (2012), A Critical Analysis of Tourism, Gender and Poverty Reduction. *Journal of Sustainable Tourism* 20(3): 437–455.

Tvedten, I. (2002), If You Don't Fish, You Are Not a Caprivian: Freshwater Fisheries in Caprivi, Namibia. *Journal of Southern African Studies*, 28(2): 421–39.

Van der Vegte, J.H., C.W. Forster and W.B. Forse (1983), Eastern Caprivi Regional Development Strategy. (Unpublished Government Document: Windhoek).

Van der Waal, B.C.W. and P.H. Skelton (1984), Check List of the Fishes of Caprivi. *Madoqua*, 13(4): 303–320.

Van der Waal, B.C.W. (1985), Aspects of the Biology of Larger Fish Species of Lake Liambezi, Caprivi, South West Africa. *Madoqua*, 14(2): 101–144.

Van Houtum, H. (2010), Human Blacklisting: The Global Apartheid of the EU's External Border Regime. *Environment and Planning D: Society and Space*, 28: 957–976.

Van Wyk, A.S. (2014), The Militarisation of the Platfontein San (!Xun and Khwe): The Initial Years 1966–1974. *The Journal for Transdisciplinary Research in Southern Africa*, 10(3): 133–151.

Vengroff, R. (1977), *Botswana: Rural Development in the Shadow of Apartheid*. London: Associated University Press.

Venning, J.H. (1914), Newly acquired country between the Zambezi and Mashi Rivers. (Shesheke: unpublished memorandum).

Vigne, R. (1998), "The Movable Frontier": The Namibia-Angola Boundary Demarcation 1926–1928. In P. Hayes, J. Silvester, M. Wallace and W. Hartmann (eds.), *Namibia under South African Rule: Mobility and Containment, 1915–46*. Oxford, Windhoek and Athens OH: James Currey, Out of Africa and Ohio University Press: 289–304.

Visser, W. (2004), Trends in South African Historiography and the Present State of Historical Research. (Paper presented at the Nordic Africa Institute, Uppsala).

Wa Thiong'o, N. (2009), The Myth of Tribe in African Politics. *Transition*, 101: 16–23.

Wallace, M. (2011), *A History of Namibia*. London: Hurst.

White, R. (1991), *The Middle Ground: Indians, Empires and Republics in the Great Lakes Region, 1650–1815*. Cambridge: Cambridge University Press.

Wilhelm, J.H. (1933), Das Wild des Okavangogebietes und des Caprivizipfels. *Journal of the South West Africa Scientific Society*, 6: 51–74.

Williams, C.A. (2011), Ordering the Nation: SWAPO in Zambia, 1974–1976. *Journal of Southern African Studies*, 37(4): 693–713.
Williams, C.A. (2015), *National Liberation in Postcolonial Southern Africa. A Historical Ethnography of SWAPO's Exile Camps*. Cambridge: Cambridge University Press.
Williams, M. (1994), The relations of environmental history and historical geography. *Journal of Historical Geography*, 20(1): 3–21.
Wilson, E. O. (2016), *Half-Earth: our planet's fight for life*. New York: Liveright.
Witt, H. (2014), The Role of Alien Trees in South African Forestry and Conservation: Early 20th-Century Research and Debate on Climate Change, Soil Erosion and Hydrology. *Journal of Southern African Studies*, 40(6): 1193–1214.
Witz, L. (2008), Review of Stolten, H.E., History Making and Present Day Politics. *African Studies Review*, 51: 186–188.
Witz, L. (2015), Hunting for Museums. *Journal of Southern Africa Studies,* 41(4): 671–685.
Witz, L., J.R. Forte and P. Israel (2016), Epistemological Restlessness: Trajectories in and out of History. In J.R Forte, P. Israel and Witz, L. (eds.) *Out of History Re-imagining South Africans Pasts*. Cape Town, HSRC: 1–30.
Wood, D. (2006), *The Power of Maps*. New York: Guilford Press.
Worden, N. (2012), *The Making of Modern South Africa, Fifth Edition*. Malden: Wiley-Blackwell.
World Travel and Tourism Council (ed.) (2017), *Travel & Tourism Economic Impact 2016 Namibia*, London.
Worster, D. (1977), *Nature's Economy: A Study of Ecological Ideals*. Cambridge: Cambridge University Press.
Worster, D. (1978), *Dust Bowl: The Southern Plains in the 1930s*. Oxford: Oxford University Press.
Yaron, G., T. Healy, and C. Tapscott (1993), *The Economics of Living with Wildlife in Namibia: Report for the World Bank*. Washington DC.
Ybarra, M. (2012), Taming the jungle, saving the Maya Forest: Sedimented counter-insurgency practices in contemporary Guatemalan conservation. *Journal of Peasant Studies*, 39(2): 479–502.
Zeller, J. and J. Zimmerer (eds.) (2003), *Völkermord in Deutsch-Südwestafrika: Der Kolonialkrieg in Namibia und seine Folgen*. Berlin: Ch. Links.
Zeller, W. (2007), Chiefs, Policing and Vigilantes: "Cleaning Up" the Caprivi Borderland of Namibia. In L. Buur and H.M. Kyed (eds.), *State Recognition and Democratization in Sub-Saharan Africa: A New Dawn for Traditional Authorities?* New York: Palgrave: 79–104.
Zeller, W. (2009), Danger and Opportunity in Katima Mulilo: A Namibian Border Boomtown at Transnational Crossroads. *Journal of Southern African Studies*, 35(1): 133–154.
Zeller, W. (2015), *What Makes Border Real – In the Namibia-Zambia and Uganda-South Sudan Borderlands*. Helsinki: Unigrafia.

List of Figures and Maps

Cover: Former Buffallo Base in the Bwabwata National Park, Photo by Sabine Hiller.
Figure 1: Proposed Nature Reserves Caprivi, Map by Ben C.W. van der Waal, 1976. NAN, CAF, 6/19/5.
Figure 2: Map of the Kavango Zambezi Transfrontier Conservation Area (Kaza TFCA), https://web.archive.org/web/20170215125139/http://www.peaceparks.org/story.php?pid=1008&mid=1073 [Archived Webpage, 15.04.2017]. Updated version provided by PPF. The information and views set out in this book are those of the author(s) and do not necessarily reflect the official or any opinion of Peace Parks Foundation, author and publisher of this map. Neither the Foundation nor any persons acting on their behalf may be held responsible for the use of said map contained therein.
Figure 3: Map of the Caprivi Strip, 2017. Map by the author and Michael Wenk.
Figure 4: Administrative authorities and political entities in the Caprivi since 1929. Maps by the author and Michael Wenk (partly based on Boden 2004).

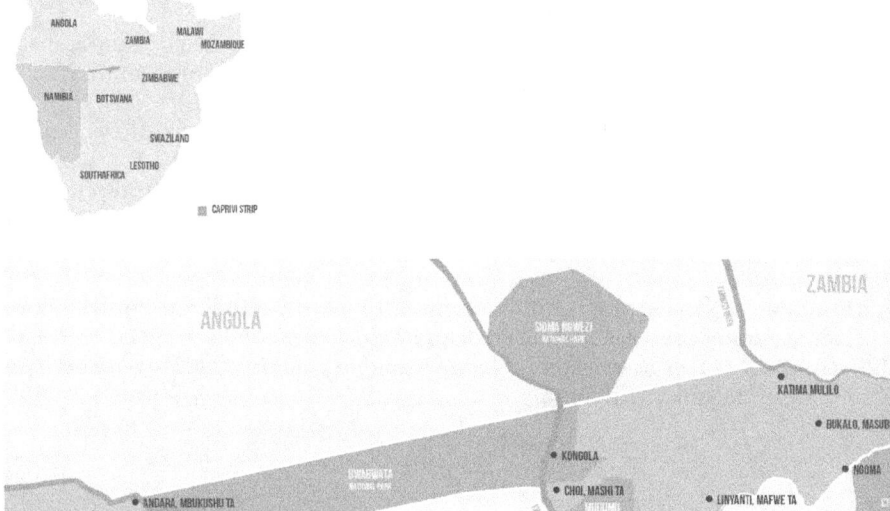

Fig. 3: Map of the Caprivi Strip, 2017. Map by the author and Michael Wenk.

1922 - 1929

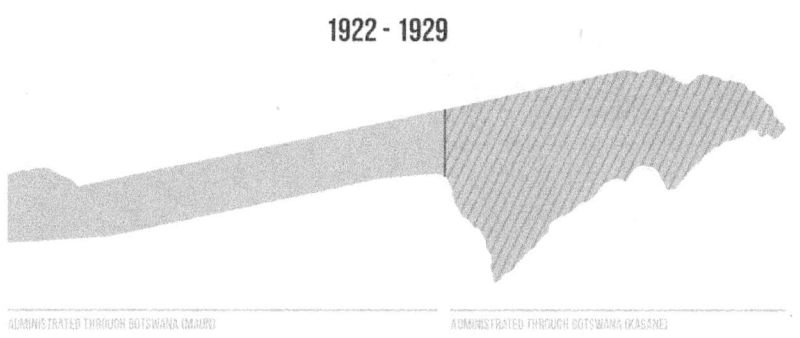

ADMINISTRATED THROUGH BOTSWANA (MAURI) ADMINISTRATED THROUGH BOTSWANA (KASANE)

1929 - 1939

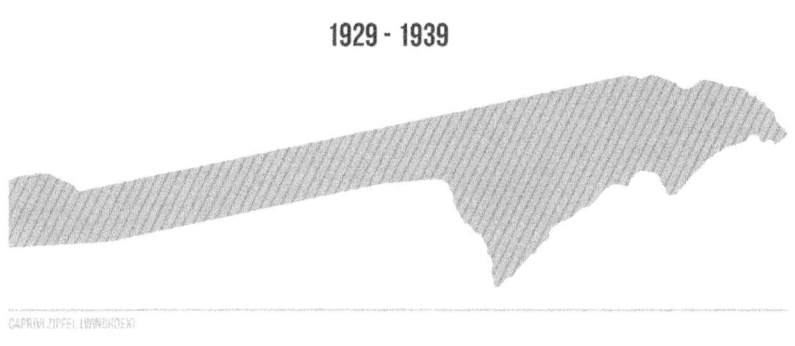

CAPRIVIZIPFEL (WINDHOEK)

1939 - 1990

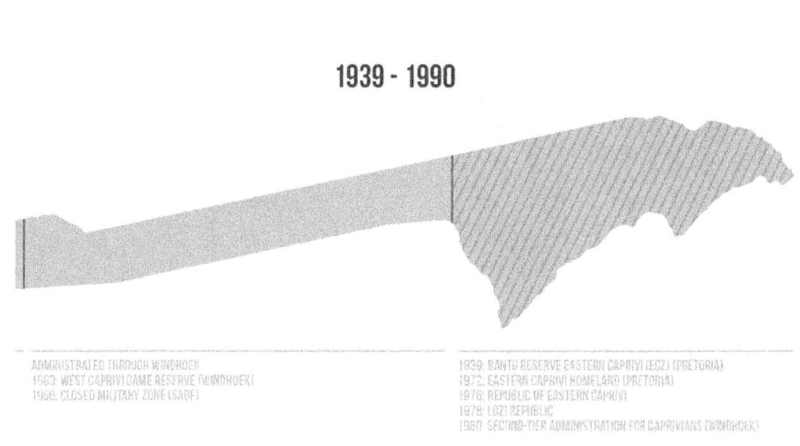

ADMINISTRATED THROUGH WINDHOEK
1963: WEST CAPRIVI GAME RESERVE (WINDHOEK)
1966: CLOSED MILITARY ZONE (SADF)

1939: BANTU RESERVE EASTERN CAPRIVI (ECZ) (PRETORIA)
1972: EASTERN CAPRIVI HOMELAND (PRETORIA)
1976: REPUBLIC OF EASTERN CAPRIVI
1978: LOZI REPUBLIC
1980: SECOND-TIER ADMINISTRATION FOR CAPRIVIANS (WINDHOEK)

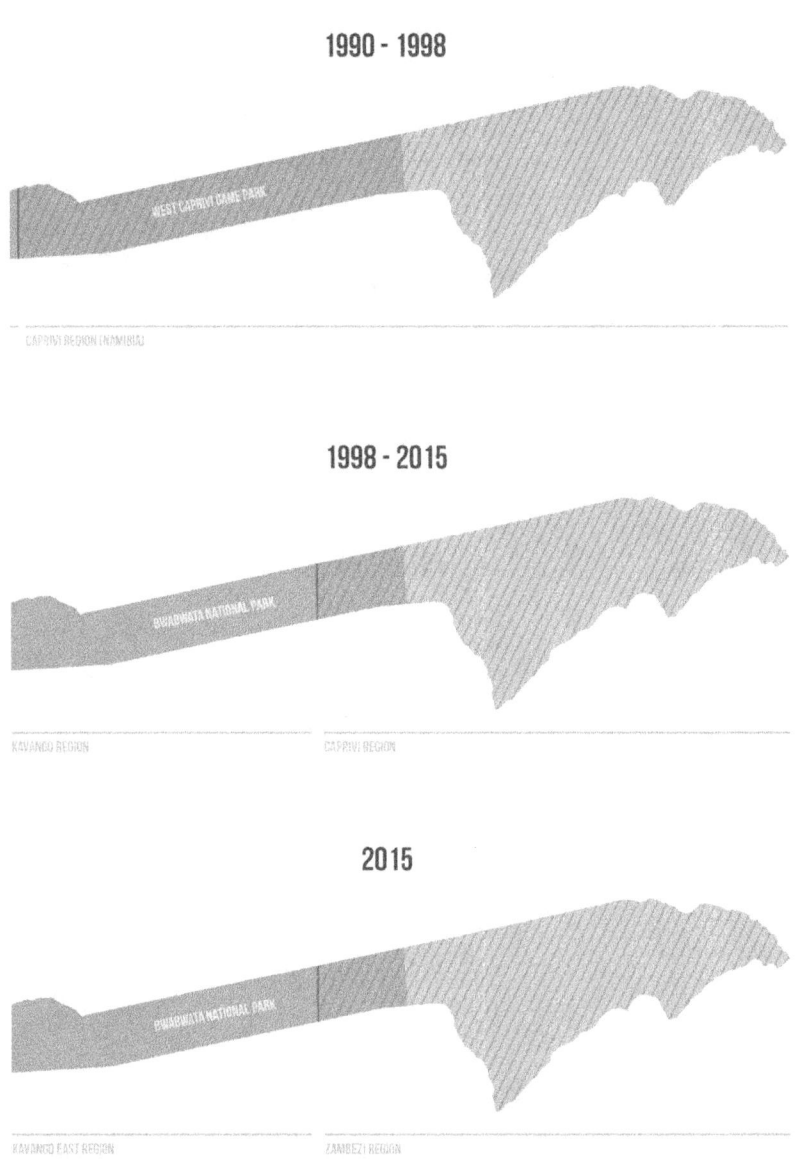

Fig. 4: Administrative authorities and political entities in the Caprivi since 1929. Maps by the author and Michael Wenk (partly based on Boden 2004).

Index

A

Afghanistan 221
African National Congress (ANC) 149
Amathole Museum 58
Amber Mountain National Park 170
Andara 30, 49, 53, 177
Angola 13, 23, 28, 38, 46f., 52f., 55, 64, 72, 83, 87, 92–94, 105, 113f., 123, 133f., 151, 153–156, 159–161, 176, 179, 181f. , 186f., 199, 201, 206, 209, 213, 217, 227
Ashforth, A. 33, 35, 49, 73–77, 81
Ashwin, J. 79, 144
Asia 133, 171
Asiwaju, A.I. 205
Australia 69, 89, 118f.

B

Bagani 119
Barotse Kingdom 53
Barrett, G. 194f., 209f.
Bechuanaland Protectorate 15, 43f., 48, 50–53, 55, 57, 61
Beinart, W. 4, 6, 12, 17f., 21, 35, 89–92, 102, 109, 116, 124, 143
Bertrand, A. 41
Biko, S. 6
Boden, G. 12, 15, 54, 55, 83, 130, 177–179, 181
Bollig, M. 12f., 21, 34f., 48, 52, 54f., 66–68, 76, 80, 102, 129, 196
Bonn 131
Boshoff, N.W. 72, 80
Botanical Research Institute, Pretoria 114
Botha, P.W. 160
Bothma, J.P. 136
Botswana 13–15, 23, 38, 43, 50f., 55, 93, 112–114, 120, 130, 138, 155, 180, 182, 186f., 199, 201, 214, 216–218, 220–222
Botswana Defence Force (BDF) 217f.
Botswana, Department of Nature Conservation 114
Breitenbach, F. 120–122, 144
Breytenbach, J. 15, 105, 133f., 148, 160, 220, 223
British Empire 32, 34, 58, 64f., 89, 91, 116, 118, 226
British South Africa Company (BSAC) 43f., 51
Brittz, E.P. 62
Bulawayo 70
Büscher, B. 3, 21, 188, 190, 192, 198, 201f., 219, 221–224
Bushmanland (Homeland) 69

Bwabwata National Park 38, 178, 211, 231f.
Bwabwata (Settlement) 55

C

Cameroon 117
Canada 186
Cape Colony 5, 118
Cape Province (South Africa) 135

Cape Town 2, 4, 7, 9, 11, 15, 27f., 65, 69, 94, 100f., 105, 119f., 122–124, 135, 148, 156, 160
Caprivi Department for Agriculture and Forestry (CAF) 28, 100, 106f., 112–115, 124, 130, 135, 139f., 147f., 150–153, 156f., 162f., 166
Caprivi Department for Native Affairs and Magistrate (CNAM) 28
Caprivi Liberation Army (CLA) 179, 181
Chadwick, M 49
Chapman, J. 41
China 2, 66
Chobe National Park 112, 130
Chobe River 40, 112f., 141
Choi 30, 38, 210f., 224
Colenbrander, A.B 70–72
Comoroff, J. 119
Comoroff, J. L. 119
Congo 52
Congo (DRC) 52
Cooper, F. 8, 33f., 39
Cuba 94, 105, 160

D

D'Amato, A. 76
de la Bat, B.J.G. 163
Democratic Turnhalle Alliance (DTA) 158, 161, 179
Denmark 180
Department of Bantu Affairs 4, 28, 32, 102, 145
Derrida, J. 29
Dobson, P. 149
Documentation Centre of the South African National Defence Force (SANDFDOC) 28
Duffy, R. 21, 175, 186, 189, 198, 218f., 221
Dzingirai, V. 175, 185f., 224

E

Edees, H. 61
Edwards, D. 113–115, 155
Elephants without Borders (EWB) 216
Ellis, S. 131, 133, 181
Eloff de Visser, L. 26, 95, 149f., 161
Etosha National Park 12, 84, 130, 135, 138, 178, 223
Europe 5, 16–18, 36f., 41, 45, 57, 61, 64, 98, 104, 147, 154, 206, 214
Evans, G. 149

F

Fanon, F. 17f.
Fisch, M. 14, 129, 179f.
Flint, L. 15, 181
Forse, W.B. 162, 164
Forster, C.W. 162, 164
Foucault, M. 29, 75
Frama Inter-trading Ldt. 134
France 187

G

Gaborone 109, 115
George (South Africa) 121

German Reich 41
Germany 18, 116, 202
Gewald, J.B. 2, 12, 32, 56–59, 62f., 70
Ghana 205
Glacken, C.J. 16f.
Gordon, R. 11, 68
Grahamstown 113
Graupner, O. 100, 134, 146, 147
Great Limpopo Transfrontier Conservation Area 220
Greenpeace 131
Grobler, M. 100
Grootfontein 68, 70, 117, 155, 180

H

Harley, J.B. 29
Harring, S. 192f.
Harris, L. 204
Harvey, D. 173, 188, 190f., 197, 203
Hazen, H. 204
Herodot 37
Hinz, M.O. 38f.
Holub, E. 41

I

Impalila Island 135, 192, 214
India 25, 34, 58, 116
Integrated Rural Development and Nature Conservation (IRDNC) 165–167, 184, 193f., 211
International Monetary Fund (IMF) 191
International Union for Conservation of Nature and Natural Resources (IUCN) 20, 115, 186, 189
Iraq 221

J

Jackson, A. 15, 50
Jehovah's Witness 52
Jonker, J. 30

K

Kafue National Park 170, 217
Kangumu, B. 12, 15, 28, 30, 32, 44, 50, 53, 56, 58f., 62, 70–72, 81f., 93, 96f., 100, 161f., 167, 176f., 179–181, 208, 215, 226
Kaokoveld 9, 13, 37, 47f., 52, 54, 67, 80, 102, 129, 136
Kariba 34, 112
Kasane 49, 57, 182, 204, 214, 216
Katima Mulilo 1, 15, 28, 41, 53, 56f., 70f., 73, 76, 79, 81, 91, 98–105, 107, 111, 119, 122, 124, 132, 134f., 138, 140, 142–144, 161f., 164–167, 169, 172, 179, 181, 187, 195f., 198f., 207, 214, 232
Katima Mulilo Magistrate 28
Kaukungwa, S.H. 96
Kavango Region 2, 12, 40, 47f., 53, 55, 69, 98, 117f., 122, 129, 136, 139, 177f., 182, 194, 225
Kavango Zambezi Transfrontier Conservation Area (KAZA TFCA) 182, 187, 197–203, 207–209, 212–217, 220f., 225, 227, 232
Kazungula 41

Kenya 52, 170, 190, 218
Kenya Wildlife Service 218
Kettlitz, K. 136, 145f., 188
Khama, I. 218
Khama II, T. 218
King William's Town 58
Koevoet 92f., 95, 100, 141, 149, 159, 161
Köhler, O. 83
Kreike, E. 13, 17, 68, 88, 90
Kruger, C.E. 14, 56, 98
Kruger National Park 3, 21, 130, 132, 135, 138, 220f.
Kumleben, M.A. 132–134
Kunene Region 9, 47, 194, 211
Kwando River 39f., 112f., 178

L

Lalu, P. 4, 7f., 10, 23, 173
Landsberg, A.G. 54
Latour, B. 89
League of Nation 44, 46, 56, 64
Leakey, R. 218
Legislative Council of the East Caprivi 96
Lester, A. 3
Lianshulu 164–167, 171
Lifumbela, S. 77
Limpopo River 9, 210, 213
Linyanti 112f., 141, 166
Liswani, K. 168
Livingstone, D. 41
Livingstone, D.N. 89, 92
Livingstone Museum 28, 201
Livingstone (Zambia) 201
London 58
Luanda 161
Luhonono (Schuckmannsburg) 49, 56
Lunstrum, E. 21, 25, 213, 218f., 221f.
Lupala Island 39
Lusaka 161

M

Macedo, D. 91
Madagascar 170, 191
Mafwe Traditional Authority 14, 30, 38, 49, 58, 96, 164–167, 169, 176f., 180f., 210
Mahango National Park 178
Maisha Consulting 221
Malan, D.F. 64
Malan, M. 64, 151
Malengalenga 91, 107, 150, 165–167, 169f., 172
Maloti-Drakensberg Peace Park 201
Mamdani, M. 8f., 48, 65
Mamili, L.S. 49
Mamili, S. 58, 76
Mandela, N. 186
Manyeleti Game Reserve 107
Marée, D. 84f.

Mashi Traditional Authority 30, 177, 179, 192, 210, 223
Massai Mara National Park 170
Masubia Traditional Authority 30, 77
Matengu, P. 107f.
Maun 57, 114
Mavhunga, C. C. 174
Mayeyi Traditional Authority 14, 30, 166f., 177, 200
Mayuni Conservancy 179, 208, 210, 212
Mayuni, J. 210f.
Mbukushu Traditional Authority 30, 49, 177
McCullers, M. 13, 35, 63, 66f., 73–75, 77, 88
McNeill, J. 22
Miescher, G. 9f., 12f., 22f., 26, 37, 45f., 48, 54f., 67, 84f., 95, 117, 135, 138, 152–154, 184
Military Intelligence Division, South African Defence Force (MID) 133f.
Mitchell, D.S. 112–114
Moore, J.W. 19f., 173, 230
Moorsom, R. 11, 48, 67, 72
Moraliswane, J. 76
Mosimane, A. 191f., 196f., 207f., 210–212
Movimento Popular de Libertação de Angola (MPLA) 93, 105, 155
Mozambique 34, 62, 133, 181, 220
M'Pacha 72, 155
Mpumalanga Province 107
Mudumu National Park 138, 142, 164–169, 228
Mugabe, R. 218
Muniango, K. 77–79
Mutwa, G. 194
Muyongo, M.A. 179–181
Myers, J.C. 33, 44, 49, 97, 99, 110

N

Nakabunze Reserve 120, 122f.
Nakatwa 165–167
Namakunde 47
Namibia Directorate of Nature Conservation and Recreation Resorts 163
Namibian Anti-Poaching Unit (APO) 138
Namibian Defence Force (NDF) 176, 179, 182, 222, 231
Namibian Ministry of Environment and Tourism (MET) 39, 132, 138, 179, 183f., 199, 217, 222
Namibian Police Force 176, 222
National Archives of Namibia (NAN) 14, 27, 49–55, 57–62, 84–86, 98, 100, 104–108, 112–115, 117, 121, 124, 130, 135f., 139f,, 144–147, 150–153, 156f., 163, 166, 188
National Archives of South Africa (NASA) 28
National Archives of Zambia (ZAR) 28
National Party (South Africa) 64
New York 58
Nkasa Lupala National Park 39, 101, 138, 164–166, 168, 228
Northern Rhodesia 43, 52f., 112
North-West University (South Africa) 155

O

Odendaal, F.H. 32, 68, 73–77, 79–84, 87f., 95–97, 106, 144, 192, 202, 227
Odendaal, W. 193
Ohangwena 46, 96
Okahandja 223

Okavango River 40, 55, 69, 84–86, 105, 112, 119, 130
Olwig, K.R. 115
Ondangwa 46, 148
Ondonga 46
Oshakati 155
Outjo 45
Ovamboland 13, 46f., 65, 67f., 72, 95f., 117, 149
Ovamboland People's Organization (OPO) 65
Ovambo People's Congress (OPC) 64
Owen-Smith, G. 194, 207, 223

P

Peace Park Foundation (PPF) 133, 186f., 198f., 201f., 208–210, 212–214, 216, 221
Peluso, N. 29, 171, 211, 218
People's Liberation Army of Namibia (PLAN) 93, 143, 148, 159, 161, 176
Planning Committee for the Eastern Caprivi 81f., 96, 120
Portugal 53
Potts, J.W. 49, 55
Pretoria 1, 4, 27f., 32, 44, 56f., 59, 62–65, 69, 73, 80f., 87f., 91f., 94, 96, 99, 103f., 109, 114, 120, 122, 131, 134–136, 145f., 148f., 156, 160–162, 181, 189, 226f.

R

Ramutsindela, M. 3, 10, 21, 175, 184, 187, 190f., 198, 200f., 203f., 206, 210, 219–224
Resistência Nacional Moçambicana (RENAMO) 181
Rhoodie, E. 1f., 33, 65–67
Rizzo, L. 9f., 13, 22, 34, 47f., 65, 67
Rundu 44, 56, 61, 84, 155, 204
Rupert, A. 133, 186
Russia 2, 66

S

Salambala Conservancy 192–194
Sangwali 30, 36–38, 101, 107, 138, 140, 142f., 168f., 201
Sedgefield 99–104, 109f., 114f., 123, 132, 146, 153, 155
Shamukumi, D.M. 40
Shesheke 41, 43, 53, 57
Shifeta, P. 231
Silva, J.A. 196, 208, 211f.
Singh, J. 126f., 174, 194, 203, 206, 208
Sitze, A. 74, 173
Smuts, J. 64
South African Air Force Museum 27
South African Air Force (SAAF) 28, 71, 92, 103f., 114, 122, 124, 133, 148, 154–156, 163
South African Defence Force (SADF) 1, 26, 28, 31, 38, 46, 62, 71, 84, 86, 88, 92, 94, 97, 100, 105, 114–116, 120, 123–126, 128f., 131f., 134, 136f., 142, 144, 148–156, 159, 161, 170f., 177f., 206, 209, 219f., 227f.
South African National Botanical Institute 155
South African National Defence Force (SANDF) 150
South African Union Defence Force (UDF) 154
Southern African Development Community (SADC) 174, 187
South West African Administration, Directorate of Nature Conservation and Tourism (NTB) 28
South West African Administration (SWAA) 28, 44, 49–56, 58, 60f., 83, 97, 117, 130, 139
South West African Police (SWAPOL) 92f., 159
South West African Territory Forces (SWATF) 28, 93, 159

South West Africa People's Organisation (SWAPO) 11, 65, 93f., 96, 105, 113, 129, 149, 158f., 161, 177, 179f.
Spierenburg, M. 187, 191, 209f., 213
Steyn, J.M. 84, 158
Stockholm 131
Stoler, A.L. 22, 173
Streitwolf, K. 14, 41–43, 56
Swart, P. 134, 163

T

Tanzania 66, 82, 93, 130, 190
Taylor, J.J. 12, 16, 22, 29, 55, 84, 97, 99f., 130, 138, 159, 177f., 182, 211f.
Thompson, J.K. 26, 135, 153
Tinley, K.L. 84–86, 144
Togo 205
Toivo ya Toivo, H.A. 65
Tomlinson, F.R. 75, 95
Touval, S. 205
Transkei (Homeland) 35, 57, 109, 119
Transvaal Provincial Administration (TPA) 100, 102, 146
Transvaal (Region) 100, 102, 146–148
Trollope, L.F. 57, 59f.
Trollope, L.T 2, 51f., 55–63, 70
Tsumeb 68, 117, 153

U

Uibasen Conservancy 211
União Nacional para a Independência Total de Angola (UNITA) 94, 105, 134, 181
United Democratic Party (UDP) 179
United Kingdom (UK) 61, 160
United National Independence Party (UNIP) 93
United Nations Environment Programme (UNEP) 189
United Nations Transition Assistance Group (UNTAG) 161
United Nations (UN) 63–65, 93, 131, 158, 160f., 180, 189
United States' Department of Defence 94
United States of America (USA) 16, 94, 131, 148f., 154, 160, 186, 191
University of Lubango 199

V

van der Byl, P. 59
van der Vegte, J.H. 164
van der Waal, B.C.W. 114, 147, 153, 156, 163f., 166
van Houtum, H. 126f., 203, 206, 214f.
Venda (Homeland) 97
Verwoerd, H.F. 35, 73, 75, 87
von Lippe-Biesterfeld, B. 186
Von Moltitz Harmse, H.J. 155
von Schuckmann, B. 41

W

Wallace, M. 1, 10–12, 46–48, 64f., 67, 92f., 95, 158–161, 175f.
Waterton Lakes Glacier International Peace Park 186
Wels, H. 187, 209f.
Werth, A. 49
Western Province (Zambia) 15

Wildlife at Risk International (WAR international) 223
Windhoek 1, 11f., 14f., 24, 28, 32, 38, 42, 44, 47–50, 52, 61, 67, 96f., 100f., 107, 115, 118, 132, 134, 137–143, 153, 155, 157–159, 161–170, 176f., 180, 183, 192f., 195, 208, 224
Witwatersrand Native Labour Association (WNLA) 16, 71, 79, 144
Witz, L. 7, 32, 37, 58, 116
Wood, D. 29, 206
World Bank 185, 191
World Wide Fund for Nature (WWF) 133, 186f., 189, 202

Y

Ya Ndemufayo, M. 47

Z

Zambezi River 41, 43, 53, 105, 112f., 135, 214
Zambia 13–15, 23, 43f., 52f., 64, 72, 92f., 113, 120, 153, 155, 161, 170, 185, 187, 201, 206, 213., 217, 219–221, 227
Zimbabwe 34, 52, 103, 114, 133, 174, 187, 200f., 213, 216, 218, 221
Zimbabwe Defence Force (ZDF) 218
Zinn, H.J. 71

www.ingramcontent.com/pod-product-compliance
Lightning Source LLC
Chambersburg PA
CBHW080923300426
44115CB00018B/2928